e
of Modern America

A History
of the American People,
1890–1945

GEORGE DONELSON MOSS

City College of San Francisco

PRENTICE HALL, Englewood Cliffs, New Jersey 07632

Library of Congress Cataloging-in-Publication Data

MOSS, GEORGE.
    The rise of modern America: a history of the American people,
1890–1945/ George Donelson Moss.
       p. cm.
    Includes bibliographical references and index.
    ISBN 0-13-181587-3
    1. United States—History—1901–1953.   2. United States—
History—1865–1921. I. Title.
E741.M675   1994
973.91—dc20   94-36595
                                         CIP

Editorial Director: Charlyce Jones Owen
Copy Editor: Ilene McGrath
Cover Designer: Bruce Kenselaar
Buyer: Nick Sklitsis
Editorial Assistant: Tamara Mann
Photo Editor: Lorinda Morris-Nantz
Photo Researcher: Rhoda Sidney
Editorial/Production Supervision
   and Interior Design: Rob DeGeorge

To the memory of my father,
who told me I could do it.

©1995 by Prentice-Hall, Inc.
A Simon & Schuster Company
Englewood Cliffs, New Jersey 07632

Printed in the United States of America

10 9 8 7 6 5 4 3 2 1

ISBN 0-13-181587-3

PRENTICE-HALL INTERNATIONAL (UK) LIMITED, *London*
PRENTICE-HALL OF AUSTRALIA PTY. LIMITED, *Sydney*
PRENTICE-HALL CANADA INC., *Toronto*
PRENTICE-HALL HISPANOAMERICANA, S.A., *Mexico*
PRENTICE-HALL OF INDIA PRIVATE LIMITED, *New Delhi*
PRENTICE-HALL OF JAPAN, INC., *Tokyo*
SIMON & SCHUSTER ASIA PTE. LTD., *Singapore*
EDITORA PRENTICE-HALL DO BRASIL, LTDA., *Rio de Janeiro*

Contents

Preface

Søren Kierkegaard, the great Danish philosopher and theologian, wrote: "Life is lived forward, but understood backwards." His observation applies to the lives of nations as well as to the lives of individuals. To understand how the United States has become the kind of nation it is, we must track backward in time, back to *fin de siècle* nineteenth-century America, when the modern epoch in American history began. The genesis of modern America, of our modern urban, industrial, and pluralistic society, can be found in the 1890s when the three mighty forces that have powerfully shaped U.S. development during the first half of the twentieth century—urbanization, industrialization, and immigration—came fully into view. Underlying these social forces was an even more powerful force driving the engines of American history: the continuous invention and application of new technologies.

The era that began amid the turmoil and stress of rapidly changing social circumstances as the nineteenth century came to an end, and that stretches to the end of history's largest war in the summer of 1945, forms a coherent unit of historical study. It constitutes a significant period in the modern history of the American people; it has its particular constellation of themes, trends, and developments; and it has its unique energy, structure, and meaning. Modern American civilization evolved during the first half of the twentieth century and acquired its characteristic look and shape during that tremendous half century. *The Rise of Modern America* is the first comprehensive historical narrative to treat the period from the 1890s to 1945 as a coherent unit of study in its own right rather than as a phase of a larger period.

The Rise of Modern America draws upon the work of many scholars who have written hundreds of books and thousands of articles concerned with all facets of American history from the 1890s to 1945. The book is a comprehensive narrative synthesis that conveys a sizable portion of what professional historians know about the modern American past. At the conclusion of each chapter is a carefully selected bibliography containing some of the finest, most readable, and accessible books that will enhance your knowledge of modern America.

The Rise of Modern America takes an innovative approach to its subject. It retains what is most valuable and relevant from traditional public policy approaches to American history. It incorporates political history, economic history, foreign policy history, and military history. These histories have usually been told from the top down, that is, they are written from the perspective of the elite groups who have held predominant power in political and economic institutions. While retaining traditional public policy approaches, I have also incorporated much demographic, ecological, and cultural history. Further, I have given much attention to the new social history that in recent times has enriched our historical literature and expanded our understanding of *what* and *who* constitute modern American history. Much of this new social history, with its focus on class, gender, race, and ethnicity, is written from the perspective of those groups who in the past were neglected or perceived as passive objects of more powerful historical agents. *The Rise of Modern America* gives much attention to immigration history, labor history, women's history, African American history, Hispanic American history, Asian American history, and Native American history.

All Americans are included in *The Rise of Modern America*. Within the traditional framework of public policy history I have created innovative multicultural structures, as diverse and dynamic as American society itself. It is a book for everyone, traditionalists and multiculturalists alike.

Historical study has its genesis and inspiration in the very human trait of curiosity. People, especially young people, are curious. They ask questions about origins: Where did I come from? Where did my parents come from? Where did my society and my country come from? If I have created the book that I intended, it will suggest answers to some of these primeval questions that define our common humanity. But if I have done my job well, *The Rise of Modern America* will be the *first* study of modern America that you read, not the only one or the last one. If historical study represents a kind of journey, my book best serves as a point of departure, not a destination.

ACKNOWLEDGMENTS

Because we continually write about large subjects, synthesize huge amounts of information, and construct elaborate analyses and interpretations of data, textbook writers are especially dependent on the expertise and support of friends and colleagues. I am extremely fortunate to be able to call upon the talents of many people who helped in many ways great and small to make this book better.

A few of the many who helped me do the book: Among my colleagues at City College: Mary Adams, Edward W. Moreno, Austin White, Richard Oxsen, Russ Posner, Tom Doyle, Stephen Moorhouse, and Glenn Nance.

Among my colleagues at the University of California, San Diego: Daniel C. Hallin, Michael Schudson, and Michael Bernstein.

Other scholars who provided invaluable help include Thomas Wolf, Laney College; Bruce Dierenfield, Canisius College; Jeffrey Kimball, Miami University, Oxford, Ohio; Garen Burbank, The University of Winnipeg; Kevin O'Keefe, Stetson University; Paul Conway, Oneonta College; Jack Colldeweih, Fairleigh Dickinson University; David Hollinger, University of California, Berkeley; and Ronald G. Walters, Johns Hopkins University.

To all of you and to those unmentioned, go my heartfelt gratitude.

Special thanks goes to Steve Dalphin, executive editor at Prentice Hall, for his uncanny ability to find books for me to write. It always surprises me when he asks me to do a book. Rob DeGeorge took charge of the demanding and quasi-magical task of transforming an ungainly manuscript into a beautiful book.

My sister, Mary Chatelier, ferreted out many original and expressive photographs from the labyrinthine confines of the National Archives.

And a very special thank you to the lovely Linda, who, for reasons that elude me but for which I am forever grateful, accompanies me on our journey through life.

CHAPTER
1

Prologue: A Society in Transition

The face of America was transformed during the last three decades of the nineteenth century. A predominantly rural nation, whose people inhabited small towns and villages, had become an urban industrial giant. As late as the 1870s, most Americans had been earning their living as farmers, shopkeepers, and small businessmen, or else as employees of farmers, merchants, and small manufacturers. By the end of the nineteenth century, large corporations increasingly dominated the economic landscape, and America was fast becoming a nation of employees. Three historical forces transformed America as the nineteenth century ran its course: industrialization, urbanization, and massive immigration. Behind these powerful forces lay the application of new technologies. Rapid technological change was the powerful engine driving the transformation of America at the dawn of the twentieth century.

A DEMOGRAPHIC PORTRAIT

The population of the United States grew from 60 million in 1890 to more than 76 million by 1900. As the twentieth century began, America was the fourth most populous nation in the world (after China, India, and Russia) and had the most rapidly growing population of any large nation in the world. The rapid rate of population growth was a function of both a high birth rate among the native-born population and the unprecedented massive inflow of immigrants. During the decade of the 1890s, over 6 million immigrants traveled to America, 75 percent of whom comprised the "new" immigration, people coming from southern and eastern Europe, principally Poland, Italy, and Russia. According to the census of 1900, 26 million of the nation's 76 million inhabitants were either immigrants or the sons and daughters of immigrants. In addition to the inflow of new immigrants, two other major population movements characterized *fin de siècle* America: People, especially farmers, continued to trek westward to farm new lands in Texas, the high plains, and California. Millions more moved from rural areas to the large towns and cities, especially in the northeastern regions of the nation. As the twentieth century began, three-fourths of the American population inhabited the eastern third of the nation, east of the mighty Mississippi River.

Even though the census of 1900 showed that nearly two-thirds of American families still resided in towns of fewer than 2,500 people, the nation had undergone a rapid growth in urban population during the 1890s. The urbanization of American society during the last decades of the nineteenth century was its most salient demographic trend. Population growth within the surging metropolises of America had been nothing short of spectacular. New York City, the commercial and cultural capital of the nation, had grown from 1.5 million people in the 1870s to 3.5 million by 1900! Chicago, which had become a city only during the Civil War, was approaching 2 million people by 1900. Other large cities showed similar dramatic increases. It was in the growing large cities of America during the 1890s where one could see the population diversity that was creating the world's foremost multicultural society. While the countryside contained relatively homogeneous enclaves of families whose forebears had emigrated from northern and western Europe, the great cities of America were increasingly populated by the world's most diverse populations.

As the twentieth century began, Americans were living longer than ever before and family size was declining. Divorce rates were increasing, but they remained quite small compared with modern figures. Of the approximately 30 million people in the work force, two-thirds were employed in nonagricultural pursuits. Of these nonagricultural workers, perhaps 12 million held blue-collar jobs in industries of various kinds. The median annual wage for a blue-collar worker in 1900 was about $500, barely enough to support a family. The industrial work force also included 5 million women and perhaps 2 million children (age 14 and below). The typical workweek was 60 hours. As the twentieth century began, millions of working-class families were enduring a life of grinding poverty with scant opportunities for themselves or their children to rise to middle-class status.

ECONOMIC GROWTH

Economic growth characterized all regions of America during the late nineteenth century, although it was most extensive in the northeastern and Great Lakes regions. Within a generation America had developed the world's largest industrial economy. Economic growth influenced the lives of nearly all Americans. Geographic and social mobility were enhanced. American manufacturing flourished during the late nineteenth century for many reasons. New natural resources were being discovered and exploited. The nation also expanded geographically as the West was wrested from the Plains Indians. Western expansion added to the size of national markets, which were also protected from foreign competitors by tariff walls erected by Congress. Additional ingredients comprised the recipe for economic growth: America raised a class of bold, skillful entrepreneurs, many from poor backgrounds, who organized and built large industrial corporations. Also the dominant values of the age promoted economic growth and material acquisition. Manufacturing also flourished because it was a time of rapid advance in basic science and technology. New machines that increased productivity appeared, and engineers harnessed new power sources.

Construction of the nation's industrial infrastructure, particularly the transportation revolution wrought by the building of the railroads, was an essential contribution to the industrial revolution. Railroads formed the most important element in American economic development for several reasons. They constituted an important industry in them-

Railroad Network, 1885

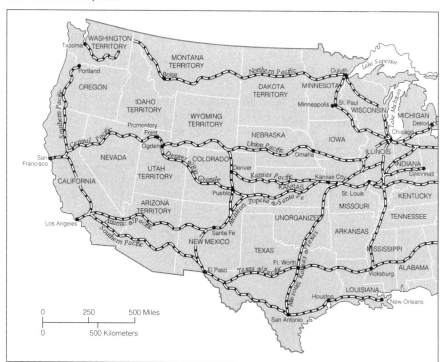

selves, the nation's first big business. During the 1880s, 7,000 miles of track were laid annually. By 1890, feeder lines, regional roads branching off the main east–west trunk lines, linked together most cities and towns in the country. As the century ended, the railroads owned 193,000 miles of tracks, more than half of the world's total trackage. As the nation's railroad industry expanded, it also became concentrated. By 1900 seven giant interregional railroad combines (including the New York Central, the Baltimore and Ohio, the Pennsylvania, and the Southern Pacific) controlled 90 percent of the nation's railroad mileage.

Railroads also stimulated the growth of a large-scale manufacturing economy. Before the national system of railroads was in place, manufacturing was confined largely to small businesses that sold to local markets. The railroads created national markets. Industrialists borrowed money, bought new machines, purchased raw materials in large quantities, hired more workers, and employed salespeople. Branch offices and new factories were opened. Those manufacturers who most successfully tapped the national markets created by the railroads became the nation's largest businesses. Railroads thus made big business possible. By 1900 the national system of railroads had created a unified continental-size national economy, the largest and most productive economy in the world.

Rapid, large-scale expansion of manufacturing enterprises formed an integral part of the American industrial revolution. In 1900 the American Gross Domestic Product (GDP) reached $40 billion, a sixfold increase in twenty years. The most impressive advances in manufacturing during the late nineteenth century occurred in the steel industry. Inventors discovered a means of mass-producing steel cheaply and thereby transformed iron manufacturing during the 1860s. The United States, which had no steel industry at the time of the Civil War, became the world's largest steel manufacturer in 1880. The steel industry was centered at Pittsburgh because of its nearness to iron and coal deposits and its easy access to both railroad and maritime transportation. Andrew Carnegie, who came to America as a penniless immigrant boy, became the steel master of America. When he retired from business in 1901, his Carnegie Steel Company was the world's largest. His personal fortune was estimated at $500 million. Carnegie devoted the rest of his life to giving away most of his vast fortune to support various philanthropic enterprises, including more than 2,500 projects such as libraries, public buildings, and foundations.

The American petroleum industry also grew rapidly during the late nineteenth century. The first producing oil well was drilled in western Pennsylvania in 1859. As the oil industry mushroomed during the 1860s, its most important product was kerosene, used mainly to light people's homes at night. One giant firm emerged to monopolize the oil refining industry in America; this was the Standard Oil Company, headed by John D. Rockefeller. Rockefeller had entered the oil business in 1863 when it was competitive and chaotic. Within a few years Standard Oil's efficient operation made it the largest refiner. Standard Oil forced railroads to grant it rebates, giving it a tremendous competitive advantage over rival refineries. It then proceeded to buy up its competition. Competitors who initially refused to sell were driven to the verge of bankruptcy and forced to sell. The Standard Oil Trust, formed in 1882, controlled 85 percent of America's oil refining capacity, and Rockefeller had become the nation's first billionaire. He too retired from business and gave away huge sums of his money to various philanthropic enterprises.

Two other important industries evolved during the late nineteenth century: the telephone industry and the electric utility industry. Alexander Graham Bell invented the telephone in 1876, and two years later the first commercial telephone exchange was installed in New Haven, Connecticut. During the last two decades of the nineteenth century, telephone use spread rapidly. By 1900, Americans were using over 800,000 telephones, mostly for commercial purposes. In that same year, the American Telephone and Telegraph Company acquired its monopoly. Thomas Edison, the most famous inventor in American history, played a key role in the emergence of both the telephone and electric utility industries. He vastly improved telephonic transmission, but his most significant achievement was his perfection, in 1879, of the incandescent lamp (what we now call the electric light bulb) at his Menlo Park, New Jersey, laboratory. At Christmastime he decorated his lab with a few dozen of the new lights, and people came long distances to see this miraculous invention of the "Wizard of Menlo Park." Here was an invention that promised to obliterate the dark, to transform the way people lived and worked.

In 1882 Edison's company built the first power station in New York, which supplied the city with electric current for lighting for 85 customers. By 1898 there were 3,000 operating power stations in the country. The Edison system employed direct current at low voltage, limiting the distance electric power could be transmitted to about two miles. George Westinghouse, another versatile inventor of the era, understood how to use alternating current; the current was stepped up to high voltages by transformers so it could be transmitted cheaply over long distances, and then it was reduced to lower voltages for safe use by consumers. He formed the Westinghouse Electric Company in 1886 to compete with Edison's company, and soon surpassed Edison as a supplier of electricity.

While entrepreneurs and inventors developed the new corporate forms of organization and the new technologies that created the American industrial infrastructure, other business leaders built extensive marketing organizations. The first advertising agencies appeared during the 1870s. Ad writers created copy and devised images to promote national sales of brand names such as Quaker Oats and Kellogg. Large department stores such as Macy's in New York and Wanamaker's in Philadelphia made their appearance. Chain stores such as the Atlantic and Pacific Tea Company (the A & P grocery) and F. W. Woolworth's "five and dimes" proliferated. As the major department and chain stores plied their urban customers with a cornucopia of goods, Montgomery Ward and Sears, Roebuck sold to rural customers through mail order catalogs. Sears's and Ward's mail order businesses could flourish only within a literate and affluent society that had evolved efficient and reliable transportation and communication networks.

As industries physically expanded, they also tended to become concentrated: fewer and fewer firms of a larger and larger size were controlling production in most of the important sectors of the economy. The primary reason for the concentration that accompanied expansion was falling prices. As prices fell, profit margins decreased and competition intensified. Rival concerns engaged in cutthroat competition, lowering their prices still further to retain or to increase market shares; successful firms either destroyed or absorbed their beaten rivals.

According to classical economic theory, cutthroat competition kept prices low and ensured that only the most efficient producers survived and prospered. In practice, however, competition often led to ruinous consequences for both a business and its customers. For example, railroads were forced to cut their freight rates to keep up with their competition. These rate reductions cut deeply into their profits, so they tried to compensate by increasing volume. To increase volume, they often resorted to illegal devices such as granting secret rebates (rates lower than their published rates) to selected large shippers such as Standard Oil while small shippers continued to pay regular rates. Railroads also resorted to bribery to coax favorable trade conditions from state governments. They often charged high prices where they had monopolies to make up for the low rates they had to offer in major competitive markets. Many railroads went bankrupt, especially during recessions and depressions. The public would not tolerate railroads' going out of business because they were the only means of transportation available, and so the courts placed bankrupt lines in the hands of receivers, who, reluctantly, kept them running, but often inefficiently.

Railroads responded to cutthroat competition and its consequences by reorganizing via mergers and takeovers; they combined lines into giant interregional systems during the 1880s. During the severe depression of the early 1890s some of these combines went bankrupt. Bankers, led by J. P. Morgan, intervened to refinance and restructure the railroad systems. The financiers saved the railroads from bankruptcy, eliminated cutthroat competition, and stabilized the nation's primary transportation system. The price paid for an orderly operating environment for the industry included higher rates for freight and passengers, banker control of many of the nation's largest railroads, and interregional monopolies.

At this time most Americans were committed to economic individual-

J. P. Morgan was one of the richest and most powerful men in America during the late nineteenth century. He reorganized railroad companies, created the world's largest steel company, and once used his vast financial resources to save the U.S. Treasury from bankruptcy.

ism and the philosophy of free enterprise. In theory they opposed government regulation of the economy; in practice they accepted considerable governmental activity in the economic sphere—protective tariffs, internal improvements, and land grant subsidies to the railroads—because these governmental actions promoted economic growth and generated jobs.

By the 1880s many Americans had been frightened by the emergence of large industrial corporations such as the giant railroad systems and the Standard Oil Trust. These businesses were too big, too powerful. They were seen as threats to society. Lacking competition, unrestrained by government, they could charge their customers whatever they wanted. Even worse, monopolists were destroying economic opportunity and threatening democratic institutions. Thoughtful citizens worried about the survivability of democracy in a society increasingly characterized by a widening gap between rich and poor. Celebration of industrialization was undercut by fear of its consequences, and many people called for government action to tame the trusts.

The first to act were midwestern farmers and merchants who pressured state legislatures to regulate railroad rates. These state efforts were generally ineffective because railroads were large regional businesses whose operations spanned several states. The Supreme Court, after initially approving such state efforts, declared state regulatory efforts unconstitutional in 1886. In 1887 Congress enacted the Interstate Commerce Act to provide a measure of railroad regulation. It called for rates to be "reasonable and just," outlawed rebates, required railroads to publish and to stick to their rate schedules, and outlawed some monopolistic practices. Most important, it created the Interstate Commerce Commission (ICC), the first federal regulatory agency, to supervise railroads, investigate complaints, and enforce the law.

In practice the ICC proved no more successful than the state regulatory commission. The ICC's chief weakness was its lack of power to set rates; it could merely take the railroads to court and try to persuade the courts to order a rate reduction. Furthermore, the ICC's small staff could handle only a few complaints. These cases were often tied up in courts by lengthy litigation, and when cases *were* resolved, they usually ended in victories for the railroads.

At the same time that some states and the federal government were trying unsuccessfully to regulate the railroads, attempts were also made to tame the trusts. As with railroad legislation, the first antitrust laws originated in the states. They were usually vague and unenforceable. Federal action came in 1890 when Congress enacted the Sherman Antitrust Act, which declared any trust or other combination found to be "in restraint of trade" illegal. Persons forming such trusts could be fined and jailed; individuals and businesses found to have suffered losses caused by illegal actions could sue in federal court for triple damages. The Supreme Court quickly emasculated the Sherman Act, however. In *United States* v. *E. C. Knight Company* (1895) it found that a sugar trust that controlled 98 percent of all domestically refined sugar was not in restraint of trade. The Court held that the E. C. Knight Co. had been formed to manufacture sugar, not to trade sugar, and was therefore a commercial activity, exempt from prosecution under the Sherman Antitrust Act. As the nineteenth century ended, business continued to centralize—and to get bigger.

LABOR

Wage earners were affected in many ways by industrialization and the rise of big business. Some effects were beneficial, others damaging. More efficient production methods enabled industrial workers to increase their output. Real wages rose 25 percent between 1870 and 1890. Work became physically less arduous, and the average workday was shortened from eleven to ten hours.

But as machines replaced human skills in shops and mills, jobs required less skill and became repetitive and monotonous. As manufacturing units grew larger, employee–employer relations became impersonal. The bargaining leverage of workers declined, and opportunities for workers to rise from the ranks of laborers and become manufacturers themselves decreased. Industrial work often proved dangerous. Nearly a million workers were injured annually in work-related accidents. In an age when *laissez-faire* attitudes dominated, there were no safety regulations or compulsory worker compensation programs. Workers and their families received no compensation, even for crippling or fatal accidents that occurred on the job. Industrialization also caused greater and more frequent swings in the business cycle. Periods of expansion would be followed by periods of depression and high unemployment.

During the 1880s and 1890s only a small percentage of industrial workers joined trade unions, and most who did were skilled artisans, such as printers and carpenters, who joined craft unions. Most of the immigrants, who made up the bulk of the industrial work force, were either unwilling or unable to join unions. Unions also excluded most African Americans and women from their ranks. The Knights of Labor, organized in 1869 by a group of garment workers in Philadelphia, managed to survive for a time. During the 1880s it led successful strikes against railroads, and its membership reached 700,000. It declined after that, mainly because the public associated it with violence and radicalism following the Haymarket riot in Chicago in 1886.

The only labor organization to establish itself during the Gilded Age was the American Federation of Labor, organized in 1886. It took a pragmatic, businesslike approach to unionism. It eschewed radicalism and politics. It concentrated on organizing skilled workers and fighting for "bread-and-butter" issues such as better wages and shorter hours. Its chief weapon was the strike. It grew steadily and had one million members by 1900.

Worker frustration and discontent mounted in the late nineteenth century. Workers felt threatened by the huge size of corporate employers, by technology, and by periodic recessions and depressions, which meant unemployment in a *laissez-faire* economy. Most of all they were frightened and angered by the stubborn arrogance of corporate employers, nearly all of whom opposed trade unions, fired workers for joining unions, and refused to bargain with union representatives. Strikes, which became frequent during the 1880s and 1890s, often became bitter, violent confrontations.

A savage railroad strike in 1877 convulsed the nation. For a time about two-thirds of the nation's railways were shut down. Violence erupted in several locations in Maryland and Pennsylvania. Workers were shot; railroad properties were sabotaged. Federal troops were called out to keep order. During an 1892 strike against Carnegie's steel factory in Homestead, Pennsylvania, a fierce battle erupted between armed strikers and company guards, claiming seven lives. This strike lasted for months before the company won, fired many of the strikers, and crushed their union.

The most important strike occurred in 1894, when workers at the Pullman Company near Chicago protested wage cuts during a severe de-

Striking steel workers at the Carnegie mills in Homestead, Pennsylvania, prepare for a clash with armed Pinkerton dectectives hired by Andrew Carnegie to break the strike.

pression. Some Pullman employees belonged to the American Railway Union, led by Eugene V. Debs, and they refused to work on trains with Pullman cars. The resulting strike tied up rail traffic in and out of Chicago. The railroad companies appealed to President Cleveland to send troops, and he did, on the pretext that they were required to ensure the movement of mail. When Debs defied a federal injunction, he was jailed for contempt of court and the strike was broken. The crushing of the Pullman strike demonstrated the power of the courts to break strikes. The strike also made Debs a national figure. In 1897 he converted to socialism and later ran for president five times on the American Socialist Party (SDP) ticket.

"NEW" IMMIGRANTS

The industrial revolution stimulated a huge increase in immigration to America and tapped new population sources. Most of the immigrants before 1890 had come from the British Isles or western and northern Europe. After 1890 large numbers continued to emigrate from these traditional sources, but the majority of immigrants arrived from southern and eastern Europe (Italy, Poland, Russia, and the Balkan countries), countries that had previously furnished few if any immigrants. These new immigrants were a predominantly peasant population pushed out of their homelands by decaying feudal economies and political and religious persecution. They flooded into America, pulled by the promise of economic opportunity and personal freedom.

Their first experiences were often harsh. They braved an uncomfortable, sometimes dangerous sea voyage and worried through inspections at Ellis Island and other immigration depots, often arriving in America with few possessions, little money, no education, and no job skills. They crowded into immigrant neighborhoods in large cities, where they found living quarters and the company of their ethnic brethren. These communities centered around old-country institutions such as the church and synagogue. Although most of these new arrivals had peasant backgrounds, few went into agriculture; they lacked the capital and knowledge required for farming, which was a specialized business in America. Also the economic possibilities and cultural attractions of the cities were more inviting than those of rural areas. The new immigrants were fed into the urban, industrial work force. They lived in tenements near the factories that employed them. Many went into construction work, digging sewers, installing utilities, and paving the streets of expanding metropolises, in which the only constant appeared to be ceaseless growth. They worked hard, often for long hours, six days a week. At night they returned to their crowded apartments in slum neighborhoods.

Even so, these harsh living and working conditions were better than what most of them had left behind. They worked no harder and earned no less than the native-born workers who were doing the same kind of work. Many immigrants acquired the income and knowledge to leave the ghetto. If they could not, their children, benefiting from educational opportunities, often achieved middle-class occupations, income, and status. There were many victors as well as victims among the immigrant groups pouring into the United States during the 1890s.

Nevertheless, the oppressive living conditions prevailing in the immigrant slums and the failure of many of the newcomers to assimilate into the mainstream of American life angered and alarmed reformers. One of them, Jacob Riis, called attention to the immigrants' plight in an influential book, *How the Other Half Lives*, published in 1890. The book consisted of sketches of life in New York's immigrant ghettos drawn from Riis's years as a reporter. His essays were illustrated with photographs. He piled one pathetic case upon another, his prose full of anger and shock. He declared the slums to be the children of "public neglect and private greed." A reformer, he advocated decent, low-cost housing as the chief means of solving these savage social problems.

A year before Riis published his spirited book, Jane Addams opened a settlement house in a slum neighborhood of south Chicago, where she and other social workers provided services to the residents, who were mainly new immigrants. She called it Hull House, and it became the largest and most famous of the hundreds of settlement houses during the last fifteen years of the nineteenth century. Hull House offered its clients a day-care center, arts and crafts, counseling, playgrounds and baths for children, cooking classes, schools, an employment referral service, and access to medical and dental care. It also brought middle-class social workers into contact with immigrants, giving those professionals an opportunity for firsthand observation of immigrant problems.

The tremendous influx of "new" immigrants also provoked a nativist backlash on the part of some old-stock native-born Americans. Nativists resented what they perceived to be a flood of poor, illiterate, and unskilled people who could never become productive citizens. A body of pseudo-scientific studies attempted to prove that immigrants from southern and eastern European countries belonged to races that were inferior to northern and western Europeans and their American descendants. During the 1880s and 1890s nativists organized for action and became a potent political force. The most influential such organization was the American Protective Association (APA), founded in 1887 primarily to promote Americanism and Protestant religions, which members equated with American national culture. Its chief targets were Roman Catholics, the Catholic Church, and Catholicism itself. Other less extremist voices joined the call for excluding "new" immigrants or at least severely reducing the size of the inflow. During the 1890s the leaders of organized labor called for the adoption of literacy tests to screen out immigrants. Congress moved to bar "undesirable" immigrants from entering the country; at various times it excluded convicts, insane people, contract laborers, paupers, anarchists, and people with serious communicable diseases.

URBAN AMERICANS

The enormous expansion of industry was the chief cause of urban growth during the Gilded Age, when modern American metropolises appeared. A steadily increasing proportion of the American urban population was made up of immigrants. By 1900, immigrant populations composed the majority of the population in several of the largest American cities. According to the 1900 census, for example, first- or second-generation immigrants made up over 80 percent of New York City's nearly 3.5 million inhabitants.

These immigrants often got blamed for all the problems that afflicted American cities of the late nineteenth century; this accusation was both exaggerated and unfair. The main cause of urban problems was the unplanned, rapid expansion of cities. Cities suffered from acute growing pains; city services could not begin to keep pace with the rate of urban growth. Severe problems with water supplies, sewage, garbage disposal, and police and fire protection arose. The worst problem was crowded, substandard housing, with its attendant physical discomfort, psychological stress, juvenile delinquency, vice, and crime. Slums spawned street gangs, epidemic diseases, and high infant mortality rates.

Gradually the basic facilities of urban living improved. Streets were paved; electric lights pushed back the dark after nightfall. Major improvements were made in urban transportation, the major innovation being the electric trolley. These streetcars changed the character of urban life. They extended the range of the traditional "walking city" from two-and-a-half miles to more than six miles, causing the geographic areas of cities to expand enormously. Population shifts occurred as the affluent classes fled from inner cities to the outer neighborhoods, the suburbs, leaving the poor immigrant working classes clustered in the downtown areas. Segregated residential patterns emerged in every city, separating people by income and economic class, which correlated with ethnic and racial divisions.

POLITICS

Politics during this era were characterized by passive presidents and strong senators. The Senate dominated the federal government. Many of its members either were political bosses preoccupied with forging alliances, winning elections, and controlling patronage, or else they were pawns of corporate interests. In either case they tended to neglect the real issues of the day. The House of Representatives was more responsive to the public interest, but it was too unstable to play an effective legislative role. Frequent, close elections meant a constant turnover in House membership, and neither party was able to control the House long enough to enact a legislative agenda. At local and state levels, corrupt political machines frequently controlled government.

Political machines stayed in power by turning out the vote on election day to support the organization's candidates. Control of elections meant power—power to distribute city jobs to supporters, to award franchises for providing city services in exchange for bribes to companies, and to award building contracts to construction companies willing to pay for them. Corrupt contractors often profited excessively from these contracts by overcharging the taxpayers and using cheap, substandard materials.

Immigrant neighborhoods formed the popular base of big city political machines. It was common for individuals to register illegally in several precincts and vote many times on election day, and often to be rewarded by machine favors—a job, a cheap rental, help in case of trouble with the police, and assistance in acquiring citizenship. Frequently a member of the political machine appeared at baptisms, weddings, and funerals. The political boss and many of his henchmen themselves were often immigrants, with whom newcomers could therefore identify, and to whose success and power they too aspired. The machine also ran ethnically balanced tickets to appeal to a broad range of nationalities and to give members of immigrant groups an opportunity to participate in politics.

Political machines often sponsored dinners, fairs, and picnic outings for their immigrant constituents, events that not only entertained the voters but also ensured their continuing political support.

Presidential elections were invariably hard fought, corrupt, and close. The two major political parties were evenly matched and nearly identical. There were few significant issue differences between them, and no ideological differences. Usually Republican presidential candidates won narrowly. Grover Cleveland was the only Democratic president to hold office during the 1880s and 1890s. Elections were not decided by the issues. Rather, voters generally voted a straight party ticket, although occasionally they were attracted by the personal qualities of a candidate.

WOMEN, CHILDREN, AND WORK

During the last decades of the nineteenth century 5 million American women entered the work force. Many became factory workers in manufacturing industries such as shoemaking, food processing, and textiles. By 1890 over 300,000 women worked in textile factories, comprising over half of the labor force. They also took jobs in business as typists, bookkeepers, and salespersons. Employers were willing to hire millions of women because in most cases they could pay them substantially less than men. Women worked for about a third to a half of what men received for

Women workers in one of the nation's "sweatshops" during the Gilded Age.

comparable work. In 1900 about 90 percent of working women were young and single. Prevailing attitudes barred married women from the work places of America; when a young working girl married, she usually had to quit her job. Female workers sometimes organized their own unions, carrying out successful strikes and achieving higher wages. Working women forged the first broad-based women's union in this country, the Women's Trade Union League (WTUL), founded in 1903. Women also entered most of the professions, albeit in small numbers. They became doctors, lawyers, engineers, and university professors. By 1900 most public school teachers and librarians were women.

Most working children labored on their parents' farms, but they also flooded into industrial occupations in the late nineteenth century. Children under age 14 worked in coal mining, textiles, and other industries. Some worked in the streets selling newspapers and shining shoes.

NATIVE AMERICANS

During the 1870s and 1880s, as the American economy expanded and the building of the railroads opened the West for economic development, the Plains Indians became victims of the westward expansion. They were conquered, their culture was fragmented, and they were deprived of much of their lands. The survivors were tucked away on arid reservations to endure a life of poverty and isolation.

Indian resistance was heroic; they held off the encroaching whites for years, but they inevitably succumbed to overwhelming firepower and vastly superior numbers. It was the destruction of the buffalo herds that fatally undermined the ability of the Plains Indians to resist the U.S. Army. Two vast herds had roamed the prairies, furnishing the Indians with food, clothing, shelter, and tools. By the 1880s these herds had been hunted to the verge of extinction, and the Plains Indians' way of life was undermined. General Philip Sheridan, the Civil War hero who commanded U.S. Army forces that conquered the Plains Indians, understood why the Indians fought, and he expressed sympathy for the people his soldiers were destroying. He wrote:

> We took away their country and their means of support, broke up their mode of living, their habits of life, introduced disease and decay among them and it was for this and against this they made war. Could anyone expect less?[1]

Plains Indians also suffered at the hands of civilian agencies entrusted with administering Indian affairs. Government agents were politi-

---

1.   Thomas C. Leonard, "The Reluctant Conquerors," *American Heritage*, 27:5 (August 1976), 34–40.

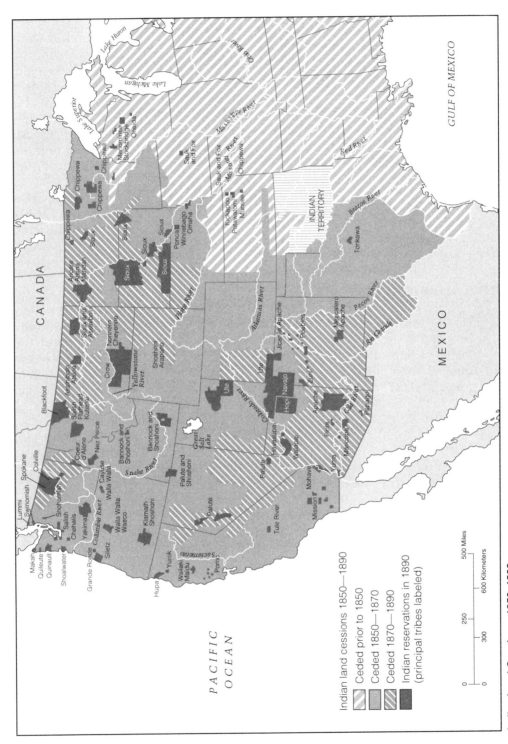

Indian land cessions 1850—1890

Ceded prior to 1850

Ceded 1850—1870

Ceded 1870—1890

Indian reservations in 1890
(principal tribes labeled)

0   250   500 Miles

0   300   600 Kilometers

Indian Land Cessions, 1850–1890

cal appointees and were often incompetent, corrupt, and indifferent to Indian welfare; they exploited the people they supposedly served. There were cases of agents' selling food supplies intended for reservation Indians to miners and pocketing the money, leaving the helpless Indians to starve.

In 1887 Congress passed the Dawes Act, designed to eliminate tribal life and to convert the surviving Plains Indians to the white man's way of life. Reservation lands were divided into small units, with each head of an Indian household allotted 160 acres. Indians who accepted the allotments and "adopted the habits of civilized life" were granted U.S. citizenship. A clause in the Dawes Act prevented Indians from selling their allotted lands for 25 years. Funds were also appropriated to provide education for Indian children. Intended as a reform to help Indians, in practice the Dawes Act proved disastrous. It shattered the remnants of Indian culture without enabling the Indians to adopt the "white man's ways." Most of the land allotments ended up in white hands, and the Indians remained dependent on government aid. The Dawes Act was the final destructive act in a long chronicle of white atrocities committed against Native Americans.

The last Indians to abandon the unequal struggle against the whites were the Chiricahua Apaches who inhabited the desert of the Southwest. Relentless warriors, they waged a bitter, savage guerrilla struggle against the U.S. Army in Arizona Territory. In 1886 the Army succeeded in capturing their chieftain, a resourceful warrior named Geronimo. The Apaches finally yielded and the nearly 300-year-old struggle between Native Americans and European invaders in North America came to an end.

There was a tragic final footnote to the Euro-American conquest of the Native American people, written in the snow at Wounded Knee, South Dakota, in December 1890. A Paiute shaman named Wovoka had developed a religion based on a ceremonial rite known to whites as the Ghost Dance. Wovoka promised his people that there would come a time when the dead would reappear and the land would be returned to Native Americans. He converted the Lakota Sioux to his new faith. U.S. soldiers attacked a Sioux religious observance. Heavily armed cavalrymen massacred the Indians as they tried to flee, butchering scores of people, including women and children.

AFRICAN AMERICANS

While Native Americans fell victim to western expansion, the status of black people in the South deteriorated in the aftermath of Reconstruction. Throughout the decade of the 1880s, the status of African Americans in the South was ambiguous. They retained legal and political rights. They voted, but they were deprived of effective political power because the Republican Party organization had been destroyed.

During the 1890s, with Mississippi leading the way, southern states rewrote their constitutions to include provisions that disfranchised most African Americans. Various subterfuges were used to circumvent the Fifteenth Amendment, the most common of which was the "understanding clause." This clause required potential voters to read and understand any section of their state constitution before registering and left enforcement of this rule to voter registrars. Registrars used it as a vehicle to disfranchise African Americans by imposing stringent standards on them, meanwhile allowing illiterate whites to register by taking their word that they "understood" the state constitution. Other exclusionary devices included literacy tests and poll taxes. Black disfranchisement ensured Democratic control of southern politics. Disfranchisement also excluded large numbers of white voters, particularly those who had formerly voted Republican.

By 1900 only 5 percent of eligible African Americans voted in the South. Disfranchisement also opened the door for legal segregation in all important areas of southern life. Elaborate segregation ordinances evolved everywhere in the South, depriving black people of equal access to public accommodations. By 1900 southern blacks were disfranchised, segregated, and deprived of equal educational and economic opportunities.

There was a tremendous increase in the amount of violence directed against black people during the 1890s. Lynch mobs roamed the South murdering hundreds of African Americans. By the end of the nineteenth century, rights acquired during Reconstruction had become a faint memory for black people.

The application of Jim Crow had been possible because the Supreme Court had retreated from its commitment to racial democracy in the aftermath of Reconstruction. In 1883 the Court nullified the Civil Rights Act of 1875, which had outlawed segregation of public accommodations. In 1896 the Supreme Court put the seal of constitutional approval upon segregation. In a notorious case, *Plessy* v. *Ferguson*, the Court sustained a Louisiana statute that segregated the races on railroads. The Court found segregation to be constitutional if "separate but equal" facilities were provided. It held that separate but equal facilities did not violate the equal protection clause of Section One of the Fourteenth Amendment. This crucial decision resolved a conflict between American professions of equality and institutionalized racism when the Court also held that segregation did not imply that black people were inferior. The timing of *Plessy* v. *Ferguson* was also important. It removed the last barrier to the general drive to deprive African Americans of rights, and in the words of historian C. Vann Woodward, the decision "unleashed the floodgates of racial aggression." Segregation would be constitutional for the next 58 years.

Out of this era of decline and danger for African Americans emerged Booker T. Washington to become the foremost spokesman for black people. Deeply concerned about the ability of African Americans to survive in racist America, he developed a strategy he hoped would lead to racial harmony and common progress. In a speech delivered at an Atlanta exposi-

Booker T. Washington, born a slave, rose to become a prominent leader in education and the foremost spokesman for African Americans during the 1890s.

tion in 1895, he preached self-help, economic progress, thrift, and racial solidarity. He told black people that if they learned to advance themselves by getting agricultural or vocational training, saving their money, and acquiring property, they would earn the respect and acceptance of whites. Washington assured white leaders that African Americans accepted disfranchisement and segregation in order to concentrate on economic gains. In return he asked southern white business leaders and politicians to support black education and hire black workers. Washington's proposed accommodationist strategy made him popular among whites and enabled him to raise millions of dollars from northern philanthropists for black technical and vocational training.

Other African American leaders, rejecting Washington's accommodationist strategies, proposed that blacks challenge racism and legal segregation, that they demand full equality now. The most prominent African American scholar in 1900, William E. B. Dubois, told blacks that they should demand the best university education available and that they should demand the right to vote in order to battle the segregation system through the political process.

During the 1890s over 90 percent of African Americans resided in the South, most of them living outside the boundaries of industrial society. Most were forced to live within an oppressive environment with no political power and with inferior legal rights. African Americans were bound by a rigid and stringent caste system that deprived them of equal opportunities, indeed forbade any expression of equality. In many regions of the South, African Americans were entrapped in a kind of economic bondage. They worked as sharecroppers or tenants, perpetually in debt, caught up in a credit system that enabled landowners, merchants, and bankers to hold them in virtual peonage.

Despite their difficult lives within an oppressive and unjust social system, many capable and hard-working African Americans achieved considerable success. They enjoyed strong, stable family lives. They established solid communities built around black churches and schools and black-owned businesses. Thousands of black farmers were able to acquire their own farms. According to the census of 1900, African Americans owned about 12 million acres of land in the South.

ASIAN AMERICANS

Chinese people first emigrated to the United States during the 1840s, when they came to California to mine gold. Initially they were welcomed. These immigrants were mostly young men who sojourned to make their fortunes in the region they called the "Gold Mountain" and who planned to return to their villages and families in China. Many came from the Toison district of Canton Province in southern China. During the 1860s perhaps 25,000 Chinese were working in California's gold fields. As the gold ore played out, some miners went on to build railroads.

During the 1860s about 12,000 Chinese worked for the Southern Pacific railroad, constructing the western half of the first transcontinental railroad, which was completed in 1869. During the 1870s Chinese immigrants in California worked in agriculture, in the fishing industry, and in service businesses such as restaurants and laundries. They were ineligible for American citizenship under a 1790 law that limited that privilege to white people. Many prospered despite considerable, often violent, anti-Chinese prejudice. In 1882 about 30,000 Chinese immigrants entered the country, bringing the national total to 150,000 concentrated mostly on the West Coast.

Many white Americans had resented the Chinese for years. Anti-Chinese prejudice was especially strong among working-class whites, who viewed the Chinese as economic competitors who took their jobs, worked for lower wages, and could be used as strikebreakers. Unions held "anti-coolie" meetings and demonstrations protesting the Chinese presence and calling for a ban on further Chinese immigration. There were violent attacks on Chinese, including lynchings, burnings, and the destroying of their homes and businesses. Pressure from West Coast politicians prompted Washington to enact the 1882 Chinese Exclusion Act, which barred most Chinese immigration to the United States for ten years. The

Chinese were the first national group to be formally barred from emigrating to America.

Japanese emigration to the United States began during the late 1880s on a small scale. By 1900 about 2,700 Japanese immigrants had reached America, most settling in California. They also encountered anti-Asian prejudice, which hindered their opportunities. White Californians began a drive to exclude Japanese immigrants that would continue intermittently until World War II.

FARMERS

The economic position of many farmers declined during the late nineteenth century, for several reasons. Ironically, one of the major reasons for agricultural decline was the fact that the American industrial revolution had enabled American farmers to mechanize, to farm larger acreages,

Harvesting wheat on one of the "bonanza farms" in western America ca. 1900.

and above all, to increase productivity. Agricultural production increased throughout the world, and the European market, which was the American farmers' major overseas outlet, shrank. Farm commodity prices tumbled. Corn, which had sold at 78 cents a bushel in 1869, brought 28 cents in 1889. Wheat brought two dollars a bushel in 1867, 70 cents in 1889. Moreover, farmers now had to pay more for equipment and other supplies because manufacturers, protected from foreign competition by tariff barriers, had raised their prices. Good land was increasingly expensive in many areas either because it was growing scarce or because the railroads and large land companies controlled it. Flour-milling and meat-packing companies forced farmers and stock owners to sell them grain and beef at lower prices. Railroads, especially in regions where they enjoyed a transportation monopoly, often charged farmers exorbitant rates to haul their crops.

Midwestern farmers organized to try to improve their economic situation. During the 1860s and 1870s they formed granges. These groups organized purchasing cooperatives and also lobbied state governments to regulate railroads, particularly to limit the shipping rates charged to farmers. These efforts were generally futile. By the late 1870s many farmers were in serious economic difficulty. Farm income continued to fall and many farmers were deeply in debt for equipment and land that they had purchased. Unable to make mortgage and tax payments, they faced the loss of their farms.

In their distress some farmers turned to currency inflation to rescue them from economic disaster. During the Civil War the government had issued "greenbacks"—hundreds of millions of dollars of paper money that was not redeemable in silver or gold. Farmers, joined by small merchants and other hard-pressed groups, called for the government to issue more greenbacks. They reasoned that currency inflation would cause price levels to rise, so their income would increase and they could pay their debts. In 1880 they formed the Greenback-Labor party, a single-issue alternative party, which attracted 300,000 votes. It faded thereafter, but the idea of easing farmers' debt burdens via currency inflation did not.

THE PEOPLE'S PARTY

In the late 1880s hard times continued and farmers continued to organize in efforts to solve their economic problems. Farmers' Alliances appeared in the Midwest and South. During the late 1880s the Alliances claimed a membership of white and black farmers that approached 2 million. They formed cooperatives and entered politics at the local level. Alliance members, encouraged by local political successes and angered by both major parties, which had continued to be unresponsive to their concerns, met in St. Louis in February 1892 to form a new national third party, the People's

Party, also called the Populist Party or the Populists. They gathered again in Omaha, Nebraska, on July 4, 1892, to choose their candidate for president and to adopt a platform. In a noisy, emotional gathering, which resembled a religious revival, they denounced bankers and business leaders who exploited the farmers and workers of the country.

The major plank in their platform was a call for currency inflation, but this was no longer a call for more greenbacks, a goal the farmers had abandoned as being unrealistic. They now wanted the free and unlimited coinage of silver to gold at a ratio of sixteen to one. They wanted to inflate the currency, expanding the money supply by requiring the U.S. Treasury to buy and to coin free of charge all silver brought to it. They wanted silver dollars to contain sixteen times as much silver, by weight, as gold dollars would contain gold. That sixteen to one ratio would ensure that silver would be more valuable as money than as a precious metal, and it would therefore remain in circulation as money, thereby inflating the currency. This money plank appealed to western silver miners as well as farmers, and it also appealed to some small business owners who saw inflation as a cure for their economic woes. Free silver also had symbolic uses: It represented the liberation of the toiling masses from economic bondage to banks and railroads. Free silver would redeem their Jeffersonian birthright and restore their claim to a fair share of society's benefits.

Other Populist planks called for government ownership of railroads and telephone lines, an income tax, a single term for the president, and the direct election of senators. Populists tried to attract the support of labor by calling for an eight-hour day, by denouncing contract labor (importing aliens as workers who took jobs from American workers and could be used as strikebreakers), and by demanding an end to the use of Pinkerton detectives to break up strikes.

At the time of the Populist movement, there was a great deal of discontent among the urban working classes. Strikes and unemployment marches were symptomatic of the seething unrest. Some angry workers made common cause with the embattled farmers from the Midwest and South. In 1894 Jacob Coxey led an "army" of about 600 unemployed workers in a march from his home in Ohio to the nation's capital. Middle-class Americans were alarmed by the growing signs of social instability in their increasingly frayed society.

The Populists nominated for president James B. Weaver, a former Civil War general and Greenback-Labor leader. Running as a third party in 1892, the Populists waged an energetic campaign. They had able leaders such as Mary E. Lease, an attorney and powerful orator, who exhorted Kansas farmers to "raise less corn and more hell." The Populists gathered over a million votes, 8.5 percent of the total. They showed strength in two regions: the South and the newer states of the Midwest. They won many local elections, elected some representatives and a few senators, and won control of the Kansas legislature. They also picked up 22 electoral votes. It was a good showing, good enough to alarm the established parties in the South and Midwest, and the Populists looked ahead to 1896.

During 1893 and 1894 the nation was mired in the worst depression in its history. Banks and businesses failed by the thousands. Railroads controlling about one-third of the trackage in the country went bankrupt. Farmers, unable to meet mortgage payments, lost their farms. Millions of industrial workers were unemployed. Late in 1894 the U.S. Treasury faced a desperate financial crisis. Its gold reserves dwindled to $41 million, not enough to pay debt obligations that would soon come due. Only an emergency bond issue that was floated by a banking syndicate headed by J. P. Morgan, which raised $62 million, saved the American government from bankruptcy.

The Populist vote increased in the 1894 elections as this party continued to demand the unlimited coinage of silver to gold at a ratio of sixteen to one. President Cleveland's failure to solve the depression discredited his administration. The Democrats in the South and Republicans in the Midwest feared they would lose their following to the Populists in 1896.

The Republicans met to nominate a candidate in St. Louis in 1896 and chose an Ohio congressman with a good record, William McKinley. They adopted a platform maintaining the gold standard and a protective tariff.

At the Democratic convention, held in Chicago in July 1896, President Cleveland lost control of the delegates, and they rallied to the candidacy of a youthful Nebraskan named William Jennings Bryan. Bryan won the nomination with a dramatic appeal for silver, ending his speech, "You shall not press down upon the brow of labor this crown of thorns; you shall not crucify mankind upon a cross of gold." The convention promptly adopted a platform calling for the "free and unlimited coinage of both gold and silver at the present legal ratio of sixteen to one" and nominated Bryan, who was only 36 years old, for president.

The Democrats' actions confronted the Populists with a Hobson's choice. If they supported Bryan and free silver, they would risk losing their identity as a political party. If they ran their own candidate, they would ensure McKinley's election and the defeat of the silver issue. Most Populists ended up supporting Bryan and the Democrats. After 1896 Populist support declined rapidly. The Democrats had co-opted the Populists' major issue and most of their followers.

In the contest between Bryan and McKinley, issues did matter. The Republicans had many advantages they could exploit during the campaign. The Democrats were saddled with Cleveland's discredited depression presidency and were on the defensive. McKinley ran a well-organized, well-financed campaign orchestrated by an Ohio businessman, Marcus A. Hanna. Hanna raised $3.5 million. His campaign organization flooded the nation with millions of pieces of campaign literature and 1,500 speakers. Theodore Roosevelt said that Hanna "advertised McKinley as if he were a patent medicine." Hanna's strategy called for McKinley to stay home, conducting a dignified "front porch" campaign. Selected delegates representing various national constituencies would be brought to his home, where McKinely would greet them and make a speech calculated to appeal to their interests. Hanna saw to it that McKinley's "front porch" speeches got national attention.

The Democrats had no money, no organization, and few prominent supporters. But they had Williams Jenning Bryan, who waged an energetic one-man campaign. He traveled over 18,000 miles and made over 600 stump speeches. Bryan had a powerful voice—loud, clear, and eloquent. He spoke, without amplification, to crowds as large as 10,000. All could hear, and most cheered. Bryan's campaign speeches were dominated by a single theme: silver. His was mainly a single-issue and regional campaign in contrast to McKinley's pluralistic and nationalistic approach.

In November McKinley won decisively, getting over 7 million votes to Bryan's 6.5 million and receiving 271 electoral votes to Bryan's 176. The Republicans also rolled up large majorities in both houses of Congress. Organization and money had beaten eloquence. Pluralism had defeated silver. Nationalism had bested sectionalism. The silver issue carried the

The Election of 1896

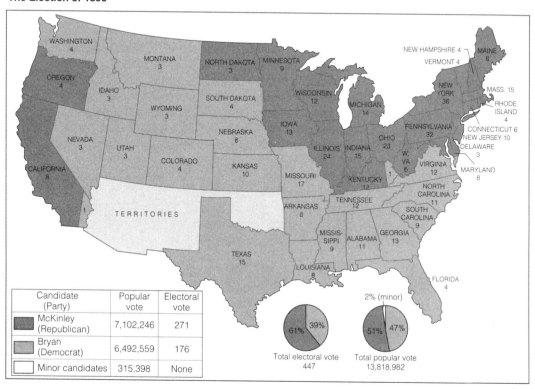

Candidate (Party)	Popular vote	Electoral vote
McKinley (Republican)	7,102,246	271
Bryan (Democrat)	6,492,559	176
Minor candidates	315,398	None

61% / 39%
Total electoral vote 447

2% (minor)
51% / 47%
Total popular vote 13,818,982

South and Midwest, but it did not travel well outside these regions. Bryan also failed to reach industrial workers. The Republicans got the support of most urban voters, most business voters, and most middle-class voters, and they carried the farm vote in several midwestern states such as Illinois and Ohio.

IMPERIALISM

For much of the Gilded Age Americans were preoccupied with internal events such as industrialization, the building of the railroads, the settlement of the West, and urban affairs. But toward the end of the nineteenth century the United States turned outward. It became involved in world affairs, built a modern navy, expanded its overseas trade, fought a war with Spain, and acquired a colonial empire. By 1900 the United States had emerged as a world power.

Many forces had converged to revive American expansionism and to direct American attention overseas. Powerful economic forces stemming from industrialization played a major role. Industrialization diversified and increased American exports, creating a search for new overseas markets and a drive to expand existing ones. Andrew Carnegie discovered he could sell a ton of steel to an English railway cheaper than English steel manufacturers could. John D. Rockefeller's Standard Oil monopoly soon dominated the European market for kerosene. Other American business leaders looked to Latin America, long a market for British manufactures. American imports also increased, many coming from American-owned enterprises in foreign lands. American investment capital poured into Canada, Mexico, and Cuba during the 1890s.

Other forces promoted expansion. Captain Alfred T. Mahan, an avowed expansionist, urged Congress to modernize and expand the U.S. Navy. In books and essays he used the example of Great Britain, the world's preeminent power, to prove his contention that sea power undergirded all great powers. He linked expanding sea power with expanding commercial ties and overseas colonial possessions. His arguments influenced many members of Congress and two future presidents, Theodore Roosevelt and Woodrow Wilson.

The missionary movements of many churches also promoted overseas activity. In their earnest desire to save souls and do good works for the greater glory of God, missionaries were servants of expansion, particularly in Asia. By the 1890s hundreds of American missionaries lived and worked in China. Reverend Josiah Strong, a Congregational minister from Ohio, actively promoted American missionary expansionism. Blending a concept of religious mission with nationalism and racial ideologies, he prophesied:

This race of unequaled energy, with all the majesty of numbers, and the might of wealth behind it—the representative, let us hope, of the largest liberty, the purest Christianity, the highest civilization . . . will move down upon Mexico, down upon Central and South America, out upon the islands of the sea.[2]

Social Darwinists also advocated American expansionism. They applied the Darwinian concept of "struggle for survival" to international power politics. They were confident that what they called the mighty American "Anglo-Saxon race" was destined to acquire colonies and to expand its influence until it dominated the world. Social Darwinist foreign policy ideas also influenced men such as Theodore Roosevelt and Henry Cabot Lodge, who helped forge America's expansionist foreign policies from 1899 to World War I.

Thus an amalgam of powerful economic, strategic, and ideological forces provided an expansionist dynamic. Together they turned a hitherto inward-looking and parochial continental power into an expansionist and international power during the last decade of the nineteenth century.

American expansion initially focused on the South Pacific. As the century came to a close, the United States gained ownership of two island chains, Samoa and Hawaii. Samoa, which lay some 4,000 miles southwest of San Francisco, commanded important shipping lanes in the South Pacific. Its splendid natural harbors of Apia and Pago Pago were desired as way stations for America's gowing trade with New Zealand and Australia.

In 1878 the United States concluded a treaty with the Samoans that gave the United States rights to a coaling station at Pago Pago. The Germans and British also negotiated treaties with Samoa, and the three nations disputed each other's interests in the archipelago. All three sent warships, and for a time war threatened among them, but they resolved their conflicts diplomatically at a conference held in Berlin in 1889. They created a three-power protectorate, which, however, proved inherently unworkable as conflicts over economic and strategic interests continued. In 1899 the Samoan archipelago was divided between Germany and the United States, with Britain gaining territory elsewhere. Germany got the two largest islands, America the remaining islands, including Tutuila, with its harbor at Pago Pago.

American involvement with the Hawaiian Islands dated from the 1820s, when New England missionaries settled there to convert the population. During the 1840s American whaling ships made Hawaii a major port of call. American cultural influence had become dominant in the islands by midcentury, and some expansionists were calling for annexation.

---

2.   Josiah Strong, *Our Country*, ed. Joseph Herbst (Cambridge, MA: Belknap Press, 1963), reprint of the 1891 rev. ed. See Chap. 14, "The Anglo Saxon and the World's Future," pp. 213–18.

In 1875 a reciprocity treaty was signed between Hawaii and the United States which lowered tariffs on both sides. These arrangements permitted Hawaii to ship sugar duty free to the United States, causing the islands' sugar industy to boom. It also tied the Hawaiian economy to mainland markets. Economic dependency became a strong force for political union with the United States. The reciprocity treaty was amended in 1887 to grant American ships exclusive right to use the Pearl River Harbor as a naval station.

By 1890 planters of American descent controlled the sugar industry and owned about two-thirds of the land. In that year changes in American tariff laws favoring domestic sugar growers caused mainland demand for Hawaiian sugar to drop sharply, plunging the Hawaiian economy into depression. Hawaiian sugar planters favored annexation with the United States to regain their lost markets. There were also other motives for annexation. In 1891 Queen Liliuokalani became the Hawaiian monarch. Resenting the growing influence of Americans, she abolished the existing constitution, which had granted Americans control of the islands' political life, and she reasserted the absolute prerogatives of the traditional Hawaiian monarchy. Her actions provoked an American-led coup in December 1892 that overthrew her government. The planter revolutionaries turned to the American minister to Hawaii, John Stevens, for help.

On January 16, 1893, Stevens, a strong advocate of annexation, arranged for 150 marines from the USS *Boston*, then in Pearl Harbor, to take up stations near Queen Liliuokalani's palace where the queen tried to regain power. The next day Stevens recognized the new revolutionary regime. The Queen yielded her authority, grudgingly. Two weeks later Stevens declared Hawaii an American protectorate and advised Washington to proceed with annexation: "The Hawaiian pear is now fully ripe, and this is the golden hour for the United States to pluck it." A delegation from the new Hawaiian government came to Washingto to negotiate an annexation treaty. In mid-February, less than a month following the coup, President Harrison submitted an annexation treaty to the Senate for approval.

The Senate had not yet voted on the proposed treaty when a new president, Grover Cleveland, took office. Cleveland, who opposed annexation, withdrew the treaty from Senate consideration. He sent a special commissioner, former Congressman James Blount, to Hawaii to find out if the native Hawaiians favored annexation. Blount reported to Cleveland that the coup against the Queen could not have succeeded without U.S. complicity and that the Hawaiians both opposed annexation and wanted their monarch restored. The president blocked annexation and tried to restore the Queen to her throne, but the Americans planters now controlling the Hawaiian government refused to step down.

In 1897 President William McKinley came to office favoring annexation. Another treaty was negotiated and sent to the Senate, which failed to approve it. It took the outbreak of the Spanish-American War to provide

The United States in the Pacific

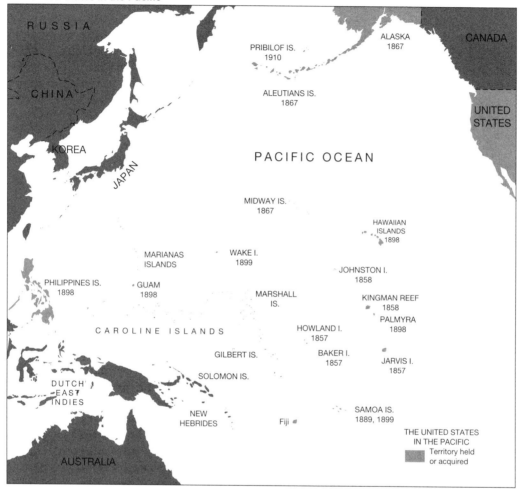

the necessary votes for the annexation of Hawaii. Advocates argued that Hawaii was needed to send supplies and reinforcements to American soldiers in the Philippines. Captain Mahan argued that the United States required Hawaii to protect the American mainland from future attacks. He also argued the United States should take Hawaii lest it fall into the hands of a hostile power such as Japan. War fever and imperialism carried the day. The annexation treaty passed. On July 7, 1898, Hawaii became an American territory.

Another major area of American interest was the Caribbean. In 1895 U.S. attention focused on Cuba when the Cubans rose in rebellion against Spanish rule. The fighting between the rebels and the Spanish troops was vicious. The Spanish commander, General Valeriano Weyler, in an effort to deny the guerrillas popular support, herded the Cuban people into concentration camps, where thousands of them perished from disease, starvation, and mistreatment. Americans, who mostly sympathized with the rebels, were appalled by General Weyler's notorious *reconcentrado* policy and its ghastly results. American newspapers also carried exaggerated and distorted accounts of Spanish activity in Cuba, further inflaming public opinion against the Spanish. Two large New York City dailies, Joseph Pulitzer's *New York World* and young William Randolph Hearst's *New York Morning Journal*, competing fiercely for readers, ran many sensational, inaccurate accounts of the war.

Irresponsible journalism may have stirred the people, but it did not cause the United States to go to war in Cuba. Other forces were at work. Anti-Spanish sentiment was intensified in early February 1898 when Cuban rebels released a private letter that had been written by Spanish Ambassador Enrique Dupuy de Lôme. In the letter de Lôme had criticized President McKinley, calling him "weak and a bidder for the admiration of the crowd."

A week after the publication of the letter, there occurred the event that probably made war inevitable. On the evening of February 15 the American battleship *Maine* was blown up in Havana Harbor. The ship was demolished and 260 sailors were killed. The cause of the blast has never been determined, but at the time Americans held the Spanish responsible. Political pressure built for America to go to war against Spain. People marched through the streets chanting, "Remember the *Maine*! To hell with Spain!" The most fervent pro-war advocates in Washington were Democratic and Populist members of Congress who invoked the "spirit of 1776," calling for a war to liberate the Cuban people from Spanish colonialism. They also identified the rebel struggle with their own efforts to escape from economic bondage.

President McKinley, wishing to solve the Cuban crisis by diplomacy and to avoid a war that he did not believe served the national interest, and backed by Wall Street bankers and business leaders who saw war as disrupting trade with Cuba, demanded that Spain revoke the *reconcentrado* policy and grant an armistice to the rebels. In early April 1898 Spain, desperately wishing to avoid a war it could never win, agreed to these terms, but it was too late. McKinley had decided to grant Congress the war it and the American people demanded. Internal political pressures had forced McKinley's hand. On April 11 he sent a war message to Congress in which he also noted the Spanish concessions that really made war unnecessary. But on April 18 Congress, in a jingoistic frenzy, issued an ultimatum directing the Spanish to vacate Cuba and ordering a naval blockade of the island. Four days later Congress followed these acts of war against Spain with a formal declaration of hostilities. The United States, surrendering to belligerent emotions, stumbled into a war it could have avoided.

The opening battle of the Spanish-American war occurred in Manila Bay in the Philippines on May 1 when Commodore George Dewey's

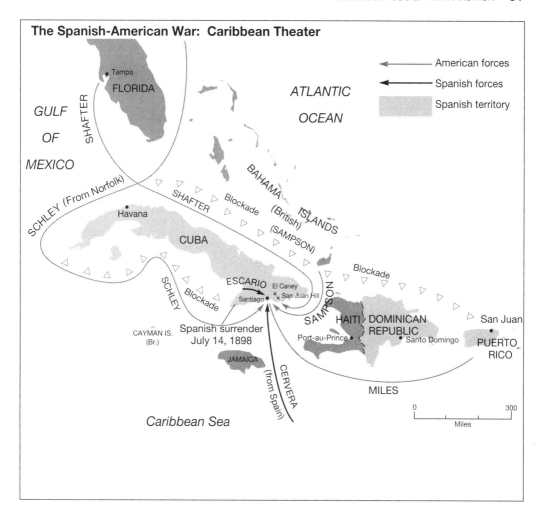

The Spanish-American War: Caribbean Theater

squadron destroyed a Spanish fleet. In August U.S. Army forces occupied Manila, the capital of the Spanish colony. An American expedition later occupied the Spanish colony of Guam, which lay 1,500 miles east of Manila.

In May the Spanish sent a fleet of seven ships to Cuba. They anchored in Santiago Bay at the southeastern tip of the island. An American fleet, discovering their presence, hovered outside the bay, waiting until the U.S. Army arrived to attack the city of Santiago and force the Spanish ships out of the bay. On June 22 about 17,000 American troops landed. This expeditionary force included the Rough Riders, a cavalry unit whose second-in-command was Lieutenant Colonel Theodore Roosevelt. The Army encountered stiff resistance from the Spanish defenders but succeeded in capturing the heights above the city and bay. Roosevelt led one of the assaults. The Spanish fleet then tried to run past the American ships, but the much more powerful American squadron destroyed it. Two weeks later the city of Santiago surrendered. Spanish power in Cuba was broken. The Spaniards sued for peace in August and the war ended. The Spanish-American war was one of the most popular wars in national history. It lasted only four months, and the United States won every battle at slight cost in lives and dollars. The war also signaled the arrival of a new imperial great power on the world scene.

At a peace conference in Paris from October to December 1898 the victorious Americans forced Spain to cede Guam, the Philippines, and Puerto Rico to the United States, for which the Americans paid the Spanish $20 million. The Spanish also ceded Cuba to the United States, but Cuba soon became an independent republic. The Platt Amendment, forced on the Cubans in 1901, made Cuba an American protectorate and curtailed Cuban sovereignty in numerous ways. What had begun as a war to liberate Cuba from Spanish colonialism turned into a war for American empire.

Ironically, before it could impose its colonial rule, the United States had to fight a war in the Philippines from 1899 to 1902 to crush a nationalist insurgency there. Filipino insurgents, led by Emilio Aguinaldo, already in rebellion against their Spanish overlords before the arrival of Dewey's fleet, had helped the Americans defeat the Spaniards. The Filipino patriots believed that they had been promised independence for their efforts, and they felt betrayed by the Paris treaty. Aguinaldo declared the Philippines to be an independent republic in January 1899 and fighting soon erupted between his and American forces. The war Americans called the "Philippine insurrection" lasted nearly three years and claimed the lives of over 4,000 U.S. troops and perhaps 220,000 Filipinos, most of them civilian casualties of American counter-insurgency warfare.

Following the suppression of the insurrection, the United States established a colonial administration in the Philippines. American teachers, engineers, nurses, and doctors flocked to the islands to modernize Filipino society. English was made the official language. In 1908 the University of the Philippines opened to train a pro-American governing elite that would gradually implement political democracy and prepare for the independence promised for the future. Linkages between American business interests and Filipino planters and merchants provided the foundation for 40 years of U.S. colonial rule in the islands as well as a growing commerce between the two countries.

In 1898 and 1899 there was much opposition to colonial imperialism within the United States. Senate opponents of imperialism nearly blocked ratification of the Treaty of Paris, which transferred Spanish colonies to the United States. Many prominent Americans joined the anti-imperialist cause, including Mark Twain, Grover Cleveland, and Samuel Gompers. The Democratic presidential candidate in 1900, William Jennings Bryan,

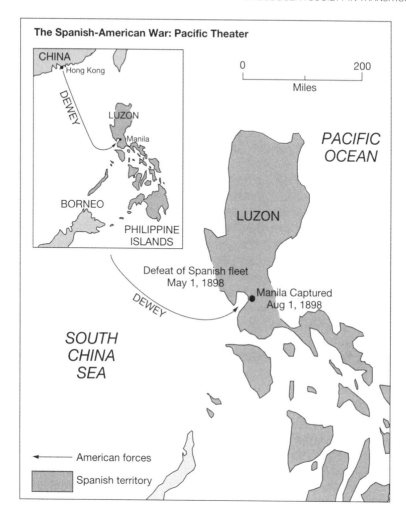

The Spanish-American War: Pacific Theater

made anti-imperialism a major issue, although President McKinley easily won reelection. If the 1900 election is taken to be a referendum on imperialism, a large majority of Americans enthusiastically embraced it.

A major reason the United States acquired the Philippines was to enhance its strategic and trading interests in the Far East, particularly in China. In 1899 Secretary of State John Hay announced a new American policy toward China called the Open Door. The Open Door policy called for equal trade in China's ports and the maintenance of Chinese "territorial integrity" at a time when most great powers had carved out spheres of influence in China and American merchants feared that they might be squeezed out of Chinese markets.

As the twentieth century began, the United States had become an imperial democracy and one of the great powers of the globe. Its world com-

U.S. troops fighting Filipino nationalists.

merce and overseas investments were expanding. Its economy was the world's largest, and its navy ranked sixth in the world. Most Americans were proud of the new role the United States played in world affairs. A few were distressed by the contradictions between democratic ideals and imperial conquests. But most Americans believed the United States had an imperial destiny and arrogantly assumed that American imperialism would benefit its victims.

SOCIAL DARWINISM

The American industrial revolution had a profound effect on how Americans felt and thought during the Gilded Age. Technological innovations revolutionized the communication of ideas. Materialistic values impinged upon literature, art, and public education. Darwin's evolutionary theories influenced American philosophers, social scientists, lawyers, and most educated people. Simultaneously Americans clung to older ideas of romantic individualism and Jeffersonian democracy. American thinking during this era remained diffuse, a mixed bag of old and new forms.

While American enterprise was expanding and consolidating, fashionable intellectual currents encouraged the exploitative drives of the people. Charles Darwin's *Origins of Species*, first published in England in 1859, began to influence public opinion in this country during the late nineteenth century. The idea that nature had ordained inevitable progress governed by the natural selection of individuals best adapted to survive in a competitive environment appealed to many Americans. The views of sugar magnate Henry O. Havemeyer represented efforts to apply evolutionary theory to the marketplace. "Let the buyer beware," he intoned. "You cannot wet-nurse people from the time they are born until the time they die. They have to wade in and get stuck, and that is the way men are educated."

The key tenets of Social Darwinism were derived from classical economics and were as old as Adam Smith. Individuals would compete fiercely within a *laissez-faire* economy. A few would succeed and grow rich. Most would fail and remain poor. Government played only the minimal role of protector of basic rights and property; it had no regulatory or welfare functions. The poor were responsible for their fate and by definition unfit. Government interference in economic affairs would be futile and impede progress, which was inevitable but incremental. Trade unions had no social or economic role to play, according to the logic of Social Darwinism. Andrew Carnegie counseled all who would heed him, "Leave things as they now are." The foremost American Social Darwinist, Yale sociologist William Graham Sumner, told his students, "It's root, hog, or die." It was each against all, struggling to survive in an economic jungle. Money and power were the clearest measures of success, increasing productivity the most obvious sign of progress.

RELIGION

The transformations in American society and culture accompanying the industrial revolution had a major impact on organized religion in the late nineteenth century. The most obvious effect was a rapid secularization of American life. Churches found themselves playing a less important social role and saw their influence decline. Even so, religious institutions continued to thrive in urban industrial America. Most churches increased their membership, especially the Catholic Church. The new immigration brought millions of Catholics to America during the 1890s.

Darwin's theory of evolution challenged the traditional religious conception of human origins. If humans evolved from apes by natural processes, then the Biblical account of creation was false and the idea of humans being formed in God's image was also untrue. A bitter controversy pitted biological science against revealed religion. Evolutionary theory did not undermine the religious faith of most Americans; they either did not learn of this theory or else dismissed it. But most American intellectuals were converted to the evolutionary theory. Some theologians reconciled the two views, arguing that evolution was merely God's way of ordering the universe.

Traditional Protestant churches in the late nineteenth century had primarily middle-class congregations. Ministers preached the Protestant ethic and personal responsibility for sin. Leaders of the Catholic Church, even though many of their communicants were slum dwellers, also echoed the social conservatism of the Protestant ministry. Even evangelists such as Dwight Moody, the foremost preacher of the time, who endeavored to reach the urban masses by establishing mission schools in slum neighborhoods, concentrated on convincing individuals to give up their sinful ways and come to Christ. All of these religious institutions and individuals focused on the Christian drama of sin and redemption at the personal level. They were unconcerned about the causes of urban poverty, vice, and crime.

But within religious ranks, some ministers tried a different approach. These "social gospelers" tried to improve living conditions as well as save souls. They advocated economic and social reform. The most influential social gospel minister was Washington Gladden. He supported trade unions, the regulation of industry, and other reforms. Some of these Christians also called for slum clearance, public housing, and the nationalization of industry.

EDUCATION

The modern American system of public education was forged during the era of the industrial revolution. Americans had long held a commitment to public education, but it was only after the Civil War that the growth of large cities provided the population concentrations necessary for economical mass education, and at the same time industrialization generated the wealth required to finance such a vast undertaking as providing education for everyone.

Steady progress occurred in public education during the Gilded Age. School attendance increased from 6.8 million children in 1870 to 15.5 million in 1900. Public spending on education rose from $63 million in 1870 to over $214 million in 1902. During these years the number of secondary schools increased from perhaps 100 to more than 6,000. By 1900 it was possible for youngsters living in cities to attend high school if their economic circumstances permitted. National illiteracy declined from 20 to 10 percent between 1870 and 1900. The goal of universal education, however, was only partially achieved during the late nineteenth century. About two-thirds of school-age children were receiving a few years of formal education by the 1890s. School sessions were often short and many students dropped out after a few years of spotty attendance. Most states did not have compulsory attendance laws, so school attendance was voluntary. The 1900 census showed the median national educational attainment to be 5.5 years of schooling.

Institutions of higher learning also multiplied during the Gilded Age. Between 1870 and 1900 the number of colleges and universities in America doubled, from about 500 to almost 1,000. Curricula expanded and diversified. Harvard's president, Charles W. Eliot, introduced the elective system, added many science and engineering courses, and experimented with new teaching techniques. Much of the expansion in college enrollments occurred as a consequence of the Morrill Land Grant Act of 1862, which created state universities in the Midwest and South.

Women attended college in growing numbers. By the end of the nineteenth century women accounted for about one-third of the 300,000 students enrolled in institutions of higher learning, with a third of these female students attending women's colleges. In the South colleges were segregated, and African Americans, both young men and women, continued to suffer from inferior educational opportunities. During the Gilded Age intercollegiate athletics became a central feature of student social life on many college campuses in all parts of the nation.

There was a tremendous demand for popular education outside the schools and colleges in the late nineteenth century. The Chautauqua movement developed to fill an important cultural gap. Started in upstate New York in 1874 as a summer course for Sunday School teachers, it grew into a massive popular education system. It presented traveling lecturers on hundreds of topics, offered correspondence courses, and published a monthly magazine. Chautauqua had hundreds of imitators. Standards on its popular lecture circuits varied and were not always high. Speakers were often chosen for their celebrity status or their skill as entertainers. Teachers too could vary from distinguished experts to assorted phonies and incompetents. To quote historian John Garraty: "Chautauqua reflected the prevailing tastes of the American people—diverse, enthusiastic, uncritical, and shallow."

MASS MEDIA

Newspapers and magazines proliferated during the Gilded Age. Technological advances in printing made possible the mass production of attractive, cheap periodicals. Increasing population and rising levels of literacy created a larger demand for printed matter. Joseph Pulitzer created the modern style of journalism and the mass-circulation daily newspaper. He built up the *New York World*, increasing its circulation to over a million in the 1890s—the largest in the world—by means of a variety of innovations and techniques. He hired talented journalists and paid them well. He went in for sensational headlines. He often sent his investigators nosing around city hall looking for scandals. He launched crusades and he held banquets and carnivals to raise funds for the poor. His paper was the first to have comics. For educated readers there was plenty of hard and serious political, economic, and international news. He also kept the price low. the *New York World* was good value at two cents an issue. Pulitzer was later imitated by an ambitious young journalist, William Randolph Hearst, who soon outdid Pulitzer when it came to sensationalism in his *New York Morning Journal*. Because of innovations in printing technology, publishers also produced high-quality weekly and monthly magazines. By the end of the nineteenth century magazines such as *Cosmopolitan*, *The Saturday Evening Post*, and *McClure's* enjoyed mass circulation.

LITERATURE AND PHILOSOPHY

In literature a new age of *realism* developed during the 1870s and 1880s, influenced by the same forces that were transforming all other aspects of American life: industrialization, the rise of cities, and evolutionary science. Novelists wrote about social problems, depicted realistic settings, and created more complex characters, taken from a wide range of classes and regions. One expression of the new realism was the local-color school. Regional writers looked to the areas they knew best for their stories and novels. For example, during the 1880s Joel Chandler Harris published his *Uncle Remus: His Songs and His Sayings*, which accurately reproduced the speech dialects of blacks in rural Georgia.

Mark Twain (Samuel Langhorne Clemens) was the first great American realist and writer from the West. The story that brought Twain his first national recognition was "The Celebrated Jumping Frog of Calaveras County," and the book that made him famous was *Innocents Abroad*, published in 1869. The latter was a travelogue that made fun of Gilded Age Americans traveling abroad. Twain was both participant and chronicler of the Gilded Age. The 1873 novel that he co-authored with Charles Dudley Warner, *The Gilded Age*, gave the era its enduring name. *The Adventures of Tom Sawyer* came out in 1876, and his masterpiece, considered by many critics to be the finest American novel, *The Adventures of Huckleberry Finn*, was published in 1884. No one surpassed Twain in creating characters, writing dialogue, and depicting a scene. He possessed a comic genius. Inside Mark Twain the funnyman who made Americans laugh uproariously at themselves and their culture beat the heart of a serious moralist. Twain was outraged, disgusted, and anguished by his age's untrammeled greed, prevalent political corruption, and heartless exploitation of the poor. His laughter at times turned bitter and mocking.

One of Twain's finest short stories is called "The Man That Corrupted Hadleyburg." It opens with a portrayal of a quiet, peaceful town. The people are not rich but they are happy, contented, and good. They care for each other. One day a stranger rides into town, deposits a sack of money in front of the post office, then dashes off. He is never seen again. The rest of the story describes what happens to the townspeople as they discover the money, try to decide what to do with it, and fall to quarreling over it. As the tale ends, Hadleyburg has become a hellish place. Its inhabitants are filled with rage and hate. They are all fighting over the money. Twain's story served as a parable for the age.

By the end of the nineteenth century some writers had moved beyond realism to *naturalism*. Naturalists concentrated on industrialization and the social disintegration of individuals that it caused. Naturalists served up stark and pessimistic portrayals of the human condition—individuals trapped in deterministic environments that degraded and often destroyed them. Naturalistic writers depicted human beings as animals governed by instincts and base passions. One of the finest naturalistic novels was Theodore Dreiser's classic *Sister Carrie* (1900). Many middle class readers were shocked and outraged by naturalism, by its pessimism and moral nihilism, and by its portrayals of individuals as passive victims of powerful natural and social forces.

There also developed in this era a new kind of American philosophy called *pragmatism*. Pragmatists asserted that ideas were true only if they worked in the world—if they were useful and achieved practical results. Experience, not logic, proved the truth of an idea. The main creators of philosophical pragmatism were Charles Peirce, William James, and John Dewey. Pragmatism inspired much of the reform spirit of the early twentieth century. James subverted Social Darwinism and *laissez-faire* capitalism by proving that social changes came about because of the willed actions of reformers, not from impersonal environmental forces. Educational reformer John Dewey and social worker Jane Addams embraced pragmatic approaches to social change.

CIVILIZATION AND ITS DISCONTENTS

As the Gilded Age ended, the majority of Americans, especially comfortable middle-class Americans, residents of small towns, shopkeepers, many farmers, and skilled workers, remained confirmed optimists, uncritically admiring of their civilization and proud to be citizens of America, no doubt the best country in all the world. However, African Americans, Asians, Native Americans, immigrants, hard-pressed western and southern farmers, and all the others who failed to achieve the good life found little to celebrate and much to protest in their increasingly industrialized and urbanized society. Giant monopolies flourished, the gap between rich and poor was widening, and poisonous slums infected every city. Shallow industrialists worshipped the almighty dollar and made getting it their re-

ligion. America's greatest poet, Walt Whitman, famed for his poetic celebration of democracy, called his fellow Americans the "most materialistic
and money-making people ever known."

Many thoughtful and well-informed middle-class people, whose own
lives were comfortable and prosperous, recoiled in horror at the social
consequences of industrialization, urbanization, and massive immigration. They were alarmed by social instability and outraged at both the
greed of businessmen and the degraded lives of the struggling masses.
Many indulged a romantic nostalgia for a vanished America of small, homogeneous communities and tranquil, orderly lives. As the nineteenth
century ended, the voices of discontent with the new industrial way of life
formed a rising chorus. Calls for reform resounded across the land.

BIBLIOGRAPHY

There are many readily available, informative books that cover various aspects of
late nineteenth-century U.S. history. The following is a select list; the books are
chosen for their readability and ease of access. Most libraries will have these
books, and they are available in paperback editions.

Robert H. Wiebe, in *The Search for Order*, has written a classic account of
the transformation of American life in the late nineteenth and early twentieth cen-
turies and the way in which middle-class intellectuals understood and reacted to
this transformation. See also Samuel P. Hays, *The Response to Industrialism,
1885–1914*. A well-written account of the Gilded Age is Ray Ginger, *The Age of Excess*. Sam Bass Warner, Jr., *A History of the American City* is the best account of the
rise of American cities in the late nineteenth century. The best-written book about
the politicians and business leaders who dominated the Gilded Age remains the
classic work of Matthew Josephson, *The Robber Barons*. The best social history of
the American industrial revolution is Thomas C. Cochran and William Miller, *The
Age of Enterprise*. Herbert Gutman, *Work, Culture, and Society in Industrializing
America* is a collection of essays reflecting the new labor history, which focuses on
the culture of work. Nick Salvatore, *Eugene V. Debs: Citizen and Socialist* is the
finest biography of the greatest figure in American socialism. Oscar Handlin, *The
Uprooted* is a classic account of the new immigrants who flooded into
America from 1890 to 1914. A fine recent study is Alan Kraut, *The Huddled
Masses: The Immigrant in American Society, 1830–1921*. Jane Addams, the pioneer social worker and humanitarian, tells in *Twenty Years at Hull House*, the
story of the first and most famous settlement house in the United States. C. Vann
Woodward, *The Strange Career of Jim Crow* is a brilliant history of the rise of legal
segregation in the South. Louis R. Harlan has written a spendid two-volume biography of Booker T. Washington. A fine book on the conflict between Europeans
and Native Americans is S. L. A. Marshall, *The Crimsoned Prairie*. Justin Kaplan,
Mr. Clemens and Mark Twain is a good biography of America's most famous
writer. Two histories of reform in broad perspective are Eric Goldman, *Rendezvous with Destiny* and Richard Hofstadter, *Age of Reform*. Ernest R. May, *Imperial Democracy* is a brief account of the emergence of the American empire at the
turn of the century.

CHAPTER
2
Progressive Reformers

Americans have been infatuated by quantitative measures as indicators of progress. At the turn of the century publicists boasted about American industrial might as measured by statistics of production: tons of steel produced, miles of railroad trackage laid, barrels of oil refined. Other boosters bragged about the huge geographic size of the country, its large cities, and its ranking as the fourth most populous nation on the planet. More thoughtful Americans concerned themselves with issues pertaining to the quality of American life. They worried about some of the negative political, social, and economic consequences of industrialization such as corporate domination of the economy, pervasive political corruption, and the masses of impoverished immigrants in all the large cities. For these "Progressives," as they called themselves, progress would be better measured by their success as reformers, as problem solvers who restored the promise of American life to all people. During the years between the Spanish-American War and the American entry into World War I, an urgent desire for change swept the nation. The combined efforts of many reformers shaped the age that historians label the Progressive Era.

MODERN SOCIETY

Progressive Era America was a time of rapid social development. Prosperity had returned after the depression and disorders of the 1890s. Farms and factories were once again prospering. In 1901 the economy approached full employment, and economic growth spurted. Farm prices rose almost 50 percent between 1900 and 1910 as farmers entered a "golden age." In 1900 the median industrial wage was about $500 per year; by 1915 it was about $800 a year and rising. A Boston newspaper in 1904 enthused: "The resort to force, the wild talk of the nineties are over. Everyone is busily, happily getting ahead."

Americans were excited by the prospects abounding in the new century. Wild celebrations everywhere had marked the beginning of the twentieth century. Americans had faith in the capacities of business enterprises and new technologies to shape a more abundant future. "New" became a favorite buzzword. Everywhere there was talk of the new city, the new art, the new democracy, and the new morality.

Another favorite theme was "mass." Americans celebrated the quantitative aspects of their national experience. They were proud of the size and scale of America—its massive economy and large population. They flocked to mass entertainment, read mass-circulation magazines and newspapers, and took mass transit from the suburbs to central cities. They even boasted of the large crowds that turned out to watch major league baseball and college football games, as if they believed national virtue resided in population statistics.

Cities grew rapidly and on a colossal scale compared with earlier eras. Downtowns became clusters of tall buildings, large department stores, warehouses, and hotels. Strips of factories radiated out from the center. As streetcar transit lines spread, American cities assumed their modern patterns of ethnic, social, and economic segregation, usually in the form of concentric rings. Racial minorities and immigrants were packed into the innermost ring, circled by a belt of crowded tenements. The remaining rings represented increasing status and affluence, radiating outward toward posh suburbs where the rich and elite classes lived. The largest cities were New York, Chicago, and Philadelphia. They had become huge industrial, urban centers whose factories and shops churned out every kind of product used by American farmers, merchants, and the growing legions of consumers.

Los Angeles, a city of 300,000, passed a series of ordinances in 1915 that created modern urban zoning. For the first time legal codes divided an American city into three districts of specified use: a residential area, an industrial area, and an area open to both residences and light industry. Other cities quickly followed suit. Zoning gave order to urban development, ending the chaotic, unplanned growth of cities that was characteristic of the Gilded Age.

Zoning not only kept skyscrapers out of factory districts and factories out of suburbs, it also had important sociological and political consequences. In southern cities zoning became another tool to extend segregation. In northern cities it was a weapon that could be used along with others against blacks and ethnic minorities—against Jews in New York City, Italians in Boston, and Poles in Detroit. In Chicago, New York, Detroit, and Cleveland, zoning laws helped confine rapidly growing black populations to particular districts, creating ghettos.

The consumer economy of the 1920s originated in the prewar era. As factories produced more consumer goods, they also spent more money for advertising. Ads and billboards promoted cigarettes, perfumes, and cosmetics. Advertising agencies grew and market research began. The first public opinion polls began as efforts to sample consumer preferences in the marketplace.

Between 1900 and 1910 almost 10 million immigrants entered the country, more than came in any other decade in American history. These newcomers continued the trend established during the late nineteenth century. Most were from southern and eastern Europe, the largest number emigrating from Italy, Poland, Russia, and Austria-Hungary. About 1.5 million were eastern European Jews, mainly from Poland and Russia. Most of these new immigrants were Catholic or Jewish. About 40 percent were illiterate, and most, coming from peasant backgrounds, arrived without money or job skills. About two-thirds were males.

These new immigrants were a diverse lot who had little in common with one another except their poverty and desire to come to America. Traffic moved both ways across the Atlantic. A large number of immigrants returned to their native land after a stay in America, either because they were disillusioned or because they had never intended to stay permanently. Those who returned to Europe were known as "birds of passage." The percentage of returnees varied with different nationalities.

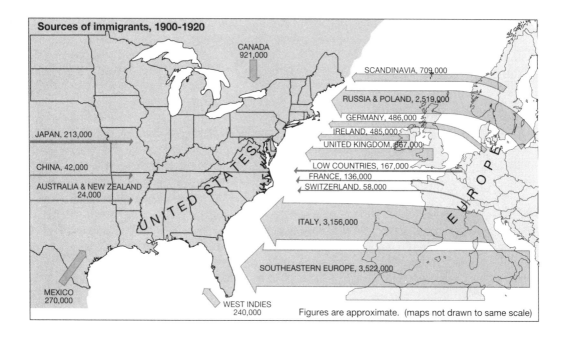

Sources of immigrants, 1900-1920

CANADA 921,000
SCANDINAVIA, 709,000
RUSSIA & POLAND, 2,519,000
GERMANY, 486,000
IRELAND, 485,000
UNITED KINGDOM, 867,000
JAPAN, 213,000
LOW COUNTRIES, 167,000
FRANCE, 136,000
SWITZERLAND, 58,000
CHINA, 42,000
AUSTRALIA & NEW ZEALAND 24,000
ITALY, 3,156,000
SOUTHEASTERN EUROPE, 3,522,000
MEXICO 270,000
WEST INDIES 240,000
UNITED STATES
EUROPE
Figures are approximate. (maps not drawn to same scale)

Those who came with their families, such as the Jews, rarely returned. Many Serbs and Poles, who tended to come as single young men, worked to earn money to buy a farm or business back home. The most numerous "birds of passage" were Italian men, thousands of whom became trans-Atlantic commuters. They worked in American industry for a year, returned to Italy, and were back in America the next year.

Despite the newcomers' tremendous cultural diversity and varying aspirations, old-stock Americans and business owners who employed them tended to lump them all into simplistic stereotypes. They were "foreigners" who had to be "Americanized," and the quicker the better. Henry Ford, the man whose technological wizardry would put the nation on wheels during the 1920s, employed thousands of immigrants in his River Rouge assembly plant near Detroit. Ford also ran an "Americanization" school, which his immigrant employees were required to attend. They were first taught to say, "I am a good American." For those who completed Ford's program there was a graduation ceremony, at which the workers acted out a giant pantomime skit. Clad in their native dress, they filed into a large "melting pot." When they emerged from the pot, they were each wearing identical American-made suits and carrying a small American flag.

Mulberry Street, New York City—the heart of the immigrant area of the Lower East Side in the early 1900s.

Nativist sentiment further intensified in the first decade and a half of the twentieth century in the wake of the continuing massive influx of new immigrants. Old-stock Americans looked down on the newcomers' appearance, behavior, and language. Racial theorists stressed the superiority of northern European "races" over those from the south and east of Europe. Some hostility toward the new immigrants reflected anti-Catholic and anti-Semitic prejudices. Nativism crystallized into anti-immigration movements that aimed to restrict the new immigration. Restrictionists failed to achieve most of their goals before World War I brought almost all immigration to a halt, but the nativists would achieve their goal of restriction during the mid-1920s.

POPULAR CULTURE

Major signs of progress in early twentieth-century American life included rising wage levels and growing leisure for workers. The average workweek for manufacturing workers had shrunk to 50 hours by 1914. By the first decade of the new century, white-collar workers worked nine-hour days Monday through Friday and a half day on Saturday. People had more money to spend and more time to enjoy spending it on recreation. Increasing income and leisure promoted a flourishing mass culture in the cities.

Spectator sports were attracting large crowds. Baseball entrenched itself as the national pastime. In 1903 the pennant winners of the two major leagues met in the first World Series. The American League Boston Red Sox beat the National League champions, the Pittsburgh Pirates, five games to three. College football was another popular spectator sport. Crowds of 50,000 or more often gathered to watch powerhouse Ivy League and midwestern teams play. On New Year's Day in 1902 the first Rose Bowl game was held in Pasadena, California; the University of Michigan overwhelmed an upstart team from Stanford 49 to zero.

Progressive reformers attacked college football for its violence and for its use of "tramp athletes," nonstudents whom colleges paid to play for them. During the 1905 season 18 players were killed and 150 suffered serious injury. Finally President Roosevelt called a White House conference to clean up college football and other sports. The result was the founding of the Intercollegiate Athletic Association, which in 1910 became the National Collegiate Athletic Association (NCAA). True to its progressive origins, the NCAA has functioned as a regulatory agency for collegiate athletics ever since.

Attendance at movies rose even faster than for spectator sports. Thomas Edison and a young assistant, William Dickson, had invented a process for making motion pictures in 1889. Commercial movies made their appearance during the 1890s. These early films were crudely made,

By the first decade of the twentieth century, "movies" had become both a mass medium and a popular art form. Film houses, called nickelodeons, offered silent films to the immigrant masses.

their audiences recruited mainly from the ranks of immigrant populations, who were crowded into the large eastern cities. Early movie houses were store fronts and parlors called "nickelodeons," a name derived from combining the price of admission with the Greek word for theater. After 1900 the new industry expanded rapidly. By 1910 there were 10,000 theaters in the country showing motion pictures, attracting a weekly audience of 10 million. The most popular films were about fifteen to twenty minutes in length and featured comedy, adventure, or pathos.

The early center of American filmmaking was New York. Then in 1909 the largest companies formed a trust to control the production and distribution of films. The next year a group of independent filmmakers discovered Hollywood, a sleepy farming community near Los Angeles. There they could escape the movie trust and take advantage of the sunshine and mild weather of southern California. Also, within a few miles of the studios could be found outdoor scenes that would substitute for almost any locale a plot might call for, whether Arabia, Sherwood Forest, or the Old South. In 1915 D. W. Griffith, the best of the new Hollywood movie makers, produced the first movie spectacular, *Birth of a Nation.*

Before 1910 band concerts were the country's most popular mass entertainment. Thousands of amateur bands offered free concerts in parks on Sunday afternoons. The most popular American band, led by John Philip Sousa, the "March King," toured the nation, attracting large crowds everywhere. Sousa was also a composer and wrote the famed "The Stars and Stripes Forever" in 1896. This robust, patriotic march became wildly popular during the Spanish-American War, making its author rich and famous.

By the end of the first decade of the new century, recorded music was taking much of the audience away from public band concerts. Recording companies were selling millions of "records." Record players became fixtures in homes that could afford them. Early recordings usually featured vaudeville skits. The first orchestral recording was made in 1906. As record sales increased, families sang less and listened more.

Ragtime, a musical idiom featuring fast syncopated rhythms, became popular, especially after 1911 when Irving Berlin wrote "Alexander's Ragtime Band." Ragtime set young people to dancing fast, abandoning the traditional waltzes and polkas. The new dances often had animal names—Fox Trot, Bunny Hop, Turkey Trot, and the Snake. The "fast set," enjoying some of these new dances, ran afoul of the moralists who worried about partners' dancing too close and becoming sexually excited (nine inches between dance partners was the approved distance).

Vaudeville, increasingly popular after the turn of the century, flowered in the decade preceding World War I. Drawing from the immigrant experience, it featured skits, songs, dances, comedy, magicians, and acrobats, all expressing the color and variety of polyglot American urban life. Vaudeville performers also expanded the limits of what was permissible in public entertainment. Vaudeville dancers bared their legs and later their midriffs. Vaudeville comics told "dirty" jokes and got away with it. The leading impresario of vaudeville, Florenz Ziegfeld, produced his famed "Follies," featuring elaborate dance numbers by beautifully costumed "Ziegfeld girls."

Popular fiction flourished along with vaudeville. Genteel novels centering around family life, often set in rural New England, were popular. Westerns also sold well. The most popular western story was Owen Wister's *The Virginian*, whose gunman hero became a prototype for later Westerns, both novelistic and cinematic. Wister was a friend of Theodore Roosevelt, who was an avid fan of Westerns and a writer of western history. Readers also enjoyed detective thrillers and science fiction, the latter featuring tales set in the future and full of spaceships, ray guns, and gravity neutralizers.

Fiction for young people sold widely. Edward L. Stratemeyer applied mass production techniques to the business of publishing popular fiction for young people. He formed a syndicate that employed a stable of writers who turned out hundreds of books in series featuring Tom Swift and the Rover boys for boys, and the Bobbsey twins for girls. Gilbert Patten created the character of Frank Merriwell, a wholesome college athlete attending Yale. The name of his athletic hero expressed the character qualities that Patten stressed: He was frank and merry by nature, and well in mind and body. Patten's books sold by the millions.

Horatio Alger's books continued to sell well during the Progressive Era, although Alger had died in 1899. Alger, like Patten, wrote fiction for adolescent boys. In more than 130 novels Alger stressed the same theme: how poor boys rose from the streets of cities to become successful businessmen. The secret of success in Alger books was always the same: moral character. Alger heroes succeeded because they were good, because they had self-discipline, and because they worked hard. Good luck often aided the hero as he made his way up in the world. Alger's novels sold by the millions during the years preceding World War I, and his name was added to the culture. Today's media frequently call attention to "Horatio Alger heroes" who rise from "rags to riches."

LITERATURE AND ART

Along with the simplistic sentimentalities of popular culture, serious art also fared well in Progressive America. Isadora Duncan and Ruth St. Denis transformed modern dance. Abandoning traditional ballet, both dancers stressed emotions, the human body, and individual improvisation. Duncan danced "the way she felt," giving expression to inner emotion and communicating ideas. Her ideas and innovative techniques swept the country. Duncan, a flamboyant personality with a zest for life, became a reigning celebrity of the age.

Greenwich Village, a seedy district of New York City, became a haven for young artists, writers, and poets committed to experimenting with new forms of expression. A group of painters, including Robert Henri, John Sloan, and George Bellows, were named by their critics the "Ashcan School" because of their interest in social realism. These artists preferred to paint the subjects they found in the Village and other parts of the city— street scenes, colorful crowds, slum children swimming in the East River, the tenements, and portraits of ordinary people. Their paintings honestly expressed the inherent beauty and vitality found in the lives of the urban masses.

In 1913 a show at the New York Armory introduced American viewers to European modernist paintings, sculptures, and prints. Americans got their first exposure to the works of Picasso, Van Gogh, Gaughin, and Cézanne among many others. The Greenwich Village crowd was dazzled and excited by the show. Traditionalists attacked the exhibits as worthless and wicked. But the artists featured in the exhibit would have a profound effect on the direction American art would take in the twentieth century, and many American painters' works would later reflect their influence.

Chicago was the center of a flourishing new poetry. Harriet Monroe started *Poetry* magazine in Chicago in 1912 and published some of the poems of many of America's most promising young poets, including Ezra Pound and T. S. Eliot. Other poets experimenting with new techniques were Robert Frost, Edgar Lee Masters, and Carl Sandburg. Sandburg's most famous poem, "Chicago" (1916), celebrated the vitality of America's second city.

The culture of the early twentieth century, both in its popular and highbrow forms, foreshadowed developments in the 1920s. Changes were underway before World War I. Evidence of ferment and change could be found everywhere—in the movie houses, in popular music, in art galleries, and in the new literary magazines. The Progressive Era was the seedtime of modern American culture.

THE ROOTS OF REFORM

Progressivism's immediate origins lay in the 1890s, when many people responded to the transformation of American life and the social problems that it generated, particularly the many undesirable consequences of industrialization. Large industrial corporations dominated their industries, controlled prices, and exploited their workers and customers. Corruption corroded government at all levels, from two-bit ward heelers on the streets to the upper echelons of the federal government. The cities, filling with a rising tide of immigrants, threatened to become home to a permanently dispossessed and alienated underclass. The great urban centers of America spawned slums, crime, and poverty. Monopoly, corrupt politics, and mass poverty challenged the central promise of American life and suggested that equality of opportunity was a myth. The American dream increasingly appeared to be beyond the reach of millions of American families. Progressive reformers, as they set out to solve these massive and often interrelated problems, did not form a unified national crusade. Rather, progressivism constituted a remarkably diverse aggregation of many, often unrelated, even mutually antagonistic, efforts to achieve political, social, and economic reform.

Progressives sought to solve problems by ending abuses of power and eliminating unfair privilege. They intended to replace the wasteful, competitive, anarchic industrial society with one that was efficient, orderly, and based on cooperation between business and government. They wanted to restore the American community that they believed had prevailed in preindustrial times, and they wanted to use modern methods and scientific techniques to bring it back. They would restrain the powerful and protect the powerless.

Progressivism's roots lay buried deep within American political traditions, but its proximate origins could be found in a series of unrelated reform movements that erupted in this country during the 1890s. One of these comprised the agrarian insurgents of the Midwest and South; these embattled farmers called for state intervention to curb the power of the railroads, banks, and other big businesses. Meanwhile within the cities the social strains caused by rapid, large-scale industrialization activated the Social Gospelers and other pioneer advocates of social justice. Also during the 1890s a literature of protest and exposure foreshadowed the Muckrakers. Henry Demarest Lloyd wrote *Wealth against Commonwealth* (1894), a scathing indictment of the Standard Oil Company. Describing the wholesale corruption of state governments carried out by Standard Oil's henchmen, Lloyd wrote, "Standard Oil did everything to the Pennsylvania legislature but refine it." A new generation of social scientists joined the assault on privileged wealth and irresponsible power. A new generation of intellectuals challenged the assumptions and precepts of Social Darwinism. The now large urban middle class, many of whose members were well-educated young businessmen and professionals, also got involved in urban reform movements during the 1890s. These concerned individuals were outraged by widespread monopoly, political corruption, and social distress. As the twentieth century began, they were increasingly involved in the proliferating reform movements that comprised the Progressive Era.

SOCIAL JUSTICE

Among the most important strands of progressive reformers were the diverse movements that have been collectively labeled the "social justice movement." Many well-educated, young middle-class women were in the front ranks of social justice activities. Florence Kelly worked to bring about safer working conditions for factory workers and was a pioneer advocate of consumer protection legislation. Jane Addams, the social worker who founded Hull House, was the most prominent woman active in social justice causes. In addition to her settlement house work, Addams worked to strengthen trade unions, abolish child labor, and achieve women's suffrage. When the United States entered World War I in 1917, Addams joined other progressive reformers opposed to American participation in the war. Between 1900 and 1915 social justice reformers could count many victories. During this period most states enacted laws that provided worker's compensation, limited work hours for women, and restricted child labor. Sometimes the courts curtailed or nullified these progressive social reforms, however.

Not all social justice reformers came from middle-class or business ranks. Industrial workers supported progressivism in some urbanized industrial states such as California and New York. They formed coalitions

A young mill worker in a textile factory ca. 1910. Child labor was a scandalous aspect of American industrial society during the Progressive era.

with middle-class reformers to press for improvements in housing and health care, for safer factories, for shorter hours, for worker's compensation, and for disability insurance. More militant members of the social justice movement moved beyond coalition politics to direct action. In 1909 the Women's Trade Union League (WTUL) and the local chapter of the International Ladies Garment Workers Union (ILGWU) waged a long, bitter strike against New York City's garment district sweatshops. After three months they gained a partial victory that resulted in the unionization of some of the sweatshops. A year later, in Chicago, Sidney Hillman led the Amalgamated Clothing Workers Union in a strike that achieved similar gains, including organizing the workers at Hart, Shaffner, and Marx, one of the largest clothing manufacturers in America.

Immigrant and working-class neighborhoods occasionally elected progressive reformers who had backgrounds in machine politics but were neither corrupt nor conservative. For example, Alfred E. (Al) Smith, a Catholic and the son of immigrants, rose through the ranks of Tammany Hall to become a progressive governor of New York. Smith worked with middle-class reformers and progressive legislators to enact labor and social welfare legislation.

Some advocates of radical change during the Progressive Era wanted more than reform; they wanted to create a fundamentally different society. They rejected progressivism for socialism. Their ranks included some immigrant Jewish intellectuals, factory workers, former Populists, western miners, and lumberjacks. A radical trade union, the Industrial Workers of the World, led by William (Big Bill) Haywood, tried to unite the nation's unskilled workers into one big union that would control their factories. It led a series of strikes in textile factories in Lawrence, Massachusetts, and in the West. It never had more than 150,000 members and never established a stable organizational structure, however, and its radical ideology kept it alienated from other trade unions. It faded into obscurity during World War I when federal prosecutors sent most of its leaders to jail for obstructing the war effort.

Most socialists of the Progressive Era supported the American Socialist Party (SDP) and its dynamic leader, Eugene Debs. American socialism grew rapidly during the Progressive Era. Debs ran for president five times. He and his party made their best showing during the 1912 election, when he polled 900,000 votes and hundreds of socialists got elected to local and state offices. In addition to those elected to city councils and county boards of supervisors, over 50 socialists served as mayors, and Wisconsin sent a socialist, Victor Berger, to Congress. American socialists published over 300 newspapers, one of which, *The Appeal to Reason*, claimed 700,000 weekly subscribers. Popular writers and journalists such as Jack London and Upton Sinclair were avowed socialists.

But American socialism and the SDP declined after 1912. By opposing American entry into World War I, socialists incurred the wrath of most patriots. Socialists suffered severe repression at the hands of the federal government. Many of its members, including Debs, were imprisoned. The party was further weakened by internal factionalism during the

A campaign poster featuring Eugene Debs, the American Socialist Party candidate for President in 1904.

1920s and lost membership to the American Communist Party. It managed to survive on the political fringes until the 1960s, when its aged leaders disbanded the remnants of a once-vital movement.

There was a more fundamental cause of the failure of the American SDP to become a mass-based political party like its counterparts in England, France, Germany, and elsewhere in Europe. Socialism never sank deep roots in American soil because its principles never attracted most American industrial workers. Most of them rejected socialist ideology. They did not want to become members of a class-conscious proletariat; they aspired to middle-class status and embraced middle-class capitalist and democratic values. They sought the American dream of a good job, money in the bank, a sturdy home, and a nice family. Many workers were devoutly religious and deeply patriotic and rejected the secularism and internationalism of the American Socialist Party.

MUCKRAKERS

Progressive reformers were aided by socially conscious journalists, writers, and artists, whom Theodore Roosevelt dubbed "muckrakers." A small army of these investigative reporters fed their middle-class readers sensational reports covering a wide range of economic, social, and political evils afflicting American life in the early twentieth century. Through their articles in *McClure's* and other slick, mass-circulation magazines millions of middle-class people became aware of the many ways the American social reality contradicted the ideal image of America. Readers were alarmed, outraged, and anguished by muckraker revelations and were often motivated to support reform efforts. Muckrakers contributed significantly to progressive reform movements. They also established a category of reportage that became an integral part of American journalism. Consumer advocate Ralph Nader used the muckraker approach to call attention to lax safety standards in the auto industry during the 1960s. The popular television show "Sixty Minutes" allows electronic journalists to perpetuate the muckraking style of reportage.

Important muckrakers included Ida Tarbell, who built on the work of Henry Demarest Lloyd and wrote a two-volume history of the Standard Oil Company, describing the ruthless, illegal methods it had employed to forge its refining monopoly. Lincoln Steffens wrote a series of articles for *McClure's*, later published as a book, *The Shame of the Cities* (1904), which exposed political corruption in several large eastern and midwestern cities. Steffens dissected the illicit arrangements between corrupt politicos and greedy businessmen eager to acquire city business and willing to pay for it. David Graham Phillip's *Treason of the Senate* (1906) depicted many senators as rich corporate servitors. John Spargo's *Bitter Cry of the Children* (1903) was a fact-filled, excruciating account of child labor in factories and mines. Burton J. Hendrick's *Story of Life Insurance* (1907) exposed scams that cheated widows out of their benefits.

The most famous muckraker was a young radical novelist, Upton Sinclair, whose realistic novel *The Jungle* (1906) highlighted the brutal exploitation of workers in the meat-packing industry. Sinclair belonged to the American Socialist Party at the time he wrote his famed novel, which vividly conveyed the filthy conditions in the packing houses where tainted and sometimes spoiled meat was processed for public consumption. In the following passage Sinclair describes how sausage was prepared:

> There was never the least attention paid to what was cut up for sausage; there would come all the way back from Europe old sausage that had been rejected and that was moldy and white—it would be doused with borax and glycerine, and dumped into the hoppers and made over again for home consumption. There would be meat that tumbled out onto the floor, in the dirt and sawdust, where the workers had tramped and spit uncounted billions of germs. There would be meat sorted in great piles in rooms; and the water from leaky roofs would drip over it. It was too dark in these storage places to see well, but a man could run his hands over these piles of meat and sweep handfuls off of the dried dung of rats. These rats were nuisances, and the packers would put out poisoned bread for them; they would die, and then rats, bread and meat would go into the hoppers.[1]

Sinclair's novel had an immediate effect. When it was published, President Roosevelt read it and promptly sent for Sinclair to ask him if the conditions he described in his novel truly existed. When Sinclair assured him that they did, Roosevelt ordered an investigation of the meat-packing industry. Federal investigators confirmed most of Sinclair's charges. *The Jungle* also helped move out of Congress a Meat Inspection Act and the Pure Food and Drug Act, two pioneer consumer protection laws enacted in 1906.

The Jungle is a classic example of muckraking. Ironically Sinclair intended to expose the horrors of working in a meat-packing plant, to show corruption in Chicago politics, and to promote socialism as the only solution to what he termed "wage slavery" under capitalism. Most of his middle-class readership, however, reacted most strongly to his lurid descriptions of the unsanitary conditions under which the public's breakfast, lunch, and dinner meats were prepared. As Sinclair noted, ruefully, "I aimed at their hearts and hit their stomachs."

WOMEN REFORMERS

When the Progressive Era began, feminists sought liberation from domestic confines and male domination. Many women joined a women's club

1. Upton Sinclair, *The Jungle* (New York: New American Library of World Literature, 1905, 1906), p. 136.

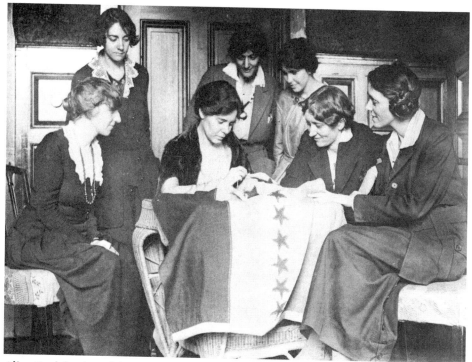

Alice Paul, leader of the National Women's Party, sews a ratification star on the party's flag to celebrate the ratification of the Nineteenth Amendment in 1920, which granted women age 21 and older the right to vote.

movement, and by 1900 the General Confederation of Women's Clubs claimed a million members. Feminist reformers brought a particularly female dimension to progressivism. Because women were excluded from politics before 1920, they tended to move into social reform. Many actively participated in the aforementioned social justice movement, where they sought◦housing reform, consumer protection, and regulations on working conditions for women and children. There was also a militant fringe to the women's movement during this time. Emma Goldman, a Russian immigrant who advocated anarchism and free love, was the most notorious feminist radical of the Progressive Era, but she had little impact on her times and made no contact with the mass of American working-class and middle-class women. She never became an American citizen and was deported during the Red Scare.

Some women joined a birth control movement led by Margaret Sanger. Sanger began her career as a nurse visiting Manhattan's immigrant neighborhoods. She distributed birth control information among poor immigrant women, and her cause attracted the interest of middle-class women who wanted to limit the size of their families. In 1921 she

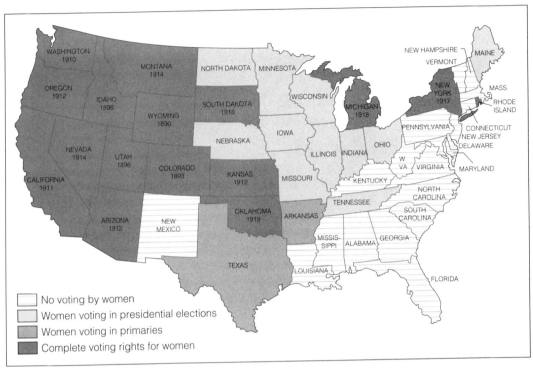

Women's Suffrage before the Nineteenth Amendment

founded the American Birth Control League, and birth control entered the realm of public discussion for the first time. Because of Sanger's efforts, many middle-class families were using contraception by the 1920s. Still, most states prohibited the sale of contraceptives, and most women during the Progressive Era opposed birth control because they believed it threatened their status as women.

The number of working women expanded rapidly during the Progressive Era. Perhaps as many as 7 to 8 million women were working by 1912. Charlotte Perkins Gilman became an advocate for women working, an early economic feminist. Gilman challenged the traditional satisfactions attributed to domesticity. She insisted that women, like men, could find full satisfaction and freedom only through meaningful work. At the time, Gilman's ideas applied mostly to the relatively small number of middle-class professional women. Most working-class women came from the ranks of immigrants, African Americans, and the rural poor, who worked mostly at low-paying, low-skill, and low-status jobs. They had no political or economic power and little chance for meaningful or creative work.

The major feminist issue of the Progressive Era was women's suffrage. The crusade for the vote had begun in the mid-nineteenth century as a spin-off from the Abolitionists' insistence that all Americans, regardless of sex or race, were equal and deserved the same rights. But male re-sistance made the struggle for women to get the vote long and hard: The Supreme Court in *Minor* v. *Happersett* (1875) ruled that women could not vote even though they were citizens. Suffragists achieved their first victo-ries at the local level. Wyoming was the first territory to grant women the right to vote. By 1912 nine states, all of them in the West, had granted women the vote. The National American Women's Suffrage Association (NAWSA), the most important suffragist organization, claimed 85,000 members in 1912.

In 1915 a talented organizer, Carrie Chapman Catt, took over the lead-ership of NAWSA, and the women's suffrage movement quickly gathered momentum. She refocused suffragist energies away from state-by-state campaigns and toward achieving a constitutional amendment, in order to place all women's right to vote beyond the reach of restrictive Supreme Court decisions. Many different women's groups worked for the cause. Militant groups such as Alice Paul's National Women's Party, influenced by radical English suffragists, used direct action tactics. The decisive factor was women's participation on the home front during World War I. Some women sold liberty bonds, worked in factories, and did volunteer medical work. Others went overseas to serve as nurses with the Red Cross in France caring for wounded American soldiers. Their efforts convinced leg-islators to propose what became the Nineteenth Amendment in 1919. It was ratified during the summer of 1920 when Tennessee became the thirty-sixth state to accept women's suffrage. The 1920 presidential election was the first in which all women age 21 or older could vote.

Because so many women had fought so hard and long for the vote, they had come to believe that achieving women's suffrage would bring the dawn of a golden era in American political life. Voting women would put a quick end to boss and business domination of politics. The moral tone of the nation's civic life would be uplifted. Those women (and some men) who expected a rapid transformation of the nation's public life were quickly disillusioned. Women did not vote as a unified movement. No women's agenda emerged. Only about one-third of eligible women voters availed themselves of the opportunity during the election of 1920. Most of these newly enfranchised women apparently voted the way their fathers and husbands did. Feminists, to their dismay, found that the vote did not bring empowerment for women; they did not attain the influence re-quired to enact the issues they favored or to change the way politics and government worked in America.

Nevertheless, attaining suffrage for women was a great victory, an overcoming of powerful and stubborn obstacles. The Nineteenth Amend-ment represented a great democratic advance, one of the crowning politi-cal achievements of the Progressive Era. Women's voting quickly came to be accepted as a normal part of the nation's political life. It was quickly for-

gotten that women's suffrage took 70 years of hard struggle and that virtually until the day it carried, powerful men denounced it and rhetorically
prophesied the end of the republic.

AFRICAN AMERICANS

The progressive reform impulse rarely extended to the 10 million African
Americans, over 85 percent of whom still lived in the South in 1910.
Southern blacks were victimized by a repressive system that disfranchised, segregated, and frequently brutalized them. In 1910 fewer than
one percent of high-school–age blacks attended high school. Southern
white political leaders, many of them progressives, perfected a demagogic
politics based on the rhetorical denunciation of blacks and on keeping
them at the bottom of the socioeconomic pyramid. During the first decade
of the twentieth century, white southerners extended and refined the systematic legal segregation of blacks and whites. Between 1910 and 1914
white mobs lynched scores of African Americans. White progressives
shared the prevailing racist view that African Americans were inherently
inferior and incapable of full citizenship. Few protested the "color line"
that everywhere separated black America from white America. Most
southern blacks resided in rural areas, working as sharecroppers and tenants and earning a median annual income of approximately $100. Many
were tied to the land by labor contracts and perpetual indebtedness to local merchants and planters. Many African Americans appeared to have
traded the legal slavery endured by their parents and grandparents for a
form of economic bondage in the Progressive Era. Institutionalized
racism and segregation also afflicted African Americans residing in northern cities. Oppression of blacks was a national and not merely a regional
problem in Progressive America.

Booker T. Washington remained the most prominent spokesman for
black people, and he continued to advocate accommodation as a policy
during the Progressive Era. Most white reformers welcomed Washington's accommodationist strategy because it urged African Americans not
to protest and to remain in their place. But to a few black progressives,
Washington appeared to be favoring second-class citizenship for African
Americans. In 1905 a group of black leaders met near Niagara Falls to endorse a more militant strategy. They called for equality before the law, voting rights, integration, and equal educational and economic opportunities
for African Americans. The chief Niagara spokesman was Dr. William E. B.
Dubois, who could not accept Washington's submission to white dominance. Dubois insisted, "The way for a people to gain their reasonable
rights is not by voluntarily throwing them away."

Dubois demonstrated that accommodation was a flawed strategy, but his militant protest strategy was ineffective. He believed that a highly educated African American elite, whom he called the Talented Tenth, would lead the way by impressing whites and setting an example for blacks. Such a strategy appealed to some white middle-class progressives, but his elitist strategy held little meaning for the African American masses, who were mainly sharecroppers and unskilled workers. When Dubois and his allies formed the National Association for the Advancement of Colored People (NAACP) in 1909, with its objective of attacking racial discrimination through the courts, its leadership consisted mainly of white progressives.

Whichever strategy they pursued, accommodation or protest, African Americans during the Progressive Era faced continued oppression. During the presidency of Woodrow Wilson, a southern progressive Democrat, the federal civil service was resegregated. African Americans struggled against long odds to achieve their portion of the American dream. Also their pride made it difficult for blacks to celebrate their American identity in a country dominated by racist whites who oppressed African Americans.

ASIAN AMERICANS

Progressive reformers were generally no more concerned about the welfare of other nonwhite minorities than they were about African Americans. Chinese Americans and Japanese Americans, mostly clustered on the West Coast, continued to experience discrimination and hostility. In 1902 Congress made the Chinese Exclusion Act permanent. In October 1906 the San Francisco school board ordered all Asian children to attend a segregated Oriental school. The Japanese government, concerned about the treatment of Japanese in foreign lands, protested this action in Washington. President Roosevelt, concerned about maintaining good relations with a rising power in Asia, intervened to persuade the school board to repeal its offensive order. An informal agreement was worked out, the Gentlemen's Agreement of 1908, according to which the school board rescinded its order against the children of Japanese subjects, and the Japanese government, for its part, agreed to restrict the emigration of peasant laborers to the United States.

Other acts against Japanese in California occurred. In 1913 progressives in the state legislature enacted an alien land law that forbade aliens to lease land for periods greater than three years. Later laws further restricted alien leases of farmland. Such laws were ineffective in practice because Japanese farmers leased lands in the names of their American-born children, and the state supreme court nullified some of these laws. In 1924 Congress, responding to political pressure from California representatives, prohibited further Japanese emigration to the United States. This irrational act profoundly insulted and angered the Japanese government, and it was, in the long run, a contributing cause of World War II in Asia.

NATIVE AMERICANS

Native Americans were ignored by progressive reformers. American Indian policy during the Progressive Era was officially guided by Dawes Act principles. Officials in the Bureau of Indian Affairs continued to pay lip service to assimilation, but under the cover of the Dawes Act they expropriated allotment lands, neglected schooling for Indian children, and tried to confine Indians to working as cheap farm laborers and domestic servants at the margins of society.

One remarkable Indian spokesman, Carlos Montezuma, became an advocate of Native American rights during the Progressive Era. A full-blooded Apache, he had been reared by an itinerant Italian musician, who treated him as a son. He went to the University of Illinois and became a prominent physician. Wealthy, learned, and articulate, Montezuma criticized Bureau of Indian Affairs policies. He formed organizations and raised funds for Indian causes, and he urged Indians to help themselves, to leave the reservations, and to stop being "papooses," dependent on the white man for survival. Proud of his Indian heritage, Montezuma also urged Native Americans to honor and retain their traditional culture and Indian identity.

MORAL REFORM

Many progressive reformers were determined not only to improve institutions, but also to improve human behavior. They set out to purge society of drinking, prostitution, and gambling. Their campaign to outlaw alcohol was their most important moral crusade. The enemies of drink drew their inspiration from a temperance crusade that stretched back to the early nineteenth century. Gradually temperance advocates evolved into prohibitionists, who believed that only total abstinence could purge the curse of alcoholism from the land. The formation of the Anti-Saloon League in 1893 marked the beginning of the prohibitionist drive, which eventually forced abstinence upon the entire nation. The League joined forces with the Women's Christian Temperance Union to portray alcoholism as a social menace which ruined lives, destroyed families, caused diseases, created poverty, and robbed the economy of productive work. Between 1893 and 1900 many states, counties, and cities outlawed or restricted the sale and consumption of alcoholic beverages. As the twentieth century began, about one-fourth of the people lived in "dry" communities. After 1900, prohibitionists concentrated their formidable energies on achieving a na-

Prohibition brought many changes to the American scene. Here the former bar of a New York hotel has been converted to a library after the advent of the Eighteenth Amendment.

tional law forbidding the manufacture, sale, and use of alcoholic beverages.

The enemies of drink got their chance during World War I when, in order to conserve food, the government forbade using grain to manufacture whiskey. Prohibitionists pressured the government into forbidding the sale of alcoholic beverages near military bases and training camps. Citizens were encouraged to abstain from drinking as a patriotic sacrifice in support of America's soldiers fighting in France. Because Germany was the enemy and many American breweries were owned by German American families, prohibitionists urged Americans to boycott beer. Prominent industrialists called for prohibition. Henry Ford enthused, "A sober worker is an efficient worker." Prominent national political leaders became converts to the cause in wartime, and Congress proposed a constitutional amendment outlawing booze. At the time that Congress enacted the proposed amendment, 26 states were already "dry," most of them in the Midwest and South, home to millions of the rural Protestants who were the driving force behind the crusade to dry up the nation.

The Eighteenth Amendment was ratified in 1919 and implemented by the Volstead Act in 1920, which strictly defined the term *alcoholic beverage* and forbade its manufacture or sale. According to the Volstead Act, any drink containing more than one-half of one percent alcohol by volume qualified as an alcoholic beverage. Such a strict definition ensured that neither beer nor wine, much less liquor, could be manufactured or sold in America. Prohibition would be the law of the land for nearly fourteen years. Not all prohibitionists were progressives and not all progressives were prohibitionists, but the Eighteenth Amendment symbolized the progressive urge to use governmental power to improve the nation's morals.

Progressives also attacked prostitution. Muckrakers exposed the "white slavery" rings that kidnapped young women and forced them into prostitution. Jane Addams wrote about the pressures of poverty that forced immigrant and black women into prostitution. In 1910 Congress enacted the Mann Act, which prohibited transporting women across state lines for "immoral purposes." By 1915 every state had outlawed brothels and the public solicitation of sex.

Most states also outlawed gambling and closed all casinos at this time. California progressives also banned professional boxing and barred betting at racetracks, forcing horse owners to close all their tracks because betting had been the source of their revenue.

EDUCATIONAL REFORM

Progressive reformers envisioned education as an important means for improving society. In order for it to do so, progressive educators demanded that schools abandon traditional nineteenth-century curricula, which stressed moralistic pieties and rote memorization. John Dewey, the foremost progressive educational reformer, stated that the chief role of public schools in a democratic society was to prepare children for productive citizenship and fulfilling personal lives. In two influential books, *The School and Society* (1899) and *Democracy and Education* (1916), Dewey expounded his theories of progressive education: Children, not subject matter, should be a school's focus. Schools must cultivate creativity and intelligence. From kindergarten through high school, children learn from experience, and curricula must be tailored to those experiences. The school should be a "laboratory of democracy."

During the Progressive Era the percentage of school-age children enrolled in public and private schools expanded rapidly. By 1920, 78 percent of all children aged 5 to 17 attended school, a huge increase over the attendance rate during the Gilded Age. School construction expanded significantly. Administration and teaching were professionalized, and salaries were raised. These gains reflected the progressive commitment to education as well as taxpayer willingness to fund the costs.

The public high school system expanded rapidly during the late 19th Century, providing clerical training to meet the demand for growing numbers of office workers around the turn of the century.

College curricula and enrollments also expanded rapidly during the Progressive Era. By 1910 there were over one thousand colleges and universities in America, more than in all other countries combined. Much of the growth in college enrollments occurred at public colleges and universities. The first community colleges appeared during this era, products of progressive educational theories. The enrollment of women at colleges and universities expanded greatly, most of them attending coeducational institutions. By 1920 women accounted for almost half of college enrollments.

CONSERVATIVE REFORMERS

Some business executives became also progressive reformers. They supported federal regulation of industries as a means of protecting themselves from more radical proposals, such as trust-busting or nationalization, as well as a bewildering variety of state regulations. Corporate leaders also saw that federal regulation could create a stable business environment by eliminating cutthroat competition and boom and bust cycles. The U.S. Chamber of Commerce and the National Civic Federation, both business and trade associations, favored limited government political and economic reform.

Most progressive reformers repudiated radical attacks on American institutions. They were committed to capitalism and rejected socialist calls for its overthrow. Most progressives, alarmed by the increasing socialist vote in the first decade of the twentieth century, intensified their commitment to moderate reform, hoping to undercut radicalism by eliminating the conditions that bred worker discontent.

Progressivism by no means touched all Americans during the age of reform. Millions of Americans opposed government regulation of business and saw nothing wrong with contemporary political structures or practices. Many powerful representatives and senators shared these views, as did the titans of the business and financial worlds. Millions still found Social Darwinist concepts an adequate justification for the American system. Progressive reformers, however, operated from the center of the political spectrum. They repudiated *laissez-faire* as obsolete and rejected radicalism as dangerous. Like Jeffersonians, they defended individual rights and equal opportunity; like Hamiltonians, they supported a strong central government to protect these rights and opportunities.

URBAN PROGRESSIVISM

Progressive reformers had a strong aversion to party politics. They wanted to scrap political machines and bosses. To improve the political process, progressives wanted to nominate candidates by direct primaries instead of party caucuses. They called for nonpartisan elections to bypass the corruption that party politics bred. To get people involved directly in the democratic process, progressives advocated three reform devices: the initiative, which enabled voters to propose new laws; the referendum, which allowed voters to accept or reject laws; and the recall, which permitted voters to remove incompetent or corrupt officials from office before their terms expired. All these mechanisms aimed to make politics more rational, efficient, and accountable to the electorate.

Traditional Jeffersonian notions of limited government eroded during the late nineteenth century because of industrialization. Corporate executives, while paying lip service to *laissez-faire* slogans, aggressively sought government aid and protection. At the same time, angry farmers called for government takeover of railroads and monopolies, and urban representatives demanded government action to correct social problems. By the dawn of the Progressive Era middle-class reformers believed that the use of government power was necessary to counter corruption, exploitation, and favoritism. Before reformers could use political power, however, they would have to reclaim government from the political machines and corporate interests that controlled it. Progressives therefore sought to gain control of the political process in order to reform society.

They started in the cities. Reformers created the city manager and city commission forms of urban government to staff municipal agencies with trained administrators instead of political cronies. They bought up public utilities so that gas, water, streetcar, and electrical companies could not corrupt city governments. These "gas and water socialists" were willing to experiment with public ownership of utilities to ensure that city dwellers obtained essential services at reasonable prices.

PROGRESSIVISM ON THE STATE LEVEL

Soon progressive reformers expanded their horizons; they moved from local to statewide efforts. They formed political coalitions to elect state legislators and governors. Reform aims varied regionally. In the urban-industrial East, progressives concentrated on breaking political machines and enacting labor reforms. In the Midwest and West they focused on railroad regulation and direct democracy.

The most successful state reform leader was Wisconsin's governor, Robert La Follette. He entered politics as a small-town lawyer with conservative Republican views, but by the time he had risen through the ranks to become governor in 1900, La Follette had become a flaming progressive reformer. He and his supporters implemented a broad reform program including direct democracy, a fair tax system, railroad regulation, labor reform, and social welfare. Wisconsin progressives also generously supported the University of Wisconsin, making it a leading public university. In turn, the university furnished many experts to staff state agencies and to study problems, enabling the government to use the resources of modern science and technology. After serving three terms as governor, La Follette was elected senator and took his progressive crusade to Washington.

California also featured vigorous progressive reform. Hiram Johnson, a San Francisco attorney, led the California progressives. He won the 1910 gubernatorial election on a promise to curb the power of the Southern Pacific railroad, which dominated the state politically and economically. Once in office, Johnson with his supporters regulated the railroad. They also created a Public Utilities Commission empowered to set rates for utilities companies operating in the state. After serving three consecutive terms as governor, Johnson, like La Follette, moved on to the U.S. Senate, where he represented California interests and became a national Republican Party leader.

State progressive reformers also enacted a range of labor protection and social welfare laws that affected industrial workers more directly than did political reforms. Many states enacted factory inspection laws, and most implemented compulsory disability insurance to compensate victims of industrial accidents. They also enacted employer liability laws. They passed laws establishing minimum age of employment, varying from

12 to 16. They also prohibited employers from working youngsters more than eight to ten hours per day. Most states enacted legislation limiting the workday for women to ten hours. In 1914 Arizona became the first state to create pensions for the elderly. However, all these laws proved difficult to enforce: Many employers refused to comply with them, and the courts often weakened or nullified them.

DIRECT DEMOCRACY

For many progressive reformers, the cure for what ailed American democracy was more democracy. They were committed to structural reforms of the political system to take government away from political bosses and special interests and to return it to the people. During the Progressive Era most states adopted the secret ballot, primaries, initiative, referendum, and recall. Progressive reformers achieved one of their major political goals in 1913 when the states ratified the Seventeenth Amendment, providing for direct election of senators, who until then had been elected by state legislators. Legislative selection of senators had often been influenced by corporate interests and manipulated by political bosses. Although direct election by voters represented a significant advance for democracy, there is no evidence that it changed the way the Senate conducted the nation's business. Most incumbents up for election in 1914, facing an electorate for the first time, won reelection. Neither the political nor ideological complexion of the Senate that convened in 1915 was much different from its predecessor.

While direct primaries did allow the voters in some states to circumvent political bosses and nominate reform candidates, in other states the machines quickly accommodated themselves to the new system, got out the vote on election day, and still got their people nominated for key offices. Part of the problem was that middle-class progressive reformers often set up a false dichotomy between the "people" (that is, voters like themselves) and the "machines," whose leaders held power because they were supported by immigrant working-class constituencies who were more numerous and when mobilized could outvote the reformers. Progressive reformers were themselves an organized interest group who functioned politically. Gradually progressives realized that direct primaries did not significantly alter political practices in the states.

Other realities of popular politics in the United States during the Progressive Era confounded reformers. Progressive political analysts tended to construct rational models of how politics worked—or how it *would* work once the proper structural reforms had been implemented and the power of the bosses and special interests was broken. To progressives, politics consisted mainly of good men running for office on the issues; an informed electorate of like-minded citizenry would respond by electing them to office, and, aided by experts, they would provide honest and efficient government that served the public interest. What this rational model failed to take into account was the cultural diversity of the American electorate, especially in urban areas. Ethnocultural issues persisted, such as whether major league baseball games could be scheduled on Sunday or the neighborhood saloon would be shut down. Such concerns mattered more to the people than did economic issues such as railroad rates or tariff schedules. Progressives also failed to understand that there was no such thing as an objective or scientific concept of the public interest. The reform program of public interest issues was itself an ideological construct that had to compete in the political arena against rival political claims.

An ironic consequence of the progressive drive to make American politics more democratic was that it may actually have made it less democratic. Coinciding with the progressive political reforms, and persisting to the present, has been a steady drop in the percentage of eligible voters who go to the polls. Before the secret ballot was implemented in most states, during the 1880s and 1890s, 80 percent or more of eligible voters routinely turned out to vote. Most eligible voters registered and most voted. Implementation of the secret ballot no doubt reduced the extent of fraud, corruption, and manipulation, but it also reduced voter turnout. Millions of ordinary urban and rural working-class men who had routinely voted in local, state, and national elections stopped voting.

Why so many Americans have not been voting is a long-standing problem that has been frequently studied. Pundits have tried to explain why America is the only rich democratic nation in the world with relatively low participation in its political processes. Many culprits have been cited: mass commercial entertainment that distracts people; busy schedules that leave no time for civic duties; the schools' failure to educate Americans in the practices of democratic politics; a political system dominated by big business; a two-party system that does not offer real choices; and the failure of many people to see any connection between what happens in their lives and the outcome of elections. It may also be that the decline of the political parties, brought about in part by progressive reforms, has contributed to the fall-off in voting. Most citizens have at best tenuous political affiliations. Accompanying the decline in politics has been an increasing privatization of life, the shrinking of the public sphere, and a loss of civic identity. Whatever factors have caused the decline in American democracy in the twentieth century, it is evident that progressive reformers, in their zeal to create a more direct democracy that empowered the people, instead created a political system that contributed to the massive apathy and alienation that have degraded American political life in the twentieth century.

PROGRESSIVISM IN PERSPECTIVE

The Progressive Era effectively ended with World War I, but a generation of reform had brought major changes. Late nineteenth-century political, economic, and social institutions had been transformed. *Laissez-faire* had vanished. Public concern for poverty and injustice had reached intense levels, yet for every underprivileged American by 1920, at least three enjoyed material comforts and freedoms unprecedented in human history.

Progressivism was characterized by a jumble of reform movements. There was no such thing as a progressive movement, only movements. Often progressives worked oblivious to one another, even at cross purposes. Progressivism's diversity of aims, means, and achievements was its most salient characteristic. Its diversity reflected the pluralism of contemporary American society and culture.

Many progressive initiatives failed or only partially succeeded. Sometimes failure came from strong opposition, sometimes from inherent flaws in the reform movement. The courts struck down key reforms, most notably laws abolishing child labor. Political reforms such as the initiative and referendum failed to encourage greater citizen participation in politics and were exploited by special interest groups. Regulatory agencies lacked the resources to perform their investigative and monitoring functions thoroughly. They often obtained their data from the companies they were supposed to police, and they were staffed by people recruited from the industries they were supposed to monitor. Some political machines survived progressive assaults, and business influence at all levels of politics remained powerful.

Even so, progressives compiled a solid record of achievement. Progressivism refashioned the nation's future. Big business became more sensitive to public opinion. The power of political autocrats was diluted. Progressive reforms protected consumers against price-fixing and dangerous products. Social reforms alleviated injustice and human misery. Expanded school opportunities enabled the children of immigrants to achieve successful careers and fulfilling lives. Progressives challenged conventional ways of thinking. They raised urgent questions about the goals and qualities of American life. They provided both a language for discussing and a method for solving public problems. They proved that concerned citizens could bring the promise of American life closer to fulfillment for millions of their fellow citizens.

BIBLIOGRAPHY

The Progressive Era has a rich bibliography. Some of the most readable and accessible books include the previously mentioned studies of reform by Eric Goldman and Richard Hofstadter. William L. O'Neill, *The Progressive Years* is a lively general account. David M. Chalmers, *The Social and Political Ideas of the Muckrakers* is the best study of the reform writers of the era. There are many fine studies of women and feminism during the Progressive Era. These include William L. O'Neill, *Everyone Was Brave*; a first-rate biography of Margaret Sanger by David Kennedy, *Birth Control in America: The Career of Margaret Sanger*; Allen Davis, *American Heroine: Life and Legacy of Jane Addams*, a fine biography of the foremost woman reformer of the Progressive Era; Aileen Kraditor, *Ideas of the Woman Suffrage Movement*, an original study of the drive to win the vote for women; and Ruth Rosen, *The Lost Sisterhood: Prostitutes in America 1900–1918*, a fascinating study of this group of women. See also the relevant chapters of Alice Kessler-Harris, *Out to Work: A History of Wage-Earning Women in the United States*. Elliot M. Rudwick, *W. E. B. Dubois: A Study in Group Leadership* is the best book about the most important black progressive. The best intellectual history of progressivism remains Morton White, *Social Thought in America: The Revolt against Formalism*. Lawrence Cremin, *The Transformation of the School: Progressivism in American Education* is the best study of an important era in education by the foremost American historian of education. Howard Quint, *The Forging of American Socialism* is a good account of socialism during the Progressive Era. Anyone who wants to know how Prohibition came to be the law of the land should read J. H. Timberlake, *Prohibition and the Progressive Movement*.

CHAPTER
3
National Progressivism

Progressivism began as a series of unrelated local reform movements during the 1890s. Gradually reformers became aware that many political, economic, and social problems could not be resolved at the municipal and county court levels, and they shifted their focus to the states, forming coalitions to seek solutions from state legislatures. By the dawn of the twentieth century, progressive reformers had begun looking to the federal government as the main engine of change. But the federal government was incapable of positive action. It was controlled by two political parties that were mainly responsive to special interests if they acted at all. The federal courts too at this time sided consistently with business interests to nullify economic and social legislation. Hence reformers turned to activist presidents to clean up politics, to tame the trusts, to provide economic security, and to promote social welfare. Two of the most successful presidencies in modern American history, those of Theodore Roosevelt and Woodrow Wilson, coincided with the surge of progressive reformism that dominated national politics from 1901 until the United States entered World War I.

THE REIGN OF *LAISSEZ-FAIRE*

During the last decades of the nineteenth century the federal government was characterized by passive presidents. Most of the powers of government were lodged in the hands of powerful senior members of the Senate and House of Representatives. In theory most Americans, being good Jeffersonians, believed in *laissez-faire* principles: The state ought to confine itself to the traditional functions of protecting life, liberty, and property and should not confer special privileges or protections on any group or individual. In practice, Americans, being good Hamiltonians, endorsed much government aid to enterprise in the form of land grants, subsidies, tariffs, military protection, internal improvements, and the postal service.

At the turn of the century the federal government was small and weak. President William McKinley's entire advisory staff consisted of six officials. The federal budget in 1897 amounted to about $300 million. Approximately 200,000 employees worked for the federal government, most for either the post office or the military services. The national state simply had no involvement in the daily lives of most of its citizens. Outside of the post office, most Americans had no dealings with any federal agency. Most citizens regarded the federal government as a remote abstraction whose reach did not extend to the communities in which they lived. Whatever government services they did depend on came from local governments. If the federal government was small, it was also cheap. People paid no direct federal taxes; the only tax most people paid was property taxes to fund local and state governments. Most citizens voted enthusiastically in presidential elections, but they viewed presidents as patriotic symbols, emblems of nationality, not as men elected to solve problems or to perform actions that could have economic or social impact on their lives.

Congress at the turn of the century was controlled by aged conservative men determined to preserve their power and the perquisites of office. In the House, Speaker Joseph Cannon ruled unchallenged. He determined committee assignments and had significant influence over appropriations and the passage of all important legislation. In the Senate the dominant figure was Nelson A. Aldrich, chairman of the Senate Finance Committee. Aldrich was himself a wealthy businessman and his daughter was married to John D. Rockefeller, Jr. To progressive reformers, Aldrich's mastery of the Senate, the most powerful branch of the government, dramatically demonstrated private capital's control of national politics.

Laissez-faire doctrines were even more firmly embedded in the federal courts, especially the Supreme Court. Most Supreme Court judges were conservative ideologues who consistently sided with business and opposed all social legislation. During the 1890s the Court nullified much regulatory legislation, gutted the Sherman Act, sanctioned segregation of black people, and nullified a progressive income tax. Most judges openly stated that the U.S. Constitution was designed to protect private property and it was their duty, as arbiters of that document, to see to it that all attacks on property were repelled. State supreme courts were also controlled by jurists who embraced conservative ideologies. Federal and state courts posed formidable barriers to legislative reform efforts during the Progressive Era.

The assault on *laissez-faire* and the growth of government that began in the 1890s derived predominantly from the fears of middle-class and working-class citizens about the growth of private power within American society. Reformers decried the emergence of powerful corporations who dominated their industries and wielded considerable political power. They viewed these corporations as bastions of irresponsible private capital who, if allowed to operate unchecked, would overwhelm public authority, undermine democracy, destabilize society, and perhaps provoke anarchy and civil upheaval.

THE ADVENT OF THEODORE ROOSEVELT

In September 1901 a deranged anarchist murdered President McKinley, vaulting young Theodore Roosevelt into the White House. As governor of New York, Roosevelt had angered Republican Party bosses by supporting regulatory legislation. They got rid of him by pushing him into the vice presidency in 1900. They never dreamed that they were giving the nation its most forceful president since Abraham Lincoln, a man who would revitalize the office, give it much of its twentieth-century character, and make it the most powerful branch of the national government.

Roosevelt did not appear presidential. He was short and nearsighted, with big teeth and a high-pitched voice. He had an upper-class background and lived on inherited wealth. Theodore had been born in New York City on October 27, 1858. His father was a wealthy New York merchant active in civic and charitable affairs; his mother was from an aristocratic Georgia family. He had been a sickly child, undersized and suffering chronic asthma attacks, but he worked hard to develop his body and participated in vigorous sports. At Harvard his small size kept him off the football team, but he did compete on the boxing and wrestling teams. In the 1880s he lived on a cattle ranch in the Dakota territory, working cattle and sharing the rugged life of his cowboys.

Roosevelt possessed enormous stores of energy and a keen mind. He had a wide range of intellectual interests. He was a serious naturalist, specializing in ornithology. He was also a successful amateur historian, author of *The Naval War of 1812* (1882) and *Winning of the West* (1889). He also inherited a sense of civic responsibility and became a professional politician. A Republican Party partisan, he held various New York state offices during the 1880s and 1890s. In 1897 President McKinley appointed him Assistant Secretary of the Navy. He resigned his office to fight in Cuba during the Spanish-American War. He gloried in military combat, viewing war as the ultimate test of a man's character. He returned from that war a hero and was elected governor of New York, then U.S. vice president in 1900.

THE BULLY PULPIT

President Roosevelt became a reform leader. Calling the White House "a bully pulpit," he frequently used the presidency to promote and dramatize progressive measures. He shared the progressive view that the Jeffersonian ideal of small government was obsolete in an age of giant industries and large cities. He was a Hamiltonian, calling for a powerful central government to regulate big business and other sectors of the massive American economy. His presidency began the federal regulation of economic affairs that has characterized twentieth-century American history. He moved against monopoly at a time when giant trusts controlled

Theodore Roosevelt.

every important economic sector. Though Roosevelt acquired a reputation as a trust buster, he believed that consolidation was the most efficient means to achieve economic and technological progress. He had no quarrel with bigness or monopoly as such. He distinguished between "good" trusts and "bad" trusts. Good trusts did not abuse their power and contributed to economic growth. Bad trusts were those few combines that used their market leverage to raise prices and exploit consumers. Roosevelt made it his prime goal to stop the bad trusts from resorting to market manipulations. If necessary he would use antitrust prosecutions to dissolve bad trusts.

The new president moved slowly at first. But in 1902 he shocked the mostly Republican Wall Street establishment when he instructed Attorney General Philander C. Knox to file suit in federal court under the Sherman Act to dissolve the Northern Securities Company. The redoubtable J. Pierpont Morgan had recently persuaded a consortium of financiers to form the holding company to control the Northern Pacific and Great Northern railroads. Government lawyers argued that the Northern Securities Company had been formed to obtain monopoly control of all rail traffic in and out of the Pacific Northwest. In truth, the holding company had been formed to protect the railroads from the depredations of Wall Street speculators. But a federal court meeting in St. Paul, Minnesota, in 1903 sided with the government and ordered the Northern Securities Company dissolved. The next year the Supreme Court, by a 5-to-4 vote, sustained the lower court's decision.

The Northern Securities Company case represented a tremendous victory for Roosevelt's administration. His stature grew enormously. He won the admiring support of Republican progressive reformers, which he retained for the remainder of his public career. Following his victory over the Morgan interests, Roosevelt launched an antitrust campaign against several of the nation's largest trusts and holding companies, including the Beef Trust, Rockefeller's Standard Oil trust, and the American Tobacco Company. In every case, the Supreme Court sustained the government's actions. It is important to understand, however, that Roosevelt preferred a cooperative relationship between big government and big business to busting up the big combines. He directed the newly formed Bureau of Corporations to work with companies when they proposed mergers. He hoped through monitoring and investigation to exert pressures on business to regulate itself. He cultivated friendly relations with prominent business and financial leaders.

Roosevelt also took a progressive stance toward labor–management relations during his presidency. In May 1902, 150,000 members of the United Mine Workers Union (UMW) struck against coal companies in the anthracite fields of Pennsylvania. The mine workers wanted a 20 percent pay raise, an eight-hour day (a reduction frm the ten ten-hour day), and a recognition of their union as the miners' bargaining agent. Company officials refused to negotiate with union leaders and the strike dragged on through the summer and into autumn. Anthracite, or hard coal, was the main fuel used for heating homes. As the strike dragged on, the price of coal shot up.

Roosevelt intervened to resolve this dangerous strike. He offered the progressive services of investigation and arbitration. John Mitchell, the president of the UMW, accepted the president's offer, but company officials rejected the proposal, refusing to meet with union representatives. George Baer, spokesman for the mine owners, asserted:

> The rights and interests of the laboring man will be protected and cared for—not by the labor agitator, but by the Christian men to whom God in his infinite wisdom has given the control of the property interests of this country.[1]

With winter approaching and city dwellers facing the prospect of acute fuel shortages, Roosevelt rallied public opinion in support of government arbitration of the coal strike. He threatened to size the mines and use Army troops to mine the coal. He sent Secretary of War Elihu Root to meet with J. P. Morgan, who had major financial interests in the Pennyslvania coal fields. Morgan and Root worked out a mediation plan and persuaded the coal field operators to accept it. Roosevelt then appointed a commission to arbitrate a settlement and pressured both sides into accepting its recommendations. The commission granted the miners a 10 percent pay increase and a nine-hour day. It did not force the companies to recognize the United Mine Workers, and it permitted them to raise their prices to cover their increased labor costs. The strike ended October 23. Roosevelt, pleased with the outcome, observed that everyone got a "square deal."

Presidential intervention in the anthracite coal strike was a significant act. For the first time in American history, the federal government had intervened in a capital–labor dispute without taking management's side. Roosevelt's enlightened role in this strike contrasts powerfully with Democratic President Cleveland's performance during the Pullman Strike of 1894, when Cleveland had used the powers of the federal government to break the strike and destroy the American Railway Union. Roosevelt also extended the progressive concept of federal regulation to labor–management relations to protect the public interest. The chief beneficiary of the square deal, however, was Roosevelt himself because the strike settlement significantly enhanced the stature of the young chief executive early in his presidency.

By 1904 Theodore Roosevelt, or "Teddy," as he was affectionately called by his many rank-and-file followers, had established himself as the

---

1. George Baer, quoted in Henry F. Pringle, *Theodore Roosevelt* (New York: Harcourt, Brace, 1931, 1956), p. 186.

most powerful and popular president since the great Abraham Lincoln. A skilled political operator, Roosevelt had also seized control of the Republican Party machinery. Corporate leaders who had previously controlled presidential nominations could only watch helplessly as the 1904 Republican national convention nominated Roosevelt by acclamation. Roosevelt selected Senator Charles Fairbanks of Indiana to be his vice-presidential running mate.

The 1904 presidential campaign was a lackluster, one-sided affair. The Democrats had nominated an obscure federal judge, Alton V. Parker, to challenge the popular incumbent. Parker never had a chance. Led by Morgan, the financial and industrial titans of the nation contributed millions of dollars to Roosevelt's campaign fund. Even if he could be troublesome, Wall Street much preferred the Republican Roosevelt in the White House to an unknown Democrat. In November Roosevelt and the Republicans rode to a landslide victory. Teddy received 7.6 million popular votes to Parker's 5 million. In the electoral vote column, Roosevelt got 336 to Parker's 140. Eugene Debs, running as the American Socialist Party candidate, received 400,000 votes, representing about 3 per cent of the total cast.

Following his landslide victory, and now president in his own right, Roosevelt pushed for the enactment of regulatory legislation, particularly of the nation's railroads. The railroad industry was by far the biggest business in the land of big businesses, and railroads remained the nation's primary means of transporting both cargo and passengers. When the new Congress convened, Roosevelt demanded that it enact railroad legislation, consumer protection legislation, and a long list of other reforms.

The fight for railroad reform was long and hard, and eventually Roosevelt won it. He displayed impressive political skill in steering the Hepburn Act through a reluctant Congress. Enacted in 1906, the Hepburn Act strengthened and enlarged the Interstate Commerce Commission (ICC). The heart of the act gave the ICC power to reduce excessive rates charged shippers, subject to review of the federal courts. For the first time since its enactment in 1887, the Interstate Commerce Commission had effective power. The authority over railroad rates had been taken from private hands and lodged with a federal regulatory agency.

Roosevelt also persuaded Congress to enact three other important reform measures. The Meat Inspection Act (1906) created a system of federal inspections and set standards to ensure that all meat shipped via interstate commerce came from healthy animals. The act also required that all meat be processed and packed under sanitary conditions. The Pure Food and Drug Act (1906) outlawed the manufacture and sale of adulterated or poisonous foods, drugs, or alcoholic beverages. This law also required that all patent medicine labels accurately describe the contents. Third, the Employee's Liability Act created a system of accident insurance for railway workers.

In 1907 a financial panic forced some large New York banks to close in order to prevent depositors from withdrawing money. Financial titan J. P. Morgan stopped the panic by providing funds to rescue some imperiled banks and by persuading financiers to stop selling securities. Roosevelt, grateful to Morgan for preventing a possible recession, allowed Morgan's U.S. Steel Corporation to buy its main competitor, the Tennessee Iron and Coal Company, giving the gigantic company monopolistic control of the steel industry.

During his last two years in office Roosevelt became more progressive, straining his relations with conservative business interests in the Republican Party. He attacked corporate leaders, whom he called "malefactors of great wealth," and he called for stricter government regulation of business and increased taxation of the rich. Although he failed to get much more legislation through Congress, Roosevelt was laying the groundwork for a new progressive reform program, which he would call the New Nationalism. During his presidency he had significantly enhanced the role of the federal government in the lives of its citizens. The growth of the modern presidency began during Theodore Roosevelt's tenure of office.

CONSERVATION

Roosevelt's most enduring contribution to progressive reform came on the issue of conservation. An avid outdoorsman, Roosevelt was a determined conservationist. He also strongly backed his friend, the chief of forestry in the Department of Agriculture, Gifford Pinchot, who shared Roosevelt's conservationist goals. In his first State of the Union address to Congress, Roosevelt passionately denounced a nation that had squandered so much of its precious natural resources by shortsighted and careless mining practices, clear-cutting forests, farming semiarid lands, and overgrazing pastures by sheep and cattle. With assistance from Pinchot and other advisers, Roosevelt proposed the first comprehensive conservation program in the nation's history.

One of the major components of this conservation program was the development of irrigation and reclamation projects, particularly in the arid and semiarid regions of the West. At Roosevelt's urging, Congress enacted the Newlands Act in 1902 for the development of western water resources. Projects were funded through the sale of public lands. Irrigated lands were sold to farmers and ranchers at low prices and on generous terms. Formerly worthless desert lands became valuable as hard-working western farmers produced bountiful crops of fruits and vegetables.

Roosevelt's greatest contribution to the cause of conservation occurred when he withdrew public lands from sale and homesteading. Congress had enacted legislation in 1891 empowering the president to

withdraw timberlands, but prior to Roosevelt's presidency few forest reserves had been created. During his presidency, Teddy added 150 million
acres of western virgin forest lands to the national forests; he also added
23 national parks and monuments including the magnificent Grand
Canyon in northwestern Arizona. In addition Roosevelt persuaded Congress to create 55 bird and wildlife sanctuaries. Altogether over 230 million acres of public land were protected and preserved for the enjoyment
of future generations. Roosevelt also used his executive authority to preserve vast areas of mineral lands and water-power sites from private development. No other nation has preserved its natural resources from
short-term private development as well as has the United States.

In 1908 Roosevelt hosted a Washington gathering of governors and
resource managers called the National Conservation Congress. This was a
significant event in the developing national conservation movement. The
congress launched a nationwide conservation program that Roosevelt,
Pinchot, and others promoted vigorously. National and state conservation
commissions were created and many private organizations promoting
various conservation causes proliferated. Roosevelt and Pinchot both favored national planning for resource management and ordered growth.
Neither was a strict preservationist. Rather, they sought to balance the

*Roosevelt's greatest achievements and most enduring legacies were his conservation ef-
forts, represented here by the magnificent trees preserved in Roosevelt National Forest,
located on the eastern slope of the Rocky Mountains in northeastern Colorado.*

needs of economic development with the desire to preserve the nation's wilderness heritage of forests, open land, lakes, and rivers. Roosevelt's great contributions to the cause of conservation stemmed from an enlightened long-term view of America's destiny. He told his fellow citizens that "we aren't building the country for a day; it is to last through the ages."

TAFT VERSUS PROGRESSIVES

Having promised in 1904 not to seek reelection, Roosevelt decided to back his good friend and political ally, Secretary of War William Howard Taft, as his successor. Roosevelt was confident that Taft would continue his reform efforts. During the summer of 1908 the Republican convention nominated Taft on its first ballot. The Democrats turned to William Jennings Bryan for the third time. The populist warhorse campaigned against the trusts and called for lowering the tariff, two Democratic staples. Bryan also made a concerted effort to get the labor vote. He promised union leaders that he would try to stop court use of injunctions against unions. Samuel Gompers, president of the American Federation of Labor, the nation's foremost trade union federation, endorsed Bryan—labor's first partisan endorsement.

Taft, aided by Roosevelt, won easily, garnering 7.7 million popular votes to Bryan's 6.4 million. Taft received 321 electoral votes; Bryan got 162. Debs, running again on the Socialist ticket, received 421,000 popular votes. In Congressional elections the Democrats gained seats in both houses. Republican progressive insurgents from the Midwest also increased their numbers. These "wild men from the west" were poised to play a more powerful role in Republican Party affairs. The still-popular Roosevelt, who could have had another presidential term had he sought it, left the country to hunt lions in Africa and to travel around the world.

Taft was an intelligent, experienced politician and was committed to progressive causes. He was an able administrator and he also retained good relations with conservative and moderate Republicans. He appeared to be the ideal successor to the energetic Roosevelt. However, he lacked Roosevelt's stamina and love of politics. He was an obese man, weighing well over 300 pounds, and he did not work hard. He was easygoing and passive; he disliked conflict and hated to impose his views on people. He intended to carry the mantle of progressivism, but he lacked the energy and political resources to do so.

At the outset of his presidency, Taft aggressively pursued a progressive agenda: He enforced the Sherman Antitrust Act vigorously and added millions of acres of land to national forests. He signed the Mann-Elkins Railroad Act in 1910, increasing the regulatory authority of the Interstate Commerce Commission over the railroad industry. He supported labor legislation. He also called Congress into special session in 1909 to lower tariff rates, an issue that Roosevelt had avoided.

Sereno E. Payne of New York, Chairman of the House Ways and Means Committee, introduced a tariff bill approved by the new president that reduced rates on most imports. It passed the House quickly by a large majority, but in the Senate, Aldrich's Finance Committee let lobbyists for various interests carve it up. By the time hundreds of amendments were added in committee, the Payne bill was no longer recognizable. Tariff reform had once again foundered on the shoals of special interest groups.

The new Payne-Aldrich Tariff Act betrayed the Taft administration's commitment to tariff reform. But President Taft had failed to exert decisive leadership. He made no effort to thwart the lobbyists or to pressure the senators to resist the special interest groups. However, a group of progressive senators, led by Wisconsin's Robert La Follette, denounced the protectionist changes, using statistical data to show that many proposed tariff rates were unreasonably high. But Taft went ahead and signed the Payne-Aldrich Tariff, calling it "the best tariff the Republican Party ever passed," even though it raised tariffs on many important imports. Taft's actions outraged La Follette and other Senate progressives, who accused him of betraying the cause of tariff reform. These midwestern insurgents suspected that Taft was deserting the progressive cause and siding with the conservative wing of the Republican Party.

Conflicts over the tariff signaled that the Republican Party was splitting into progressive and conservative factions. Following the tariff battle, House progressives challenged the autocratic power of Speaker Joseph "Uncle Joe" Cannon, whose control of committee assignments and debate schedules allowed him to determine the fate of most House legislation. Taft initially backed the insurgents, then changed his mind and supported Cannon. His reversal angered House progressives and they joined their Senate colleagues in denouncing the president as an apostate reformer.

Taft also alienated progressive conservationists when he permitted Secretary of the Interior Richard A. Ballinger to open one million acres of forest and mineral lands for private development. He also fired Gifford Pinchot for protesting Ballinger's sale of some public water-power sites in Alaska to private interests. Taft was not opposed to conservation; he was backing Ballinger mainly as part of a political feud with Pinchot, but progressives viewed Pinchot's dismissal as an ominous sign that Taft was betraying the conservationist cause. The Ballinger–Pinchot controversy got even more complicated when Pinchot traveled abroad to seek out his old friend Roosevelt. Without consulting Taft, Roosevelt sided with Pinchot, angering the rotund president, who resented his former friend's lack of confidence in his presidency.

As the split within Republican ranks widened, Taft cast his lot with the conservatives, with whom he was personally more comfortable. During the Republican primaries for the midterm elections of 1910, Taft backed conservative candidates wherever they were opposed by progressives. In almost every election, the administration's candidate lost. Now in full revolt against their own president, progressive Republican leaders talked openly of leaving the GOP to form a new party if Taft were renominated in 1912.

During this intramural political wrangling, Roosevelt sided with the progressives. After returning from his world travels, Roosevelt denied any presidential ambitions, but he did speak out on the issues. He was easily the most famous living American, and his speeches made headlines. During a speech given at Osawatomie, Kansas, on August 31, 1910, Roosevelt came out in favor of a comprehensive progressive program he called the New Nationalism. He attacked "lawbreakers of great wealth" and called for a broad expansion of federal power. He asserted that progress must come through the national government. In a series of speeches Roosevelt expounded on the principles of the New Nationalism: strict regulation of big business, progressive income and estate taxes, workman's compensation, legislation to protect working women, curtailing of child labor, and a host of structural reforms to make the political system more responsive to the voters. He also called for a close working partnership between the federal government and state and local governments. When the 1910 election results were tallied, they registered a significant victory for Roosevelt and the progressive wing of the Republican Party and a smashing defeat for Taft and the Old Guard. The Democrats, many of them advocates of progressive reforms, won control of the House of Representatives for the first time in nearly twenty years. A bipartisn coalition of progressive Democrats and Republicans controlled the new Senate. In addition, most governors elected in 1910 were Democrats.

THE ELECTION OF 1912

On January 11, 1911, progressive Republican leaders met in the Nation's capital to form the National Republican Progressive League. They elected Senator Bob La Follette of Wisconsin to head their new organization. At a conference held in Chicago later in the year the new Progressive League chose La Follette as its favored candidate for the Republican presidential nomination in 1912.

Paralleling the growing Republican Party split between progressives and conservatives, there occurred a break between Taft and Roosevelt in October 1911, when the president ordered an antitrust suit against U.S. Steel, forcing the giant company to sell off its Tennessee Iron and Coal Company. Roosevelt reacted angrily because he thought the suit unwarranted. Also he had approved U.S. Steel's acquisition of the Tennessee Iron and Coal Company during the financial panic of 1907. Taft's actions made Roosevelt appear either a supporter of monopoly or, worse, a dupe of big business. He attacked Taft's action publicly, denouncing Taft for betraying the reform cause, and early in 1912 he announced that he would be a candidate for the Republican presidential nomination. Progressive leaders rallied to Roosevelt's banner.

Roosevelt threw himself into the campaign. He was clearly the choice of the Republican Party rank and file. He was victorious in all the states that held presidential primaries—he even beat President Taft in his home state of Ohio—but Roosevelt could not win the nomination through the primaries because not enough states held primaries on those days. President Taft's forces controlled the party machinery and came to the Republican convention in Chicago with a small majority of the delegates. Roosevelt's forces challenged the credentials of 254 of Taft's delegates, some of whom had been chosen under dubious circumstances. The fate of Roosevelt's candidacy, the fate of the Republican Party, and the outcome of the 1912 presidential election depended on the selection of those 254 contested delegates. The Taft-controlled credentials committee awarded 235 of the disputed delegates to Taft and only 19 to Roosevelt. Having won control of the convention, Taft's forces beat back all efforts to seat more of Roosevelt's delegates and secured Taft's renomination, narrowly, on the first ballot.

Roosevelt, outraged, was convinced that the nomination that was rightfully his had been stolen from him by the political bosses. He decided to run for president as the head of a third party. In August delegates gathered in Chicago in the same convention hall where Taft had emerged victorious six weeks earlier to create the Progressive Party. On the evening of August 6, in an emotional atmosphere that resembled a revivalist camp meeting, delegates who were mostly Republican progressives nominated Theodore Roosevelt as their presidential candidate and adopted his New Nationalism as the party platform. The delegates also chose California governor Hiram Johnson as Teddy's vice-presidential running mate. Roosevelt, in a rousing acceptance speech, told the delegates that we "stand at Armageddon and battle for the Lord." Teddy pronounced himself "as strong as a bull moose" and urged adoption of the New Nationalist program, including regulation of corporations, a national presidential primary, the elimination of child labor, a minimum wage, women's suffrage, and many other progressive reforms. Roosevelt's candidacy made it official: The Republican Party had split. Conservative Republicans supported President Taft's bid for reelection. Progressive Republicans, now formed into the Progressive third party, supported Roosevelt's candidacy.

The Democrats meanwhile had held their 1912 convention in Baltimore. The leading candidate for nomination was Champ Clark of Missouri, a veteran Democratic leader and currently Speaker of the House. Clark was a disciple of William Jennings Bryan and also had the backing of media magnate William Randolph Hearst, who was a power within the Democratic Party. Clark had won most of the delegates during the primaries and came to the convention heavily favored to win the Democratic nomination. But he was challenged by a political newcomer, Woodrow Wilson, the progressive reform governor of New Jersey, who for most of his adult life had been a college professor and administrator. A third candidate was Congressman Oscar Underwood of Alabama, who ran as a favorite son candidate and showed strength in other southern states.

When the Baltimore convention began on June 25, 1912, Underwood and Wilson appeared to have no chance against Clark. On the initial ballot Clark won a large majority of delegates, but he failed to get the two-thirds vote required for nomination. (The Democratic Party retained the two-thirds rule adopted in 1836 to give southern delegates extra clout in choosing the party's presidential nominees.) For several successive ballots the Underwood and Wilson delegates held firm to deny Clark the nomination. Then on the fourteenth ballot Clark made a deal with Tammany Hall to win the votes of the New York delegation. Outraged, the idealistic Bryan, still the most popular leader in the Democratic Party, switched his support to Wilson. For three more days the candidates continued to battle fiercely for delegates. Finally, on the forty-sixth ballot, Underwood's supporters switched to fellow southerner Woodrow Wilson and the nomination was his. Wilson chose Governor Thomas R. Marshall of Indiana for his vice-presidential candidate.

The Socialist Party nominated its perennial candidate, Eugene Debs. The stage was set for one of the most significant elections of the twentieth century, one in which the American system was subjected to a thorough evaluation, and an election in which alternative public policy options were rigorously debated and offered to the voters.

There were four significant candidates in the race: on the Right, the Republican candidate was the incumbent President Taft; on the Left, Eugene Debs ran on a Socialist slate calling for the nationalization of monopolies; in the Center stood two candidates—the Democratic nominee Woodrow Wilson, and the Progressive Party leader, former President Theodore Roosevelt, both of whom claimed the mantle of progressive reform. Neither Taft nor Debs had a chance to win; the outcome turned on the battle between Wilson and Roosevelt.

Roosvelt ran on his New Nationalism program; Wilson countered with a progressive program he called the New Freedom. Both candidates embraced progressive principles, and there were similarities in their appeals, but there were also significant differences between them because they represented different varieties of progressivism. The candidacies of Roosevelt and Wilson revealed a deep ideological cleavage that had evolved within national progressivism. Their most important difference expressed a philosophical division within progressive ranks over the fundamentals of progressive government. Roosevelt would not destroy the trusts, which he saw as efficient means to organize production. He favored establishing regulatory commissions staffed by experts who would protect consumer rights and ensure that concentrations of economic power performed in the public interest.

Wilson, whose New Freedom drew heavily upon the ideas of progressive legal reformer Louis Brandeis, believed that concentrations of economic power threatened liberty and foreclosed economic opportunity. He wanted to break up trusts to restore competition, but he did not want to restore *laissez-faire*, which he believed to be obsolete. He favored what Brandeis called "regulated free enterprise." Also Wilson did not favor the cooperation between big government and big business inherent in Roosevelt's New Nationalism. He spoke passionately, sometimes in evangelical tones, of the need to emancipate the American economy from the power of the trusts, declaring that government should provide for the man on the make, not for the man who has it made. The Democratic platform, which had been drafted partly by Bryan, also called for structural reforms to make the political system more democratic and for a downward revision of tariff schedules.

On the central issue of the 1912 campaign, however, the role of the federal government in promoting the economic security and social welfare of the American people, Wilson and the Democrats were mostly silent or took refuge in vague generalities. The absence of social justice planks in the Democratic platform derived mainly from the party's ancient Jeffersonian allegiances. Democrats still adhered to states' rights doctrines and a general policy of modified *laissez-faire* at the federal level. Wilson was suspicious of both big business and big government, regarding them both as potential threats to liberty. If regulation were necessary, Wilson would have the states do it. In 1912 the Democratic Party position was that if laws were needed to protect working people, they would come from state governments, not from Washington.

As he traveled the campaign trail in search of votes, Wilson highlighted the major themes of his New Freedom program. He would unleash the entrepreneurial energies of the American people by abolishing special privileges and restoring competition to the American system of free enterprise capitalism. He would achieve these goals by lowering tariffs, reforming the banking and currency systems, and strengthening the Sherman Antitrust Act.

Roosevelt dismissed Wilson's prescription for economic renewal as hopelessly reactionary and infeasible. Roosevelt reminded his audiences that big business was here to stay and that was a good thing. Large corporations were more efficient and more productive than small enterprises. They contributed greatly to national wealth and gave America a competitive edge in world markets. Roosevelt insisted that efforts to destroy large corporations were probably impossible and would undermine national prosperity. He accepted a corporate-dominated economy, but one strictly monitored and regulated by a powerful central government in order to prevent trusts from abusing their power. Teddy called for the creation of a federal trade commission to regulate the nation's large corporations. He hedged on the tariff by calling for the creation of a nonpartisan tariff commission to make "scientific adjustments in rates," which could be either up or down. Roosevelt, in keeping with the spirit of his New Nationalism, called for a host of social justice measures protecting farmers, women, children, and workers.

Election results showed Wilson the winner with only 42 percent of the popular vote—he was a minority president, but he carried 40 states and captured 435 of 531 electoral votes. The Democrats also won control over both houses of the Congress that would convene in 1913. Two-thirds of the gubernatorial elections also went to Democratic candidates. Roosevelt got about 27 percent of the popular vote, carrying 6 states with 88 electoral votes. Taft, who stayed at the White House and refused to make even one campaign speech, finished a distant third with 23 percent of the vote and 9 electoral votes. Debs, campaigning nationally, pulled down 902,000 votes, about 6 percent, the best ever by a socialist. Debs received the votes of many citizens who were not socialists but who knew Debs to be an honest man and a champion of the dispossessed.

The split in the Republican Party along with Theodore Roosevelt's failure to win over the Democratic progressives and thus forge a majority coalition of reform forces made Wilson's electoral victory possible. Had the Republican Party been united behind a Roosevelt candidacy, he

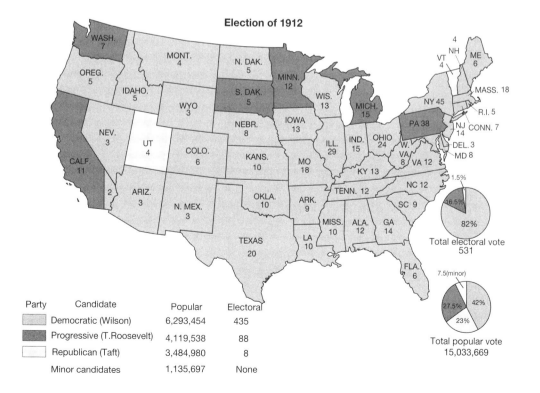

Election of 1912

Party	Candidate	Popular	Electoral
	Democratic (Wilson)	6,293,454	435
	Progressive (T.Roosevelt)	4,119,538	88
	Republican (Taft)	3,484,980	8
	Minor candidates	1,135,697	None

Total electoral vote
531

Total popular vote
15,033,669

would have won handily. Even Taft running on a progressive slate with Roosevelt's support would probably have prevailed. Wilson, however, was able to maintain traditional Democratic constituencies and his New Freedom also kept Democratic progressives within the party fold. Partisan political alignments more than the issues determined the outcome of the 1912 election.

A SCHOLAR IN POLITICS

Wilson made an unlikely president. He had been born in Staunton, Virginia, on December 29, 1856, the son of a stern Presbyterian minister. He grew up in South Carolina and Georgia during the era of the Civil War and Reconstruction. After becoming an attorney, he opted for an academic career. He received a Ph.D. from Johns Hopkins University and became a professor of history and political science. (Wilson is the only U.S. president ever to have earned a doctorate.)

During a lengthy and distinguished academic career, Wilson taught at several colleges and universities. From 1885 until 1902 he was a professor of history and government at Princeton University. He became an authority on the U.S. Constitution and was one of the most eminent American scholars of his generation. He wrote several scholarly books, of which his most renowned study was *Congressional Government* (1885). In this work Wilson stated that the separation of powers in the U.S. Constitution made responsible leadership impossible. He advocated revising the Constitution to create a national government modeled along the lines of the British cabinet system. However, after observing Theodore Roosevelt transform the presidency from a passive office to a dynamic and powerful one from which he led the nation and promoted reform causes, Wilson changed his mind. He realized that a strong president could provide responsible leadership and could bend the Congress to his will, which corresponded to the will of the people.

Wilson entered politics in middle age. In 1902 he became president of Princeton University, where he upset traditionalists with curriculum reforms. He resigned his presidency in 1910 during a dispute over university policy, intending to return to the classroom. But in 1910 the New Jersey Democratic Party needed a candidate for governor, and Wilson consented to run. The party bosses who secured his nomination needed his respectability, and they assumed he could be managed if he won. After winning the governorship, however, Wilson repudiated the bosses and embraced progressivism enthusiastically. He directed the passage of a host of legislative reforms that significantly improved politics in a state notorious for boss rule and corporate domination. His accomplishments in New Jersey enabled him to win the Democratic Party presidential nomination in 1912.

Woodrow Wilson, the "schoolmaster in politics," was an eloquent champion of progressive reform causes. He is shown here making a campaign speech during the election of 1912.

Wilson's manner reflected his religious and academic background. Tall, lean, and stiff, he looked sternly through his glasses at the world and its inhabitants. He could be aloof and often spoke self-righteously. Yet he proved to be an effective, even charismatic political leader. He took control of his party in Congress. He was a brilliant speaker; he could inspire support and intense loyalty with vivid religious imagery and ringing evocations of American principles in which he devoutly believed. Because he was steeped in the democratic and Judeo-Christian ideologies that under-girded progressivism, he could espouse reforms in moving, compelling, and irresistible phrases.

THE CLIMAX OF PROGRESSIVISM

In a brilliant inaugural address, the new president spelled out his pro-gressive reform agenda to the American people. His top priority was tariff reform, long a Democratic Party staple and long a failed promise. Wilson called the new Congress into special session to revise the tariff. Breaking with tradition, he went in person to deliver a forceful message to a joint session of Congress, urging quick passage of the tariff bill. Wilson was the first president to address a joint session of Congress, the first to focus pub-lic attention directly on the lawmakers.

Tariff rates had been rising for years and had appreciably increased living costs for millions of Americans. Farmers had complained for years that protective tariffs raised their operating costs and lowered their com-modity prices. All previous efforts at tariff reform, such as Taft's ill-fated ef-fort in 1909, had been blocked by Senate protectionist forces. Now Oscar Underwood, Chairman of the House Ways and Means Committee, steered the administration's tariff bill through the House. It reduced substantially duties on hundreds of items and placed many more on the free list. The measure passed easily by a vote of 281 to 139, with a lot of progressive Re-publican support.

In the Senate, once again the lobbyists for special interests de-scended on the senators, like so many Furies, to press their amendments to maintain the protectionist rates. But unlike the lethargic Taft, President Wilson was prepared to battle the lobbyists. He made a dramatic appeal to the American people, telling them: "The public ought to know the extraor-dinary exertions being made by the lobby in Washington. Only public opinion can check it and destroy it." Voters strongly responded to his ap-peal, and the Senate passed the measure with the reductions intact. The new president played a major role in bringing about the first reduction in tariff rates since the Civil War.

Wilson signed the new law, the Underwood-Simmons Tariff Act, Oc-tober 3, 1913. It reduced average import tax rates from about 40 to 29 per-cent across the board. Costs of living and of doing business for millions of Americans declined immediately. Imports to America increased dramati-cally. Reduced rates also meant that tax revenues declined sharply; be-cause tariff fees were the federal government's principal source of revenue, the new tariff bill levied a graduated income tax to replace its lost income, an option made possible by the recent ratification of the Six-teenth Amendment. The tax was small by today's standards. Incomes under $4,000 per year were excluded, a provision that exempted over 90 percent of American families in 1914, the first year the tax was in effect. The income tax was originally intended to be a tax only on the affluent and wealthy. People in the $4,000 to $20,000 income brackets had to pay one percent income tax. The rate rose gradually to a top rate of 7 percent on incomes exceeding $500,000 per year. Such rates did not take much wealth from rich people and most Americans never noticed it, but the income tax had made its debut. Passage of the tariff reform was a major political victory for the rookie president. It gave him great leverage over Democratic leaders in Congress and won him the trust and respect of most Americans, who sensed that an effective leader was in power who could keep the progressive faith and fulfill his campaign promises.

Wilson next turned his attention to another salient Democratic campaign promise: reform of the nation's banking and currency systems. Again, the new president intervened directly in the legislative process; he worked closely with key Democratic leaders in the House and Senate to ensure passage of the kind of measure that he wanted. Carter Glass of Virginia, Chairman of the House Banking Committee, introduced the federal reserve bill in early September. The House approved it quickly, but there was a long and tough battle to get the administration's bill through the Senate relatively unscathed. Wilson persisted and the Senate approved the measure the day before Christmas.

The Federal Reserve Act constituted the most important progressive reform measure of Wilson's presidency. It created the nation's first centralized banking system since Andrew Jackson had destroyed the Second Bank of the United States. It created twelve regional banks to hold the reserves of member banks throughout the nation. These district banks had authority to lend money to member banks at low interest rates called the *discount rate*. By adjusting this rate, the regional banks could adjust the amount of money a bank could borrow and thereby increase or decrease the amount of money in circulation. In response to national need, the banks could either loosen or tighten credit by lowering or raising the discount rate. More elasticity was structured into the money supply, and interest rates for farmers and small business owners would be lower. A Federal Reserve Board, whose five members were appointed by the president with the approval of the Senate, ensured that the banking industry would be regulated in the public interest. The nation still uses the Federal Reserve system, although its powers have been significantly changed by subsequent legislation. The head of the Federal Reserve Board has the power to determine interest rates and the rate of monetary growth and is the most powerful nonelected official in Washington.

Following his victories on the tariff and banking bills, Wilson went after Congress to achieve his third and final major reform commitment: strengthening the Sherman Antitrust Act. Three measures, including one introduced by Henry Clayton of Alabama, cleared the House. The Clayton

Act amended the Sherman Antitrust Act by outlawing monopolistic practices such as discriminatory pricing (the practice of a company's trying to destroy a smaller firm by lowering its prices in that company's market while keeping higher prices elsewhere) and interlocking directorates (the management of two or more competing companies by the same executives). Officers of corporations convicted of antitrust violations could be held individually responsible. The Clayton Act also exempted trade unions and agricultural organizations from antitrust laws, and it curtailed the use of court injunctions during strikes.

These acts, especially the Clayton Act, encountered serious opposition from the business community, including many small businessmen who had supported Wilson and the Democrats. They thought that these antitrust measures went too far; besides, it was proving impractical to try to prohibit by law every conceivable method of restraining trade. Facing both a practical and political problem, the Wilson administration executed a major ideological shift. Wilson dropped his support for antitrust legislation and supported instead a measure introduced by Congressman Raymond Stevens of New Hampshire that created a federal trade commission. On September 26, 1914, Wilson signed the Federal Trade Commission Act, which created the Federal Trade Commission (FTC), replacing the Bureau of Corporations. The FTC was empowered to study corporate practices and issue cease-and-desist orders against unfair trade practices. The chief purpose of the new agency was to monitor business practices and proscribe unfair practices *before* they had put their competition out of business and cheated their customers.

Ironically, Wilson had been forced to abandon a key plank in the New Freedom program, antitrust, in favor of a New Nationalist plank, a federal trade commission, which had been pushed by his arch political rival, Theodore Roosevelt. By 1914, corporate mergers were so extensive that restoration of free enterprise was impossible short of drastic antitrust actions that were unthinkable to Wilson and his key domestic adviser, Brandeis, who favored the trade commission concept. Wilson and Brandeis accepted economic concentration and embraced Rooseveltian concepts of expanding the government's regulatory powers to prevent harm to the public interest.

SOCIAL JUSTICE

During the first two years of his presidency, Wilson had been unconcerned about social justice legislation designed to provide federal protections for the exploited and disadvantaged classes of industrial America. Wilsonian progressivism was not responsive to the concerns of poor, weak, or helpless Americans. The President had no interest in helping African Americans and, in fact, supported the resegregation of the federal civil service. Gradually, his interests turned toward social legislation. His shift toward the New Nationalism and embracing of the Federal Trade Commission Act signaled a change of direction. He realized that the national government had a positive role to play in promoting social welfare and enhancing economic security. Wilson also understood that he faced defeat in the 1916 election unless he supported a vigorous slate of New Nationalist reforms. The Democratic Party was still the minority party; unless Wilson could attract a large number of Roosevelt progressive Republican voters, he would lose to the Republican Party candidate, who would be backed by a reunified party.

In 1916 Wilson supported a whole range of social justice measures. These included the Federal Farm Loan Act, which created banks to lend money to farmers at low interest rates, and the Adamson Act, which gave all railroad workers an eight-hour day and time-and-a-half for overtime. Soon after signing the Adamson Act, Wilson signed a progressive tax measure that raised income tax rates, created a federal estate tax, and imposed excess profits taxes on large corporations. This represented the first effort in American history to use the tax powers of the federal government to effect a redistribution of wealth from the "haves" to the "have nots." Wilson further courted progressive social reformers by backing laws outlawing child labor and granting federal employees worker's compensation. He also appointed Louis Brandeis to the Supreme Court, a controversial appointment because Brandeis was an outspoken critic of big business and also the first Jew ever appointed to the Court.

As Wilson approached the election of 1916, his presidency had been one of the most significant and successful in American political history. His reform ideas set the direction of federal economic policy for much of the twentieth century. All major progressive reform initiatives were enacted. Ironically, a major reason for the decline of progressivism that occurred after 1916 was that it was a victim of its own success. Its agenda was implemented—and exhausted. The "schoolmaster in politics," with scant prior political experience, in the judgment of many historians turned out to be the greatest president since Abraham Lincoln.

BIBLIOGRAPHY

There is a solid body of historical literature on national politics during the Progressive Era. Two classic studies of national progressivism are George Mowry, *The Era of Theodore Roosevelt* and Arthur Link, *Woodrow Wilson and the Progressive Era*. An imaginative comparative study of the two greatest progressive reform leaders, Theodore Roosevelt and Woodrow Wilson, is John M. Cooper, Jr., *The Warrior and the Priest*. John M. Blum has written two fine studies: *The Republican Roosevelt* and *Woodrow Wilson and the Politics of Morality*. The best one-volume biography of Roosevelt is William H. Harbaugh, *The Life and Times of Theodore Roosevelt*. David G. McCullough, *Mornings on Horseback* is a finely crafted account of the youthful Roosevelt. Edward A. Weinstein, *Woodrow Wilson: A Medical and Psychological Biography* shows how Wilson's personality and medical condition influenced his political career. Donald E. Anderson, *William Howard Taft* is the most balanced biography of the twenty-seventh president. David Thelen, *Robert La Follette and the Insurgent Spirit* is a spirited study of one of the most important progressive leaders who never quite made it to the White House. Robert Wiebe, *Businessmen and Reform* is an original account of progressive reformers within the business community. Two books written by intellectuals during the Progressive Era that influenced presidents include Herbert Croly, *The Promise of American Life*, which influenced Roosevelt, and Walter Lippmann, *Drift and Mastery*, which influenced Wilson. Gabriel Kolko, *Triumph of Conservatism* is a radical account of federal regulatory policies.

CHAPTER
4
America and the World

In the aftermath of its war with Spain, the United States pursued an interventionist foreign policy. It fought a war to crush a nationalist rebellion in the Philippines and joined other imperial powers to suppress the Boxer uprising in China. It sent its troops into many Latin American nations: Cuba, Panama, the Dominican Republic, Nicaragua, Haiti, and Mexico. Progressive foreign policy aimed to promote overseas trade and investment, to maintain regional order, and to fulfill the imperatives of the American missionary impulse to redeem the world. The foreign policy elite who formulated progressive foreign policy believed that northern Europeans and their American descendants belonged to a superior race destined to dominate and to "civilize" the darker-skinned people of Latin America, Asia, Africa, and the Pacific islands. In 1917 the United States reached beyond the Caribbean and Pacific regions to intervene in Europe to ensure an Allied victory over Germany. World War I was a transforming experience for the United States, opening a historic opportunity for America to assume primacy among the world's nations.

MANAGING THE AMERICAN EMPIRE

U.S. foreign policy during the Progressive Era was determined mainly by American expansionism during the 1890s and the acquisition of an overseas empire. Progressive diplomatists were concerned with the opportunities and problems encountered in managing, protecting, and expanding the American empire, which reached from the Caribbean to the Far East. The American empire during the period between the Spanish-American

War and World War I faced threats from restless nationalists, commercial rivals, and other expansionist nations.

Although Cuba did not become an American colony after the war with Spain, the United States dominated the new nation. American troops remained in Cuba until 1902, and Cuba was governed by General Leonard Wood, formerly the commander of the Rough Riders. To get rid of the American forces, Cubans were forced to accept the Platt Amendment, which was incorporated into the new Cuban constitution and later ratified as a treaty. The amendment conceded American hegemony over Cuba and impaired Cuban sovereignty. Cuba could make no treaties with another nation without U.S. approval. Cuba granted the United States the right to intervene "to maintain order and preserve Cuban independence." Cuba also had to lease a naval base at Guantanamo to the United States. The Platt Amendment governed United States–Cuba relations until 1934. Cubans protested it to no avail. When a rebellion occurred in 1906, President Roosevelt intervened to reestablish a U.S.-controlled provisional government, supported by 5,000 American troops, that ruled for 28 months. Over the next 15 years, whenever political instability occurred in Cuba, the United States sent the Marines ashore to maintain order and protect American lives and property.

The 30-year-long American protectorate left its mark on Cuba. Americans helped Cubans improve transportation, develop a public school system, create a national army, increase sugar production, and raise public health levels. An American physician, Dr. Walter Reed, working with Cuban physicians, proved that mosquitoes carried yellow fever germs, and American sanitary engineers eradicated the disease from the island. At the same time, American investments in Cuba reached $220 million by 1913, and American exports to the island reached $200 million by 1917. The Platt Amendment, the U.S. Marines, and U.S. investments made a mockery of Cuban sovereignty for decades. The Cuban nation developed with a colonial mentality. Cuban patriots nurtured a resentment toward the United States that in time became anti-Americanism.

Expanding American interests in the Caribbean and Asia made building an interoceanic canal across Central America an urgent American priority. Two obstacles had to be overcome before it could be constructed. First, the Clayton-Bulwer Treaty (1850) with the British, requiring Anglo-American control of any Central American canal, had to be cancelled. In 1901 Secretary of State John Hay and Lord Pauncefote, the British ambassador to the United States, signed the second Hay-Pauncefote treaty, giving America the right to build and fortify a transisthmian waterway. Second, a route for the canal had to be acquired. One possible route lay across the Colombian province of Panama, where a French company, the New Panama Canal Company, owned the right-of-way, having inherited it from the failed De Lesseps company, which had tried to build a canal during the 1880s. Only 50 miles separated the two oceans along this route, but

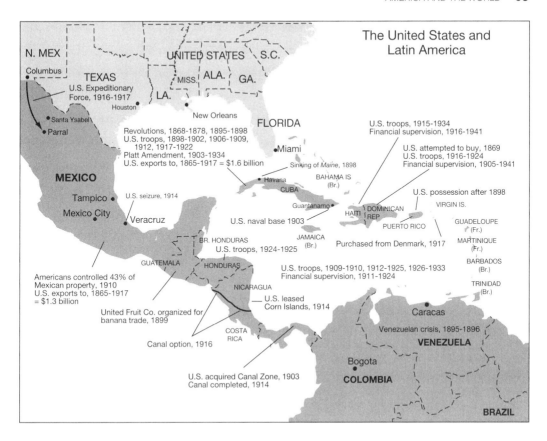

The United States and Latin America

N. MEX
Columbus
TEXAS
U.S. Expeditionary Force, 1916-1917
Houston
Santa Ysabel
Parral

UNITED STATES S.C.
MISS. ALA. GA.
LA.

New Orleans
FLORIDA
Miami

Revolutions, 1868-1878, 1895-1898
U.S. troops, 1898-1902, 1906-1909, 1912, 1917-1922
Platt Amendment, 1903-1934
U.S. exports to, 1865-1917 = $1.6 billion
Sinking of *Maine*, 1898
Havana
CUBA
Guantanamo
U.S. naval base 1903

BAHAMA IS (Br.)

U.S. troops, 1915-1934
Financial supervision, 1916-1941

U.S. attempted to buy, 1869
U.S. troops, 1916-1924
Financial supervision, 1905-1941

U.S. possession after 1898
VIRGIN IS.

HAITI DOMINICAN REP
PUERTO RICO
GUADELOUPE (Fr.)
MARTINIQUE (Fr.)

MEXICO
Tampico
Mexico City
Veracruz
U.S. seizure, 1914

JAMAICA (Br.)
Purchased from Denmark, 1917

BARBADOS (Br.)

BR. HONDURAS
U.S. troops, 1924-1925
GUATEMALA HONDURAS

U.S. troops, 1909-1910, 1912-1925, 1926-1933
Financial supervision, 1911-1924

TRINIDAD (Br.)

Americans controlled 43% of Mexican property, 1910
U.S. exports to, 1865-1917 = $1.3 billion

NICARAGUA
U.S. leased Corn Islands, 1914

United Fruit Co. organized for banana trade, 1899

Caracas
Venezuelan crisis, 1895-1896
VENEZUELA

Canal option, 1916
COSTA RICA

Bogota
COLOMBIA

U.S. acquired Canal Zone, 1903
Canal completed, 1914

BRAZIL

the terrain was rugged and posed serious health hazards. Another possible route traversed Nicaragua. It was 200 miles long, but it would be an easier challenge because much of it included Lake Nicaragua and other natural waterways.

President Roosevelt considered both sites and chose the Panama route. His decision was influenced by the lobbying of Philippe Bunau-Varilla, a French engineer living in Panama who had directed the now defunct French canal project. On January 18, 1903, a commission agreed to pay the New Panama Canal Company $40 million for its right-of-way and equipment. Congress subsequently approved the Panama route. On January 22, 1903, Secretary of State John Hay negotiated a treaty with Tomas Herrán, the Colombian *charge d'affaires*. By its terms, the United States received a 99-year lease on a 6-mile-wide zone across the isthmus of Panama; in return the United States granted an initial payment of $10 million to Colombia and $250,000 annual rental. But on August 12, 1903, the Colombian senate unanimously rejected the Hay-Herrán treaty because the senators wanted more money and because the agreement, which severely infringed upon Colombian sovereignty, was unpopular with the

Colombian people. The senators wanted an initial payment of $15 million from the United States and also tried to extract $10 million from the New Panama Canal Company.

President Roosevelt could have negotiated an agreement with the Colombians, who were eager to have the United States build the canal, but the imperious Roosevelt angrily denounced them, broke off negotiations, and sought to get the right-of-way by other means. Panamanians, also eager for the Americans to build the canal, learning of the Colombian rejection and urged on by New Panama Canal officials, rose in rebellion on November 2, 1903. Roosevelt had previously given Bunau-Varilla indications that the United States would accept a Panamanian revolt.

That same day an American fleet, led by the cruiser USS *Nashville*, arrived in Colon, Panama's Caribbean port. When Colombia landed 400 troops at Colon on November 3 to suppress the rebellion, however, the American Navy did not interfere, disappointing the Panamanian rebels, who had hoped for American help. Forced to rely on their own resources, the Panamanians outmaneuvered the Colombians by bribing their leader into taking his troops back to Colombia. With the soldiers gone, the revolution succeeded. Joyous Panamanians declared their independence on the evening of November 3, and at noon the next day Secretary of State John Hay recognized the sovereign Republic of Panama. On November 18 Hay and the new Panamanian minister plenipotentiary, the resourceful Philippe Bunau-Varilla, negotiated a treaty, the Hay-Bunau-Varilla Treaty, granting the United States a zone 10 miles wide "in perpetuity" across the isthmus for the same money that Colombia had previously rejected. The New Panama Canal Company then received its $40 million for its right-of-way and properties. On February 24, 1904, the U.S. Senate overwhelmingly approved the new treaty. American public opinion also overwhelmingly approved the new treaty and the means required to achieve it.

Construction of the canal began in 1904 and the 50-mile-long canal opened to seafaring traffic on August 15, 1914. From opening day, the merchant ships of many nations and vessels of the U.S. Atlantic and Pacific fleets traversed the big ditch. Americans celebrated the opening of the canal by staging a world's fair honoring it, the Panama-Pacific Exposition held in San Francisco in 1915. Building the canal was a tremendous engineering feat that served the national interest economically and strategically. The United States fortified the Canal Zone, and guarding the canal and its approaches became a vital U.S. strategic interest. The terms of the treaty negotiated by U.S. and Panamanian officials made the Canal Zone an American colony. Panama was a sovereign nation in name only because of American control of the canal and a strip of Panamanian soil stretching across the heart of that small country.

Roosevelt's arrogant intervention in the internal affairs of Colombia, while popular with most citizens of the United States, frightened and angered Latin American nationalists who viewed the Panama Canal as a symbol of "Yanqui" imperialism. In 1922 the United States paid Colombia $25 million in return for Colombia's recognition of Panamanian independence, a payment humorously dubbed "canalimony." In 1978 the United States and Panama concluded treaties that provide for turning over the Canal Zone to Panama in the year 2000.

Following his acquisition of the Canal Zone, Roosevelt turned the rest of the Caribbean into an "American lake." He was aided in these actions by the British, who were concerned with improving relations with the United States and tacitly accepted the American sphere of influence. London, perceiving the shifting power balance in the Western Hemisphere, gracefully acceded to American hegemony in Latin America. British acceptance of American dominance in the Caribbean signaled a growing Anglo-American accord that cleared the way for U.S. regional expansionism without fear of British opposition and that blossomed into a full-fledged Anglo-American alliance during World War I. Both world powers benefited from their "great rapprochement."

Roosevelt said, "Speak softly and carry a big stick." He used the stick, but he seldom curbed his noisy rhetoric. In 1904 he announced his Roosevelt Corollary to the Monroe Doctrine, a warning to Latin American countries to put their governments and finances in order to forestall European intervention in their affairs. Roosevelt warned:

> Chronic wrongdoing . . . may in America, as elsewhere, ultimately require intervention by some civilized nation, and in the Western Hemisphere the adherence of the United States to the Monroe Doctrine may force the United States, however reluctantly, in flagrant cases of such wrongdoing or impotence, to the exercise of an international police power.[1]

The Roosevelt Corollary to the Monroe Doctrine transformed that hallowed prohibition on European intervention in the Western Hemisphere into a firm assertion that the United States henceforth would arrogate to itself the role of regional policeman.

Roosevelt and his progressive successors, Taft and Wilson, frequently implemented Roosevelt's corollary. Between 1900 and U.S. entry into World War I, American troops intervened in Cuba, Panama, Nicaragua, the Dominican Republic, Haiti, and Mexico. American officials took over customs houses to control tariff revenues and government budgets, renegotiated foreign debts with American banks, and trained national armies—and they conducted elections. Frequent U.S. interventions into Nicaraguan affairs between 1907 and 1933 made that small and poor Central American country a U.S. protectorate.

Mexico appeared especially threatening to the progressive managers

1.   Theodore Roosevelt, quoted in Henry F. Pringle, *Theodore Roosevelt* (New York: Harcourt, Brace, 1931, 1956), p. 207.

of U.S. foreign policy. In 1910 revolutionaries overthrew Porfirio Diaz, an aged dictator who had maintained a favorable environment for U.S. and other foreign investments for 40 years. During the next seven years the Mexicans changed governments several times as revolutionary factions struggled for power. At various stages of the Mexican revolution, American lives and property appeared to be imperiled.

But President Wilson appeared less concerned about protecting the U.S. investment in Mexico of one billion dollars than he was guiding the Mexicans to establish an American-style political democracy. In the summer of 1913 Wilson attempted to remove General Victoriano Huerta from power and replace him with a government led by Venustiano Carranza, the leader of the Constitutionalists. When an arms embargo failed to work, Wilson sent American naval vessels to the Mexican gulf ports of Vera Cruz and Tampico. On April 21, 1914, Wilson, learning that a merchant ship carrying arms for Huerta's forces was arriving at Vera Cruz, ordered a force of 800 U.S. sailors and Marines to enter the city and seize the customs house to interdict the arms shipment. Local Mexican forces fought the American invaders in the streets of Vera Cruz. Nineteen Americans and hundreds of Mexicans died in the battle. Although the U.S. invasion was intended to overthrow General Huerta, the American actions offended Mexicans of all political persuasions, who viewed the U.S. actions as an affront to their nationalism and a threat to their independence. Appalled at the bloodshed that he had provoked, a chastened Wilson permitted mediation of the U.S.–Mexican dispute by Argentina, Brazil, and Chile. Mediation failed, but Huerta abdicated and fled to Europe in July 1914. Carranza took power. Wilson withdrew American forces from Vera Cruz and extended diplomatic recognition to the new leader.

The Mexican revolution soon turned violent again when one of Carranza's generals, Francisco "Pancho" Villa, broke from the Constitutionalist ranks. Sporadic fighting occurred between Carranza's and Villa's forces during 1915. On March 9, 1916, General Villa, who perceived Wilson to be an ally of Carranza, led his forces across the border and attacked the American town of Columbus, New Mexico, killing seventeen Americans. Wilson reacted to the daring raid by ordering the U.S. Army under the Command of General John J. "Black Jack" Pershing to invade Mexico and capture Pancho Villa. Seven thousand American soldiers advanced 350 miles into Mexico without ever spotting Villa's elusive forces. Instead, Pershing's soldiers found themselves fighting Carranza's forces. Again Wilson's military intervention had managed to anger and frighten all Mexicans. On February 5, 1917, only when it became evident that the United States would soon enter World War I, did Wilson withdraw the U.S. Army from Mexico. Only impending war in Europe forced Wilson to abandon his self-righteous and futile efforts to direct the political destiny of Mexico. The chief legacy of Wilson's meddling has been Mexican resentment and mistrust of the United States.

The United States policed the Caribbean region during the progressive years for several reasons. American security and prosperity required order in these small, poor nations. Washington would not tolerate disorders that might threaten its new canal across Panama. Order also protected America's growing commerce and investments in Latin America. Between 1900 and 1917, American exports to Latin America increased from $132 million to $309 million. Imports from Latin America increased even more. American investments in Caribbean countries in sugar, tobacco, bananas, coffee, transportation, and banking expanded rapidly. Progressive diplomats also projected their reform urges; they wanted to remake Latin American societies in the image of the United States. Progressive idealists assumed that all people, if given the chance, wanted to be like Americans and that they would thereby be greatly improved. President Woodrow Wilson asserted "every nation needs to be drawn into the tutelage of America."

A salient characteristic of American foreign policy between the Spanish-American War and U.S. entry into World War I was insensitivity to the nationalism of other people. Americans did not understand or take seriously the Filipino resistance to American colonial domination, Cuban anger over the restrictions of the Platt Amendment, Colombian outrage over U.S. support of the Panamanian insurrection, or Mexican resentment over Wilsonian interventionism. The American empire that evolved comprised few colonies; it was mainly an informal empire, characterized by economic and political control instead of formal annexation and governance. This informal American empire, administered by paternalistic military officers, bankers, and reformers, many of whom displayed a contempt for the native people's culture, politics, and economies, wounded their national pride and infringed upon the sovereignty of their governments—all in the name of national security, profits, democracy, and saving souls.

American foreign policy toward Europe during the Progressive Era was governed by three principles: (1) Europeans should not intervene in Western Hemisphere affairs now that American military force backed the Monroe Doctrine. (2) America should stay out of European affairs. When Roosevelt intervened to mediate a conflict between France and Germany over Morocco in 1906, he was criticized for entangling the United States in a European problem. (3) American interests were best served by international cooperation with the British, the world's preeminent power.

Possession of the Philippines and implementation of the Open Door policy had thrust the United States into Asian affairs. American policy toward Asia during the Progressive Era was dominated by relations with Japan, a rising Asian power. When imperial conflicts over Manchuria and Korea provoked Japan and Russia to war in 1904, Japan scored quick victories. President Roosevelt attempted to mediate an end to the war at a conference in Portsmouth, New Hampshire, in 1905, trying to preserve the balance of power in the Far East. He failed. Later that year the Taft-Katsura Agreement conceded Japanese control of Korea in exchange for a Japanese promise not to attack the American colony in the Philippine Islands. Roosevelt sent the American "Great White Fleet" on a world tour in 1907 and 1908 to impress the Japanese with American naval might. The Japanese were duly impressed, gave the Americans a lavish welcome, and began building bigger ships as soon as the Americans left. In 1908 the Root-Takahira Agreement recognized Japanese interests in Manchuria in exchange for another Japanese pledge to respect American colonial possessions in Asia.

Despite these agreements, United States–Japanese relations were not harmonious. The Japanese were offended by the racist mistreatment of Japanese in California during the progressive years. American economic activities in China also alarmed the Japanese, who worked to increase their economic concessions in that country. In the long run, Japanese–American relations would founder on conflicts over China, and the result would be World War II in Asia.

EUROPE GOES TO WAR

War erupted in Europe in August 1914, to the surprise and horror of most Americans. It had many causes, including decades of imperialistic rivalries over trade and colonies. By the first decade of the twentieth century the great powers of Europe had joined one of two rival coalitions, each armed to the teeth. The Triple Alliance joined together Germany, Austria-Hungary, and Italy. The Triple Entente combined Britain, France, and Russia.

All members had economic and territorial ambitions that had involved them in the affairs of unstable countries and provinces in the Balkan peninsula. A series of crises in the Balkans had caught the great powers of Europe in a chain of events that propelled them to war. Within the Balkans, Slavic nationalists sought to build a major power by prying territories from the Austro-Hungarian Empire and adding them to Serbia. One of these territories was Bosnia, which contained a large Serbian population. On June 28, 1914, at Sarajevo in Bosnia, the heir to the Austrian throne, Archduke Franz Ferdinand, was assassinated by a Serbian terrorist, Gavrilo Princips.

Austria, backed by Germany, delivered an ultimatum to Serbia. Serbia appealed for help from its major ally, Russia. When Austria declared war on Serbia in late July, Russia began mobilizing her vast armies. Germany asked Russia to stop her mobilization. The Russians refused and the Germans, convinced war was coming, declared war on Russia August 1 and on Russia's ally, France, two days later. Germany quickly followed these declarations of war with an invasion of neutral Belgium that was

World War I, 1914–1918

part of a preconceived plan to attack the French in order to defeat them quickly and avoid fighting a two-front war, against France in the west and her ally Russia to the east. Germany's attack on Belgium brought the British into the war on August 4. Later Turkey and Bulgaria joined Germany and Austria-Hungary. Japan joined the Entente powers, as did Italy in 1915, after being freed from the Triple Alliance. (Germany and the nations allied with it were called the Central Powers. The nations allied in the Entente were called the Allies.) Six weeks after the assassination at Sarajevo, Europe was at war.

UNNEUTRAL NEUTRALITY

When the war began, nearly all Americans assumed that the United States would never become involved. There appeared to be no vital American interests at stake; it was a European war over European issues. The war was considered "none of our business." No one expected it to last more than four to six months; it should be over by Christmas, said the pundits.

President Wilson's response to the outbreak of war was an effort to isolate America from its effects; he declared America to be neutral. In a speech delivered before the Senate he urged his countrymen to be neutral in their thoughts as well as acts. The United States, he asserted, would stand as an inspiring example of peace and prosperity in a deranged world. He also feared that if the United States did not remain neutral, its "mixed populations would wage war on each other." The war, he said, was one "with which we have nothing to do, whose causes cannot reach us."

Wilson's appeal for neutrality and unity at home proved impossible to attain. Ethnic groups took sides. Many German-Americans and Irish-Americans sided with the Central Powers while Americans of British, French, and Russian ancestry cheered the Allies. A large majority of Americans were drawn to the Allied side; they viewed the war as a struggle between democracy and autocracy. Germany's invasion of neutral Belgium at the outset of the war convinced many Americans that Germans were international outlaws, barbarian defilers of helpless innocents. Clever British propaganda reinforced this view of Germans as enemies of civilization.

America's economic ties to the allies also made genuine neutrality impossible. War orders from France and Britain flowed in to American farms and businesses, producing a roaring wartime prosperity. In 1914 U.S. exports to the Allies totaled $753 million; in 1916 that figure soared to nearly $3 billion. During that same period, trade with Germany tumbled from $345 million to a paltry $29 million. Much of the war trade with the Allies was financed with credit extended by U.S. banks, which loaned the Allies $2.3 billion during the neutrality period. The Germans received only $27 million. President Wilson had initially banned bank loans to all belligerents in the hopes of shortening the war, but he reversed himself when he saw that the war was going to be a protracted struggle. Also he understood that the Allied war trade had become important to the American economy. If credits were not made available to the Allies, their purchases of American goods would fall sharply, hurting manufacturers, farmers, and workers in this country.

Germany viewed the commercial and financial ties between the United States and the Allies as giving its enemies access to supposedly neutral American arsenals and credits. Wilson responded to German complaints by insisting that if America cut its ties with the Allies, that would be an unneutral act favoring the Germans, since under international law the British, who controlled the seas, could, at their own risk, trade with neutrals. He maintained that it was Germany's responsibility to stop the trade with an effective blockade of the Allies. Wilson's view that American neutrality policy accorded with international law was true, but British control of the seas turned this policy in favor of the Allies.

Wilson and nearly all his leading advisers were pro-Ally in the general sense that they preferred an Allied to a Central Powers victory. They believed that American interests and ideals would fare better in a postwar world that was dominated by the British rather than one that was dominated by Germany. Wilson envisioned a world made safe for progressive foreign policy principles of free-market capitalism and political democracy. He believed that only a free and prosperous world order could ensure perpetual peace.

Although it is accurate to say that popular pro-Ally sentiments, economic and financial ties to the Allies, and Wilson's pro-Ally preferences made genuine neutrality impossible, it is important to stress that Wilson did not seek to bring the United States into the war. He wanted desperately to avoid war, and he crafted a foreign policy that for nearly three years avoided war while at the same time protected vital American interests and national honor. Repeatedly, Wilson sent his personal representative, Colonel Edward House, to Europe to try to mediate an end to the conflict. In early 1917 Wilson cried, "It would be a crime against civilization if we went in." No modern president has felt a greater horror of war and none tried harder to avoid engulfing his people in war than this profoundly religious and idealistic leader.

But Americans got caught in an Allies–Central Powers conflict. The British were determined to use their sea power to cripple the German economy and undermine its war machine. An integral part of the British naval strategy against Germany was to sever its trade with neutrals such as the United States. Britannia, ruling the waves, declared a loose, illegal blockade of Central Powers ports. The British defined contraband broadly to include foodstuffs and strategic raw materials. (Contraband was trade with belligerents that was forbidden to neutrals, traditionally arms and munitions.) They also harassed neutral shipping. American ships hauling goods to Germany seldom reached their destination. To neutralize German submarines, the British violated international law by arming their merchant ships, hauling armaments in passenger ships, and flying the flags of neutrals, including the U.S. flag.

President Wilson frequently protested British violations of American neutral rights. He told English leaders that neutrals had the right to ship noncontraband goods to all belligerents and pointed out that the British definition of contraband was contrary to an international agreement that the British themselves had signed. The British defused American protests by easing their blockade periodically and by paying American companies for confiscated cargoes. Two other factors prevented American—British relations from deteriorating seriously despite British violations of American neutral rights. First, expanding Allied purchases of American goods more than made up for the lost Central Powers markets; the American war economy continued to expand. Second, the Germans too violated American neutral rights, by sinking ships and killing people, acts that made British offenses appear mild by comparison. British violations of international law were annoying, sometimes outrageous, but the English never sank any American ships nor killed any American citizens.

Germany, for its part, was determined to sever Allied–American trade. The German navy had conceded control of the seas to the British navy at the outset of the war. To try to cut the commercial links between the United States and the Allies, Germany resorted to submarine warfare. In February 1915 the German government announced that it was creating a war zone around the British Isles, a submarine counterblockade: All enemy ships entering the war zone would be sunk. They also warned all neutrals to avoid the war zone lest they be attacked by mistake, and they cautioned passengers from neutral nations to stay off enemy passenger ships. President Wilson reacted to this edict quickly and firmly. He told the German leaders that if any American property or lives were lost in the war zone, Germany would be held to "strict accountability." His message amounted to an ultimatum, a threat of war if the German attacks killed Americans.

International law in force at the time required commerce destroyers to warn merchant or passenger ships before attacking them in order to allow passengers and crew to disembark safely. Such rules assumed that passengers and merchant crews were civilians, innocent noncombatants, and therefore exempt from attack. These rules predated the development of the submarine, however. If submarines surfaced to warn ships, they would lose their chief advantage, surprise. Any merchant or passenger ship could easily outrun a surfaced submarine and avoid its torpedoes. Moreover, a surfaced submarine was an easy target for deck gunfire and was vulnerable to ramming, and the time it took for crew and passengers to debark usually gave a ship's radioman opportunity to call in nearby destroyers to attack the waiting U-boat. Wilson refused to acknowledge the limitations of submarines that made it impossible for them to warn their intended targets and still function effectively. To Germans it appeared that Wilson's strict accountability policy denied them effective use of the one weapon they possessed that could disrupt the Allies' ties with American producers and bankers and enable Germany to win the war. Engaged in a brutal struggle for national survival, the Germans deeply resented Wilson's policy with its dated, legalistic views of submarine warfare. Here lay a conflict between Germany and the United States that had ominous potential.

AMERICA GOES TO WAR

Since the Germans had promised not to attack American ships in the war zone, an agreement they honored until 1917, the issue became the right of Americans to sail and work on belligerent ships. Germany's sinking of the British luxury liner *Lusitania* forced the issue. The ship had left New York on May 1, 1915, carrying 1,257 passengers and also hauling 4.2 million rounds of rifle ammunition. Before the liner set sail, New York newspapers carried announcements from the German embassy warning passengers that Allied ships were "liable to destruction" in the war zone. Passengers ignored the warning. On May 7, off the southern Irish coast, a German submarine torpedoed the *Lusitania*. The ship sank quickly, carrying 1,198 people to their death, including 128 Americans.

Most Americans were horrified and outraged by the attack. Wilson angrily dismissed the idea that because the ship was hauling ammunition, the Germans were justified in killing nearly 1,200 innocent people. Still neither the American people nor Wilson wanted war over the incident. Wilson steered a middle path between Secretary of State William Jennings Bryan, who wanted to forbid Americans from traveling on belligerent ships and to prevent Allied passenger ships from hauling ammunition, and Theodore Roosevelt, who was ready for war with Germany over the incident. Wilson sent a note to the German government insisting on the right of Americans to travel on belligerent ships. He also demanded that German submarines protect passenger ships and pay for U.S. losses. When Wilson refused to consider banning American travelers on Allied passenger ships, Bryan resigned. His replacement, Robert Lansing, supported Wilson's position.

At first the Germans refused to apologize for the sinking of the *Lusitania* or to curb their submarines. Further notes were exchanged. To avoid war with America, the Germans eventually expressed regret for the loss of life and agreed never again to attack a passenger ship without warning. To charges from his critics that he was pursuing a double standard which favored the Allies, Wilson replied that the British were violating only property rights whereas the Germans were violating human rights and murdering civilians.

On August 30, 1915, a German submarine torpedoed another British liner, the *Arabic*, and two Americans were killed. The Germans hastened to apologize and pledged never again to attack passenger liners without warning. The *Arabic* incident fueled a debate in this country over the propriety of American passengers' riding on belligerent ships. Critics of Wilson's strict accountability policy wanted the President to require American passengers to travel only on American ships in the war zone, in the belief that such an order would avoid further incidents and the risks of war. They sponsored a congressional resolution prohibiting Americans from traveling on armed merchant ships or passenger ships hauling contraband, but the resolution failed to pass either house.

In March 1916 a German submarine attacked a French channel steamer, the *Sussex*, mistaking it for a minesweeper. Four Americans were injured. An angry Wilson ordered the Germans to restrict their submarines or he would sever diplomatic relations. The Germans, embarrassed by the incident and not wishing war with the United States, pledged not to attack merchant ships without warning. They observed the "*Sussex* pledge" for the rest of the year. Relations with Germany stabilized during 1916. "Strict accountability" was working. Meanwhile the British stepped up their blockade activities, and their violations of U.S. neutral rights escalated. Relations between the United States and the British deteriorated as relations with Germany improved. A nearly genuine neutrality prevailed for much of 1916.

Seeking reelection in November 1916, Wilson faced a formidable challenge from the Republicans. The party was reunited, its Progressive Party insurgents having returned to the fold. Republicans nominated an able candidate, Supreme Court Associate Justice Charles Evans Hughes, formerly a reform governor of New York. The 1916 presidential campaign was bitter, revealing deep divisions within America. Hughes attacked Wilson's social policies and accused him of not defending American neutral rights adequately against German assaults. The Democrats accused Hughes of being pro-German, and Wilson implied that anyone who thought he was pro-British was disloyal. The key issue in the campaign was American foreign policy toward the warring powers. The Democratic Party campaigned on the slogan "He kept us out of war," referring to the *Sussex* pledge. Also Wilson's admirable record of achievement as a domestic reformer appealed to progressive voters in both parties.

Hughes was favored to win when the campaign began, but he proved a poor campaigner. He was not a good speaker, and he inadvertently offended California progressive Republican leaders and lost the presidency. In a close election, California, normally Republican, went for Wilson, giving him a narrow victory. A difference of fewer than 4,000 votes in California would have removed Wilson from the White House. His party fared no better. The Democrats retained a narrow majority in the Senate, but in the new House there would be 216 Democrats, 210 Republicans, and 6 independents. It was not clear at election time which party would control the new Congress.

Despite the campaign slogan, Wilson knew that American neutrality was precarious as long as the war continued. A German submarine skipper could provoke a crisis at any time by ignoring the *Sussex* pledge. Wilson sent Colonel House on another mission to European capitals to find a formula that could serve as a basis for a cease-fire. He also appealed directly to the heads of the warring governments for "a peace without victory." His peace efforts failed because of events beyond his control.

The German government made a fateful decision to resume unrestricted submarine warfare on February 1, 1917. Henceforth all ships, belligerent or neutral, warship or merchant, would be attacked on sight in the war zone. The Germans, whose situation had grown desperate, had decided to take a calculated risk, what they called their "gambler's throw." The British blockade was severely pinching the German and Austro-Hungarian economies. Inflation was rampant and starvation widespread in both countries. The Germans gambled that an all-out submarine war would enable them to cut off shipments of vital foodstuffs and ammunition to the Allies, permitting Germany to win the war before enough American troops could be mobilized and ferried across the Atlantic. They knew their decision would provoke American entry into the war, but they assumed that they would win the race against time. They also believed that they were fated to lose a long-running war of attrition, for the Allies had superior resources—more population, more manufacturing capacity, and Allied sea power gave them access to their overseas colonies and the American arsenal. So they chose their "gambler's throw."

Wilson, as was expected, promptly severed diplomatic relations in response to Germany's direct challenge to American neutrality. But he did not ask Congress for a declaration of war immediately. British Prime Minister Lloyd George and Senate Republican leader Henry Cabot Lodge accused Wilson of cowardice. The Germans began sinking American ships. During February and March of 1917 German submarines sank scores of Allied merchant ships. On April 1 the British had only a six weeks' supply of grain on hand. Coal, sugar, and potatoes were scarce. The British people were feeling the privations of war. Once mighty lords of international banking, the British by the spring of 1917 had mortgaged themselves heavily to American creditors in purchasing huge quantities of ammunition. The British treasury was approaching bankruptcy. Lloyd George feared that a combination of hunger, bankruptcy, and submarine warfare might force the British to accept Germany's peace terms, enabling them to win their "gambler's throw."

The French were also suffering that spring of 1917. General Robert Nivelle had tried to break the stalemated slaughter in the trenches with a spring offensive against the Germans at Champagne. The French fell into a trap set for them by German commander General Ludendorff and were slaughtered. After sustaining two weeks of massive losses under hellish conditions, the French soldiers mutinied. Nivelle was dismissed in disgrace. The French, exhausted and demoralized, were incapable of continuing the war much longer without help.

Spring 1917 was also a fateful season for the other major Allied power, Russia. After nearly three years of war, the Russians had lost millions of men; Czarist generals had herded unarmed peasants into fierce battles only to have them slaughtered like sheep. The civilian population had also been subjected to severe privation and suffering. The Czar's government, aloof from the Russian people, could neither provide moral leadership nor organize the war effort efficiently. Having lost control of his army, the Czar abdicated on March 15. Two days later Russia became a republic for the first time in its history; a provisional government came to power led by Alexander Kerensky, who pledged to honor Russian treaty and commercial obligations and to continue the war.

The German Chancellor, Theobald von Bethmann-Hollweg, watched Russian political developments closely. Aware that Russia was riven with factionalism, he decided that Germany ought to support the most extreme groups within Russia to promote chaos and cripple the Russian war effort. He arranged for a small group of radical Russian exiles living in Switzerland to return to Russia. The radicals, led by a man calling himself V. I. Lenin (his real name was Vladimir Ilich Ulyanov), traveled across Germany on a sealed train; they were forbidden to get off the train while it was in Germany, since Bethmann-Hollweg wanted to make sure the radical political virus would infect only Russia. In mid-April Lenin and his small band of "Bolsheviks" got off the train at Petrograd's Finland Station. In November 1917 Lenin led a rebellion that toppled Kerensky's fragile government and took Russia out of the war. Lenin's goal was to establish a Communist state in Russia and to promote a socialist revolution that would sweep across Europe in the wake of war. Germany was one of the first countries to experience a Communist uprising.

In late February the British gave President Wilson a secret telegram they had intercepted and decoded, which was addressed to the German minister in Mexico from German Foreign Secretary Arthur Zimmermann. The telegram instructed the minister to tell the Mexican government that if Mexico joined a military alliance against the United States, Germany would help the Mexicans recover their territory lost to the United States in 1848 in the Mexican-American war. Wilson took the Zimmermann note seriously. At the time, U.S.–Mexican relations were severely strained because Wilson had twice ordered American troops into Mexico during the Mexican revolution, and the two countries had verged on war. Soon after learning of the note, Wilson went before Congress seeking what he called an "armed neutrality." He hoped, by arming American merchant ships, to forestall war. As Congress debated his request, he released the Zimmermann note to the media. A wave of anti-German sentiment swept the country. Public opinion moved closer to war.

But a group of antiwar senators, including Robert La Follette, filibustered Wilson's armed neutrality proposal to death. Furious, Wilson excoriated them as a "little group of willful men, representing no opinion but their own, who have rendered this great nation helpless and contemptible." He then armed the ships on his own executive authority. But his action could not prevent German submarines from sinking American merchant ships. Cries for war resounded across the land.

Since the German decision to resume submarine warfare in mid-January, Wilson had hesitated to take the country to war for many reasons. He confided to a friend: "It was necessary for me, by very slow stages indeed and with the most genuine purpose to avoid war to lead the country on to a single way of thinking." Since the war had begun, Americans had disagreed about America's relationship to it and what course of action the nation should take. Also, in the spring of 1917 America stood at the end of nearly two decades of divisive political and social upheaval. The concentration of economic wealth and power, the many progressive efforts to tame the trusts, the serious strikes, and the arrival of over 12 million immigrants since 1900 had opened deep social fissures. Wilson did not want to burden American society further with the strains of a major war effort. He knew what the war was doing to the political and social structure of the European belligerents. He asserted that "Every reform we have won will be lost if we get into this war." The President also feared the problems posed by the presence of millions of foreign-born residents in the country. He was particularly worried about the loyalty of those who had recently emigrated from Germany and the other Central Powers nations. If America went to war against Germany, could it count on the loyalty of its citizens who had recently come from the Fatherland?

But the time for decision had come. On March 20 Wilson met with his cabinet; its members unanimously favored war with Germany. The next day Wilson announced a special session of the newly elected Sixty-fifth Congress to begin on April 2, where he would give his war message. The President then secluded himself to prepare his speech.

He went before a hushed Congress the evening of April 2, 1917, to deliver a solemn, subdued speech. Missing were Wilson's usual rhetorical flights and resounding cadences. He recounted the many German violations of international law and American rights. He condemned German sabotage and spying within the United States and denounced the proposed German alliance with Mexico. He urged Congress to "formally accept the status of belligerent which has thus been thrust upon it."

Wilson then informed the assembled legislators what war would mean and what he intended to do. He planned to lend billions of dollars to the Allied nations already at war with Germany, to increase taxes to finance the costly American war effort, and to implement conscription. He also made it clear that he would insist more than ever on the preeminence of a strong executive. Although he acknowledged the loyalty of most Americans of German birth, he warned "if there should be disloyalty, it will be dealt with a firm hand of repression." An explosion of applause from the audience greeted that remark. As he neared the end of his speech, Wilson, with matchless eloquence, explained American war aims:

The world must be made safe for democracy. Its peace must be planted upon the tested foundations of political liberty. We have no selfish ends to serve. We desire no conquest, no dominion. We seek no indemnities for ourselves, no material compensation for the sacrifices we shall freely make. We are but one of the champions of the rights of mankind. . . .

It is a fearful thing to lead this great peaceful people into war, into the most terrible and disastrous of all wars, civilization itself seeming to be in the balance. But the right is more precious than peace, and we shall fight for the things which we have always carried nearest our hearts,—for democracy, . . . for a universal dominion of right, . . . and make the world itself at last free. To such a task we can dedicate our lives and our fortunes, everything that we are and everything that we have, with the pride of those who know that the day has come when America is privileged to spend her blood and her might for the principles that gave her birth and happiness and the peace that she has treasured. God helping her, she can do no other.[2]

Wilson asked the Congress to commit the country to a distant war that had already butchered 7 million men and promised to add millions more names to the ledger of death before it ended. He had called for high taxes and the drafting of millions of young Americans who would be sent into that war. He had asked Congress to accept the expansion of presidential power, and he had called for the enforced loyalty of all Americans in a cause to which millions of his fellow citizens were hostile or indifferent.

Wilson's request for a war resolution provoked an extended debate among members of Congress that lasted four days. The outcome was a foregone conclusion. The proponents of war knew they had an overwhelming majority of the votes. But that reality did not inhibit the enemies of war who spoke against the resolution. The supporters of the resolution shared Wilson's view of the war as a struggle between the forces of democracy and the forces of autocratic tyranny, with America aligning itself on the side of virtue in a profound ideological conflict to make the world a safe place for democratic nations. Some members of the Senate, like Warren G. Harding of Ohio, voted for war to uphold American rights which had been violated by German submarines.

Opponents of the resolution considered it hypocritical to demand war in the name of democracy. They considered the European conflict a contest between rival imperialisms. As they saw it, only territory and markets were at stake, not democratic principles. They also pointed out that many ardent supporters of the war were among the most determined opponents of progressive reform efforts to make American institutions more democratic. Some midwestern progressive opponents of war viewed the conflict as benefiting the rich at the expense of ordinary citizens. Republican Senator George Norris of Nebraska passionately declared:

---

2. Taken from a copy of Wilson's War Message found in Armin Rappaport, *Sources in American Diplomacy* (New York: Macmillan, 1966), pp. 211–12.

belligerency would benefit only the class of people who . . . have already made millions of dollars, and who will make many hundreds of millions more if we get into the war. . . . War brings no prosperity to the great mass of common patriotic citizens. . . . We are going into war upon the command of gold . . . I feel that we are about to put the dollar sign on the American flag.[3]

Norris's progressive colleague, Senator Robert La Follette, echoed his views. La Follette also charged the Wilson administration with having forced the war upon America by pursuing a pro-British neutrality policy. Other foes of war adhered to traditional isolationist views; they believed intervening in a European war was contrary to American interests and values. Aged Isaac Sherwood, a Civil War veteran who retained vivid memories of the killing during that fratricidal war, could not bring himself to support American entry into what he called "a barbarous war 3,500 miles away in which we have no vital interest." On April 6 Jeannette Rankin, the first woman ever to sit in Congress, spoke with tears coursing down her cheeks: "I want to stand by my country, but I cannot vote for war."

Six senators and fifty representatives finally voted against American entry into the war, more than opposed any other war resolution in American history. There were others who opposed the war but voted for it anyway. But all opponents of the war resolution made it clear that their opposition would cease once war was officially declared.

Wilson took the United States to war in the spring of 1917 for many reasons: to defend democracy, international law, morality, and the nation's honor. Wilson stressed these idealistic war aims in his stirring peroration. The United States also went to war to protect its commerce and national security. Further, Wilson and his advisers feared that the Allies could lose the war if the United States did not enter on their side. Another reason for entering the war was to ensure an American role at the peace conference. Wilson hoped to be a major influence in shaping the postwar world along progressive lines. Wilson took the United States to war not only to win the conflict, but also to shape the future.

The decisive event that brought the United States into World War I was the German decision to resume unrestricted submarine warfare in early 1917. This decision nullified Wilson's neutrality policy based upon "strict accountability" and forced Wilson to choose between war and appeasement. Wilson's critics have cited his rigid conception of international law, which did not fit the reality of submarine tactics. They have also faulted his unyielding defense of the right of Americans to travel on belligerent ships, even those hauling contraband. But most Americans supported his neutrality policy, and when he told the people on April 2, 1917, that "neutrality was no longer feasible nor desirable," most supported his request for war.

---

3.   Quoted in David Kennedy, *Over Here: The First World War and American Society* (New York: Oxford University Press, 1980), p. 19.

OVER THERE

The United States had been preparing for combat during the years of neutrality. As early as 1915 President Wilson began planning a large military buildup. His proposals triggered a great debate within the nation over preparedness. Many congressmen and senators opposed the buildup. Pacifist progressives led by Jane Addams formed an antiwar coalition, the American Union Against Militarism. Businessmen like Andrew Carnegie, who in 1910 had established the Carnegie Endowment for International Peace, helped finance peace groups. Henry Ford spent half a million dollars in 1915 to send a "peace ark" to Europe to urge the European powers to accept a negotiated settlement.

Despite opposition from pacifists both in and out of government, Congress enacted the National Defense Act of 1916, which increased the size of the National Guard and established summer training camps for soldiers. Also the Navy Act established a three-year naval expansion program. To finance these expensive preparedness measures, Congress enacted the Revenue Act of 1916, a progressive tax increase that called for a surtax on high incomes and corporate profits, a tax on large estates, and increased taxes on munitions makers. Despite these preparedness activities, the United States was not ready for war in the spring of 1917. The Army was small and equipped with obsolete weapons. Its most recent military action had been trying, and failing, to catch the elusive Pancho Villa in the wilds of northern Mexico. Its war planning was out-of-date, concerned with fending off a Japanese attack on the West Coast and a German invasion of the Caribbean.

Soon after the United States entered the war, Congress enacted a Selective Service Act implementing conscription. Antidraft forces challenged the constitutionality of the draft, but the Supreme Court quickly upheld it as a proper exercise of the "implied powers" principle. It required that all males between the ages of 20 and 30 register for the draft. In 1918 the draftee ages changed to between 18 and 45. By war's end, 24 million men had registered for the draft, nearly 5 million had been conscripted, and 2 million had been sent to fight in France. Millions of draft-age men got deferments because they worked in war industries or had dependents. Over 300,000 evaded the draft by refusing to register or not responding when called. About 300,000 men volunteered for duty. The typical "doughboy" was a draftee, 22 years old, white, single, and with a seventh-grade education. Eighteen percent of American troops who served in World War I were foreign-born, mostly from the European countries at war.

About 400,000 black men were drafted or volunteered. The American military, reflecting the society from which it was recruited, was segregated during World War I. African American soldiers were kept in all-black units and not allowed to enter many programs. They were not al-

Black troops fought in all-black, segregated units during World War I. This photo shows troopers from the 369th Infantry Regiment, who saw heavy combat on the Western Front in 1918.

lowed to become aviators or to join the Marines. A separate officers' training program provided African American Army officers, who were never allowed to command white soldiers.

Even though the United States entered the war belatedly and on a smaller scale than the other major combatants, its armed forces played a major role in the war. The Navy performed crucial service. In April 1917, when America entered the war, German submarines were sinking Allied merchant ships at a rate of 870,000 tons per month. American destroyers, teamed with their British counterparts, reduced and eventually stopped the submarine threat. American naval planners helped to develop the convoy system, in which destroyers and other warships escorted merchant ships across the Atlantic, effectively screening out German submarines. American troop ships were convoyed to France, and all 2 million men arrived safely. Since Germany's plan for winning the war crucially depended on submarines, the U.S. Navy made a major contribution to the Allied victory.

When American troops arrived in France, General John J. "Black Jack" Pershing, the commander of the American Expeditionary Force

(AEF), would not allow them to join Allied units. He refused to let American soldiers be fed into the mincing machine. Allied commanders had locked themselves into suicidal trench warfare, producing years of stalemate and ghastly casualty rates. Zigzag trenches fronted by barbed wires and mines stretched across the 200-mile-long Western Front, which ran from the French channel coast, curving across northeastern France, to the Swiss border. In front of the trenches lay a region called "no man's land," cratered by heavy artillery bombardments. Allied soldiers, upon order, would charge the German lines on the other side of this deadly frontier; rapid-fire machine guns mowed them down and chlorine gas poisoned them. Little territory would be gained yet the human cost was great. Then it would be the Germans' turn to be ordered to die in a futile charge. The stalemated slaughter went on for over three years. Before the advent of the Americans, the blood of millions of German, French, and British soldiers had spilled over the killing fields of northeastern France.

At the Battle of the Somme in 1916 the British and the French launched their greatest offensive of the war, with 600,000 men killed or wounded to gain 125 square miles of territory. The Germans lost 500,000 men defending that small piece of blood-stained ground. The Germans also tried to break the impasse in 1916 by laying siege to a crucial French fortress at Verdun. The German strategy at Verdun was simple and horrible: besiege the fort indefinitely, bleed France dry, and rely on the numerical superiority of German manpower to guarantee eventual victory. The siege ended six months later with 350,000 French and 330,000 German soldiers dead. The front had not moved.

The entry of American men and materiel into World War I determined its outcome. With both sides on the verge of exhaustion, the arrival of fresh American forces tipped the balance decisively toward the Allies. Had America not entered the war, a German victory was possible. American forces began combat in March 1918 when the Germans launched a great spring offensive, their armies now strengthened by the arrival of thousands of battle-hardened veterans from the Eastern Front. In late May advance units reached the Marne River near the village of Chateau-Thierry, 50 miles from Paris. Early in June 27,500 American soldiers fought their first important battle, driving the Germans out of Chateau-Thierry and nearby Belleau Wood. The size of the American forces expanded rapidly. In early July, near the Marne, 270,000 Americans joined the fighting, helping to flatten a German bulge between Reims and Soissons. On July 15 the German army threw everything into one final effort to smash through to Paris, but in three days they were finished. Chancellor Bettmann-Hollweg said: "On the eighteenth, even the most optimistic among us knew that all was lost. The history of the world was played out in three days." The war had turned in favor of the Allies.

Between September 12 and 16 the American First Army, now 500,000 strong and fighting with French forces, wiped out a German

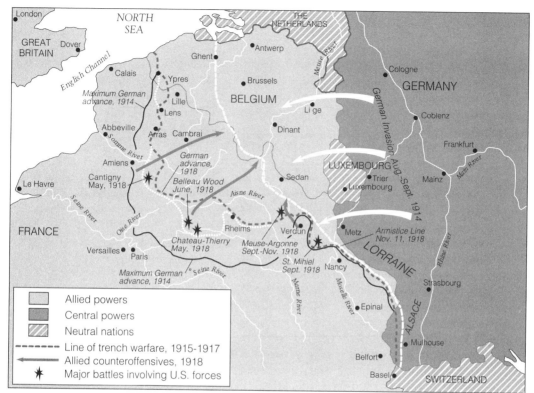

The Western Front

thrust at Saint-Mihiel. Two weeks later the Americans began their most important battle of the war: 1.2 million "doughboys" launched the Meuse-Argonne offensive. In 40 days and nights of heavy slugging in the region of
the Argonne forest, the Americans eventually fought their way through
the formidable defenses of the Hindenburg Line. To the West, French and
British forces staged similar drives. On November 1 the Allies broke
through the German center and raced forward. On November 11, with
German armies in full retreat and the German submarine threat destroyed, Germany signed an armistice. They were also lured toward an
armistice by offers of a generous peace from President Wilson. After four
years of killing, the war had ended. The Allies were victorious. The Americans had lost 48,909 men and another 230,000 had been wounded. Losses
to disease, mainly influenza, eventually ran the death total to over
112,000.

Ten months before the Armistice Wilson, in a speech to Congress,
had outlined a peace plan called the Fourteen Points. The first five points
incorporated liberal principles upon which the peace must be based:
open negotiations, freedom of the seas, free trade, disarmament, and a

The most important campaign in which American doughboys fought was the Meuse-Argonne Offensive in the fall of 1918. In forty days and nights of continuous fighting, U.S. troops sustained heavy casualties on their way to victory.

colonial system designed to serve the needs of subject peoples. The next eight points called for territorial transfers within Europe to implement the principle of "self-determination," which would permit all people possessing a distinct history, language, and ethnic identity to live under governments of their own choosing. The fourteenth point created an international agency to oversee the new order:

> a general association of nations . . . formed . . . for the purpose of affording mutual guarantees of political independence and territorial integrity to great and small states alike.[4]

In the final weeks of the war Wilson lured the Germans into overthrowing the Kaiser and surrendering by promising them a peace based on the Fourteen Points. He then pressured the Allies into accepting the Fourteen Points, somewhat modified, as the basis for conducting the impending peace conference. It was brilliant diplomacy by Wilson. His efforts made him immensely popular among Europeans. He was the savior who had delivered them from a murderous war and promised a just and lasting peace.

---

4. Taken from a copy of The Covenant of the League of Nations found in Rappaport, *Sources in American Diplomacy*, p. 218.

THE HOME FRONT

The war experience had a profound effect on American lives and institutions. Government had to quickly mobilize a vast military force, gear the economy for war, and prepare the American people to meet the rigorous demands of belligerency. The state had intervened in American life in unprecedented ways, and tremendous power had been concentrated in Washington. Business and government became partners for the duration of the war. Hundreds of new government agencies, staffed mostly by businessmen, came into being to manage the war effort. Many of these agencies clamped controls on the economy. The Railroad Administration took over operation of the nation's railroads when they broke down under the strains of wartime usage. The federal government also took over operation of the telephone and telegraph companies to avert strikes. The largest and most powerful wartime agency was the War Industries Board (WIB), created in July 1917 and headed by a friend of Wilson's, financier Bernard Baruch. The WIB coordinated the war economy, allocating resources, directing purchasing, and fixing prices.

Inexperience and inefficiency caused waste and delays in mobilizing the American economy, but Wilson proved to be a strong war leader, and America eventually delivered enough men and materiel to win the war. About 25 percent of American production went into the war effort. Farmers enjoyed boom years; they put more acreage into production, bought new farm machinery, and watched farm commodity prices soar. Farm income rose from $7.6 billion in 1914 to nearly $18 billion at the war's end. Steel production doubled in wartime. The gross national product more than doubled between 1914 and 1920.

The most serious wartime economic problem was rampant inflation. One cause was increased demand for goods created by Allied and U.S. government purchases. The major cause, however, was government refusal to set price controls or to ration scarce commodities. The cost of living doubled between 1914 and 1920. Of the $34 billion cost of the war, the government financed one-third through taxes, and the remaining two-thirds came from borrowing, including the selling of Liberty Bonds to the people. The War Revenue Act of 1917 established a graduated personal income tax, a corporate income tax, an excess profits tax, and an increased excise tax on several items. Despite the higher war taxes, corporate profits in wartime reached historic highs. Net corporate income rose from $4 billion in 1913 to over $7 billion in 1917.

Organized labor prospered in wartime also. The president of the American Federation of Labor, Samuel Gompers, gave a no-strike pledge to the Wilson administration during wartime. He and other labor leaders also served on wartime government agencies. The National War Labor Board protected the right of workers to organize unions and to bargain collectively. Union membership rose from 2.7 million in 1916 to over 4

During the war, thousands of women, hitherto excluded from many industrial occupations, found work in war industries. The wartime economic performance of women was a major factor in their getting the vote in 1920.

million in 1919. Wages rose and many workers won an eight-hour day, but sharp inflation cancelled most of the economic gains made by workers.

Disadvantaged groups also benefited in wartime. With 16 percent of the work force off fighting the war and with immigration curtailed, war industries turned to women, African Americans, and Hispanic Americans. Women entered many industrial trades hitherto closed to females. The movement of women into previously all-male job categories generated controversy. Women often were paid less than men for the same work and were excluded from unions. When the war ended, most of the wartime gains women had made were lost.

War-generated economic opportunities opened up for African Americans also. About 500,000 blacks fled poverty and oppression in the South, heading north for Detroit, Chicago, and New York City, where the war industries were located. Most African American migrants were young unmarried males in search of work.

New jobs and improved living opportunities for blacks in wartime provoked a white backlash. The Ku Klux Klan revived. There were savage race riots in several cities: During the summer of 1919 race riots rocked over twenty northern cities. The worst violence occurred in Chicago, where on a hot July day an incident at a beach started the rioting. Stabbings, burnings, and shootings went on for days. Thirty-eight people died and over 500 were injured before the National Guard restored order.

CIVIL LIBERTIES IN WARTIME

Civil liberties were also a casualty of war. The targets of abuse were German-Americans, whose loyalty was suspect, and Americans who refused to support the war effort. These dissenters included pacifists, conscientious objectors, socialists, tenant farmers in Oklahoma who rebelled against the draft, and progressive reformers like Robert La Follette and Jane Addams.

Soon after the United States entered the war, President Wilson appointed George Creel, a progressive journalist, to head a Committee on Public Information (CPI), a government propaganda agency created at Wilson's request to promote the war effort. It hired writers, scholars, filmmakers, and artists to mobilize public opinion in support of Allied war aims and to arouse anti-German sentiments. Creel enlisted 75,000 "four-minute men," who gave short patriotic speeches at public gatherings explaining war aims and celebrating American national virtues. CPI members urged people to spy on their neighbors and report "suspicious" behavior to the authorities.

For a time there was vigorous debate between the supporters of the war and antiwar critics. Creel Committee speakers were the most prominent defenders of the American effort. Wilson himself provided the most potent ideological defense of the war when he called it a struggle to preserve democracy. Linking the war to democracy made it a crusade, tying it to the ancient doctrine of American mission. World War I became a war to save democracy, to save Europe from itself, and to redeem mankind. America would send its young manhood to rescue the Old World from itself. The child of Western Civilization would save its parents. Wilson, an eloquent student of American history, tapped deep ideological wellsprings of emotion, giving the war transcendent meaning. Most Americans embraced the notion of a great war to make the world a safe place for democratic governments. Against Wilson's and the Creel Committee's defenses of the war, the arguments of critics, however plausible, were ineffective. Isolationist, populist, and humanitarian arguments collapsed. The champions of war easily won the battle to define the symbolic meaning of the war and to win the allegiance of most citizens.

But their propaganda victory had its costs. Congress passed repressive legislation, strongly endorsed by President Wilson, to curb dissent in wartime. The Espionage Act, enacted into law June 5, 1917, gave the government powerful tools for suppressing opponents of war. It levied fines of up to $10,000 and prison terms as long as twenty years for obstructing military operations in wartime, and up to $5,000 in fines and five-year sentences for use of the mails to violate the law. It also prohibited any statement intended to impede the draft or promote military insubordination, and it gave the Postmaster General power to ban from the mails any publication he considered to be treasonous. Armed with the powers of the Espionage Act, Postmaster General Albert Burleson barred many German-American and socialist publications from the mails, thus hindering their activities.

The Sedition Act, enacted in 1918, was more severe than the Espionage Act. It made it a crime to obstruct the sale of war bonds or to use "disloyal, profane, scurrilous, or abusive" language against the government, the constitution, the flag, and the military uniforms. It made almost any publicly voiced criticism of government policy or the war effort a crime punishable by fines, imprisonment, or both. The Justice Department prosecuted over 2,000 people under the two acts, and many more people were bullied into silence. Jane Addams came under Justice Department surveillance. The most famous victim of wartime repression was Eugene Debs, the Socialist Party leader. Debs, who opposed the war, delivered a speech to a Socialist convention gathered in Canton, Ohio, on June 16, 1918. He spoke for over two hours. His speech was a general indictment of the American economic system and a call for socialism. He mentioned the war in only one passage:

> The master class has always declared the wars; the subject class has always fought the battles. The master class has had all to gain and nothing to lose, while the subject class has had nothing to gain and all to lose—especially their lives.[5]

Justice Department agents in the audience wrote down his words, and within two weeks he was indicted by a federal grand jury for violating the Sedition Act on ten different counts. During his trial in September Debs acknowledged the offending remarks. His defense consisted solely of the argument that the Sedition Act violated the First Amendment and was therefore unconstitutional, and his remarks were therefore within the boundaries of constitutionally protected free speech. His defense failed because the Supreme Court had previously upheld the constitutionality of both the Espionage and Sedition Acts on the grounds that in time of war the government can legitimately curb free speech.

A jury convicted Debs on three counts of obstructing the draft, and he was sentenced to ten years in federal prison. His attorneys appealed the conviction, but on March 10, 1919, the Supreme Court sustained his conviction. Debs began serving his sentence in April and remained in jail until December 1921, when he was pardoned by President Harding. While in prison, Debs ran for president on the Socialist Party ticket in 1920, campaigning from his jail cell. He got 920,000 votes, the most he ever received in his five presidential campaigns.

State and local governments also joined the war against dissent. Officials removed what they considered pro-German books from schools and

---

5. Quoted in Ray Ginger, *Eugene V. Debs: The Making of an American Radical* (New York: Collier Books, 1949), pp. 376–77.

libraries. Iowa refused to allow any foreign languages to be taught in its public schools. Teachers who questioned or challenged the war were dismissed.

Encouraged by government actions, vigilante groups and superpatriots went after alleged enemies and traitors. They became proficient at bookburning, spying on their fellow citizens, harassing schoolteachers, vandalizing German-owned stores, and attacking socialists. Radical antiwar figures were frequent vigilante targets. In April 1918 a Missouri mob seized Robert Prager, a young man whose only crime was that he had been born in Germany. He was bound in an American flag, paraded through town, and then lynched. A jury acquitted his killers on the grounds that they had acted in self-defense.

The federal government, which encouraged and supported the campaign to crush dissent, concentrated its fire on the American Socialist Party and the Industrial Workers of the World, both of which openly opposed the war. By the end of the war many leaders of both radical organizations were in jail and their organizations were in disarray. Neither organization ever regained the following it had enjoyed before the war.

RED SCARE

Wartime suppression of dissent spilled into the postwar era with the Red Scare of 1919 and 1920. During this turbulent period the targets of government prosecutors and vigilantes were Communists or Communist sympathizers, many of them aliens, suspected of plotting to overthrow the government. The Bolsheviks had come to power in Russia in November 1917, and after the war Communism did appear to be spreading westward. Communist uprisings occurred in Hungary and Germany. Americans fearfully looked at a Europe in chaos—shattered economies, weakened governments, and hungry millions struggling to survive in a world where democracy appeared more imperiled than ever. In 1919 the Soviets established the Comintern to promote world revolution, and in that year two Communist parties were formed in the United States. War had disrupted American race relations and family life; inflation and unemployment were high. Nervous Americans, aware that a small, disciplined band of revolutionaries had come to power in Russia, worried that revolution might come to the United States.

Dramatic events occurring in 1919 intensified fears of revolution, provoking the Red Scare. Thousands of strikes broke out, idling over 4 million workers. A general strike in Seattle was particularly alarming. In May dozens of bombs were mailed to prominent business and political leaders in various cities, although none of the intended targets was killed or injured. Revolutionary anarchists plotting to undermine the government were suspected of sending the bombs, but police never caught the conspirators. In September the Boston police, who belonged to an American Federation of Labor (AFL) local, went on strike. For a few days the streets of Boston belonged to rioters and looters. The governor of Massachusetts, an obscure Republican politician named Calvin Coolidge, became famous when he sent a terse telegram to Samuel Gompers, the president of the AFL, which read, "There is no right to strike against the public safety by anyone, anytime, anywhere." He also called out the Massachusetts National Guard, which restored order and broke the strike.

The most serious strike occurred in the steel industry when 350,000 workers walked off their jobs. The strikers wanted union recognition, a reduction in their seven-days-a-week, twelve-hours-a-day work schedule, and pay increases to offset inflation. Management refused to negotiate any of their grievances and moved to break the strike. The companies hired strikebreakers, goon squads to assault workers, and launched a propaganda campaign to convince the public that the strike was a Bolshevik conspiracy.

In mid-1919 Attorney General A. Mitchell Palmer stepped forward to save America from Red revolution. A progressive Democrat, ambitious to get the 1920 Democratic presidential nomination, Palmer claimed that America was in imminent peril of revolution:

> The blaze of revolution was eating its way into the homes of the American workmen, its sharp tongues of revolutionary heat . . . licking the altars of churches, leaping into the belfry of the school bell, crawling into the sacred corners of American homes, burning up the foundations of society.[6]

To combat the Red menace, Palmer hired a young lawyer named J. Edgar Hoover to direct a new Bureau of Investigation. Hoover placed thousands of people and many organizations under surveillance. State and local governments took various repressive measures as well. Vigilantes, many of them war veterans, also swung into action.

In January 1920, using information collected by Hoover, Palmer ordered raids in 33 cities across the land. Federal agents, assisted by local police, broke into homes and meeting halls and arrested about 6,000 people. The Palmer raids were preemptive: Palmer and Hoover intended to catch the conspirators plotting their revolutionary actions and to seize their maps, weapons, and the conspirators themselves before they could carry out their plans. There were wholesale violations of civil liberties. Many of those arrested were neither radicals nor Communists, nor had they committed any crime. Eventually most of them were released. However, about 550 aliens were deported for having violated immigration laws.

Investigators never uncovered a revolutionary plot; it apparently existed only in the imaginations of Palmer and Hoover. When Palmer's pre-

6.   Quoted in Mary Beth Norton et al., *A People and a Nation: A History of the United States*, 2nd ed., Volume II: Since 1865 (Boston: Houghton Mifflin, 1986), p. 669.

diction that there would be a revolutionary uprising on May Day in 1920 proved mistaken, he lost credibility. Some progressives also criticized his disregard of constitutional rights and due process. The Red Scare died out as the strikes ended, the Communist threat in Europe receded, and the nation returned to normal peacetime activities. Palmer's presidential bid collapsed.

One episode from the Red Scare has endured. On April 15, 1920, a paymaster and his guard were shot dead during the robbery of a shoe factory in South Braintree, Massachusetts. Three weeks later Nicola Sacco, a shoe worker, and Bartolomeo Vanzetti, a fish peddler, both Italian immigrants and committed anarchists, were charged with murder. Both men were armed at the time of their arrest. The evidence against them was contradictory. During their trial, witnesses for the prosecution perjured themselves, and there were indications that the police had tampered with some of the evidence used against them. Furthermore the judge in the case, Webster Thayer, was biased against the defendants. At one point in the proceedings he called them "anarchist bastards."

When a jury convicted them of murder and Judge Thayer sentenced them to death, many believed Sacco and Vanzetti were innocent; they felt the two men had been convicted because they were radical immigrants. They had been convicted for what they were, not for what they had done. The case generated significant political controversy, and the Massachusetts governor appointed a special commission to review the case. After a careful examination of the trial, the commissioners concluded that justice had been done, although they reprimanded Judge Thayer for his derogatory remarks about the defendants.

The case of Sacco and Vanzetti assumed international proportions, engaging the passions of men around the globe. Anatole France, a Nobel Prize–winning author, entered an eleventh-hour plea for their lives. All in vain. Despite the worldwide protests, both men were electrocuted August 23, 1927. By then millions of people in this country and around the world were convinced of their innocence. To this day, scholars of the case continue to debate its merits. Some believe Sacco and Vanzetti were innocent victims of political vengeance. Others cite evidence establishing their guilt. It is impossible to resolve the issue, so the debate goes on.

The Red Scare left many other casualties besides Sacco and Vanzetti. Thousands were sent to prison, suffered civil rights violations, or were deported. Dissent was stifled; critics were afraid to speak out. The give and take of free debate, essential to maintaining the health of democracy, was curtailed. Reformers no longer criticized institutions or proposed reforms. The radical movement in America was badly wounded by combined wartime and Red Scare repression. The government's campaign against its critics marred Wilson's otherwise excellent record as a war leader. His intolerance toward opponents of his war policies revealed both his lack of faith in democracy during wartime and a willingness to use repressive methods to stifle opposition. A legacy of repression, intolerance, and narrow conformity carried into the 1920s.

THE PEACE CONFERENCE

While the nation was in the throes of the Red Scare, President Wilson journeyed to Paris to try to implement his Fourteen Points. He faced many obstacles, some erected by his political rivals and some created by his own political errors. Wilson was the first president to go abroad on a diplomatic mission during his term of office; his decision to go was controversial. Republican opponents suspected that Wilson wanted to get all the credit for the peace settlement; they accused him of having a "messiah complex." He also left behind some serious domestic problems. Many farmers, businessmen, and trade unions were unhappy with some of his war policies.

Wilson erred by making a blatantly partisan appeal to the voters for the election of a Democratic Congress in 1918 on the eve of his departure for France. The voters, concerned with domestic issues, particularly inflation, promptly elected Republican majorities to both houses of Congress. The outcome of this election meant that any treaty Wilson brought back from Paris would have to be ratified by a Republican-controlled Senate. Wilson also lost political stature in the eyes of foreign leaders with whom he would soon be negotiating. He made further errors by not appointing any prominent Republican leaders to the delegation accompanying him and by not consulting with the Senate Foreign Relations committee before he left for Paris.

At Paris he confronted more obstacles. The Allies were determined to impose a harsh peace on the defeated Germans. The French Premier Georges Clemenceau, the British Prime Minister David Lloyd George, and the Italian leader Vittorio Orlando, along with Woodrow Wilson, were the dominant voices at the conference. The Allied leaders had signed secret treaties during the war and they came to Paris intending to enlarge their empires at Germany's expense. They dismissed Wilson's liberal war aims as foolish and irrelevant. Clemenceau viewed Wilson's idealism as a species of political theology. Referring to Wilson's peace plan, Clemenceau said: "God gave us Ten Commandments and we broke them; Wilson gives us Fourteen Points. We shall see."

Most of the conference sessions were held at Versailles, a suburb of Paris. The delegates met behind closed doors, repudiating one of the Fourteen Points, which had called for open diplomacy. The victors demanded and got a clause in the treaty making Germany absolutely responsible for the war and creating a reparations commission to determine the huge bill Germany would have to pay. (The commission later set the figure at $33 billion!)

Wilson fought hard for decolonization and self-determination, but he had to make many concessions to imperialism. Former German colonies were placed in a mandate system which gave the French, British, and Japanese access to their resources. Japan gained influence over Germany's former sphere in China at Shantung and many of its former Pacific island colonies. France occupied Germany's Rhineland. Still Wilson was able to carve several newly independent nations out of the remnants of the Austro-Hungarian empire—Austria, Hungary, Yugoslavia, Czechoslovakia, and Poland. He also helped to erect a *cordon sanitaire* of new nations—Finland, Estonia, Latvia, and Lithuania—along the western border of Russia in order to contain Communism.

Wilson also fought hard for the League of Nations charter. He was willing to sacrifice many of his Fourteen Points because he reasoned that the League would moderate the harsh peace terms, contain imperialism, and ensure collective security in the postwar era. He wrote most of the new international organization's charter. He created a League of Nations dominated by a permanent council of the major powers, an assembly for discussion and debate among the member nations, and a World Court. The heart of the League's covenant was Article X, the collective security provision, which provided for League members to "respect and preserve as against external aggression the territorial integrity and existing political independence" of all members. Wilson also insisted that the League of Nations charter be incorporated into the body of the peace treaty, forming an integral part of it.

German representatives signed the Treaty of Versailles in June 1919 under protest, giving up chunks of their territory, 10 percent of their population, all their colonies, and a huge portion of their wealth. It was a vindictive, humiliating peace imposed on the defeated Germans. Many commentators, including the famed British economist John Maynard Keynes, foresaw the seeds of another war sown in the harsh terms imposed by the peacemakers at Versailles.

While the peace conference was still in session, Senator Henry Cabot Lodge, chairman of the Senate Foreign Relations Committee, circulated a resolution signed by 39 senators, more than enough votes to block ratification, stating that the League charter did not protect American national interests. Wilson responded by writing into the League covenant language that exempted the Monroe Doctrine and U.S. internal matters from League jurisdiction.

FIGHT FOR RATIFICATION

As the terms of the treaty became known in the United States, criticism of it mounted from several sides. Many progressives attacked Wilson's betrayal of so many of his Fourteen Points. There was nothing in the Versailles

Treaty about freedom of the seas, free trade, or disarmament. Other liberals attacked the closed sessions, the concessions to imperialism, and the huge reparations imposed on Germany. Senator La Follette said the treaty's provisions confirmed his view that World War I was nothing more than a struggle between rival imperialisms. Conservative critics such as Senator Lodge feared the League would limit American freedom of action in the postwar world. Isolationists feared Article X would obligate the United States to provide armed forces to preserve collective security in the postwar world.

Wilson returned home to face his critics and to defend the treaty. He defended his concessions as necessary compromises and pointed out that the League of Nations would eventually right all wrongs in the postwar era. Senator Lodge was unimpressed; he organized Senate opposition to the Treaty of Versailles. He introduced fourteen reservations, modifications that he wanted made in the League charter, before he would approve the treaty. These reservations included exempting U.S. immigration policy from League decisions and giving Congress the right to approve any League resolution that implemented Article X.

The 49 Republican senators formed three distinct factions in the debate over ratifying the impending treaty. Twenty-three shared Lodge's view that all fourteen reservations would have to be implemented before they could support the treaty. They were called "strong reservationists." Twelve would support the treaty if some of the reservations were implemented. This group was known as the "mild reservationists." Fourteen isolationists opposed the treaty in any form and determined to oppose it with or without reservations. These senators formed the "irreconcilables."

In the fall of 1919 President Wilson went on a nationwide speaking tour to rally public support for the treaty; he hoped to pressure the Senate into ratifying it. In Pueblo, Colorado, the President became ill following an eloquent speech which left his audience in tears. He was taken back to Washington, where he suffered a thrombosis which left him partially paralyzed. For several weeks he was incapacitated, unable to perform his duties as president. Even after he made a partial recovery, his judgment remained impaired. He refused to consider compromising with his Republican opponents in the Senate, and he demanded absolute loyalty from his Democratic supporters.

In November 1919 the Senate voted twice on the treaty. Before the votes were taken, the Senate Democratic floor leader, Gilbert Hitchcock, told the President that the treaty could not pass without reservations. He suggested that "It might be wise to compromise." Wilson responded curtly, "Let Lodge compromise!" The first vote was on the treaty with Lodge's fourteen reservations attached. The Senate rejected it 39 to 55. Then a vote was taken without the reservations. It also failed, 38 to 53. The "irreconcilables," absolutely opposed to American entry into the League of Nations, voted against it both times. Senators representing midwestern and eastern states voted against the unamended version. Democratic senators from the South favored it. Western senators were divided.

AMERICA AND THE WORLD **127**

A third vote was taken in March 1920, with the reservations attached
to the treaty. Wilson continued to insist that all Democrats oppose the
treaty in amended form, refusing all efforts at compromise. Although 21
Democrats defied Wilson's order, the third vote fell seven votes short of
the necessary two-thirds majority, 49 to 35. Had Wilson permitted Democrats to compromise with Republicans who favored mild reservations, he
would have probably gotten the required two-thirds majority and the
United States would have joined the League of Nations. Wilson's refusal to
compromise doomed the treaty.

Wilson's refusal to compromise had many causes—his personal dislike of Lodge, the illness that had impaired his judgment, and partisan political considerations. But there was a more fundamental cause of his
refusal and of the Republican senators' unwillingness to accept the treaty
without amendments. The fundamental conflict between Wilson and
Lodge was based on two competing conceptions of the national interest.
Was the national interest best served, as Wilson believed, by endorsing
collective security? Or was it best served, as Lodge believed, by continuing
to travel the traditional American path of unilateralism, as expressed in
Washington's Farewell Address and the Monroe Doctrine? Looking out
on the postwar world, many senators preferred unilateralism, which
meant nonalignment and free choice over the binding commitments of
collective security mediated through the League of Nations. Woodrow
Wilson had a bold vision of a new world order based on internationalist
collective security arrangements, but he was unable to find the arguments
or concoct the formula that would enable him to bring the requisite number of senators along with him.

Historians have speculated on the long-run significance of the failure
of the United States to join the League of Nations. The United States
emerged from World War I the preeminent world power economically
and financially; it also had the potential to be the world's number one military power. Had the United States joined, the League of Nations would
have been a stronger and more prestigious agency. During the 1930s
when aggressor nations began to disrupt the world order, the League of
Nations, if bolstered by American membership, might have more effectively maintained collective security and curbed aggression. World War II
might have been avoided or at least curtailed. If these speculations have
the ring of truth, then the failure of the United States to ratify the Treaty of
Versailles and join the League of Nations was a colossal world tragedy.

THE WAR EXPERIENCE

World War I was a brief, intense experience for the American people that
had a profound and enduring effect on their lives and institutions. During
the war the federal government intervened in the economy and influenced
the lives of Americans in unprecedented ways. The wartime cooperation of

Europe after Versailles

business and government stimulated the growth of trade associations that during the 1920s lobbied to protect their interests and minimize competition. The suspension of antitrust laws in wartime fostered the growth of monopoly and oligopoly that flourished during the 1920s. War accelerated the emergence of the modern corporate economy with its complex, usually cooperative relations with the central government. The war effort was a modernizing experience that ended forever the old *laissez-faire*, voluntaristic order that had emerged from the nineteenth century.

The war also afforded American businessmen many world economic opportunities. They reduced the outflow of capital from this country by purchasing billions of dollars of American stocks and bonds sold on the market by foreign belligerents desperate for cash. They also reclaimed many of the dollars spent repatriating these securities by selling huge quantities of foodstuffs and ammunition to the Allies. When the Allies had exhausted their dollar accounts, American banks advanced them billions in credits, reversing America's historic credit dependency on European investors. Also Americans moved to take over markets previously dominated by Europeans, particularly in Latin America at the expense of the British and Germans.

America emerged from the war as the world's preeminent economic power. In the 1920s the United States produced about half of the world's coal and steel, and over 70 percent of its petroleum. American trade accounted for about 30 percent of the world's commerce. American corporations opened subsidiaries in foreign lands. European companies, strained by the war, fell behind their U.S. rivals. America had also become the world's leading creditor. New York replaced London as the world's banking center. U.S. financiers and investors loaned billions of dollars to businesses and governments in Europe and Latin America.

Although the Versailles settlement disillusioned many Americans about the war and the United States did not join the League of Nations, the nation did not revert to isolationism after the war. American observers attended all League meetings and America usually supported League actions, but it was wary about intervening in European affairs, given Europe's postwar economic and political disorder. America preserved its freedom of action.

The war changed the public mood. Photographs and films had revealed the brutal, deadly reality of trench warfare, dramatically different from the soaring rhetoric of President Wilson's speeches. Veterans wanted only to return home and forget about their war experiences. Americans wearied of idealistic crusades and became cynical about their internationalist commitments. They turned inward, closing out the larger world. The baseball scoreboard became more important to them than news of the world, and it was a lot more fun.

The war split the progressive movement, destroying the reform coalition. Most progressive intellectuals ultimately supported the war, sharing Wilson's belief that it was a war to save democracy. A left-wing progressive minority, however, led by Jane Addams, retained its pacifist beliefs. Progressivism emerged from World War I shaken and weakened. Progressives who had viewed the war as a grand opportunity for America to reform the world—a chance to bring peace, democracy, and progressive capitalism to Europe—also became disillusioned. Many lost enthusiasm for crusades both at home and abroad. Some reformers felt betrayed by European imperialists who had used the Paris conference to turn a glorious victory into a sordid settlement perpetuating world problems and sowing the seeds of future wars. Progressivism had lost its innocence.

BIBLIOGRAPHY

John Dobson, *America's Ascent: The United States Becomes a Great Power, 1890–1914* charts the rise of the United States to world prominence during the Progressive Era. David McCullough, *The Path between the Seas: The Creation of the Panama Canal, 1870–1914* is a beautifully rendered account of the Panama Canal project. Howard K. Beale's classic *Theodore Roosevelt and the Rise of America to World Power* remains the best book on progressive foreign policy. All facets of the American experience during World War I have been written about. The best account of the causes of U.S. entry into the war is Ernest R. May, *The World and American Isolation, 1914–1917*. Ross Gregory, *The Origins of American Intervention in the First World War* is a short, lively account. A classic study of America and the war is Daniel M. Smith, *The Great Departure: The United States and World War I, 1914–1920*. Wilson's official biographer, Arthur Link, has written a good account of the President's diplomacy, *Wilson the Diplomatist*. The best military history of American involvement in World War I is Edward M. Coffmann, *The War to End All Wars*. A. E. Barbeau and Florette Henri have written *The Unknown Soldiers: Black American Troops in World War I*. The role of women in the war has been recorded by Maurine W. Greenwald in *Women, War, and Work*. The best account of the home front in the war is David Kennedy, *Over Here: The First World War and American Society*. The attack on civil liberties in wartime is recorded in H. C. Peterson and Gilbert Fite, *Opponents of War, 1917–1918*. The best account of the Red Scare and the man who led the attack on it is Stanley Coben, *A. Mitchell Palmer: Politician*. The best account of the fight over the League of Nations is Thomas A. Bailey, *Woodrow Wilson and the Great Betrayal*.

CHAPTER
5
The New Era

The 1920s was a complex, vital decade, an era of conflict and contrast. Americans during the 1920s were forward-looking and reactionary, liberal and repressive, progressive and nostalgic. A majority of Americans enjoyed unprecedented material abundance and leisure, but poverty plagued millions of small farmers, industrial workers, and nonwhite minorities. Prosperity eradicated neither poverty nor social injustice from the land.

The most important trend of the 1920s was the emergence of a new mass consumer culture that fostered changes in the ways many Americans worked, lived, and cared for one another. It also brought changes in manners, morals, and personal identities. Consumerism also shifted the American sense of community—from communities based on shared values toward communities based on shared styles of consumption. But beneath the surface unity of mass consumerism and participation in new leisure activities, cultural conflicts and tensions seethed. American society was fragmented along many fault lines—urbanites versus rural folks, WASPs versus ethnics, white against black, and perhaps the profoundest divide: between those who embraced a modernist culture and those who retained traditional values.

The 1920s was a decade of great accomplishments in art, science, and technology. Creative American writers, musicians, and artists flourished. It was also a decade characterized by stunts, fads, contests, and commercial promotions. Ballyhoo artists prospered, as did criminals who made millions from the illegal liquor trade. It was a time of prosperity, social change, and personal liberation. It was also an age that featured an upsurge in religious fundamentalism, the Ku Klux Klan, nativist immigration restriction, and repression of radicalism. Crime rates and church attendance both soared during the decade.

The 1920s also marked a beginning, a time when millions of Americans adapted to urban patterns of existence. They centered their new urban lifestyle around ownership of automobiles and participation in the new urban mass culture. While many urbanites abandoned their former rural, agrarian way of life, they retained some of its values. It was a time of transition. During the 1920s the major historical developments of twentieth-century American life—technological change, urbanization, the development of bureaucratic modes of organization, and the growth of the middle class—accelerated rapidly. Between the end of World War I and the stock market crash in 1929, the shape of modern America emerged; the historical forces driving the rise of the urban nation accelerated. The New Era was the first recognizably modern decade.

A MOBILE PEOPLE

The 1920 census confirmed the major demographic trend underway in this country since the American Revolution: A majority of American families had left the countryside and moved to the city. Of the 106 million people living in America in 1920, 52 percent resided in towns and cities with a population of 2,500 or more. America had become an urban nation. That movement from the hinterlands to the cities accelerated during the 1920s. By 1930, 69 million of the 123 million inhabitants of the United States resided in urban areas while 54 million lived in the countryside. The emigration of African Americans from the rural South to northern cities, spawned by the opportunities for work in war industries, continued during the 1920s. A sizable number of Puerto Ricans came to America during the 1920s, as did Mexicans fleeing poverty, oppression, and political instability in their native land.

Because the United States severely restricted immigration after 1921 and because the birth rate dropped sharply among middle-class families, the growth of the population during this decade slowed to the smallest rate recorded since census taking began in 1790. But while national population growth rates slowed, the rate of urban population growth accelerated, especially in the nation's largest cities. The five American cities whose population exceeded a million in 1920—New York, Chicago, Philadelphia, Detroit, and Los Angeles—collectively increased their population by 50 percent during the decade.

During the 1920s, for the first time in American history, the farm population showed a net decline. More than 13 million rural Americans left the countryside and moved to the urban frontiers. Construction of interurban highways and the advent of mass ownership of automobiles permitted rapid growth of suburban communities that sprang up around the large metropolitan centers. The other great demographic trend, as old as the republic itself, continued as millions of families kept moving west, al-

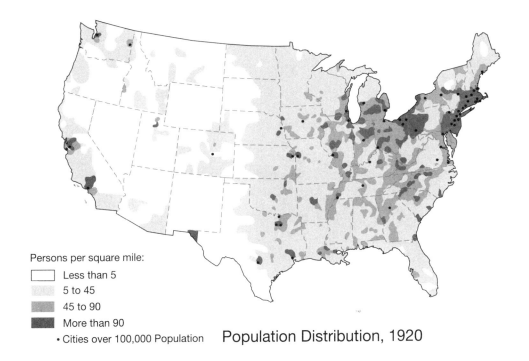

Persons per square mile:
- [ ] Less than 5
- 5 to 45
- 45 to 90
- More than 90
- • Cities over 100,000 Population

Population Distribution, 1920

though during the 1920s they made the trek in cars and passenger trains rather than covered wagons and horses. California often appeared to be the favorite destination of these 1920s migrants.

THE CONSUMER ECONOMY

The decade is famed for its prosperity, but the "Roaring Twenties" economy began slowly. Along with postwar disorder and the Red Scare, Americans suffered severe economic difficulties during 1920. The government's heedless decontrol of the economy and mass discharge of veterans in 1919 contributed to the downturn. High inflation continued to plague consumers. As 1920 ended, a sharp recession occurred, brought on in part by the Federal Reserve Board's restrictive monetary policies. Financial crisis ensued. Prices dropped, consumer demand fell, and exports declined as war markets closed, and farm income plunged. Unemployment soared—from 2 or 3 percent to over 12 percent, the highest rate since the severe depression of 1892 to 1894. Railroads went bankrupt, coal mines closed, and many New England textile mills shut their gates. Americans had their first contact with "stagflation," high prices combined with high unemployment. Recovery began in late 1922. Year One of the prosperity decade was 1923. This prosperity, although uneven, continued until the collapse of the securities industry in 1929, one of the longest epochs of good times in American economic history.

During these seven good years, industrial output nearly doubled and the gross domestic product (GDP) rose 40 percent, from $63 billion to $87 billion. These figures represented in real dollars an annual increase in GDP of 5.6 percent, a rate unmatched for a comparable length of time in American history! National per capita income increased by 30 percent, from $520 to $681. Real wages for factory workers increased by 11 percent during the 1920s while hours worked per week declined from 47.5 to 42. The size of the middle class increased rapidly during the decade. White-collar workers increased substantially, from 10 million in 1920 to over 14 million in 1929, whereas the number of farm workers declined and blue-collar and service workers increased only slightly. By the end of the decade white-collar workers accounted for about 30 percent of the jobs in the American labor force of 50 million workers.

For the first time in world history a significant percentage of a population earned enough money to buy a growing spate of goods and services and had enough leisure time to enjoy them. This first-ever consumer economy was based on a large and prosperous middle-class society. In sociological terms, the New Era created an entirely new middle-class social structure based on consumerism.

Prices remained stable, even dropping for some items during the late 1920s. In an economy with no inflation and no rise in living costs, increased GDP meant significant increases in consumer purchasing power and rapidly rising living standards. By the mid-1920s a typical middle-class household owned an automobile, a radio, a phonograph, a washing machine, a vacuum cleaner, a sewing machine, and a telephone. A generation earlier only the rich could have afforded these possessions, and they would have used technologically inferior versions.

The application of new technologies to productive processes was the key to the extraordinary American economic expansion of the 1920s. The continuous-flow assembly line, pioneered by Henry Ford at his River Rouge auto factory near Detroit, became standard in most American manufacturing plants. Electric motors replaced steam engines as the basic energy source in factories. By the end of the decade electricity supplied 70 percent of all industrial power. Efficiency experts broke down manufacturing processes into minute parts in time-and-motion studies to show how men and machines could maximize output. Frederick W. Taylor, trained as a civil engineer, was the most prominent of these time-and-motion experts. Output per man-hour, the basic measure of productivity, increased an amazing 75 percent over the decade. In 1929 a work force only slightly larger than the one employed in 1919 was producing almost twice as many goods.

Most of this explosive growth occurred in industries producing consumer goods—automobiles, appliances, furniture, clothing, and radios. Dozens of new consumer products flowed from factories and shops. New alloys, chemicals, and synthetics such as rayon and cellophane became commonplace. People bought more preserved, processed, and canned foods as well as machine-fashioned clothing. Americans found a whole new spectrum of products to buy—cigarette lighters, wristwatches, heat-resistant cookware, and sheer rayon stockings. The electric power industry expanded, so that by the end of the decade nearly 70 percent of American homes were electrified. Radio broadcasting was an insignificant industry at the beginning of the decade; it had become a big business by its end.

Service industries also expanded to accommodate the new affluence and leisure. Specialty stores, restaurants, beauty shops, movie theaters, and service stations proliferated. Henry Ford's slogan "Buy a Ford and Spend the Difference" best expressed the spirit of the New Era's rampant consumerism. The construction industry was both a major cause of and a significant participant in the new age of prosperity. Cities and suburbs expanded, and roads and highways proliferated. The value of both residential and commercial construction rose from $10 billion in 1920 to $18 billion in 1929.

Skyscrapers became a distinctive feature of every large American city. Skyscrapers were a uniquely American contribution to urban landscapes, necessitated largely by a sharp rise in land values generated by industrial expansion and rapid population growth. New York led the way. The Empire State Building, completed in 1930 and rising 1,250 feet into the sky, had 102 stories and space for 25,000 offices! The skyscraper became a major symbol of the new American mass culture, and the mighty metropolis on Manhattan Island was the dynamic center of American civilization, serving as both its commercial and its cultural capital.

Air transportation was another industry that expanded at a prodigious rate during the 1920s. American aviation had grown rapidly during the war; both the Army and the Navy had developed aviation services, and over 1,000 U.S. military aircraft had been sent to war in France. During the 1920s dozens of aircraft factories turned out thousands of planes each year. Air routes for mail, cargo, and passengers proliferated. By the end of the decade there were more than 50,000 miles of airline routes in the United States. In a Ford trimotor plane passengers could fly from New York to San Francisco, with several stops along the way, in 24 hours.

One of the crucial developments of the New Era amounted to a revolution in communications. Key industries flowered from small beginnings—film, radio, and telephones. Automatic switchboards, dial telephones, and teletype machines connected the business world into information networks of unprecedented speed and efficiency. Urban middle-class households now had phones; families spent the evening listening to radio programs. At least once a week most urban families went to the movies; by 1929 the average weekly attendance in movie theaters had reached 90 million!

THE ADVENT OF THE AUTOMOBILE

The automobile led the parade of technological marvels that made the American way of life the wonder of the world during the 1920s. During this decade Americans bought 15 million new cars. Efficient production methods dropped the price of new cars sharply, making what had been a plaything of the rich affordable to the middle class and even some working-class families. Many families that could not afford a new car bought a used one.

The man who put America on wheels was a Michigan farm boy who taught himself to be a mechanic. Henry Ford had two key insights: The first, in his words, was "Get the prices down to the buying power." He installed continuously moving assembly lines which enabled him to manufacture 9,000 cars per day by 1925. The second insight was to pay his workers top wages. The assembly line had increased worker productivity significantly, but it also simplified jobs, making them boring and fatiguing. Absenteeism and high worker turnover became serious problems for Ford. In 1914 he raised wages to $5.00 per day, making Ford employees the highest paid industrial workers in the world. Absenteeism and

Henry Ford (right) beside the first automobile he built in 1896. His son, Edsel, inspects the ten millionth (!) "Model T" Ford car which rolled off the assembly line in 1924.

turnover practically disappeared. Ford's sales and profits soared. Between 1921 and 1925 more than half of all new cars sold in America were Model Ts. During those years Henry Ford netted $25,000 a day. He owned the entire Ford Motor Company and became the nation's second billionaire.

He also became a folk hero. His simple tastes, his dislike of bankers, and his disdain for society inspired mass affection for him. For millions of people, Ford's achievement symbolized the wonders of the American system. He had given the American people a marvelous machine at an affordable price, he was an inspiring example of a poor boy's rise to riches, and he paid his employees well. A serious grass-roots boom promoted him for president in 1923.

Although uneducated and ignorant of most things outside the automotive business, Ford, because he was famous and successful, spoke out often on public issues. His views derived from his nineteenth-century rural roots. He condemned drinking, dancing, and the use of tobacco. He held nativist views and published anti-Semitic propaganda. He denounced modern art and once proclaimed that "History is bunk." Ironically, mass ownership of automobiles and road building were fast destroying the old-fashioned rural America that Ford cherished.

A new Ford Model T cost as little as $285 in 1925, and the joke went that you could get it in any color you wanted as long as it was black. New or used Fords were affordable to factory workers earning $1,200 annually and by office workers earning $2,000. For many car buyers, owning an automobile was more urgent than owning a home or the other consumer items of the era. An interviewer once asked a rural housewife why her family owned a car but not a bathtub. Her reply: "Bathtub? You can't go to town in a bathtub!"

Mass ownership of automobiles profoundly altered American culture. Traffic jams, speeding tickets, and auto accidents became permanent features of the American scene. Young people out for a drive could escape the watchful eyes of parents, and moralists feared that automobiles were becoming "bedrooms on wheels." Most of all, the motor car symbolized a new age of social equality. The average man could own America's most important status symbol. The son of an east European peasant could now drive along the same highways and enjoy the same scenery as the son of a rich man. Henry Ford, the man who had put America on wheels, had accomplished a capitalist revolution. Marxists would be hard put to convince an American factory worker at the wheel of his new Ford that he was being ground to dust by capitalist exploiters. The car became the supreme symbol of the 1920s' version of the American dream.

The manufacture of automobiles had a multiplier effect on the American economy. Much of the output of the steel industry, the glass industry, and the rubber industry went into making cars. The automobile stimulated extensive road construction and spawned many service industries

A sign that Americans had entered the Age of the Automobile. Traffic jams clogged the streets of all large cities by the 1920s and even began spilling into the suburbs, as shown here.

that catered to drivers. Congress enacted a Federal Highway Act providing federal money for states to build highways. The Bureau of Public Roads began planning a national highway system. Service stations and a new kind of hotel, a motor hotel, later shortened to "motel," made its appearance. Insurance companies, previously concerned with life insurance, added auto insurance to their policy lines. The automobile industry was directly or indirectly responsible for the employment of 4 million people in 1929. According to historian James T. Patterson, "Automobiles were to the 1920s what the railroads had been to the nineteenth century, a major force affecting the entire economy."

The oil industry, which had sold mostly kerosene to light people's homes, shifted production to gasoline, an unimportant product before the advent of the automobile with its internal combustion engine. During the early 1920s oil companies could not produce gasoline fast enough to meet the demands of a people taking to the roads. An "energy crisis" occurred. Long lines of angry motorists formed at the gas pumps. The price of a gallon of gas doubled, from 20 to 40 cents. The crisis faded in 1924 when Standard Oil gained access to British-controlled oil in Iraq.

The automobile also altered urban residential patterns. People now drove downtown to work and shop instead of catching a trolley. Suburbs, previously located within the outer neighborhoods of cities, now evolved as satellite cities, often 10 to 20 miles away from the central city. Los Angeles was the first American metropolis to develop during the age of the automobile. It took shape as a series of neighborhoods and shopping districts sprawling over a large geographic area, all connected by long streets and highways. One observer called the metropolis "a series of suburbs in search of a city."

THE BUSINESS OF AMERICA

The most distinctive feature of the new consumer economy was its stress on advertising. The advertising industry, which had developed during the Gilded Age and centered on Manhattan's Madison Avenue, became a big business during the 1920s. The earnings of ad agencies rose from $1.8 billion in 1921 to $3.4 billion in 1926. Clever ad writers manipulated public taste and consumer spending with increasing effectiveness. Advertisers sought to create consumer desire for new products by identifying them with the good life; sometimes they employed psychology to appeal to consumer needs, fears, anxieties, and sexual fantasies.

Advertisers viewed human beings as infinitely suggestible, infinitely manipulable. Edward Bernays, who became America's leading public relations expert during the 1920s, believed that opinions were formed by groups, not by individuals. He insisted that advertisers appeal to group leaders. Sell a new product by getting celebrities or socially prominent people to endorse it. Hire Babe Ruth to sell athletic equipment to kids. Hire a movie actress or debutante to sell cigarette smoking to women. Bernays believed strongly in the ability of an educated elite to use the persuasive power of advertising to sell the growing cornucopia of consumer goods to the gullible masses. Bernays once snorted, "The average person does not know what he wants until we tell him."

One adman became a best-selling author. Bruce Barton, who wrote *The Man Nobody Knows* (1925), expounded a new gospel of business. The man nobody knew was Jesus of Nazareth. According to Barton, Jesus was the greatest salesman who ever lived and "the founder of modern business." This Madison Avenue Jesus "picked up twelve humble men and created an organization that won the world."

Advertisers encouraged credit buying to boost sales. The new consumerism was thus enhanced by advertising and fueled by credit. Installment buying or time-payment plans flourished. Of the millions of new automobiles sold annually during the prosperous 1920s, over 80 percent were purchased on credit.

During the 1920s the communications revolution and the expansion of advertising combined to create a consuming public that possessed up-to-date information about products, services, fads, and fashions. People spent much time and energy learning about the latest products and trends—wanting to "keep up with the Joneses." Advertisers employed the new media to create a new human species: *Homo consumerins.* Descartes, the great French philosopher, had once stated, "I think; therefore I am." A new generation of eager Americans with money to spend and time to play collectively stated, "We consume; therefore we are." Most middle-class Americans who sampled the wonders of the New Era pronounced them good and wanted more. Pundits noted that abundance would soon engulf all Americans and put an end to poverty. Then all Americans would have a stake in the system; class, racial, and ethnic tensions would melt away. There could be no envy and no conflict in a land where there was plenty for all.

National chain stores advanced during the 1920s at the expense of small, local businesses. Atlantic and Pacific Tea Company (A & P) and Safeway dominated the retail food market. A & P had 15,000 stores as the decade ended. Woolworth's "five and dimes" and giant drug chains like Rexalls spread coast to coast. J. C. Penney opened thousands of clothing stores. As the 1920s ended, retail chain stores in many fields had opened outlets in nearly every town and city. They offered good value and courteous service and generated huge profits from volume sales.

Corporations continued to be the dominant economic unit of the 1920s. Large corporations often had a million or more individual stockholders, and one individual rarely held more than a few percent of the stock. Most corporations generated large profits from volume sales during the 1920s, enabling them to finance their expansions and freeing them from dependence on bankers and financiers. Professing a new ethic of social responsibility, corporate managers ran their giant firms independently of any external controls. As businesses expanded their output of goods and services, the nation's financial institutions also grew rapidly. Assets of banks, insurance companies, and savings and loan associations doubled during the decade.

Big business grew bigger during the 1920s. The consolidation drive that had begun during the Gilded Age continued through the Progressive Era despite its antitrust activity, then accelerated during the war years and climaxed during the New Era. Another wave of mergers swept the corporate world, over 8,000 between 1920 and 1928 as thousands of small firms, unable to compete with big companies, were taken over. As the decade ended, about 200 giant corporations owned half of the nation's wealth. In almost every manufacturing sector huge, integrated companies were in control—in automobile manufacturing, steel milling, oil refining, meat processing, flour milling, mining, railroading, and other industries. They dominated not only production but also marketing, distribution, and financing. Antitrust activities faded in an age of economic giants and continuing centralization.

As corporations grew larger, the managerial revolution in American business that had been underway since 1900 was completed. Corporate bureaucracies were organized along hierarchical lines. Gone was the age of titans, when owners of large companies directed their operations. Ownership was divorced from management. Salaried professional managers hired by boards of directors controlled companies whose owners were thousands of individual and institutional stockholders uninvolved in the management of these giant firms. Executives and managers ran the corporations in trust for the owners, whose only interests were raising dividends and increasing capital gains.

Many of the nation's largest companies that dominated their industries during the 1920s established research and development divisions as integral components of the corporate structures. Many of America's leading universities, which were also growing rapidly during the decade, served as research centers for industry and trained a whole generation of engineers, technicians, and scientists who staffed the new corporate R&D laboratories. American businesses took the world lead in developing new product lines and improving existing products. European companies, lacking both the financial resources and the trained staff, could not begin to keep up with their American competitors.

While business prospered during the 1920s, labor suffered through a lean decade. Even though the economy was expanding, employment was rising, and wage levels rose steadily throughout the decade, membership in AFL unions declined sharply. AFL membership stood at 5 million at war's end but by 1929 had fallen to 3.6 million. There were many reasons for this decline in trade union power during prosperous times. Public opinion was indifferent or even hostile to trade unions, especially when they went on strike. Government hostility also hindered the growth of unions. The Justice Department frequently used court injunctions against striking unions, and the Clayton Act's provisions designed to protect unions proved useless. Corporations took actions to wean their employees away from unions. They instituted company unions, profit sharing, group health and life insurance, pensions, and company-sponsored social events. These benefits and services were all expressions of the new welfare capitalism of the 1920s. Companies also engaged, often successfully, in "open shop" drives to eliminate trade unions where they were already established.

While companies moved successfully to weaken or eliminate trade unions, the American Federation of Labor itself was increasingly inept in defending the interests of its members. Its aging and conservative leadership could not adapt to technological changes that eliminated many skilled jobs. In the new mass-production industries such as automobiles, the AFL either did not try to organize workers or else their efforts failed. Most AFL unions during the 1920s appeared content to try to protect the economic security of skilled craftsmen, the elite workers who comprised the backbone of the trade union federation.

This combination of welfare capitalism, hostility to unions, and the AFL's loss of militancy meant a decade of relatively peaceful labor–management relations. The number of strikes declined sharply. Meanwhile the status of organized labor plummeted.

Organizational activities fostered by progressive reformers before and during the war flourished during the 1920s. Business and professional associations worked to protect their members' interests. Retailers and small manufacturers formed trade associations to exchange information, to coordinate planning, and to promote their industries. Farm bureaus and farm cooperative associations lobbied for government help and tried to stabilize declining commodity prices. Lawyers, engineers, doctors, teachers, scientists, and other professionals formed associations and societies to promote their interests. The progressive organizational impulse had turned to professionalism.

Uniformity and standardization, the dominant characteristics of modern mass production processes, became major cultural influences. An Iowa farmer bought the same kind of car that an auto worker in Detroit or a business executive in Los Angeles purchased. They also bought the same groceries, the same health and beauty aids, and the same underwear. They listened to the same radio programs, saw the same movies, and read the same comic strips. Regional differences in lifestyles and speech accents declined. Americans began to look, act, and sound more and more alike. Consumerism fostered conformity in manners and morals.

THE BUSINESS OF GOVERNMENT

With the upsurge in prosperity, most Americans shed their fears of big business and ceased complaining about the depredations of large corporations. John D. Rockefeller, previously denounced as a robber baron and an enemy of democracy, became a celebrity, praised for his philanthropy. Part of the new acceptance of oligopoly was attributable to the public's perception that big business contributed to rising productivity, higher wages, and improved living standards. Popular approval of big business was also encouraged by skilled business publicists who projected a corporate image of ethical concern and social responsibility. An ethic of service replaced the older predatory, "public-be-damned" attitudes of Gilded Age buccaneers. A spokesman applied the language of religion to corporate enterprise: "Through business, . . . the human race is finally to be redeemed."

Both the legislative and executive branches supported business during the 1920s. Congress lowered corporation taxes in 1921 and raised tariff rates a year later. Secretary of the Treasury Andrew Mellon got Congress to slash federal spending from a high of $18 billion in 1918 to $3 billion in 1925, generating a surplus that was used to retire part of the national debt. He persuaded Congress to reduce income taxes on the wealthy in 1926. In 1921 the government returned the railroads, modernized at taxpayers' expense, to their private owners. Government-built merchant ships were sold to private shipping companies at a fraction of their cost. Regulatory agencies such as the Federal Trade Commission and the Interstate Commerce Commission were staffed with businessmen, who took a protective stance toward the industries they were regulating.

The federal government's role in the economy increased during the 1920s. Republicans widened the scope of federal activity, and the number of government employees nearly doubled between 1921 and 1929. Herbert Hoover led the way in the Commerce Department, establishing new agencies to make the housing, transportation, and mining industries more efficient. Government encouraged corporations to develop welfare programs for employees. Agencies also devised new federal machinery to arbitrate labor disputes. Despite their use of the rhetoric of *laissez-faire*, the Republican administrations of the 1920s expanded the apparatus of the federal bureaucracy pioneered by progressive reformers. They applied Theodore Roosevelt's conception of business–government cooperation, although the presidents in this decade viewed government as a passive servant of business rather than as the active regulator that Roosevelt had championed.

Progressivism declined during the 1920s for several reasons. Many intellectuals and writers deserted the progressive cause. Urban middle-class people, who had formed the major constituencies for reform politics during the Progressive Era, were no longer interested in muckraker exposés or reform causes; they now embraced the new business ideologies of the 1920s with their emphasis on production, consumerism, and welfare capitalism. Most important, progressive political leaders lost control of the major political parties. The Republican Party during the 1920s was controlled by eastern and midwestern industrialists and financiers. Within the Democratic Party Wilsonian progressivism was discredited. Worse, the Democrats, torn apart by cultural conflict and disunity, could not provide national leadership or a coherent political program. Within the Democratic fold the eastern and midwestern urban factions battled the mostly rural southern and western factions for control of the party. Antitrust activities and the commitment to social justice waned.

But progressivism survived in Congress and expanded its range of concerns. A group of midwestern congressmen and senators, sometimes joined by southerners and northern urban liberals, supported labor legislation, aid to farmers, and other progressive measures. Progressivism survived also at state and local levels. Several states enacted workmen's compensation laws and old age pensions. City planning and zoning commissions controlled urban growth in a professional manner. Also social workers provided help for the urban poor.

The Supreme Court was dominated by conservative jurists during the 1920s, headed by Chief Justice, and former President, William Howard Taft. Many of its decisions protected business from rigorous regulation, weakened trade unions, and nullified social legislation. In *Hammer* v. *Dagenhart* (1918) and *Bailey* v. *Drexel Furniture Company* (1922) the Court nullified the child labor acts of 1916 and 1919 on the grounds that they infringed on the right of states to regulate wages, hours, and working conditions. In *Adkins* v. *Children's Hospital* (1923) the court overturned a minimum wage law for women on the ground that it infringed upon women's freedom of contract.

THE ELECTION OF 1920

Electoral politics during the 1920s continually demonstrated the strong popular appeal of Republican, pro-business candidates. At the 1920 Republican convention, a lightly regarded candidate, Senator Warren G. Harding of Ohio, got the presidential nomination because the leading contenders were deadlocked. His genial personality and lack of strong views made him an appealing compromise choice. He conducted a clever campaign tailored to the public mood, which had turned against both domes-

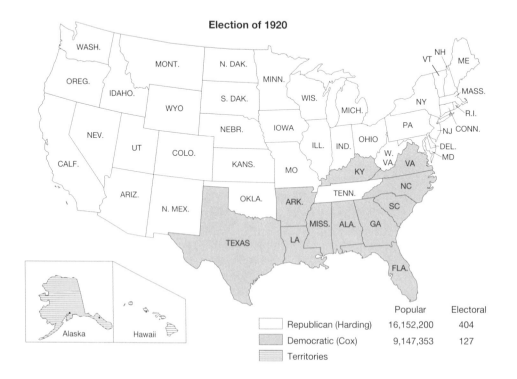

Election of 1920

		Popular	Electoral
Republican (Harding)		16,152,200	404
Democratic (Cox)		9,147,353	127
Territories			

tic reform and Wilsonian internationalism. Harding coined a new word to describe public yearnings; he told an audience that Americans wanted "not nostrums but normalcy." "Normalcy" was not good usage, but it made for good politics in the 1920 campaign.

Harding and his running mate, Calvin Coolidge, a journeyman professional politician made famous by his role in crushing the Boston police strike, easily defeated their Democratic opponents, Governor James Cox of Ohio and Franklin Roosevelt, formerly Assistant Secretary of the Navy and a distant relative of the late President Theodore Roosevelt. Cox was saddled with Woodrow Wilson's discredited administration, and his own support for American membership in the League of Nations had become unpopular by the fall of 1920. Harding and Coolidge rolled to a landslide triumph. Harding received over 16 million votes, more than twice as many as any previous candidate. His 61 percent of the popular vote was also a historic high. His huge majority also came from women voters. The 1920 election was the first in which the Nineteenth Amendment, enfranchising women, was in force. Feminists were disappointed when only about 25 percent of eligible women voted and moreover most voted the way their husbands did. Cox and Roosevelt managed to attract only 9 million votes.

THE HARDING PRESIDENCY

President Harding selected capable men to serve in key cabinet positions. His appointees included Secretary of State Charles Evans Hughes, Secretary of Agriculture Henry C. Wallace, Andrew Mellon at the Department of Treasury, and Herbert Hoover at the Department of Commerce. Harding relied heavily on his cabinet advisers; he had a conception of government-by-cabinet in contrast to his strong-willed predecessor, President Wilson, who rarely sought advice from anyone.

Although a traditional Republican, Harding showed considerable moderation and flexibility and was responsive to some progressive reform concerns. He established a modern budgeting system for the government, supported an anti-lynching measure, approved legislation aiding farmers, responded to some labor concerns, and supported civil liberties. He also pardoned Eugene Debs, the Socialist leader imprisoned for his opposition to the war, and invited him to the White House for a visit following his release.

Harding's administration is best remembered for its many scandals. Although honest himself, Harding inadvertently appointed many men to office who were incompetents, crooks, or both. Most of these miscreants were recruited from the ranks of the Ohio Gang, a noisome group of political camp followers who trailed Harding to the banks of the Potomac. The leader of the Ohio Gang was Harry Daugherty, Harding's campaign manager in 1920, a corrupt professional politician and lobbyist whom Harding appointed Attorney General. Members of the Ohio Gang often met at a residence on K Street known as the Little Green House. Here they drank bootleg whiskey, played poker, and hatched schemes to rip off the taxpayers. Harding's loyalty to Daugherty and his gang of thieves corrupted his presidency and ruined his historical reputation.

One of the more serious scandals involved Charles Forbes, head of the Veterans Bureau, who eventually went to Leavenworth for fraud and bribery. Among his crimes: he sold off medical supplies intended for soldiers who had been badly wounded in the war and he kept the money. In another scandal Daugherty stood trial for accepting bribes; he was probably guilty as charged, but he beat the rap by refusing to testify at his trial, claiming that if he testified, he would have to implicate the now dead President Harding. Jesse Smith, a close friend of Daugherty, collected bribes from gangsters who were convicted of violating federal Prohibition and income tax laws and who sought presidential pardons. Smith committed suicide rather than face trial. The most notorious scandal revealed that Secretary of the Interior Albert Fall had accepted bribes from oil companies in exchange for his leasing public oil lands to them illegally. It is known as the Teapot Dome Scandal, named for the site of a federal oil reserve in eastern Wyoming which had been turned over to the Mammoth Oil Company. After a Congressional investigation unearthed the criminal activity, Fall was tried, convicted, fined $100,000, and sent to prison. He was the first cabinet member in American history to serve time for wrongdoing committed while in office.

In the summer of 1923 neither Harding nor the American people knew about his administration's extensive corruption, although there is evidence suggesting that Harding was becoming suspicious and fearful. He confided to journalist William Allen White, "I have no trouble with my enemies. . . . But my friends, . . . they're the ones that keep me walking the floor nights." Harding left the nation's capital to try to escape his travail, embarking on a transcontinental tour in late June 1923. He suffered from a nervous disorder and was deeply depressed. His travels took him to the Midwest, into the Northwest, up to Alaska, and then back to Vancouver. After finishing a speech in Vancouver, the President, seriously ill, collapsed. Nevertheless, the presidential entourage continued on to San Francisco. On the evening of August 2, 1923, while resting in his room in the Palace Hotel, Harding died suddenly of a cerebral embolism, a blood clot that lodged in his brain. The sudden death of a popular president came as a great shock to the nation, and millions mourned the passage of a kindly, genial man who appeared to be the appropriate leader for a country seeking "normalcy" in the wake of world upheavals. In the years after his death, investigations and trials exposed the corruption and thievery riddling his administration, and Harding's reputation plummeted. Historians rate him as among the republic's least successful presidents.

KEEPING COOL WITH COOLIDGE

At the time of Harding's death, Coolidge was vacationing at the family home in Plymouth, Vermont. Early on the morning of August 3, by the light of a kerosene lamp, John Coolidge, the local justice of the peace, administered the presidential oath of office to his son, now the thirtieth president of the United States. The new president, a rural Puritan and scrupulously honest, moved quickly to clean up the corruption mess in Washington. Coolidge dismissed Daugherty and replaced him with Harlan Fiske Stone, the respected dean of Columbia Law School and future Supreme Court justice. Stone led the investigations, indictments, and trials that purged the government of crooks and thieves.

But mostly Coolidge kept the Harding administration in place and continued Harding's policies. Coolidge had close ties with the Hamiltonian wing of the party, the powerful industrialists and financiers who controlled the Republican Party during the 1920s. Coolidge admired successful corporate leaders and bankers and was devoted to the principles of *laissez-faire*. He believed in low taxes, free enterprise, and a minimalist state. He stated that "if the federal government disappeared, the average citizen would probably never notice the difference." He also said, "the man who builds a factory builds a temple." Andrew Mellon became his mentor in fiscal and financial affairs. He was unresponsive to the occasional progressive reform legislation coming from Congress, usually vetoing the measures.

THE 1924 ELECTION

Coolidge proved to be an able politician, popular with the American people. He had a notion that the White House belonged to the American people, and he spent hours most days greeting folks who stopped by for a visit. Because of a medical condition, he required much sleep, up to ten hours each night plus a nap during the day. He was the least energetic of modern presidents, working perhaps four or five hours a day, with weekends off. Coolidge quickly took control of the Republican Party and easily gained his party's 1924 presidential nomination. His restoring of integrity to the national government and the nation's rising prosperity ensured his election.

Coolidge was also aided by the Democratic Party, which nearly tore itself apart at its nominating convention. Northern big-city Democrats, who represented ethnic constituencies, largely Jewish and Catholic, sought a resolution condemning the Ku Klux Klan. Southern, rural, and some midwestern state delegations controlled by the Klan defeated the resolution. Northern Democrats also sought a plank in the party platform calling for the repeal of the Eighteenth Amendment, which had imposed

Prohibition on the country, but southern and rural delegates, strong supporters of Prohibition, defeated that proposal.

The intraparty cultural conflict peaked in the fight over who would be the Democratic Party's presidential candidate in 1924. Southern Democrats, dry (politicians who favored retaining Prohibition were called "drys," those favoring repeal were called "wets"), anti-immigrant, and pro-Klan, rallied to the candidacy of William Gibbs McAdoo. Eastern big-city Democrats supported Governor Alfred E. "Al" Smith of New York. Smith was a Catholic, a "wet," and a leader of Tammany Hall. Smith and McAdoo fought it out for 103 ballots in the longest and most acrimonious convention in American political history. Finally, the convention, in desperation, turned to a compromise candidate to break the deadlock. They chose John W. Davis, a conservative corporation lawyer associated with Morgan banking interests. He was inexperienced, a political unknown, and hopelessly incapable of providing his party or his nation with effective leadership.

With the two major parties controlled by conservative pro-business forces, progressives formed a new third party. It was the Progressive Party reborn. They chose as their presidential candidate the old progressive warhorse Robert La Follette. Progressives adopted a platform calling for government ownership of railroads, government development of hydro-electric power plants, direct election of the president, and a host of labor and social reforms. His Progressive candidacy contrasted sharply with the pro-business platforms of the major parties.

The election results were predictable. It was 1912 in reverse. The two pro-business candidates got most of the votes. Coolidge won easily, defeating Davis and La Follette in the popular vote. Coolidge got more votes than Davis and La Follette combined, 15.7 million to 8.4 million for Davis and a mere 4.8 million for La Follette. In the electoral vote column Coolidge got 382 to Davis's 136, while La Follette carried only his native Wisconsin. In an electoral contest in which only 52 percent of the eligible electorate cast ballots, "Coolidge prosperity" had received a strong popular endorsement. The Republicans also retained large majorities in both houses of Congress. Conservatism reigned. At the level of presidential politics, national progressivism appeared mortally ill, if not dead. It was time to "keep cool with Coolidge."

CONGRESSIONAL POLITICS

If one focused only on presidential politics during the 1920s, one would get a simplistic picture of conservative Republican domination. Shift the focus to Congress, and the political picture becomes more complex. One also discovers that progressive reform forces in both parties retained considerable popular appeal in various regions of the country and occasionally succeeded in enacting major legislation, sometimes over presidential vetoes. Progressive forces themselves were often divided, usually along regional or interest group lines. Northern urban liberal reformers often worked at cross purposes with southern agrarian reformers. Farm Bloc progressives, usually Republicans, often succeeded in protecting farmers' interests. They got tariff rates increased on agricultural imports. They also succeeded in delaying or decreasing Secretary of the Treasury Andrew Mellon's efforts to cut income tax rates and estate taxes. Congress also enacted bonuses for World War I veterans over Coolidge's veto in 1924.

The most serious economic problem afflicting the nation during the prosperous 1920s was the continuing depression in most sectors of American agriculture. It had begun in 1920 when commodity prices collapsed shortly after the end of the war and world agricultural output increased. Prices remained low throughout the decade. Aggregate farm income fell from $10 billion in 1919 to an average of $6 billion per annum for the years 1923 to 1929. The decline in farm income as a proportion of national income fell from 15 percent in 1920 to 9 percent in 1929. Falling commodity prices were not the only problem farmers faced during the hard times of the 1920s. Farm costs rose sharply during this time as the price of farm equipment kept rising. Taxes and interest charges also rose; net farm indebtedness more than doubled during the decade. Most farm families were not vigorous participants in the 1920s consumer economy; millions of farm families in fact sank into poverty.

Farmers responded to economic distress by seeking government relief just as they had done during the Populist revolt of the 1890s, but during the 1920s they formed the Farm Bloc. Progressive congressmen and senators fought for policies responsive to agricultural interests; the politics of protest were abandoned. Farmers had become another interest group. Farm organizations sent lobbyists to Washington to pressure the politicians. Congress responded with a series of measures, most of which were accepted by Harding during 1921–1923. The most important bill extended credits to farmers at low rates of interest. Farmers also sought relief from farm surpluses that were depressing commodity prices and keeping farm income down. Various schemes were proposed, including a plan for the government to buy all major staple crops produced for the market at a fixed price. A bill proposed by Congressman Gilbert N. Haugen of Iowa and Senator Charles L. McNary of Oregon that embodied the principle of government purchases of crops at a fixed price passed both houses of Congress only to be vetoed by President Coolidge. A later version of McNary-Haugen was also vetoed by Coolidge in 1927. Many of the nation's farmers, now an organized interest group with major political influence in Congress, had embraced the progressive notion that the federal government had an obligation to protect the economic security of all classes.

The large majority of women appear to have remained relatively indifferent to politics during the 1920s despite having recently received the franchise. Only about 25 percent of eligible women voted, and their voting patterns resembled those of men. Most women voted for Republicans and prosperity during the decade. Still, a minority of politically active women leaders considerably enhanced their political influence. The number of women delegates to the major party national conventions steadily increased throughout the 1920s. Eleven women served in the House of Representatives. Two women, both Democrats, Nellie Taylor Ross of Wyoming and Miriam M. "Ma" Ferguson of Texas, succeeded their husbands as governors. Hundreds of other women won elections to state and local offices and a few were appointed to serve as state and federal judges.

THE ELECTION OF 1928

President Coolidge chose not to run in 1928, for health reasons. Had he sought another presidential term, he would easily have been reelected. The country was prosperous, most people content, convinced that the wonders of the New Era would continue indefinitely. When Coolidge stepped aside, Herbert Hoover came forward to wear the mantle of prosperity. Hoover was an apt candidate for the Republicans. He combined the traditional ethic of personal success through hard work with a progressive emphasis on collective action. Born poor on an Iowa farm and orphaned at 9, he had worked his way through Stanford University. He graduated with its first class in 1895 amid the worst depression in American history. By the time he was 40, Hoover was a multimillionaire mining engineer. He retired from business to begin a second career in government service. During and after World War I Hoover distinguished himself as the U.S. food administrator and as head of general relief for Europe. He served as Secretary of Commerce under Harding and Coolidge. In both administrations he was a highly visible, active cabinet officer.

Hoover was not a traditional Republican conservative; he was a progressive who expanded Theodore Roosevelt's New Nationalist concept of business–government cooperation. As Commerce Secretary he had promoted business, encouraged the formation of trade associations, held conferences, and sponsored studies—all with the aim of improving production and profits. In his speech accepting the Republican nomination for President in the summer of 1928, the confident Hoover proclaimed that America would soon be the first nation in the history of the world to abolish poverty.

The Democrats, who remained factionalized and conflicted, nominated New York Governor Alfred E. "Al" Smith. He was the only candidate of national stature available to the Democrats in 1928. Smith's background contrasted dramatically with Hoover's. Whereas Hoover had rural, Protes-

Al Smith waving to supporters during his 1928 presidential campaign.

tant roots and a business background and had never run for office; Smith was from immigrant stock, raised on the streets of a Manhattan slum, and his political career was rooted in machine politics. Smith was also the first Roman Catholic to run for president on a major party ticket.

Hoover ran on a platform pledging to continue Republican prosperity for four more years. He had an easy campaign. The nation was peaceful and prosperous. Most Americans were content with the present and looked to the future with optimism. Hoover made only about a half dozen speeches during the entire campaign. He reminded the voters that the good times coincided with the Republican ascendancy, and he promised their continuance. Unwilling to challenge the public's complacent view of

Coolidge prosperity, the Democrats adopted a similar, conservative program. Smith appointed his friend John J. Raskob, the president of General Motors, to manage his campaign. The weak, "me too" strategy adopted by Smith and Raskob failed. Nothing Smith could say or do convinced businessmen or most voters that he was a better choice than Coolidge's heir apparent. Smith also lost votes in some regions because of his religious affiliation, his political machine connections, his urban background, and his attacks on Prohibition.

Smith nevertheless waged a vigorous campaign. He struck back at bigots who charged that his Catholicism made him a servant of the Pope. But he was overwhelmed by the prosperity wave that Hoover rode to an inevitable landslide victory. Hoover won the popular vote, 21 million to 15 million for Smith, and in the electoral vote he received 444 to Smith's 87. Hoover carried 40 of the 48 states. He even won several states of the Old South, including Virginia, North Carolina, Tennessee, Texas, and Florida. The Republicans also rolled up large majorities in both houses of Congress. It was a Republican sweep.

After this defeat, its third shellacking in a row, the Democratic Party appeared on the verge of extinction. But the epitaphs sounded were premature. Prosperity had defeated Smith, and, although no one in November 1928 could know, prosperity was about to end. Hoover's overwhelming victory concealed a significant political realignment taking form. Catholic working-class voters in the big cities, who were not sharing in the 1920s' prosperity, were switching from Republican ranks to the Democrats. Coolidge had carried the twelve largest cities in 1924, but all twelve voted for Smith in 1928. Farmers in the Midwest, upset over continuing low prices for farm commodities, also voted for Smith. Smith also got about half the black vote in northern cities. A new coalition of northern blacks, ethnics, urban workers, and dissatisfied farmers was in the making. This coalition waited upon the economic collapse that was just around the corner.

BIBLIOGRAPHY

The best book ever done on the 1920s is Frederick Lewis Allen's famed *Only Yesterday: An Informal History of the 1920s*, a relatively brief, entertaining account that highlights the frivolity and disillusionment of the era. William E. Leuchtenburg, *The Perils of Prosperity* is the best scholarly history of the New Era. A fine recent account is Geoffrey Perrett, *America in the Twenties*. Isabel Leighton, editor, *The Aspirin Age* is a fine collection of essays on various events and personalities of the 1920s and 1930s. Elting E. Morison, *From Know-How to Nowhere* is a remarkable account of the development of American industrial technology during the 1920s. James J. Flink, *The Car Culture* is the best study we have of the impact of mass ownership of automobiles on American life. The best biography of the man who put America on wheels is Allen Nevins and F. E. Hill, *Ford: The Times, the Man, and the Company*. George Soule, *Prosperity Decade: From War to Depression, 1917–1929* is the best short economic history of the 1920s. Irving Berstein,

The Lean Years: A History of the American Worker, 1920–1933 is the best 1920s labor history. On advertising, see Roland Marchand, *Advertising the American Dream: Making Way for Modernity, 1920–1940.* John D. Hicks, *The Republican Ascendancy* is a solid survey of the political history of the 1920s. The most balanced treatment of the Harding presidency is Robert K. Murray, *The Harding Era.* The best biography of Calvin Coolidge is Donald McCoy, *Calvin Coolidge.* Allan J. Lichtman, *Prejudice and the Old Politics: The Presidential Election of 1928* is an excellent treatment of the cultural conflicts that underlay American political life during the 1920s.

CHAPTER
6
The Roaring Twenties

As Americans rushed headlong into modernity during the 1920s, propelled by the accelerating forces of technological and societal change, they had to cope with tensions and conflicts that seethed within their culture. Within the cities which had become the centers of American life, people enthusiastically embraced the new consumerism, the latest fads and fashions, and the flourishing popular culture. In the countryside, where traditionalists held sway, people strongly resisted, or tried to resist, those powerful currents of modernity that appeared to be undermining traditional family and religious values. Consequently a kind of cultural schizophrenia prevailed in 1920s America; Americans managed to be both happy to embrace modernity and content to wax nostalgically for that "ole time religion" and the simpler, more tranquil, and more innocent way of life that it represented. The new was here to stay, but the old yielded ground slowly and grudgingly. A generation of Americans, nervous about rapid social change and the erosion of traditional values, tried in many ways to preserve the old while embracing the new.

It was in the cities and suburbs of the "Roaring Twenties" that the new mass consumer culture flourished. Urbanites dined out, went to movies, and attended sporting events. They embraced fads such as crossword puzzles, Mah-Jongg, miniature golf, and marathon dancing. Most speakeasies (illegal bars and clubs during Prohibition) were located in cities where patrons could drink, wear garish clothes, and listen to jazz. Cities were also the center of a growing social and cultural pluralism in American life; women, immigrants, racial minorities, and religious denominations all struggled to adapt and to succeed. America's towns and villages, on the other hand, remained mostly homogeneous WASP (white Anglo-Saxon Protestant) enclaves.

WOMEN, WORK, AND FAMILY LIFE

Family life changed. Birth control became more effective and more widely practiced during the 1920s. Birthrates and family size dropped sharply. Average family size shrank from six or seven members in 1900 to four or five members by 1930. Divorce rates rose sharply. In 1920 there was one divorce for every eight marriages; by 1929 the ratio of divorces to marriage was 2 to 7. Young people were spending more years in school, lengthening adolescence and postponing the time when they would enter the work force. High school enrollment quadrupled between World War I and 1930. By 1929 one-third of all high school graduates were going on to college, more women than men.

Schools and peer groups played a much more important role in socializing children than before the war. Classes, sports, and social clubs brought young people of the same age together. A middle-class youth culture made its appearance with its own values, consumer preferences, and lifestyles, often conflicting with those of their parents. Prolonged adolescence led to strains on the family as youngsters rebelled against parental authority and their Victorian moral standards. Middle-class youngsters, freed from having to go to work at an early age, went on a spree. Novelist F. Scott Fitzgerald recorded the heavy drinking, casual sexual encounters, and constant search for thrills and excitement among upper-class youth in *This Side of Paradise*. The theme of rebellion characterized this generation of "flaming youth."

Improved nutrition, health care, and easier lives caused average life expectancy to increase from 54 to 60 years during the decade. The number of people aged 65 and older increased by one-third between 1920 and 1930; the elderly were the most rapidly growing demographic group in the population. Retirement communities sprang up in the warm climes of Florida and southern California. It was also during the 1920s that median female life expectancy exceeded male life expectancy for the first time in history. Lengthened female life expectancy was caused mainly by the reduced dangers of pregnancy and childbearing. Infant mortality rates decreased by two-thirds also.

The elderly emerged during the Twenties as a large, growing population category with distinct needs and preferences. Many of the elderly were poor because of forced retirement and the lack of pensions. In the 1920s few private employers and no government provided pension plans. Progressive reformers of the 1920s developed ways of meeting the economic needs of some of the elderly poor. Most states implemented old-age pensions during the decade, and the principle of old-age support through pensions, insurance programs, and retirement homes was established. Foundations were laid for a national program of old-age insurance, which was implemented during the Thirties.

The new lifestyles of the 1920s had a major effect on the lives of women. Middle-class women had fewer children to rear. Their houses often had central heating and hot water heaters. They used vacuum cleaners, electric irons, electric sewing machines, electric stoves, and washing machines to lighten domestic duties. They bought preserved foods, ready-made clothing, and mass-produced furniture. Women were no longer domestic producers or beasts of burden as their mothers and grandmothers had been. They were now household managers and were responsible for much of their family's consumer spending.

Although domesticity remained the most common realm of women, millions joined the labor force during the 1920s. In 1920 about 8 million women worked outside the home; by 1930 about 11 million had jobs. But traditional patterns of gender discrimination continued during the 1920s. Women earned about half of what men did for comparable work; most women worked in "female jobs" where few males were found—teachers, nurses, typists, bookkeepers, clerical workers, department store sales clerks, waitresses, maids, and hairdressers. The number of women working in factories, 2 million, did not increase during the decade. The number of women in some professions declined. Although women earned about one-third of all graduate degrees awarded during the 1920s, they made up only 4 percent of college faculties. The professions remained mostly male bastions.

Before the 1920s most working women had been young, single females from poor backgrounds who had to work. A few had been middle-class careerists, mostly unmarried doctors, attorneys, scientists, or academics. During the 1920s, however, married women entered the labor force in significantly increased numbers. Some married women were responding to the pressures of poverty; more were working to supplement family income and to enhance their family's lifestyle. Most married working women claimed they worked because of economic necessity, but their definition of need reflected new consumer values. Their families "needed" radios, a new car, and a larger home. Nevertheless, only about 10 percent of married women worked outside the home during the 1920s.

Feminists continued to be active during the 1920s. With the battle for the vote won, they concentrated on issues involving women in the workplace, such as greater economic opportunity and equal pay. Alice Paul, leader of a new organization, the National Woman's Party, supported an equal rights amendment introduced in Congress in 1923. Some feminists, including the League of Women Voters, opposed the equal rights amendment because they believed that women needed special legal protections, particularly laws guaranteeing them a minimum wage and setting a ceiling on their work hours. They feared the courts would nullify these protective laws for women if the equal rights amendment were ratified. The drive to enact the ERA during the 1920s failed. So did feminist campaigns to improve the economic status of women and to abolish child labor. Feminists succeeded in getting the Sheppard-Towner Act (1921) passed, which authorized federal aid to states to establish maternal and infant health care programs. Also feminists continued to be involved in local and state progressive reform politics, pushing for consumer protection legislation and for the inclusion of women on juries.

A generational change had a major effect on feminism during the 1920s. New images of femininity emerged. Young women were more interested in individual freedom of expression than they were in political reform or social progress. Some adopted what H. L. Mencken called the "flapper image." Short skirts and bobbed hair, signals of sexual freedom, spread on college campuses and in offices. Young women rouged their cheeks, smoked cigarettes, swore, drank at parties, danced to the beat of "hot jazz" combos, and necked in the back seats of automobiles. Premarital sex increased and became less scandalous as Victorian inhibitions declined.

There was another important consequence of the sexual revolution of the 1920s: The modern custom of "dating" replaced the old Victorian practice of calling. No longer did young women of marriageable age invite young men to their homes in the presence of chaperones. Automobiles and city life created new possibilities; besides, many modern homes lacked parlors or porches. Young men increasingly invited young women out on dates, to attend a movie, maybe have dinner in a nice restaurant, or just go for a drive along the lake in his flivver.

Dating also shifted the social initiative from women to men. Because it was assumed that a proper young lady did not work and the man did, he paid. Dating was incorporated into the new consumer culture of the 1920s; it became an act of consumption in which the woman sold her company to the highest bidder. Dating also became competitive, placing a premium on the young lady's physical appearance (her "looks") and her personality. Physical beauty and personal vivacity became valuable marketable commodities in the dating game. It was important for women to have many dates with different men, and for men to be seen in fashionable places with attractive women. Women who dated were also expected to neck and pet; men expected these favors in return for having spent money on them.

Popular female movie stars such as Clara Bow, the "It Girl," and Gloria Swanson, a passionate screen lover, became role models for young women. The mass media promoted the flapper image as a new woman whose manners and morals resembled those of her male counterparts. As one critic put it, "there was now a single standard for men and women, and that a low one." Women, especially young middle-class women, were liberated from many social restraints of the prewar era. Flappers competed with men on the golf course and in the speakeasies. They expected sexual fulfillment before and during marriage.

It is important not to exaggerate the extent to which women participated in the new trends of the 1920s. A contemporary survey of over 2,000 middle-class women found that only 7 percent of them had engaged in premarital sex. The typical American woman of the 1920s did not work outside the home, and she lived in a household that could not afford most of the new labor-saving appliances of the age. The average housewife-mother spent about 50 hours per week performing household duties. The typical girl continued to play with dolls and was socialized in traditional ways to become a housewife and mother as her mother had before her. Boys continued to play "cowboys and Indians" and grew up to head their families and compete in the marketplace as their fathers had done. According to feminist historian June Sochen, "In the 1920s, as in the 1790s, marriage was the only approved state for women."

AFRICAN AMERICANS

African American sharecroppers fled the deteriorating southern agricultural economy for northern cities, continuing a trend that had begun during the war. African American newcomers to city life were forced to squeeze into northern ghettos as they discovered that better neighborhoods were closed to them. As African American families moved into these cheaper neighborhoods, the remaining whites usually moved out. The black population of New York, Chicago, and Detroit doubled during the decade.

Even though the black unemployment rate was high, at least double the rate of white workers, and the wage level generally lower, the living standard for northern urban blacks was considerably higher than that of African Americans in the rural South. Northern urban blacks also found that segregation in the cities was generally less thorough than in the South. Community life formed around the black churches, mostly Protestant. Many blacks opened small businesses, and a solid black middle class emerged in New York, Chicago, and other northern cities during the 1920s. African Americans also acquired political influence at the local level because of their population concentration. In 1928 Oscar DePriest of Chicago, a Republican, became the first black Congressman elected in the twentieth century.

Thousands of northern African Americans during the early 1920s joined a black nationalist movement led by a Jamaican immigrant, Marcus Garvey. This was the first mass movement of African Americans. Garvey denounced all whites as corrupt and preached a doctrine of black separatism. He promoted race pride and black capitalism and told his listeners that Jesus had been a black man. He also fostered a "back to Africa" campaign and founded a steamship line to foster emigration. Garvey was attacked by African American leaders like Dubois. Although a charismatic leader and a rousing speaker who could energize blacks, Garvey proved an incompetent businessman. He lost the money of his investors when his steamship company went bankrupt. In 1923 he was convicted of mail fraud and sent to federal prison. Two years later President Coolidge pardoned him but deported him; Garvey held a British passport. Garvey's movement quickly disintegrated but he had tapped a wellspring of black grievances and aspirations.

HISPANIC AMERICANS

Hispanic emigrants also poured into America's cities during the 1920s. *Campesinos* from northern Mexico, fleeing rural poverty and revolutionary disorder, moved into California and the southwestern desert states. During the decade an estimated 300,000 to 400,000 Mexicans emigrated to the United States, flocking to the growing cities of Los Angeles, Tucson, and San Antonio. By 1925 Los Angeles had the largest Spanish-speaking population in North America except for Mexico City. These Mexican immigrants also confronted residential segregation, and they crowded into low-rent inner city districts to form their own communities or *barrios*.

As European immigration declined because of America's restrictive immigration policies that gradually went into place during the 1920s, the demand for Mexican labor increased. Because the Mexican immigrants were poor and unorganized, they had little bargaining leverage but a great need for work. They worked for low wages, often entire families, and were forced to live under primitive conditions. Families crowded into hovels and shacks, without running water or indoor toilets. The children often had to work in the fields and so had scant opportunities for attending school. Despite encountering racism and segregation, some urban Mexican Americans established profitable businesses, joined the middle class, and saw their children get good educations.

During the 1920s thousands of Puerto Ricans moved to mainland America. They represented a surplus rural population attracted by economic opportunities in the states. Puerto Rican communities formed in Brooklyn and Manhattan. These migrants found work in hotels, restaurants, and domestic service.

NATIVE AMERICANS

Ironically, Native Americans, who had the priority claim to being "American," ranked at the bottom of the social ladder during the 1920s and endured the most severe hardships. These first Americans were last in taking advantage of the opportunities created by the prosperous consumer economy of the 1920s. Thousands of American Indians died each year from disease, starvation, suicide, murder, and alcoholism. The infant mortality rate was the highest of that of any major ethnic group within the United States. The Native American unemployment rate was the highest and the longevity rate the lowest for any group.

Federal Indian policy was characterized by indifference and neglect. Government officials continued to implement the Dawes Act policy of assimilation and maintained their cruel efforts to eliminate all traces of Native American art, language, diet, and religious practices. Few American Indians attended school or were able to get good jobs. Most Native Americans during the 1920s were confined to reservations, where they lived in shacks without running water, indoor plumbing, or central heating. Most endured a hard, poor life with no real chance of escape or improvement. Their children could expect the same.

THE ETHIC OF PLAY

Even as they tried to preserve old values, many Americans were irresistibly attracted to the new order. During the 1920s millions of Americans turned enthusiastically to varieties of recreation, as both participants and spectators. In 1929 Americans spent over $4 billion on play, a figure that would not be surpassed until the 1950s. The entertainment industry became big business as promoters hurried to satisfy the great American need for fun. Fads flowered and ballyhoo flourished.

Fashions and fads flashed across the recreational landscape during the Twenties. Early in the decade it was Mah-Jongg, a game imported from China, played with sets of tiles. In 1924 and 1925 crossword puzzles seized the popular fancy. Every newspaper and mass circulation magazine carried crossword puzzles. A new card game invented by a group of American socialites, contract bridge, became popular. In the late 1920s it was miniature golf that was the rage. By 1930 an estimated 30,000 miniature golf courses hosted millions of players each week. Throughout the decade various dance crazes such as the Charleston and Black Bottom attracted millions of enthusiasts.

GOING TO THE MOVIES

Americans became avid moviegoers during the 1920s. Motion pictures became a major art form, a mass medium, and big business. Almost every community had at least one movie theater. Movie houses ranged from small-town storefronts to big city luxury palaces. In 1925, 60 million people attended movies each week. By 1930 the figure had reached 100 million, nearly twice the average weekly church attendance.

The most popular movies were grand spectaculars such as *The Ten Commandments* (1923), slapstick comedies starring Charlie Chaplin, and adventure films like *Robin Hood* (1925), starring Douglas Fairbanks. Movie romances also had large audiences. John Gilbert and Greta Garbo were the most famous screen lovers of the silent film era, their passionate lovemaking enthralling audiences everywhere. Moviegoers idolized and often identified with film stars, who ranked among the reigning celebrities of the 1920s. Mass circulation gossip magazines offered lurid details of their private lives to credulous fans.

The most ballyhooed movie star of the 1920s was Rudolph Valentino, an Italian immigrant whose passionate Latin machismo caused women in the audience to sigh and faint. Valentino's films played upon sexual fantasies and thrilling encounters with evil. In his most famous role he played an Arab sheik, a combination kidnapper and seducer, who lifted women into his arms and carried them into his tent. When he died of ulcers at age 31 in 1926, his New York funeral was a public spectacle. Crowds lined up for over a mile to file past his coffin. Police had to fend off thousands of weeping women who tried to throw themselves on his corpse.

The 1920s was the great age of silent films. The beginning of their

Rudolph Valentino was Hollywood's greatest romantic idol during the 1920s (pictured here with co-star Nita Naldi).

end came when sound was introduced in *The Jazz Singer*, starring Al Jolson, in 1927, although studios continued to turn out silent films into the 1930s. Sound had its hazards, however, for some of the great silent screen stars turned out to have squeaky or harsh voices unsuitable for talking films. John Gilbert was sound's most famous casualty. The great screen lover had to retire from moviemaking for want of a voice.

SPECTATOR SPORTS

Spectator sports also boomed in the 1920s. Each year millions of fans packed stadia and arenas to watch college football, major league baseball, auto racing, boxing, horse racing, and tennis. Sporting events provided excitement, thrills, and drama. Sportswriters and radio sportscasters described athletic contests and reported results. Many sportswriters were also ballyhoo artists, promoting and hyping ball games and boxing matches.

Baseball was the most popular spectator sport of the 1920s. Attendance at major league games increased vastly early in the decade when owners introduced a livelier ball that enabled powerful hitters to belt home runs into the stands, and sometimes out of the park. More than 20 million spectators attended games in 1927. The most popular baseball player of the 1920s, the most famous athlete-celebrity of his era, was George Herman "Babe" Ruth. The Babe hit 60 home runs in 1927 and led the New York Yankees to a World Series sweep over the Pittsburgh Pirates. Ruth was legendary for his off-the-field exploits as well. He was a glutton for food, drink, and women. The Babe missed almost two months of the 1925 season because of a mysterious illness, which was publicly diagnosed as a stomachache but was in reality venereal disease picked up during a nighttime adventure. People tended to forgive the Babe for his transgressions, for he was a remarkable athlete and he also spent a lot of his time visiting with youngsters and signing autographs.

Second in popularity only to Ruth was Jack Dempsey, a powerful fighter with a lethal punch who was heavyweight champion from 1921 until 1926. Dempsey's fights were often savage brawls and drew huge gates. In a fight with Luis Firpo, an Argentine slugger, Dempsey got knocked out of the ring. He managed to crawl back through the ropes and knock Firpo out in the third round. In 1926 Dempsey lost his title to Gene Tunney, a skilled boxer, via a decision, and he failed to regain the title in a rematch the following year at Soldier Field in Chicago. The second Dempsey–Tunney fight drew 145,000 fans, the largest crowd ever to see an athletic event in the United States.

Other athletes enjoyed celebrity status in the 1920s. William "Big Bill" Tilden was a champion tennis player. Earl Sande was the finest jockey. Man O' War was a great equine champion, considered one of the greatest racehorses ever. Gertrude Ederle, a 17-year-old schoolgirl, became the first woman to swim the English Channel—and set a new record doing it. She returned to New York to receive a stupendous ticker tape parade. The greatest college football player of the decade was Harold "Red" Grange, a running back for the University of Illinois, and three-time All-American. Grange was a talented broken-field runner who thrilled spectators with his long touchdown runs. He was a celebrity when still in college, receiving lucrative offers from movie studios and real estate promoters. During his first year in professional football, fans urged him to run for Congress, although he was only 22 years old.

Black athletes during the 1920s were barred from major league baseball and were rare in other professional sports. African American baseball players did have opportunities to play on all-black professional teams, however. African American athletes had their best opportunities to participate in major sports in high school and college, although most were forced to attend segregated institutions. At the 1924 Olympic Games in Paris, DeHart Hubbard won a gold medal in the men's long jump, becoming the first African American athlete to win an Olympic gold medal.

AN AMERICAN HERO

The greatest hero of the 1920s was neither a movie star nor a professional athlete; he was a young aviator named Charles Augustus Lindbergh. In May 1927 Lindbergh flew solo nonstop across the Atlantic from New York

In a hero-worshipping age, Charles A. Lindbergh was the greatest hero of all for his solo flight across the Atlantic in May 1927. Here, he stands before "The Spirit of St. Louis," the plane in which he made his historic flight.

to Paris in $33\frac{1}{2}$ hours in a small monoplane named "The Spirit of Saint Louis." His feat was the greatest news story of the decade. President Coolidge sent the cruiser USS *Augusta* to bring Lindbergh home to the wildest celebration of the decade.

Lindbergh was a handsome, modest middle-class midwesterner who did not try to cash in on his fame. His quiet personality, at variance with the frantic hype and ballyhoo of the decade, caused Americans to honor him more. Lindbergh's flight also represented a triumph of American industrial technology, a point that Lindbergh made repeatedly. It was the machine that had been specially configured for the long flight, as much as the man, who made the crossing possible. A contemporary observer also suggested that the intense emotional response Lindbergh provoked in this country was a reaction to his clean-cut appearance, WASP background, and moral character. In an age of ballyhoo and change, Lindbergh affirmed traditional values. Will Rogers, an actor and humorist, said Lindbergh's flight proved that "someone could still make the front pages without murdering anybody."

RELIGIONS IN CONFLICT

Most of the "new" immigrants coming to America from the 1890s until America closed its doors in the late 1920s were either Catholics or Jews. By the 1920s nearly 25 million Catholics resided in the United States and Catholicism had become the nation's largest religious denomination. Immigration had dramatically increased the size and influence of the Catholic Church in America, an increase that provoked an intensely hostile response from millions of American Protestants. Anti-Catholicism was a major nativist current flowing through the 1920s culture. Al Smith's 1928 presidential bid aroused unprecedented hostility among Protestants in the South and Midwest.

Millions of Jews also emigrated to the United States during the 1890s–1920s. In 1890 there were about 400,000 Jews living in the United States; in 1920 there were over 4 million. Just as was the case with Catholics, the large influx of Jews to America and the rapid assimilation of many of them into the middle-class mainstream provoked an intense hostility among established Americans. Anti-Semitism was also a major nativist component of the 1920s culture. Although most Eastern European Jews had arrived in America poor, they rose more rapidly than any other group. By the 1920s Jews had become prominent financiers, doctors, lawyers, writers, artists, and scholars. Most Jews were more liberal politically than the American population as a whole. They achieved prominence as labor leaders, civil libertarians, and philanthropists.

If there was conflict and tension among Protestants, Catholics, and Jews, there was also much intramural conflict within Protestant denominations. Many Protestant churches were split into liberal and conservative factions. Liberal churches experienced loss of membership as fundamentalist churches grew rapidly during the 1920s. Some Protestant churches were influenced by the new business culture of the Twenties. Church leaders talked about productivity; some hired efficiency experts and referred to ministers as "salesmen of God." Some businessmen viewed churches as businesses with a product to sell—salvation.

During the 1920s millions of Americans turned to religious fundamentalism. They sought certainty in a rapidly changing society by joining evangelical Protestant churches, which embraced a literal interpretation of the Bible. Unquestioning faith in the revealed word of God brought fundamentalists both a means of salvation and protection against a materialistic and skeptical social order. The leading fundamentalist of the early 1920s was Billy Sunday, who had been a ballplayer, a pitcher in the major leagues. Sunday was a fiery, charismatic preacher. When he pitched the gospel, hundreds, even thousands, would come forward, moved by the sheer force of his fervent rhetoric. Sunday preached against many of the fashionable trends of the 1920s; he condemned smoking, drinking, dancing, adultery, and the movies. Another famous evangelist of the 1920s, a Canadian named Aimee Semple McPherson, was known for her faith-healing sermons emanating from Angelus Temple in Los Angeles. The Angelus Temple was an inspiring structure, built at a cost of $2 million, and seating over 5,000. The faithful came to hear McPherson preach the gospel, save souls, and heal the sick. Fundamentalists like Sunday and McPherson provoked laughter and ridicule from modernists who considered them mountebanks and their followers antiquated morons. Fundamentalists responded to their critics by calling them sinners and infidels, who lived degenerate lives while on this earth and were doomed to spend eternity suffering the everlasting torments of hellfire and damnation.

Fundamentalists, who were most numerous and politically influential in southern states, campaigned for laws prohibiting the teaching of Darwinian evolutionary theory in public schools and colleges. They did not want young people being taught that human beings had evolved by natural processes over vast stretches of time from lower forms of life, a theory contradicting the Biblical version of Divine creation. Tennessee was one state that passed an anti-evolutionism law.

THE MONKEY TRIAL

In 1925 scientific theory and revealed religion collided in a courtroom in Dayton, Tennessee. By teaching his class evolutionary theory, John Scopes, a young high school biology teacher, deliberately violated the state's anti-evolutionism statute to provide a test case. The trial became front-page news in the summer of 1925 when prominent public figures involved themselves on both sides of the controversy. William Jennings Bryan, three-time presidential candidate and longtime spokesman for traditional values, joined the prosecution. Clarence Darrow, the country's most successful trial lawyer and prominent reformer, headed a defense team of civil libertarians who had volunteered their services because they believed that an important constitutional issue was at stake in the "Monkey Trial." It was also covered by radio, which was fast becoming a mass medium.

The emotional highlight of the trial came when Darrow cross-examined Bryan about his beliefs. Darrow exposed Bryan's ignorance of science and his fundamentalist religious views. The old Populist insisted that Eve had been created from Adam's rib and that a whale had swallowed Jonah. He told Darrow, "If God wanted a sponge to think, a sponge could think." He also quipped, "It's better to know the Rock of Ages than the age of rocks." Liberal intellectuals and educated, secular people laughed at Bryan's simplistic ideas. H. L. Mencken, a prominent journalist covering the trial, savagely satirized the old man's beliefs, delighting sophisticated readers on college campuses.

Bryan and the fundamentalists won their case in court. The Tennessee state prosecutor won a conviction against Scopes on the grounds that the legislature had the right to determine what was taught in public schools within the state. Darrow appealed the conviction, but the Tennessee state supreme court sustained the state's right to ban the teaching of unpopular theories even if they were valid scientifically. The court also outmaneuvered the defense attorneys when it overturned Scopes' conviction on a procedural technicality that prevented the defense from taking the case to the U.S. Supreme Court. Tennessee's anti-evolutionism law remained on the books, as did similar laws in other states.

Additional states soon passed anti-evolutionism laws. Publishers removed accounts of Darwinian theory from high school biology textbooks. By 1930, 70 percent of high school biology classes did not teach evolutionary biology, far more than in 1920, when the fundamentalists began their crusade. Modernists might scoff at Bryan's antiquated views, Darrow might have reduced the old man's ideas to intellectual rubble, but Bryan and his fundamentalist cohorts won the battle to influence young people's minds, which was the most important issue at stake in the "Monkey Trial."

THE REVIVAL OF THE KLAN

In another reactionary movement of the 1920s, the revived Ku Klux Klan, millions of Americans defended traditional values against the forces of change. The new Klan was founded in 1915 by William J. Simmons, an Atlanta insurance salesman. Simmons claimed he was reviving the terrorist organization that had intimidated and brutalized blacks during Reconstruction in order to purge southern culture of what he termed corrupting influences. The new Klan adopted the earlier organization's cloth hoods, mystical terms, secrecy, and vicious tactics, and it achieved a far larger membership than the old Klan. Simmons also added some innovations to the new organization. Unlike the original Klan, Simmons prohibited Jews, Catholics, and aliens from joining. He also adopted the burning cross as a symbol; the Reconstruction Klan had not burned crosses.

The new organization spread nationally and during the early 1920s the "Invisible Empire" claimed 5 million members. The 1920s Klan represented a powerful current in the political and social mainstream, often allying itself with Protestant church congregations and local leaders in southern and midwestern communities. It achieved significant political influence in various regions of the country and wielded power within the Democratic Party in several states. At its peak it had considerable strength in urban areas. It was especially strong in Indiana, Ohio, and Illinois. The Klan membership in California during the 1920s was far larger than its membership in deep South states such as Alabama and Mississippi.

The new Klan also sought a broader range of targets than did its predecessor. It tapped powerful nativist sentiments that asserted native, white Protestant supremacy not only over blacks, but also over immigrants, Catholics, Jews, radicals, and anyone who violated the Klan's sense of moral order. They intimidated, beat up, and occasionally murdered blacks. They administered vigilante justice to bootleggers, prostitutes, and

The "invisible empire" of Ku Klux Klan members marching in full regalia in front of the nation's capitol in 1926.

adulterers. They campaigned against Catholic and Jewish political candidates. Klansmen considered parochial schools to be a threat to the Protestant nation and tried to close them down. They forced schools to adopt Bible readings and to stop teaching evolutionary theory. They beat up trade union organizers and harassed immigrant families.

During the mid-1920s the Klan went into rapid decline. Scandals helped undermine its appeal. Some members became involved in bootlegging and racketeering. One of its leaders, Grand Dragon David C. Stephenson, a political power in Indiana, was convicted of murdering a young woman whom he had kidnapped and raped. After he went to prison, he exposed some of his political associates. Klan membership and Klan power in Indiana evaporated. The Klan's last hurrah was helping to defeat Al Smith in 1928. By the end of the decade the Klan's brand of coercive, exclusive patriotism gradually lost much of its appeal within a pluralistic society.

CLOSING THE DOOR

Another powerful reactionary current flowing through the early 1920s sprang from native-born Americans' prejudices against the "new" immigrants, those from southern and eastern Europe. Since the 1880s nativist organizations, labor leaders, and some progressive reformers had urged an end to unrestricted immigration. Nativists complained that these newcomers were inherently inferior, with alien habits and beliefs which they did not abandon, and that they polluted native stock. They also feared that Catholic private schools would undermine the American system of public education. Labor leaders charged the "new" immigrants with lowering wage levels, raising unemployment, refusing to join unions, and working as strikebreakers. Some reformers argued that the immigrants crowding inner city slums exacerbated urban problems, supported corrupt political machines, and formed a permanent underclass of unassimilable aliens.

The drive to restrict immigration gained momentum during and after World War I. Over President Wilson's veto, Congress enacted a Literacy Test Act in 1917 which required immigrants to be literate in any language. The Red Scare strengthened anti-immigrant movements by heightening fears of radical aliens importing revolutionary ideologies and tactics. Businessmen, who had previously championed free immigration because it gave them a pool of low-wage workers, installed assembly-line technologies that cut labor costs and decreased their need for workers.

Social scientists also joined the cause of immigration restriction when they misinterpreted the findings of intelligence tests the Army had given draftees during World War I. They found that recruits from southern and eastern European countries scored much lower than soldiers whose ancestors had come from the British Isles, northern, and western

Europe. The tests really measured educational levels attained and the cultural opportunities experienced, but scientists assumed that they measured innate intellectual abilities, confirming the nativist assumption that the "new" immigrants were of lower intelligence than old-stock Americans.

When immigration after the war threatened to reach the prewar level despite the literacy test, Congress enacted restrictive legislation that reduced immigration generally, sharply curtailed immigration from southern and eastern Europe, and excluded Asians. In 1921 Congress enacted the Emergency Quota Act, according to which immigrants equal to 3 percent of the number of foreign-born residents of the United States could enter each year. This number amounted to about 350,000 people, since there were 11.7 million foreign-born Americans according to the 1910 census. Each country's portion of the 350,000 was determined by the number of its nationals already resident in the United States. For example, there were about 1.3 million Italians, which amounted to 11 percent of the foreign-born population in 1910; Italy therefore got 11 percent of the 350,000 slots, 38,500 places, for the year 1922.

The Emergency Quota Act was a temporary measure. Following extensive study and hearings, Congress enacted a comprehensive measure in 1924, the National Origins Act, which would define U.S. immigration policy for the next 40 years. The act phased in a more restrictive system that reduced the "new" immigration to an annual trickle and banned Asians altogether, but it allowed sizable numbers of immigrants from northern and western Europe to continue to enter America.

By its terms, beginning in 1925 immigration equal to only 2 percent of the foreign-born population living in the United States in 1890 could enter the country. Since the 1890 population had been about 7.5 million, only 150,000 people could enter annually. This law both sharply reduced total immigration and further limited "new" immigration because most southern and eastern Europeans residing in the United States had arrived after 1890. For example, of the 7.5 million foreign-born residents in the country in 1890, only 450,000, 6 percent, were Italians. Hence Italy's 1925 quota came to only 9,000 slots compared with 38,500 under the Emergency Quota Act.

Congress amended the National Origins Act in 1927 to establish an immigration system that kept the 150,000 annual quota but further reduced the number of "new" immigrants allowed to enter. Starting in 1929, each nation's quota was based not on a percentage of the foreign-born population living in the United States, but on the national origins of the entire European population of the country according to the 1920 census. For example, there were about 3.8 million Americans of Italian descent residing in the United States in 1920, counting both those born in Italy and their descendants born in America. They composed 4 percent of the 96 million total European population in 1920, so Italy got 4 percent of the

150,000 immigration slots available in 1929, or 6,000 openings. Between 1900 and 1910, before the country adopted restrictive immigration policies, about 1.6 million Italians had come to the United States, an average of 160,000 annually. All southern and eastern European nationalities suffered similar sharp reductions in their quotas. What had been a flood before World War I became a trickle after 1929.

In practice, the national origins quota system reduced immigration below the 150,000 allowed annually because it assigned large quotas to western and northern European nations that did not use all of their assigned slots each year. Most of Great Britain's annual 65,000 slots went unused during the depression years of the 1930s, and these unused slots did not transfer to other nations. Meanwhile in Italy and other southern and eastern European countries, which had small quotas, a huge backlog of potential immigrants built up.

The national origins system was designed to preserve the ethnic and racial status quo that had prevailed during the 1920s. It also reflected current nativist assumptions and prejudices. America sent a message to the world with its new immigration policy: If you were white, Anglo-Saxon, and preferably Protestant, you were welcome. If you were Catholic, Jewish, or Slavic, a few of you could come each year. If you were Asian, you were excluded. America, which had opened its doors to the people of the world as no nation ever had, now closed the "golden door" to all except a few favored nationalities. The national origins system severely compromised the inspiring verse on the base of the Statue of Liberty, "Give me your tired, your poor, your huddled masses yearning to breathe free."

Religious fundamentalism, the Ku Klux Klan, and immigration restriction represented reactionary efforts by traditionalists to preserve an older, simpler, and (from their perspective) purer America against spreading modernism and urban-industrial values. Traditionalists attempted to sustain old values in the midst of a dynamic materialistic, hedonistic, and pluralistic society.

THE AGE OF THE SPEAKEASY

In their heedless pursuit of fun, Americans in the 1920s became lawbreakers and supporters of organized crime. Americans had voted for Prohibition, which took effect January 1, 1920. Initially the law was effective; per capita liquor consumption dropped sharply. Prohibition was especially effective in the South and Midwest, where it had strong popular support. But the Prohibition Bureau, charged with enforcement of the law, had a small budget and only a few thousand agents, many of whom were inept, corrupt, or both. After 1925 enforcement declined in urban areas. Smuggling and home manufacture of liquor increased. Many people made beer, wine, and "bathtub" gin. Foreign booze was brought across the nation's long borders and shorelines. Local police stopped enforcing Prohibition in many cities.

Illegal drinking became a big business with millions of customers, and criminal organizations moved into the illicit liquor industry. The most notorious of these crooked businesses was headed by Al Capone, whose mob seized control of the liquor and vice trade in Chicago. Capone maintained his power for years through bribery, threats, and violence. During the 1920s more than 500 gangland murders occurred on the streets of Chicago, many involving Capone's hired gunmen. Capone's organization took in an estimated $60 million a year. He was immune from local reprisals but ran afoul of the FBI. Capone was convicted of income tax evasion and sent to prison in 1931. He died years later of syphilis.

Americans during the 1920s were caught between two conflicting value systems. They retained traditional ethics of hard work, thrift, and sobriety, and at the same time they embraced the new ethic of play. They turned to mass entertainment provided by nightclubs, movies, sports, and radio. They also took up individual hobbies and amusements such as photography, stamp collecting, playing and listening to music, and camping. Most such activities were neither illegal nor immoral, but millions of Americans were willing to break the law or reject traditional morality if such restrictions interfered with their pursuit of pleasure.

POPULAR WRITERS

During the 1920s Americans read millions of books, but most did not read serious works of literature. Most critically acclaimed writers of the 1920s whose reputations have endured and whose books have become classics did not sell well during the decade. The most popular writers of the 1920s, whose books sold millions of copies and who perennially topped the best-seller charts, included Geneva "Gene" Stratton-Porter, Harold Bell Wright, Zane Grey, and Edgar Rice Burroughs.

Gene Stratton-Porter became rich writing novels that affirmed traditional values during a transitional era. Her books championed the virtues of optimism, a love for nature, and triumph over adversity. Harold Bell Wright, formerly a minister, was a prolific writer, turning out a book every two years for twenty years. He used his novels as didactic vehicles to preach the gospel of hard work and clean living. Zane Grey, a dentist turned writer, was the most popular of the 1920s novelists. His books went on the best-seller lists every year during the decade, and total sales for the era exceeded 20 million copies. His novels were usually set in a highly romanticized version of the Old West, and many of them were transformed into Western movies. Grey wrote more than 50 novels and was the most widely read novelist of his age. Edgar Rice Burroughs made his fame and fortune as the author of the Tarzan books. Burroughs' novels were purely escapist fare—stories about the adventures of a white man in Africa who had been reared by apes. Tarzan became the inspiration for cartoons, comic books, and dozens of films starring several different athletic actors.

Americans during the Twenties were also enthusiastic readers of newspapers. The trend toward consolidation in the industrial economy also occurred in the newspaper business. Ownership of newspapers was increasingly concentrated in the hands of a few media magnates such as William Randolph Hearst. Even though newspaper readership increased by millions during the decade, in 1929 there were 2,000 fewer papers than in 1919. Tabloid newspapers made their appearance during the 1920s, led by the pioneer in the field, *The New York Daily News.* Tabloids sensationalized and simplified news stories and also contained lots of comics, sports news, features, photographs, and puzzles.

THE LOST GENERATION

The most impressive cultural achievement of Americans during the 1920s was a vast outpouring of literature. American literature enjoyed its most creative era since the American Renaissance of the 1840s and 1850s. Urban America produced a generation of literary intellectuals who attacked the new consumer culture and its values. Many of the young writers had been involved in the war and came home traumatized and disillusioned by the great crusade to save democracy. The war experience shattered their lives and destroyed their progressive idealism. They were bewildered by rapid social change and appalled by the shallow materialism of the New Era. They condemned the excesses of the new business civilization and lamented the loss of American innocence.

One of the new writers was Ezra Pound, who developed new forms of poetic expression. He abandoned rhyme and meter to use clear, cold images that powerfully conveyed reality. Pound called the Western world that had waged four years of destructive warfare a "botched civilization, an old bitch gone in the teeth." He wrote of the hellish experience of American soldiers fighting on the Western Front and then coming home to a society they found empty and disillusioning.

T. S. Eliot, born in St. Louis, moved to England and later became a British citizen. His greatest poem, published in 1922, is "The Waste Land." It is a long, difficult work expressing Eliot's profound despair about modern life and its loss of faith. He evoked images of sterility and fragmentation depicting contemporary civilization as a spiritual and moral wasteland. "The Waste Land" became an anthem for the disillusioned writers of the postwar generation. Eliot also composed "The Hollow Men" (1925), a biting description of the emptiness of modern man's existence.

From the depths of their profound disillusionment this generation of

F. Scott Fitzgerald was a seminal author during the Jazz Age whose lifestyle often reflected the spirit of the times. He is pictured here with his wife, Zelda, and their daughter, Scottie.

young writers forged a major new literature. The symbol of this "lost generation" was F. Scott Fitzgerald. In a fine novel, *The Great Gatsby* (1925), Fitzgerald told the tragic story of Jay Gatsby, a romantic believer in the American dream who was destroyed by an unscrupulous millionaire, Tom Buchanan. Buchanan had Gatsby killed because he had fallen in love with Buchanan's wife, Daisy, a "vulgar, meretricious beauty" who did not deserve Gatsby's passion. Fitzgerald told his generation that innocent America where the dreams of men came true had been corrupted. Money and power had become the arbiters of fate.

Fitzgerald's own life was filled with sadness. He had married an attractive socialite, Zelda Sayre, and the two lived extravagantly, beyond his means. He had to write popular stories to pay his bills. He later became an alcoholic; Zelda had an emotional collapse and had to be institutionalized. Fitzgerald ended his days as a Hollywood script writer; he died of a heart attack in 1940.

Many young American writers and artists fled the United States to live and work in Rome, Berlin, London, and especially Paris. In Paris they lived along the left bank of the Seine. They lived cheaply and mixed with other writers, artists, and Bohemians. They wrote by day and talked, drank, and made love by night. Ernest Hemingway was the best writer of these young expatriates. He had grown up in the Midwest and worked as a newspaper reporter. During the war he was an ambulance driver on the Italian Front, where he was seriously wounded by an artillery shell. After his recovery and return to America, he worked for a time as a reporter. Then in 1922 he settled in Paris to write. His first novel, *The Sun Also Rises* (1926), captured the amorality and sense of the meaninglessness of life among expatriate drifters of the postwar era. *Farewell to Arms* (1929), his finest novel, portrayed the horrors and confusions of the war. Like Hemingway, the main character in the story, Frederick Henry, is wounded on the Italian Front, and Hemingway uses Henry's wound to symbolize the disillusionment and the psychic damage done by a pointless war. It was Hemingway's style—direct, terse, simple, a style that evoked powerful feelings—that made him the most important American writer of his generation. Hemingway was a muscular, athletic man who loved the outdoors and participated in strenuous sports. He boxed, fought bulls, and hunted lions in Africa. He also survived a plane crash in Africa. The Hemingway lifestyle created a legend and made him a cult hero, the celebrity writer. Many people were more interested in the life of the artist than they were in his art.

Sinclair Lewis was the most popular serious writer of the 1920s. His first major work, *Main Street* (1920), sold well and drew critical acclaim. It depicted the ignorance, smugness, and meanspiritedness of small town life. Two years later he brought forth *Babbitt*, his most famous novel. George Babbitt represented the archetypal businessman of the 1920s. Babbitt was a booster, gregarious, and narrowly conformist in his opinions, but beneath the noisy clichés hid a timid man who wanted to do better but was afraid to try. Both book titles passed into the language. "Main Street" symbolized the complacent bigotry of small-town life, and "Babbitt" became a symbol of middle-class materialism and conformity. Lewis, a social satirist with great descriptive powers, masterfully depicted the sights and sounds of 1920s American life. His scathing satire skewered the fads and foibles of his era. In other works he attacked the medical profession, religious evangelists, and manufacturers. His books sold well, making him rich and famous. Lewis became the first American writer to win a Nobel Prize for literature.

H. L. Mencken was another prominent American writer of the decade. Mencken was a middle-aged journalist and language scholar who founded the *American Mercury*, a sophisticated magazine that carried modern poetry, short stories, reviews, and satire. Mencken savagely satirized every aspect of American life. Anything sacred or significant to traditionalists was fair game for Mencken. At one time or another he went after the Ku Klux Klan, Rotary Clubs, funerals, the Boy Scouts, motherhood, home cooking, Prohibition, democracy, and religious fundamentalism. He especially disliked religious people, all of whom he called "Puritans." He defined a Puritan as someone "who lives in mortal fear that somewhere, somehow, someone might be enjoying himself."

Mencken was at his best ridiculing politics and politicians. He regularly launched all-out assaults on the men in the White House and other prominent politicians. His readers laughed uproariously as he called Bryan "a charlatan, a mountebank, a zany without sense or dignity." He called Woodrow Wilson a "bogus liberal." Harding was a "numskull," a "stonehead," and Coolidge was "a cheap and trashy fellow," a "dreadful little cad." Mencken's Hoover became a "pious old woman, a fat Coolidge." He coined the word "booboisie" to describe the complacent middle-class majority. He wrote about the great American "boobocracy" and the "boobocratic" way of life. Once when a young woman, upset by his diatribes, asked him why he bothered to live in the United States, Mencken replied, "Why do people go to zoos?"

Mencken was a professional iconoclast. His satires were amusing but never profound. His chief talent was his marvelous flair for language. He appeared to believe only in his own cleverness and a good turn of phrase. Mencken also very much reflected the spirit of the 1920s. When the Depression brought hard times in the 1930s, Mencken, in his accustomed way, satirized Franklin Roosevelt. No one laughed and Mencken faded from public view.

The literary explosion of the 1920s was broad, rich, and diverse. It included novelists Sherwood Anderson and John Dos Passos, who showed how the new technologies had undermined traditional values of craftsmanship and community. American dramatists Eugene O'Neill, Maxwell Anderson, and Elmer Rice created the modern American theater. Women writers made major contributions to the literature of the 1920s. Edith Wharton wrote a scathing indictment of wealthy easterners in *The Age of Innocence* (1921). Willa Cather and Ellen Glasgow wrote novels focusing on the problems besetting women in the Midwest and South.

THE HARLEM RENAISSANCE

African American writers also flourished during the 1920s. Harlem (a part of New York City), the largest black city in the world during the 1920s, became a cultural mecca, site of the "Harlem Renaissance." African American newspapers, magazines, and theater companies flourished. William E. B. Dubois was the dominant intellectual voice of Harlem. James Weldon Johnson, scholar, novelist, and poet, was another significant voice.

Langston Hughes, the leading poet of the Harlem Renaissance, wrote excitedly of the gathering of young African American poets, novelists, painters, and composers. Poets Countee Cullen and Claude McKay both

Harlem was almost a city in itself—consisting of over a half million people during the 1920s. Here, young black writers and artists gathered to celebrate a new pride in black people and black culture. Langston Hughes was one of the most gifted of the young black writers congregating in the black mecca.

wrote militant verses urging African Americans to challenge bigotry in all its forms. Jean Toomer was an outstanding realistic novelist and short story writer. Alain Locke wrote of a "New Negro" coming into being who would shed his dependency and become a participant in American civilization. Zora Neale Hurston wrote novels, short stories, and essays. Other writers addressed the issue of black identity—how to retain pride in their African heritage and come to terms with themselves as Americans. Hughes wrote:

> We younger Negro artists who create now intend to express our individual dark-skinned selves without fear or shame. If white people are pleased, we are glad. If they are not, it doesn't matter. We know we are beautiful.[1]

Art and music also thrived during the Harlem Renaissance. Plays and concerts were performed. All were part of the ferment. Historian David Lewis commented, "You could be proud and black, politically assertive, economically independent, creative and disciplined . . . ." Although the center of African American intellectual and artistic life during the Twenties was Harlem, the new black cultural awareness spread to other cities, where theater groups and poetry circles flourished.

---

1.   Quoted in Mary Beth Norton et al., *A People and a Nation: A History of the United States,* 2nd ed., *Volume II: Since 1865* (Boston: Houghton Mifflin, 1986), p. 703.

THE JAZZ AGE

The Jazz Age, as the 1920s was sometimes called, owed its name to the music created by African American musicians working in New Orleans at the turn of the century. By the 1920s it had spread to the rest of the country. White musicians learned to play jazz, and white audiences gathered to listen and to dance. Jazz was endlessly experimental, and the best jazz musicians were inspired improvisers. Jazz provided a way for African Americans to express symbolically their resentments and frustrations at the constraints imposed on their lives, and it also expressed their joy and a sense of community. Jazz also served as a call for freedom and rebellion. It appealed to young middle-class whites rebelling against the Victorian restraints imposed by their parents.

Gifted African American jazz musicians such as trumpeter Louis Armstrong, trombonist Kid Ory, and blues singer Bessie Smith became famous during the 1920s. Phonograph records and radiocasts popularized their music. Music recorded by African American artists and bought by millions of blacks gave African Americans a distinctive place in the new consumer culture. Jazz also gave a big boost to the pop record industry. Most important, it gave America its most distinctive art form. Paul Whiteman, the best-known band leader of the 1920s, popularized jazz music for predominantly white audiences.

Popular songwriters, some working in the jazz idiom or blending jazz with traditional musical forms, occupied a central place in the culture. Thousands of songs expressed the spirit of the age, the values, and the important personal concerns. Records, radio, and movies greatly expanded the availability of new popular music. Music could be heard everywhere, although the creative heart of pop music during the 1920s could be found in Tin Pan Alley, an area of clubs, ballrooms, and composition offices in Manhattan. Some of the great masters of popular songwriting were active during the decade, including Irving Berlin, the king of Tin Pan Alley. Other great popular songwriters were Jerome Kern, Ira Gershwin, Cole Porter, and Fats Waller. George M. Cohan was a versatile artist—singer, dancer, actor, and writer. Many of the songs of these creative artists have endured, providing valuable historical clues to the inner life of the era.

It was during the 1920s that popular songs took on their modern form, a subjective, personal idiom expressing the singer's private feelings. A recurrent theme of 1920s' songs was a lost love, a lost romance that the singer still felt. Another was the hope that true love would come along someday; still another theme was a love that was all-possessive. Other songs were upbeat, happy, expressing the gaiety and fun-loving aspects of a decade in which many people devoted themselves to the serious business of going to parties. Cole Porter, the most talented of the Twenties' lyricists, expressed the new morality of the era in witty verse. It is the popular songs of the Twenties that comprise one of its richest cultural legacies.

THE RISE OF RADIO

Radio hardly existed when the Twenties began, but within a few years the new electronic medium enjoyed explosive growth. Over 500 stations were launched in 1922. The Radio Corporation of America (RCA), which had begun the first commercial broadcast station to promote the sales of its radios, organized the first national radio network in 1926 and called it the National Broadcasting Company (NBC). In the early years of radio, music dominated the airwaves. It was radio that popularized jazz and the hit songs coming out of Tin Pan Alley.

Although musical programs continued to dominate the airwaves, radio diversified and expanded its programming as the 1920s developed. Radio began covering major sporting events, including the World Series and major college football games. Important boxing matches, especially heavyweight championship fights, were aired to the growing American radio audiences. Soon comedy shows, dramatic shows, soap operas, and quiz shows were added to the network repertoire of programs.

By the mid-Twenties most radio stations were devoting a few minutes each evening to broadcasting national news. By 1930 about half of American households owned at least one radio. By the end of the 1920s radio had become a mass medium and a big business. Advertisers were paying thousands of dollars for a minute's worth of prime-time advertising. The Radio Act of 1927 formally established the principle of federal regulation

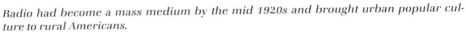

Radio had become a mass medium by the mid 1920s and brought urban popular culture to rural Americans.

of the broadcast industry and also created the Federal Radio Commission to license stations.

THE FLOWERING OF AMERICAN CULTURE

In all cultural realms the 1920s was one of the most creative eras in American history. In addition to those responsible for the literary outpouring, the evolution of jazz, and the wide circulation of popular songs, there was Georgia O'Keefe, who worked to develop a distinctive American style of painting, and O'Keefe's husband, Alfred Stieglitz, who developed photography as an art form. Composer Aaron Copeland built orchestral and vocal works around native themes and folk idioms. George Gershwin blended jazz, classical, and folk musical forms in compositions including "Rhapsody in Blue" (1924) and "Concerto in F" (1925). In architecture, the American skyscraper boom expanded. Midwesterner Frank Lloyd Wright built homes, churches, and schools in a distinctively American style, called the "prairie style," in which he merged the environment and the structure.

There is a paradox at the heart of the cultural flowering of the Roaring Twenties. All the serious writers and artists railed against the conformity and materialism of the age. They wrote scathingly of the flawed promise of American life. They attacked technology, mass production, and the forced, frantic pace of modern existence. They were oblivious to politics and social reform, retreating into individualism, into writing and other forms of artistic expression. But despite their disillusionment and alienation, or perhaps because of them, they created a first-rate body of artistic works. They were in the forefront of the modernist revolt against Victorian standards and traditional esthetic forms. Ironically, contemporary critics of the 1920s wrote some of the finest of the American prose and poetry. Their best work suggested, despite their complaints and condemnations, that America had come of age intellectually and artistically during the 1920s. Their dominant motifs were experimentalism and innovation. In literature and art it was a wonderfully creative time that powerfully expressed the adolescent exuberance of the modernist spirit. Americans were now in the forefront of world literature and popular culture.

BIBLIOGRAPHY

There are many fine studies of American social and cultural life during the 1920s. Lois Scharf and Joan M. Jensen, eds., *Decades of Discontent: The Women's Movement, 1920–1940* has several articles about feminist concerns of the 1920s. A fine study of young people in the 1920s is Paula Fass, *The Damned and the Beautiful: American Youth in the 1920s.* Kenneth S. Davis, *The Hero: Charles A. Lindbergh* is a good biography of the preeminent cultural hero of the times. Robert Creamer, with *Babe*, has written the best biography of the greatest baseball player of the

1920s. Nathan I. Huggins has written the finest account of black culture during the 1920s, *Harlem Renaissance*. Ray Ginger, *Six Days or Forever* is a marvelous account of the famous Scopes Monkey Trial that took place in 1925. Andrew Sinclair, *Prohibition: The Era of Excess* records the social consequences of the Noble Experiment. Roderick Nash, *The Nervous Generation: American Thought, 1917–1930* is a fine intellectual history of the 1920s. Gilbert Seldes, *The Seven Lively Arts* is the best cultural history of the 1920s. Robert Sklar, *Movie-Made America: A Cultural History of American Movies* has excellent chapters on the movie industry of the 1920s. Frederick L. Hoffmann, *The Twenties: American Writing in the Postwar Decade* is the best general study of the great American writers of the 1920s. Arnold Shaw, *The Jazz Age: Popular Music in the 1920s* is a wonderful account. Also see Marshall Stearns, *The Story of Jazz*. Barbara H. Solomon, ed., *Ain't We Got Fun? Essays, Lyrics, and Stories of the Twenties* is an entertaining popular history. For the early history of radio see Erik Barnouw, *A Tower in Babel: A History of Broadcasting in the United States, Vol. 1, To 1933*.

CHAPTER
7

The Great Depression

The prosperous 1920s gave way to economic disaster during the 1930s. The spectacular collapse of the securities markets in this country during the fall of 1929 catalyzed the process of economic disintegration historians label the Great Depression. The boosterism of the 1920s collapsed along with stock values, commodity prices, and real estate prices. President Hoover, who had ridden the last wave of 1920s prosperity to an overwhelming electoral victory in 1928, found himself confronting an unprecedented national crisis. Millions of his fellow citizens faced massive unemployment and underemployment, failing businesses, and farm commodity prices so low that it did not pay to harvest the crops. The American economic collapse of the early 1930s triggered a worldwide crisis of capitalism that gripped most of the leading industrial countries and Third World producers of raw materials for years. International trade declined sharply. Most nations devalued their currencies in a vain effort to maintain their export markets. Internationalism weakened and aggressive nations such as Germany, Italy, and Japan took advantage of the situation to conquer weak and vulnerable countries. Within the United States American voters during the election of 1932, perceiving Hoover's vigorous efforts to combat the effects of depression as ineffective, turned to the Democratic candidate, New York governor Franklin Delano Roosevelt, to lead them out of the morass of depression.

THE HOOVER ERA

No American presidency ever began as favorably as Herbert Hoover's. His administration would crown one of the most successful careers in the history of the Republic. The poor orphan boy had risen to become rich, fa-

mous, and the most admired man in public life. His experiences as businessman, wartime food and general relief administrator, and cabinet officer had prepared him thoroughly for the presidency. Hoover's career
combined the idealistic and the pragmatic; he was the utopian who got
things done in business and government.

America in March 1929 was peaceful and prosperous. Its economy
was preeminent in the world, and New Era living standards were the highest in human history. Poverty persisted in America, but Hoover had declared repeatedly during his campaign for the presidency that the United
States was putting poverty on the road to extinction. He had proclaimed,
"We shall soon be in sight of the day when poverty will be banished from
this nation." All families would soon have "two cars in every garage and a
chicken in every pot." His inaugural address celebrated the American
standard of living: "We have reached a higher degree of comfort and security than ever before existed in the history of the world."

Hoover also espoused an energetic philosophy of government firmly
grounded in the progressive tradition of Theodore Roosevelt: "The election has again confirmed the determination of the American people that
regulation of private enterprise . . . is the course rightly to be pursued in
our relations to business." He concluded his inaugural address with a
ringing affirmation of his faith in American progress: "I have no fears for
the future of our country. It is bright with hope." These words came from
the heart of a man who knew no failure in life.

Some voices dissented from Hooverian optimism. They voiced concern about the rampant speculation in the stock market. Hoover himself
had at times fretted about the speculative mania that siphoned off investment funds into unproductive channels, but he had done nothing about
it. He regarded agricultural problems and tariff reform to be more pressing, and he called Congress into special session to tackle farm and tariff
problems. Congress enacted the Agricultural Marketing Act that Hoover
had requested, but it failed to raise farm prices or to pass his tariff proposals.

But Hoover did get much of his legislative program enacted during
the eight months of his presidency preceding the stock market collapse,
many of them progressive measures. Congress outlawed any further
leases of public oil lands to private developers. Appropriations for Native
American educational and health services were increased. Hoover created a commission to study ways of abolishing poverty in America and to
usher in what he called a "Great Society." These and other progressive
measures suggest the direction in which Hoover was moving. They indi-
cate what might have been had the stock market not crashed and plunged
Americans into the long dark night of the Depression that transformed
the Hoover administration into an ordeal of frustration and failed policies.

THE GREAT CRASH

During the summer of 1929 the economy slipped. Construction starts declined as new building permits were down 65 percent. Business inventories increased sharply as consumer spending slackened. During August industrial production and wholesale prices dropped. Unemployment rose. The economy was sliding into a recession. Simultaneously, the Federal Reserve Board, responding to its critics who had called for a tighter monetary policy to discourage speculation in the stock market, raised its discount rate hoping to dampen gently the speculative orgy. But higher interest rates did not slow the traffic in brokers' loans; unfortunately, they did contribute to the recessionary downturn because they reduced borrowing by consumers and investors.

The stock market ignored the recession; stock prices continued to climb during August and September as stock averages soared to historic highs. On September 3 the price of a share of A.T. & T. common stock was $304 and General Electric was up to $396, triple its price eighteen months earlier. The biggest gainer of the decade, RCA, reached $450. As the economy faltered, business leaders, blinded by the Great Bull Market, forecast a quick recovery.

The Crash began Wednesday morning, October 23, 1929, when millions of shares of common stock were suddenly offered for sale at the New York Stock Exchange by brokers executing sell orders from their customers. Key issues slumped in heavy trading. Although no one panicked that day, brokers noted nervously that the market had lost $4 billion. Speculative stocks had taken a beating and many blue chips were off as much as five points.

No one knows for sure why thousands of investors chose that particular morning to sell their holdings. The national mood was confident. Hoover's presidency had been successful. There were no political or economic crises anywhere to frighten investors. The mild recession was not considered serious, nor likely to last long. There was no conspiracy to rig the market. There was no shortage of investment funds. Banks and corporations had plenty of money, which they were eager to lend despite the new tight money policy. Higher interest rates had not deterred speculators.

The market had shown weaknesses in September but had rallied, and September ended a positive month. Sharp losses occurred the first week in October, but the market again rallied. Losses occurred during the week preceding the Crash but had caused no alarm. On both October 21 and 22 the market closed on the upside. The selling and huge losses of October 23 caught everyone by surprise. That night optimism vanished at the world's most important financial center. The bulls all became bears. The floodgates opened on Thursday, October 24, "Black Thursday." Prices fell and did not recover. Bedlam reigned on the floor. Brokers shouted themselves hoarse seeking vanished buyers. At times, there were no takers of stocks at any price. Hysteria and panic prevailed. People screamed, shouted, and wept.

Although the origins of the selling wave of October 23 remain mysterious, its consequences proved to be catastrophic. That afternoon a group of New York's leading financiers formed a pool to buy stocks and stem the panic. A pool member walked on the floor of the exchange and bid $205 for 25,000 shares of U.S. Steel then selling for $193. For a moment that dramatic gesture worked. Selling stopped, prices steadied. Some believed the panic to be over.

A flood of reassuring statements came the next day. John Maynard Keynes, the world's foremost economist, declared the decline a good thing, for it had eliminated speculators and money would now be channeled into productive enterprises. New York governor Franklin Roosevelt expressed confidence in the stock market. President Hoover declared, "The fundamental business of the country is on a sound and prosperous basis." These official optimists failed to restore confidence. Stock prices held for a few days only.

New torrents of selling occurred the following week. Many investors were forced to sell to cover their debts. Tuesday, October 29, was the worst. In one of history's greatest avalanches of panic selling, more than 16 million shares were dumped on the market. Stock averages lost almost 40 points. In a single day as much money in capital values vanished as the United States had spent fighting World War I. The October 30 headline of *Variety* trumpeted, "Wall St. Lays an Egg." By month's end, over $15 billion in stock values had been lost. At year's end, losses reached $40 billion, representing 60 percent of the total value of stocks listed on the Exchange when the Crash began.

As 1930 began, some businessmen still exuded optimism because no one had yet connected the Wall Street disaster to the general economy. They believed that the market crash had merely ruined the lunatic fringe of margin speculators without harming the people who produced and distributed goods within the economy. The notion that the basic economy remained healthy after the securities collapse underlay Secretary of the Treasury Andrew Mellon's famed remark:

> Let the slump liquidate itself. Liquidate labor, liquidate stocks, liquidate the farmers, liquidate real estate. . . . Values will be adjusted, and enterprising people will pick up the wrecks from less competent people.[1]

---

1. Quoted in Robert Sobel, *The Great Bull Market: Wall Street in the 1920s* (New York: Norton, 1968), p. 145.

A cartoon dated October 29, 1929, portraying the Crash on Wall Street as the Day of Judgment.

CAUSES OF THE GREAT DEPRESSION

As 1931 began, the recession which had begun during the summer of 1929 had become a depression, the first to afflict America in 40 years. The year 1931 was Year One of the Great Depression.

The Depression had multiple causes, including several flaws inherent in the prosperous economy of the 1920s. A fundamental defect of the 1920s' economy was the unequal distribution of wealth. Average per capita disposable income rose about 10 percent during the 1920s, but income of the wealthiest Americans rose 75 percent during the same period. The Federal Trade Commission reported that the richest one percent of the population owned 60 percent of the nation's wealth. The savings of the top 60,000 families exceeded the savings of the 25 million poorest families. Cuts in corporate and personal income taxes, which benefited mainly business and wealthy people, increased the inequality of income distribution. Because a rising portion of national income went to upper-income families, the economy became increasingly dependent on their spending and saving for continued growth. With wealth concentrated at the top, much income went into investments, luxury purchases, and stock speculation instead of spending for consumer durables. The wealthy had more money than they could spend; farmers, workers, and the bulk of middle-class families together did not have enough money to keep the economy growing in 1928–1929.

Because profits rose faster than wages, businessmen increased their production of goods by investing some of their profits for plant expansion at a rate greater than the capacity of consumers to buy the goods. The gap between production and consumption of goods widened in durable goods industries such as automobile manufacturing and housing construction, which had become the mainstays of the 1920s consumer economy because so many other businesses depended on them. Construction, autos, steel, and many other major industries had overbuilt. In 1928 and 1929 sales lagged, inventories rose, production decreased, and unemployment increased.

Farmers did not share fully in the expanding consumer economy. They had never recovered from the collapse of commodity prices after World War I. Most farmers had been in recession since 1921. They had received 16 percent of national income in 1919, but ten years later they were receiving only 9 percent. Agricultural overproduction became chronic during the 1920s as farm income declined relatively. Because of their lowered income, farmers' purchasing power remained weak during the 1920s.

Industrial wages rose about 10 percent during the decade, but workers also earned a smaller share of national income at the end of the decade than they did when it began. Technological unemployment caused by businessmen's installing new labor-saving machinery in their factories threw thousands of people out of work each year. Unemployment remained high throughout the 1920s, averaging about 7 percent. Since unemployment insurance and federally funded welfare payments did not exist during the 1920s, sustained unemployment meant poverty and severely curtailed purchasing power.

In the fall of 1929 there were about 3 million people out of work, many of them in textiles, coal mining, lumbering, and railroads. These "sick industries" all suffered from overexpansion, declining demand, and inefficient management. Impoverished unemployed workers could not participate in the consumer economy. The closing of a coal mine or a textile factory also blighted communities and regions that depended on them, creating depressed areas and further diminishing purchasing power.

Another inherent weakness of the New Era economy lay in the realm of international economic policy. During World War I the United States became the world's leading creditor nation because European nations incurred huge losses of wealth and borrowed billions of dollars from American banks and the U.S. Treasury. But the United States never adjusted its trade relations to accord with the financial realities of the 1920s. A debtor nation must export more than it imports to earn foreign exchange with which to pay its foreign debts. A creditor nation has to import more than it exports to provide nations that owe it money an opportunity to earn funds with which to pay its debts. Throughout the 1920s the United States annually ran trade surpluses with its major European and Latin American debtors. Also it enacted higher tariffs to protect its industries and farmers from foreign competition, thereby making an equal exchange of goods between the United States and its debtors impossible. What kept these unsound commercial relations going was credit. American lenders, aided by the "easy money" policy of the Federal Reserve Board, extended credit to foreign businesses and governments to enable them to pay off debts and to buy American goods.

When the Crash occurred, many American lenders who had suffered losses refused to make new foreign loans and called in existing ones as they matured. Credit cutoffs caused foreign debtors to default and to stop buying American goods, so American exports dropped sharply. American farmers were hurt most, because many of them sold a large part of their crops abroad. Sharply declining international trade following the stock market collapse was a major cause of the Great Depression.

Weaknesses within the corporate structure also helped cause the Depression following the Crash. Many holding companies (corporations created to own stocks in other corporations instead of owning physical assets) had been set up within the electric power, railroad, and securities industries. Promoters used these holding companies to get control of many companies in a given industry and to sell huge stock issues. Holding company was pyramided upon holding company until a small company at the top of the pyramid controlled hundreds of companies at its base. Many of these elaborate structures collapsed after the Wall Street panic because the operating companies at the bottom of the pyramids stopped earning dividends. When these dividends stopped, the "upstream" companies in the pyramid collapsed because they had issued bonds whose interest had been paid by dividends from the "downstream" operating companies. With their bonds defaulting, the holding companies collapsed. A flurry of lawsuits and investigations exposed some holding company promoters as con artists. Samuel Insull, who had built an elaborate holding company empire in electric utilities, fled the country to escape arrest for embezzlement. He later returned, had to stand trial, and was acquitted. A giant investment trust, Goldman, Sachs, and Company, sold one billion dollars worth of securities in 1929; after the Crash its portfolio dwindled to zero! Sometimes these disastrous liquidations engulfed banks who had invested heavily in pyramided holding companies. Speculative and sometimes fraudulent holding companies were a weak link in the business sector. Their collapse ruined thousands of investors and shattered confidence in the soundness of the American financial system.

Many banks, even if they never invested in holding companies, got into serious trouble during the 1920s. Long before the Crash, bank failures had reached epidemic proportions in the Midwest and Southeast. Between 1921 and 1928 over 5,000 mostly small rural banks had failed. There were several causes: mismanagement, fraud, inadequate regulation, and economic decline in their operating regions. Often a bank failure would set off a series of devastating runs on nearby banks as depositors scurried to withdraw their funds, ensuring those banks' failures. These panicky runs often caused formerly sound banks to go down along with the weak, crooked, and mismanaged ones. Weaknesses in the U.S. banking industry were a major cause of the Depression following the stock market collapse.

The most spectacular flaw in the 1920s' economy was the stock market itself. The Great Bull Market, which began in 1924, rose continually for five years, peaking in September 1929. The stock market came to dominate American economic life. Newspaper headlines quoted stock numbers daily; nearly everyone followed the market. It became the greatest celebrity of a hero-worshipping age, a symbol of economic health and emblem of the superiority of the American way. Because the market occupied a central place in the public consciousness, its collapse had a profoundly negative psychological effect far greater than the immediate financial disasters it caused. It confused and frightened people, shattering their confidence in the economy and the men who managed it, even though most Americans did not own a single share of stock and suffered no direct loss from the Crash.

What had kept the market rising for years had been the continuous entry of new investors who bought mostly common stocks. Abundant money to fuel the market came from many sources, both foreign and domestic. Institutional investors dominated, but thousands of small investors also played the market. Banks speculated with depositors' funds. Businessmen invested their profits. The easy money policy of the Federal Reserve Board kept credit readily available at low interest rates, encouraging investment. In 1928 and 1929 thousands of small speculators were lured into the market by low margin requirements. (Margin is the amount of down payment required for purchasing a portfolio of stocks from a broker.) Margins as low as 10 percent were available to clients. Brokers' loans increased spectacularly as people swarmed in to buy stocks on margin. These margin-account speculators helped drive stocks to their historic highs on the eve of the Crash.

The unperceived danger inherent in the market was that the boom was always self-liquidating. A continuous inflow of new investors was required to generate the demand that bid up stock prices and created the capital gains which most investors sought. When, for reasons that are unknown and unknowable, on the morning of October 23, 1929, the customary buyers did not show up and thousands of investors telephoned in sell orders, the market dropped sharply. That day's selling was a signal for massive selling to begin, both for those who wanted to sell and those who had to sell because their stocks, purchased on credit, were no longer safely margined. The rout was on; prices plummeted because there was no one or no instrument to stop them. The Federal Reserve's tools proved helpless. Pooling failed. Only direct government intervention to close the markets might have stopped the panic, but no one proposed such a drastic measure.

In the weeks following the Crash newspapers carried sensational stories of ruined speculators committing suicide by leaping from upper-story windows at their banks and private clubs. There was, in reality, no suicide wave in the aftermath of the collapse. More people killed themselves during the summer of the Great Bull Market than in the winter following the Crash. The myth probably arose because any suicides of businessmen at the time of the Crash were attributed to financial losses, whereas in more prosperous years such deaths went unnoticed. It was during the years 1932 to 1934, the worst years of the Depression, that the suicide rate rose, and most suicide victims of the Great Depression were ordinary working-class and middle-class people in despair, not bankrupt securities speculators.

If the suicide rate after the Crash did not rise, the embezzlement rate did, or at least the number of trials for business crimes. Investors, smarting from their losses, demanded audits of company books and management policies. These audits often led to indictments and trials such as the Insull case. Embittered investors discovered that formerly admired financial wizards had been swindlers.

The central question is: What role did the market collapse play in causing the Depression? Did the Crash cause the Depression or was the Crash only a symptom of the coming collapse? Although few could see it at the time, the panic on Wall Street was a major cause of the Great Depression, for it exposed many of the underlying weaknesses inherent in the 1920s economy. Deep-rooted faults surfaced, compounded by foreign influences, faulty economic knowledge, political errors, and irrational behavior.

The Crash curtailed the purchasing power and investing capacity of the wealthy classes upon whom the consumer economy had come to depend for growth, because many rich people lost money in the market. The collapse also shook their confidence in the economic system, making them less willing investors. Loans to foreign governments that had kept international trade and debt repayments flowing stopped, causing massive defaults on bond payments and loss of foreign markets for American exporters. Investors, exporters, and farmers who sold their crops abroad lost income and purchasing power. Jerry-built holding companies collapsed. Investment trusts depreciated to nothing. Bank failures escalated. Credit dried up. Corporations that had lost money in the stock market had to curtail investment, decrease production, and eventually lay off workers. As workers were fired, purchasing power dropped further, starting another round of cutbacks and layoffs. In sum, the stock market crash immensely damaged the economy in many ways and was both catalyst and major cause of the Depression.

Governmental financial policy also contributed to the coming of the Great Depression. Easy availability of credit and low interest rates encouraged speculation in the market, and the government did nothing to regulate these. After the Crash, the Federal Reserve Board raised interest rates and tightened credit, further weakening a severely deflated economy. A more enlightened monetary policy might have shortened and ameliorated the downturn; instead the "Fed" helped cause the Crash and then made the Depression worse with its bumbling policies.

Within a year after the Crash the American economy had passed from recession into depression. Business confidence spiraled down with the business cycle. A nation of boosters had been transformed into anxious pessimists by a disastrous chain of events triggered by the collapse of the Great Bull Market.

THE SHRINKING OF THE AMERICAN ECONOMY

As the Depression deepened, statistics embodied a litany of human disaster. Between 1929 and 1933 about 100,000 businesses failed. Investment declined from $7 billion to less than $2 billion. Corporate profits fell from $10 billion to less than $1 billion. The gross national product dropped from $80 billion to $42 billion as the economy shrank to half its former size. Manufacturing also declined by half. Wholesale prices shrank by almost 40 percent. Almost 6,000 banks went under during those four years, and they took with them millions of savings accounts representing $25 billion in savings. By 1933 the Dow-Jones average for industrial stocks stood at 32 points, about 10 percent of its value on the eve of the Crash.

When the Crash occurred, unemployment stood at about 3 million. It climbed steadily thereafter as an average of 100,000 workers lost their jobs every week during the first three years after the Crash. Some large corporate employers laid off all their full-time employees. By March 1933 unemployment had soared to 13 million, about one-fourth of the work force. At least that many more were working part-time and for reduced wages. During the depths of the Depression about half the American work force was either unemployed or underemployed. Labor income fell 40 percent during those four dismal years.

Scenes of misery abounded in the industrial cities. A million unem-

Unemployment, 1929-1945

Source: Historical Statistics of the United States,
Colonial Times to 1970

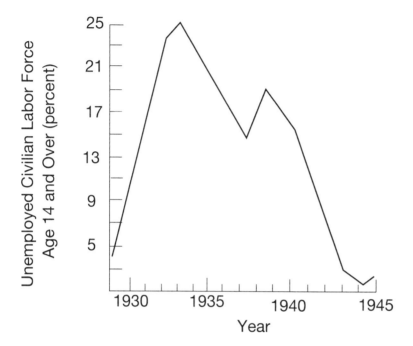

ployed men and women trudged the sidewalks of New York. Unemployed office workers sold apples on street corners at five cents apiece. People sat forlornly in employment offices keeping watch for nonexistent jobs. Diets deteriorated, malnutrition became all too common, and weakened people easily contracted diseases. People stopped going to doctors. The incidence of epidemic diseases like tuberculosis, typhoid, and dysentery increased. Unable to pay heating bills, people huddled together in cold tenements. Many doubled up in crowded apartments. Often those unable to pay rent were evicted. Homeless people built shanty towns on vacant lots, in gullies and canyons, and in forests on the edge of cities. Other wanderers slept in parks and doorways. Bread lines and soup kitchens manned by charities proliferated. People stole food from grocery stores, rummaged through garbage cans and city dumps, and begged for food. In 1932 New York City hospitals reported 29 victims of starvation and 110 people dead of malnutrition. Most were children.

In rural areas, troubled by economic difficulties as far back as the 1920s, the Depression made conditions far worse. Between 1929 and

Unemployed workers during the Great Depression selling apples for 5 cents apiece.

1933 the already low farm income dropped by one-half. Farmers responded to falling prices by producing more, but their increased productivity depressed prices further, and their troubles were compounded by the loss of foreign markets because of tariffs and economic collapse in Europe. Falling income, droughts, plagues, bank failures, unpaid mortgages and taxes, bankruptcies, and foreclosures ruined farmers. In some regions of the rural South and Southwest the economy collapsed from a combination of economic and natural disasters, depriving the rural poor of an economic base. Many poor tenant farmers and their families became transients, hitting the road in search of jobs or food. Those that remained on the land struggled to survive on incomes of $300 to $400 per year.

The Depression also brought ecological disaster to the Great Plains region. Between 1929 and 1933 scores of dust storms howled across the land each year. These black blizzards brought darkness at noon and transformed an area stretching from the Oklahoma panhandle to western Ne-

Bread lines were commonplace during the depression years of the early 1930s. Here, unemployed workers wait in line for a meal furnished by The Brass Rail Restaurant.

braska into a giant "Dust Bowl." Drought-parched fields and pastures turned into sand dunes. Searing summer heat killed thousands of people, cattle, fish, and birds. Millions of people were forced to flee the stricken regions. Nature alone was not to blame for the Dust Bowl. The arid lands west of the 98th meridian were not suitable for intensive agriculture or livestock grazing. Sixty years of ecological abuse had stripped the Great Plains of its natural vegetation by the time the droughts struck. Denuded of its native sod, the land lay helpless when the hot dry winds came. One-third of the Great Plains just blew away during the early 1930s. Grit from the Nebraska plains collected on window sills at the White House. Sailors swabbing the decks of ships in New York harbor swept away bits of Montana.

Many Americans found Depression conditions difficult to understand. The nation's productive capacity was unimpaired. Factories were intact, farm productivity was higher than ever, and workers were desperately eager to work. Yet economic paralysis was everywhere. The contradiction of poverty amidst plenty made little sense to a people reared on the gospel of hard work and self-help. Farmers produced too much wool and cotton in the countryside and yet unemployed workers wore ragged clothing in the cities. Dairy farmers poured fresh milk on the ground, and wheat farmers refused to market their crops, yet people starved in the cities.

The Depression savagely struck farm families. Farm commodity prices plunged disastrously, and it was impossible for many tenant farmers and sharecroppers to make a living. Families like this one hit the road to join the thousands of other homeless wanderers.

The Great Depression forever marked the generation of Americans who had to endure a decade of deprivation. Years later, long after prosperity had returned and most middle-aged Americans enjoyed affluent lives, many still retained vivid memories of their Depression experiences. They remembered the humiliation, and most of all they remembered the insecurity and fear. Deep down they also feared that it could happen again, that the bottom could once more fall out and they would lose everything. The Depression left invisible scars.

HOOVER BATTLES THE DEPRESSION

Far more than any previous president, Hoover committed the power and financial resources of the federal government to battling the Depression. Previous presidents had left fighting depressions to the private sector. Grover Cleveland had confined his actions to maintaining the gold standard during the severe depression of the 1890s. Hoover, eschewing *lais-*

*The Dust Bowl, triggered by years of poor land management and drought, brought eco-
logical and economic disaster to the Great Plains region.*

sez-faire, accepted governmental responsibility for reviving the economy
and saving the capitalist system. His actions paved the way for the New
Deal of the mid-1930s; some New Deal proposals extended programs begun by Hoover.

Both Hoover and Franklin Roosevelt inherited the progressivism of
Theodore Roosevelt and Woodrow Wilson. Franklin Roosevelt had been
one of the Democratic Party leaders who had tried to persuade Hoover to
accept his party's presidential nomination in 1920. At the time, Roosevelt
said of Hoover, "He certainly is a wonder and I wish we could make him
president of the United States. There could not be a better one."

A few weeks after the Crash President Hoover began a series of anti-
depression measures. His approach reflected his progressive faith in voluntary business–labor–government cooperation. He held meetings with
prominent business, farm, and labor leaders, and they complied with his
request to hold the line on production and wage levels in order to prevent the stock market collapse from spreading to the general economy. He
requested and got an income tax cut from Congress to stimulate demand.
He persuaded the Federal Reserve Board to lower interest rates to stimulate borrowing. Most important, the President expanded federal public
works projects to stimulate regions with slack economies. Hoover was the
first president to cut taxes, reduce interest rates, and use public works
projects to try to stimulate the economy and prevent downturns in the

business cycle. Roosevelt and his New Dealers would later make extensive use of all these inflationary devices.

Hoover's anti-depression program, along with declining federal revenues caused by economic contraction, unbalanced the federal budget. Despite strong bipartisan pressure from Congress to keep the budget balanced, Hoover accepted deficit financing as necessary to combat the economic downturn. From 1931 to 1933 Hoover's budgets ran deficits totaling $6.5 billion; the national debt rose from $16 billion to $22.5 billion. Deficit spending in peacetime was unprecedented and Hoover incurred much criticism for his efforts. During the 1932 presidential campaign Democratic candidate Roosevelt repeatedly attacked Hoover for his profligacy; "I accuse the present administration of being the greatest spending administration in peacetime in all our history." Roosevelt pledged a 25 percent reduction in government spending and a balanced budget.

Hoover's anti-depression program not only failed to generate economic recovery, it failed to arrest the downward spiral of the business cycle. Industrialists who had earlier pledged to hold the line were forced to cut production in the face of declining sales and mounting inventories. They also cut wages, hours, and discharged employees. Lowered interest rates failed to stimulate borrowing, and tax cuts failed to stimulate spending. Public works projects offset only a portion of the decline in the construction industry. Although Hoover had made unprecedented use of federal power and battled the Depression across a wide front, there were limits to the actions he was willing to take. He opposed using federal funds for unemployment relief. He insisted that relief efforts remain in the hands of local governments, with supplemental aid from private charities such as the Red Cross and the Salvation Army.

Amid the rising tide of depression, the 1930 elections occurred. The Democrats blamed the Republicans both for causing the Depression and for failing to cure it. They also criticized Hoover for his refusal to allow federal unemployment relief. The Democrats won control of the House, but the Republicans retained narrow control of the Senate. The Republicans were clearly weakened by the Crash and the economic downturn that followed. The Democrats made a decisive comeback from their 1920s' doldrums and realized that they could win in 1932. In New York, Governor Franklin Roosevelt won reelection to a second term and positioned himself to win the Democratic presidential nomination in 1932.

THE COLLAPSE OF EUROPEAN ECONOMIES

During the first half of 1931 economic conditions improved. President Hoover confidently proclaimed the Depression to be over. But in July the economy nose-dived again, skidding to new lows. The summer decline coincided with the collapse of European economies, which was caused largely by the withdrawal of American credits and the loss of American markets. These effects of the American Depression dealt body blows to weak European economies only partially recovered from the ravages of World War I. Germany and Austria, the two weakest links of the continental economy, were the first to fail. The contagion of collapse spread to the rest of Europe, then to its colonies. Great Britain was forced off the gold standard, a move that destabilized all national currencies. The international free market was replaced by controlled national economies that instituted high tariffs, import and export quotas, and managed currencies,

President Hoover, shown here on the day of his inauguration, battled the Great Depression vigorously, but ultimately his efforts failed to rid the country of depression or to even arrest the downward spiral.

devices implemented to gain advantage over trading partners and to insulate national economies from the effects of worldwide deflation.

The American scene of mass unemployment, bankruptcy, and deprivation occurred on a world scale. In Britain long lines of unemployed waited for relief benefits. German peasants starved in their fields. Millions of Frenchmen were reduced to one meal a day in a country famed for its abundant harvests and fine food. But in no other country were the effects of depression as severe as in America. Nowhere else did production decline so steeply, unemployment climb so high, currency deflate so severely, and recovery take so long. President Hoover, understanding the interrelatedness of the American and European economies, moved to combat the European crisis. He persuaded Congress to grant a one-year moratorium on all intergovernmental debt payments to try to save the international credit system. He failed. Germany defaulted on its reparations payments to France and Great Britain; both in turn defaulted on war debt payments to the United States.

The effects of default were devastating financially and psychologically because Americans viewed debt repayments as moral as well as contractual obligations. To Americans, default represented betrayal by former allies whom they had rescued from the brink of defeat in 1918. The United States became more isolationist, increasingly reluctant to join cooperative efforts to solve international economic and political problems. "America first" nationalistic attitudes strengthened.

The European collapse further weakened the American economy, causing President Hoover thereafter to insist that the main causes of the American Depression were foreign. He believed that his anti-depression program was working and that the American economy was on the road to recovery when it was derailed by the European depression. It is true that an American upturn occurred during the spring of 1931, before the European collapse, but Hoover failed to see that it was the loss of U.S. credits and markets that had toppled the weak European economies. The main causes of the U.S. Depression were internal and can be found in the many weaknesses of the 1920s' economy exposed by the stock market collapse. President Hoover saw only half of a central truth: The international economic crisis of the early 1930s revealed how interdependent the capitalistic economies of the Western world had become. The Great Depression of the early 1930s was a worldwide capitalist crisis.

THE DEPRESSION DEEPENS

Sharp declines in foreign trade following the European collapse devastated the already depressed American farm sector. Declines in farm prices were greatest for wheat, cotton, and tobacco, which were the major U.S. export crops. Hoover spent much time trying to solve farm problems, but he could never solve the fundamental problem of overproduction. Programs extended credit to farmers. Emergency funds were allotted to feed starving livestock in drought-stricken states. The Federal Farm Board purchased surplus wheat and cotton and turned the surplus over to the Red Cross, which then processed the crops and distributed flour and clothing to needy rural families. It was a generous gesture, but farmers needed higher commodity prices, not handouts. The Farm Board, however, did not have the authority to order production cuts or make cash payments to farmers. Neither the President nor Congress was willing to devise farm programs that would curb production or increase farm income with subsidy payments as demanded by rural spokesmen.

As farm income fell, and taxes and mortgage payments remained fixed, thousands of farmers lost their lands. Government's failure to raise farm prices or to prevent foreclosures provoked direct action among militant midwestern farmers. In Iowa during the summer of 1932 Milo Reno formed the Farmers' Holiday Association, which organized a farmers' strike. Members refused to ship their crops to market, in order to force commodity prices up. They also blockaded highways to stop trucks from hauling nonmembers' produce to markets. Wisconsin dairy farmers dumped milk along roadsides and battled with deputy sheriffs. In Storm Lake, Iowa, farmers forcibly halted a foreclosure sale. In Bucks County, Pennsylvania, farmers forced an auctioneer to sell a farm for $1.18, bought it, and returned it to the former owner. These direct action tactics signaled the growing radicalism of farmers facing desperate economic circumstances and ineffective government programs.

Industrial workers too suffered the ravages of depression. Detroit was especially hard hit as the market for new cars fell drastically. By fall 1932 approximately 350,000 people, half of the city's workers, were out of work. At Ford's River Rouge assembly plant only about one-quarter of the 1929 work force was still on the job in 1933. The Communist Party organized a march of unemployed workers to the gates of Ford's factory to ask for jobs. Company guards opened fire upon the marchers, killing four men and wounding others. Other industries sharply curtailed production and discharged workers by the thousands. Layoffs generally were by seniority. Young people, minorities, and unskilled workers were often the first fired and the last to be rehired. Many of the economic gains these groups had made during the prosperous years of the 1920s were undone by the depression of the 1930s. And for many still working, wages and hours were slashed severely.

By the fall of 1931 unemployment approached 8 million, representing 18 percent of the work force. As unemployment reached massive proportions, private charities and municipal relief agencies proved inadequate to meet the ever-growing demands on their resources. States inevitably were forced to intervene. New York, under the leadership of Governor Roosevelt, took the lead among states in accepting responsibility for unemployment relief. The New York state legislature created an agency to help city and county governments handle their relief burdens. Other states followed. But in time, as the army of unemployed swelled to unprecedented size, state funding also proved inadequate. As 1931 ended, with the economy continuing to shrink, it was evident that only the federal government had the financial resources to provide relief for unemployed workers and their families. In the winter of 1931 and 1932 New York City families on relief got $2.39 per week, which social workers admitted could not meet the needs of the smallest budget. In Houston, city officials no longer processed relief applications from black and Hispanic families, reserving what funds they had for whites only.

President Hoover, beset by a deteriorating economy and rising popular discontent, launched another recovery program in December 1931. Important measures included the Glass-Steagall Act (1932), which reformed the banking system, increasing the amount of money in circulation. The Federal Home Loan Bank enabled some homeowners to refinance their mortgages and save their homes. The heart of Hoover's second-phase program was the Reconstruction Finance Corporation (RFC), a lending authority funded by $500 million from the U.S. Treasury and authorized to borrow an additional $1.5 billion from private sources. The RFC made large loans to banks, insurance companies, and railroads, many of whom were in financial difficulty during the Depression. The New Dealers would later expand the RFC and use it extensively to fight the Depression.

Hoover also tried to use psychological tools to fight the Depression and promote recovery. He tried to use publicity releases to stimulate optimism about American economic prospects. He stated, "The worst has passed" and "Prosperity is just around the corner." But by 1932 the only thing around most corners was the lengthening bread lines of unemployed men and women. As the Depression lengthened, the President's upbeat statements made him appear out of touch with reality or, worse, a cynical manipulator. Had Mr. Hoover been able to engineer a recovery, these efforts at ballyhoo and prophecy would probably have worked. President Roosevelt and his New Dealers were successful in using similar techniques to promote optimism because they were accompanied by some improvement in business conditions in 1933 and 1934.

Still Hoover continued to resist federal aid for the unemployed. He was not a cruel or insensitive man, nor did he embrace Social Darwinist tenets. He deplored the suffering that hard times inflicted on millions of his fellow citizens, but he deplored even more what he believed would be the consequences of federal relief: mass demoralization and the creation of a large class of welfare recipients permanently dependent on government handouts, which would undermine the American way of life. The President's ideological rigidity on this crucial matter provoked bitter criticism from the Democrats and the opposition press. Hoover was denounced as the man who fed starving Europeans after the war but refused his countrymen funds with which to buy their families food. He could rush food to starving cattle but not to people. These charges stung the President and badly damaged his public image. He yielded a little in the summer of 1932, when he supported amendments to the RFC that allowed it to lend $300 million to state and local agencies for relief purposes. But large-scale federal unemployment relief had to await the New Deal.

Many other politicians of both parties as well as prominent Americans shared the President's concerns about relief. Franklin Roosevelt publicly worried that direct relief would undermine the character of workingmen. Congress in 1932 voted down a measure to funnel federal relief funds to the states, with Democratic senators providing 40 percent of the votes that killed it. The traditional American view of relief yielded slowly, even in the face of massive economic decline and vast human suffering.

As President Hoover and his critics debated the relief issue, one group of unemployed sought to dramatize their plight and seek financial

The rout of the Bonus Marchers. In late July 1932, President Hoover ordered the U.S. Army to disperse the marchers and their families from public lands, where they had set up a shanty town in the nation's capital.

aid. In May 1932 about 15,000 World War I veterans converged on Washington to support a demand that veterans were making of Congress for early payment of an insurance bonus due them in 1945. They needed the money in 1932 to pay debts and feed their families. As their leaders lobbied on Capitol Hill, the veterans set up camps on marshy flats across the Anacostia River. Congress refused to grant the estimated $250 million, contending it was too costly.

After this defeat most of the veterans went home, but about 2,000 people remained. They became squatters, trespassers, living in the Anacostia camp and occupying vacant public buildings. They were a nuisance, even an embarrassment, but they posed no serious threat to public health or safety. On July 28 Hoover ordered the police to evict all squatters from government buildings. At one site a conflict occurred, several policemen were injured, and police shot and killed two veterans. Following this violence, the President ordered the Army to drive the veterans out of Washington. Under the command of General Douglas MacArthur, the Army deployed cavalry, infantry, tanks, tear gas, and machine guns. The soldiers cleared the buildings and then attacked Anacostia Flats. Using overwhelming force, the Army forcibly dispersed the veterans and their families. They tossed tear gas at the defiant veterans and burned their shanties to prevent their return.

After the Army had completed its mission, General MacArthur called the veterans "a mob . . . animated by the essence of revolution." President Hoover claimed that most of the veterans were Communists and criminals. Neither a grand jury probe nor an exhaustive Veterans Bureau investigation found evidence to sustain these charges, however. More than 90 percent of the marchers had been veterans; 70 percent had served overseas, and 1 in 5 was disabled. What they wanted was jobs and food for their families. The Bonus Marchers were mostly poor and unemployed yet patriotic Americans petitioning their government for relief during hard times, hoping that their World War I military service gave them a claim for special treatment. They were at first rejected, and later some of them were attacked by their government. The *Washington News* editorialized:

> What a pitiful spectacle is that of the great American government, mightiest in the world, chasing unarmed men, women, and children with army tanks.[2]

THE 1932 ELECTION

President Hoover's callous handling of the Bonus Marchers hurt him politically, but the deteriorating economy and the failure of his anti-depression programs did far worse damage to his reelection prospects. Hoover

2. Quoted in Arthur M. Schlesinger, Jr., *The Crisis of the Old Order, 1919–1933* (Boston: Houghton Mifflin, 1957), p. 265.

wanted renomination and no Republican rivals challenged him. He appeared confident that his program would soon bring recovery. But there was little enthusiasm for Hoover or his program at the Republican convention, although it was tightly controlled by the President's men and gave the incumbent a first ballot nomination by acclamation. Many Republicans were frankly pessimistic about Hoover's reelection prospects with the millstone of depression hanging so firmly around his ample neck. Many Republican congressmen and senators, not wanting to be associated with a loser, ran independent campaigns.

The Democratic contest was much more exciting. New York Governor Franklin D. Roosevelt was the front runner for the nomination. He had formidable political assets: a famous name, a good record as a progressive governor of the most populous state, and strong support in all regions of the country. His principal challenger was Alfred E. "Al" Smith, Roosevelt's former mentor who had preceded him as New York's governor. Smith, whom Hoover had beaten decisively in 1928, fervently sought his party's nomination again, confident he could avenge his loss and lead the nation back to prosperity. He also had millions of supporters among the party faithful.

Roosevelt would come to the convention with a majority of delegates, but short of the necessary two-thirds required for nomination. Smith's strategy was to get enough votes (along with the votes pledged to other candidates) so that he could prevent Roosevelt's getting a first ballot victory. There were several candidates waiting in the wings if Smith succeeded in stopping Roosevelt and deadlocking the convention. The most important of these challengers was John Nance Garner, Speaker of the House, who was championed by William Randolph Hearst, a Democratic Party titan because of his great personal wealth and his control of a vast media empire. Garner was a small-town banker and realtor from Uvalde, Texas, who had worked his way up through party ranks via the seniority escalator. "Cactus Jack," as he was nicknamed, was a populist, a dry, and an isolationist.

Roosevelt had appeared unstoppable in the spring; he won all the early primaries. Then Smith beat him in Massachusetts; and Garner, with Hearst's help, beat him in California. Roosevelt's momentum slowed. When the convention opened in Chicago in late June, all was uncertainty. The stop-Roosevelt coalition, led by Smith, came within a whisker of victory. Through three ballots Roosevelt fell about 100 votes short of the two-thirds majority needed to nail down the nomination, and he could not break through that barrier. His support in several southern states was wavering. After the third ballot the convention recessed. Roosevelt's backers had a few hours in which to try to save his candidacy. During those hours a bargain was struck that saved the nomination for Roosevelt. The key figure in the deal was Hearst. He agreed to switch California's delegation from Garner to Roosevelt if Roosevelt would accept Garner as his vice-presidential running mate. James A. "Big Jim" Farley, Roosevelt's campaign manager, accepted Hearst's offer, the convention reconvened, and a fourth ballot was taken. The leader of the California delegation, William Gibbs McAdoo, rose to cast the Golden State's 44 votes for Roosevelt. Within minutes, Roosevelt had the nomination.

Roosevelt flew to Chicago to make his acceptance speech. It was an aggressive speech, peppered with criticisms of the Hoover presidency. He drew his loudest applause when he proclaimed that "the theory that government helps the favored few" had been discredited and that his administration would do "the greatest good for the greatest number." Roosevelt called for economy in government, a balanced budget, and lower taxes, sounding more conservative than President Hoover. He also advocated progressive measures, including expanding of public works, production controls for agriculture, and federal relief for the unemployed. He pledged to help the "forgotten man" find meaningful work and regain his lost standard of living. Near the end of his speech Roosevelt told the delegates, "I pledge you, I pledge myself, to a New Deal for the American people." The press seized upon that figure of speech and the New Deal became a popular slogan for Roosevelt's anti-depression program. As he finished, an organ blasted out the notes of "Happy Days Are Here Again"; Roosevelt's campaign had found its theme song. A radical journalist, unimpressed by the candidate or his speech, wondered if the country would be better off with a whole new deck of cards instead of just a new deal from the same old capitalist deck.

One feature of both conventions provides insight into the politics of Depression America. Prohibition remained a major issue with both parties. Both parties contained wet and dry factions, although there were more wets among the Democrats and more drys among the Republicans. After a ferocious debate over the issue, the Republicans adopted a plank keeping Prohibition, but they also proposed another constitutional amendment that would permit each state to determine whether it wanted to be wet or dry. The Democrats also had a rousing debate on the subject before adopting a plank calling for repeal of the Eighteenth Amendment. Walter Lippmann wondered why the delegates spent so much time on the Prohibition issue instead of addressing the many urgent economic problems created by the Great Depression. John Dewey grumbled:

> Here we are in the midst of the gravest crisis since the civil war and the only thing that the two national parties seem to want to debate is booze.[3]

Will Rogers quipped that the debate over Prohibition didn't matter much anyhow since "neither side could afford the price of a drink."

3. Quoted in William E. Leuchtenburg, *Franklin D. Roosevelt and the New Deal* (New York: Harper & Row, 1963), p. 9.

Both Hoover and Roosevelt began their campaigns in August. Both campaign organizations spent heavily for media exposure, mostly for radio time. Hoover had the support of most of the nation's newspapers and radio stations, and he had more money to spend than Roosevelt. But these advantages could not offset the fatal disadvantage of being the president in office when financial and economic disaster struck the nation. The Democrats could have won the 1932 presidential election with any candidate nominated. The 1932 election was no contest from the outset.

Neither candidate succeeded in arousing the voters. Hoover's efforts failed completely. Roosevelt's speaking style was cool, controlled, and priggish. He conveyed no deep understanding of the economic crisis that was imperiling the American way of life. His cheerful confidence and statements of faith in the capacity of American institutions to revive and prosper were superficial, uninformed by statistical data or economic theory. He appeared to lack understanding of complex economic and financial processes. He had no program to offer the American people, merely a collection of miscellaneous proposals. Many who heard him speak during the campaign must have shared Walter Lippmann's opinion of the candidate as "A pleasant man who, without any important qualifications for the office, would like very much to be president."

Roosevelt's campaigning disappointed progressive intellectuals, especially his habit of backing off from a position if it was attacked. A pattern emerged during the campaign: Roosevelt would attack Hoover in general terms; Hoover would strike back, refuting Roosevelt by citing statistical data; Roosevelt would beat a retreat, shifting the argument as he backed away. By the end of the campaign, Roosevelt had eaten so many of his own words that the voters had difficulty discerning any important issue differences between him and the incumbent. Hoover ridiculed Roosevelt's habit of waffling on the issues, calling him a "chameleon in plaid." In 1932, Franklin Roosevelt neither looked nor sounded like a Messiah.

Roosevelt did not offer the American people a New Deal during the 1932 campaign because it did not then exist. The phrase was merely empty rhetoric. He and his advisers concentrated on winning the election; programs to combat the Depression and promote recovery would come later, after he had won and had forged his administration. It was also unnecessary for Roosevelt to offer specific programs; he knew that he was winning without them. So he played it safe. He blamed Hoover and his party for causing the Depression, condemned them for failing to solve it, and promised to solve all problems if elected.

Roosevelt understood that the central issue in the campaign was Hoover's failed program. Roosevelt avoided specific commitments and resisted all efforts by journalists and the embattled Hoover to pin him down. He did on occasion propose a few general programs—federal unemployment relief, more public works, production controls for farmers, and expansion of the Reconstruction Finance Corporation's lending authority to include small businesses. But the main purpose of these proposals was to attract votes, not solve economic problems. The only specific commitments he made during the campaign were promises that he never kept: balance the budget, cut taxes, and reduce spending 25 percent. At times his campaign utterances were contradictory, such as calling for spending for public works and unemployment relief at the same time that he promised to cut taxes, reduce spending, and balance the budget. But always, Roosevelt's trump card was to deplore the effects of the Depression on the American people. His strategy worked brilliantly.

Compared with Roosevelt's clever performance, Hoover's reelection campaign was pathetic. No longer calm or confident, Hoover sounded harassed and peevish as he faced an increasingly skeptical and hostile electorate. He was an uninspiring speaker, reading his speeches in a nasal monotone that failed to arouse audiences or even to hold their attention. He failed to project much concern for the mass of ordinary citizens mired in Depression miseries. He did, in fact, care about them, but he lacked the emotional resources and rhetorical skill needed to convey sympathetic understanding to his audiences. He became defensive, lashing back at Roosevelt, journalists, and other critics.

Hoover was a proud, stubborn man, unaccustomed to failure. He could neither acknowledge the failure of his program nor devise alternatives, bound as he was by ideological blinkers. Long before election day it was obvious to most observers that Hoover's reelection campaign had failed. He rarely left Washington during the final weeks, and when he did, crowds frequently jeered and booed the harried leader. Much hostility toward him personally pervaded the stricken land. The Great Engineer, the Horatio Alger hero of 1928, stood before the electorate in 1932 as the condemned killer of the American Dream. He became the butt of countless Depression-spawned jokes. Vaudeville comedians, upon hearing that business was improving, asked, "Is Hoover dead?" His name became a derisive prefix—Hoovervilles were shanty towns inhabited by the homeless; Hoover blankets were newspapers the unemployed wrapped themselves in for warmth; and Hoover hogs were jackrabbits put into hobo stew. On the final day of his campaign Hoover's motorcade was stinkbombed.

On election day the voters repudiated both Republicans and President Hoover by decisive majorities. In the popular vote Roosevelt rolled up almost 23 million to Hoover's 15.8 million. In the electoral vote column Roosevelt got 472 votes to Hoover's 59, and he carried 42 of 48 states. No Republican incumbent had ever been beaten so badly except William Howard Taft in 1912, but Taft's decisive defeat had been caused by divisions within his party. The 1932 election represented a Democratic Party victory as well as a personal triumph for Roosevelt. The Democrats attained their largest majorities in both houses of Congress since before the Civil War, winning the House with 312 seats to 123, and the Senate with 59

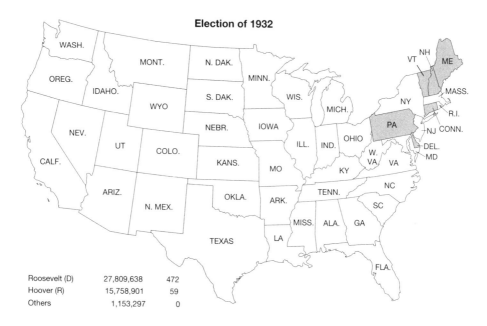

Election of 1932

Roosevelt (D)	27,809,638	472
Hoover (R)	15,758,901	59
Others	1,153,297	0

seats to 37. The 1932 election was the most dramatic turnabout in American political history. Roosevelt had beaten Hoover even worse than Hoover had beaten Smith. Hoover had won forty states in 1928; he got six in 1932. Roosevelt won millions of nominally Republican votes in northern and western states. Of the 3 million first-time votes cast in the 1932 election, Roosevelt got about 80 percent. These new voters were mostly young urban dwellers, many of them the children of "new" immigrants coming of age. These "ethnics" became an important voting block in the emerging Democratic coalition.

The political reversal of 1932 was both historic and long-lasting. The Republican Party had been the party of the normal majority since 1894 and had dominated national politics for the first three decades of the twentieth century. Since 1932 the Democrats have been the normal majority party, although their coalition has weakened since the late 1960s. Only two Congresses since 1932 have held Republican majorities. A major realignment of political parties occurred during the 1932 election, catalyzed by the Crash, the Great Depression, the Republican political failures, and demographic change.

The large majority who voted for Roosevelt and his party in 1932 could not know what programs they were voting for. Mainly they voted for an attractive political personality who expressed faith in American institutions and the American people and who promised immediate action. Millions, including many who had voted for Hoover in 1928, were repudiating Hoover, his party, and his failed policies, rather than endorsing a not

yet existent New Deal. Republicans had been given three years to whip the
Depression and they could not; conditions were worse than ever on election day 1932, and only President Hoover could see an upturn coming
soon. Many voters felt that the Democrats could do no worse and maybe
they would do better. American voters in 1932 were more certain of what
they didn't want than what they were getting when they cast their ballots
for the Hyde Park patrician, driving the fallen Horatio Alger hero from the
White House.

For the United States it was politics as usual amid the severest economic crisis in the history of the Republic. Most Americans, despite three
years of economic depression with no end in sight, remained politically
passive in 1932. Organized labor was quiet. Only Communists tried to organize the unemployed masses. The Communists, partially subsidized by
Moscow, staged unemployment marches, rent strikes, and hunger riots.
Party membership increased between 1930 and 1932, but Communism attracted few industrial workers, however hard-pressed they may have
been. The Communist Party made special efforts to recruit African American workers but could attract only a few. Probably in the view of most
African Americans it was tough enough being black in America without
being a "Red" too. The most obvious achievement of the Communists was
to frighten some conservatives, who believed that a "Red" revolution was
building in America. Despite hard times and government failures, there
was little protest or rebellion in Depression America, and those few that
did occur neither changed the conditions they challenged nor posed any
threat to authorities. Neither the power nor legitimacy of government at
any level was ever challenged by more than a handful of people. Discontent yes, but not even the preconditions for revolution had appeared in
Depression America.

Both the Socialist Party and the Communists ran presidential candidates in 1932. Their candidates articulated radical indictments of the
American capitalist system and offered socialist alternatives. Together the
two radical parties polled fewer than one million votes, less than 2 percent of the votes cast. Much more expressive of popular political views in
the depths of economic depression were the 16 million voters who cast
their ballots for Mr. Hoover, despite hard times, his failed program, and
his lackluster campaign.

Far more Americans were demoralized by economic depression
than were radicalized by their searing experiences. Clinging to traditional
individualistic values, they could not see economic collapse as a collective
failure, as a crisis of institutions. They assumed personal responsibility for
their predicament, blaming themselves instead of the American system
and its leaders for their impoverishment. Others, overwhelmed by disaster, were incapable of anger or rebellion. Dispirited, they remained at
home or sat on park benches muttering to themselves. They suffered in silence, alone and isolated. Many hit the road or rode the rails, joining 2

million other rootless individuals seeking a job, a meal, a shelter, or merely a sense of motion. Along with these homeless migrants of despair there were others who, rejecting all secular saviors, awaited divine deliverance from their earthly afflictions.

INTERREGNUM

The four-month interval between Roosevelt's election in November 1932 and his inauguration on March 4, 1933, proved to be the most painful winter of the Great Depression. Unemployment climbed past 13 million. Each month thousands of farmers and businessmen went bankrupt. Across the land destitute families shivered in darkened, heatless rooms without adequate food, clothing, or medical care. Recovery appeared nowhere in sight. A Roosevelt adviser, Rexford Guy Tugwell, wrote in his diary, "Never in modern times, I should think, has there been so widespread unemployment and such moving distress from cold and hunger."

As the Depression continued to deepen and its miseries multiplied, the search for scapegoats escalated. Who was to blame for the economic collapse? Inevitably and implacably millions of Americans reached the same conclusion: If businessmen and Republican Party leaders were responsible for the prosperity of the 1920s, they were surely responsible for the poverty of the early 1930s. The reputation of financiers, industrialists, economists, and politicians plummeted. A Senate investigating committee, chaired by Ferdinand Pecora, probed the investment practices on the New York Stock Exchange and discovered that Wall Street titans had rigged investor pools and often profiteered at the expense of their customers and their firms. Inside traders had frequently bought stocks below the market price paid by the general public.

Pecora's committee failed, however, to prove its suspicion that a conspiracy of "short sellers" had caused the market to collapse, despite wide circulation of such rumors. (Selling short is an investment strategy used by speculators to profit from a declining stock market. They contract to sell stocks they do not yet own in the future at their current price. If the price of the stock drops before delivery date, speculators buy the stock at the lower price and deliver it to the buyer who has contracted to pay the earlier higher price. The short seller pockets the difference as profit for having guessed accurately that the market would drop.) Pecora's committee did succeed in exposing many financiers as ruthless, crooked men who sold out their customers and their banks to save their own financial skins. The committee's investigations were among the many Depression era events that destroyed the American financier as folk hero.

The social irresponsibility of some prominent businessmen also contributed to the public's disillusionment with the business community. During a time when millions of families were living in dire poverty, many businessmen continued to collect large salaries and manipulate their investments to avoid taxes. Some falsified their tax returns and others refused to pay taxes. Henry Ford, Detroit's largest employer and the richest man in America, refused to accept any responsibility for the army of jobless workers filling the city. A nation that had regarded its financial and business leaders with awe in 1929 turned on them furiously now that their magic capabilities to generate wealth had vanished.

Congressional investigations, grand jury indictments, and trials of businessmen during the Depression paralleled the "witch hunts" for Communist subversives during the McCarthy era of the early 1950s. A similar need existed during the early 1930s to simplify and personify a grave disaster that, in reality, was vastly complex and caused by a bewildering variety of forces and circumstances. It provided bleak comfort to confused and hungry citizens to believe that an evil conspiracy of greedy inside traders selling short had engineered the stock market crash for their own profit and then panicked when it got out of control, destroying the securities market and causing the Depression. In fact, no one planned the Crash and no one understood precisely why the market had fallen so sharply, why the Depression ensued, or why it was so severe and seemingly interminable.

Many who angrily scapegoated businessmen also despaired of the political process, which appeared incapable of coping with economic crises. During its "lame duck" session from December 1932 through February 1933 Congress failed to enact a single important piece of economic legislation. The national government appeared to have been reduced to farcical ineptitude at a time when there was an urgent need for effective measures to combat economic calamity.

NADIR

During that harrowing winter of 1932 and 1933, with the economy depressed and government paralyzed, some observers feared that the American system of political economy was dying. The European depression proved that the capitalist malaise was worldwide. Only the Soviet Union, undergoing rapid industrialization during the 1930s, had an expanding economy and labor shortages. During the Great Depression over 100,000 unemployed Americans, responding to ads a Soviet company had placed in American newspapers, applied for work in the Soviet Union. About 6,000 obtained jobs and left the stagnant American economy to live and work in the Soviet Union, apparently preferring a job under Communism to joblessness in capitalist America. Some American voices were heard calling for an end to political democracy and the creation of a directorate to make the "tough" decisions necessary to restore prosperity and order. These calls for "strong" leadership in time of crisis sounded the siren song of an American-bred Fascism fearing economic collapse and the rise of radicalism. Perhaps it could happen here?

Meanwhile President Hoover and President-elect Roosevelt were playing a political game. The outgoing president invited Roosevelt to attend a conference on European debt problems. They met on November 22, 1932. Hoover, believing that the main causes of the American Depression were foreign, gave foreign economic policy a higher priority than did Roosevelt, who correctly saw that the Depression's main causes were domestic. Their meeting was unsuccessful. Roosevelt, suspecting Hoover was trying to get him to endorse his policies, avoided making any commitments. He did not want to be identified with the failed policies of a discredited leader. Hoover and Roosevelt had another inconclusive meeting in January 1933. Hoover believed that Roosevelt did not understand the economic situation and thought him a shallow demagogue. The two men, formerly good friends, had come to dislike each other intensely.

Roosevelt spent most of the four months before his inauguration meeting with advisers, forming his government, and drafting his legislative agenda. He was forging the New Deal. Many of his assistants came from academic backgrounds. They were college professors recruited from the social science faculties at Columbia and other prestigious Ivy League universities. These scholars would form the "brains trust" of the Roosevelt Revolution that was about to descend upon Washington.

At a time when the political leadership of the nation appeared helpless, with a repudiated leader still holding office and the President-elect without power, there occurred an event that nearly eliminated the New Deal before it could begin. On February 15, 1933, three weeks before his scheduled inaugural, Roosevelt came to Miami to attend a reception. Sitting on the top of the back seat of an open car in a city park, Roosevelt gave an informal speech to a crowd of well-wishers and then slipped down into the car seat. At that moment the mayor of Chicago, Anton Cermak, came up to the car to ask a political favor of Roosevelt. Roosevelt leaned forward to hear what Cermak was saying. A short, dark man, standing on a box 30 feet away, began firing a pistol at Roosevelt. Cermak was fatally wounded, and four others were hit by bullets. Roosevelt escaped the deadly assault unharmed, and the assassin was immediately captured and jailed. The man who had tried to kill the President-elect was Guiseppe Zangara, a little man with a consuming hatred of all rich and powerful people.

Roosevelt shrugged off the frightening incident. He believed that if fate intended him to die at the hands of an assassin, he would. He showed courage and poise, dismissing the murderous assault with jokes and smiles. Roosevelt also expressed remorse at the death of Cermak and sympathy for the others wounded during the shooting. It is sobering to reflect on what direction the history of the United States during the years of grave economic crisis at home and international disorder abroad might have taken had Zangara succeeded in killing Roosevelt. Would the American system of middle-class democracy and capitalism have survived?

As the spring of 1933 approached, the nation appeared to be heading for financial collapse. Another epidemic of bank failures swept the land. As February 1933 ended, banks all over the country closed their doors; they either were bankrupt or had closed to avoid bankruptcy. Panicky depositors stood in long lines for hours waiting to withdraw their money. They believed that their dollars would be safer in shoe boxes, under mattresses, or in tin cans buried in their back yard than in bank vaults. By March 3, the day before Roosevelt's inaugural, 38 states had shut down all their banks and the remaining 10 states were moving to close theirs. Normal business and commerce ground to a halt. People reverted to bartering for necessary goods and services. On that same day the New York Stock Exchange suspended all securities trading and closed down. Financial paralysis crept across the nation; it was the lowest ebb of the commercial spirit in American history.

BIBLIOGRAPHY

There are many good books written about the stock market crash, the causes of the Great Depression of the 1930s, and the Depression's impact on the American people. Robert Sobel, *The Great Bull Market* and John Kenneth Galbraith, *The Great Crash* are two short studies of the coming of the Great Depression. Gordon Thomas and Max Morgan-Witts have written a colorful social history of the Crash called *The Day the Bubble Burst*. The impact of the Depression on the life of people is vividly expressed in Studs Terkel, *Hard Times*, a collection of interviews with hundreds of people who recall their difficult experiences. David Shannon, ed., *The Great Depression* is an excellent collection of primary sources about life during the economic crisis. The finest economic history of the Great Depression, which explains why it was so severe and lasted so long, is Michael Bernstein, *The Great Depression: Delayed Recovery and Economic Change in America, 1929–1939*. Another fine account of the Depression experience is Caroline Bird, *The Invisible Scar*. Two classic studies from the 1930s have endured: Robert S. and Helen Merrell Lynd, *Middletown in Transition*, a sociological study of a midwestern city in the Depression; and James Agee and Walker Evans, *Let Us Now Praise Famous Men*, a powerful documentary in words and pictures of poverty-stricken Alabama sharecroppers. John Garraty, *The Great Depression: An Inquiry into the Causes, Course, and Consequences of the Worldwide Depression of the 1930s* is a fine recent study that puts the Depression into comparative perspective. Two good recent biographies of Herbert Hoover are David Burner, *Herbert Hoover: A Public Life* and Joan Hoff Wilson, *Herbert Hoover: Forgotten Progressive*. Roger Daniels, *The Bonus March* and John Shover, *Cornbelt Rebellion* are fine accounts of 1932 radical protest movements.

CHAPTER
8
The New Deal

When Franklin Delano Roosevelt assumed the presidency on March 4, 1933, the United States and most of the world were gripped by the iron hand of depression. Roosevelt himself was largely an unknown quantity, and the New Deal existed only as upbeat political rhetoric. Over the next five years Roosevelt and the New Dealers proceeded to design and implement an energetic legislative program to alleviate the effects of depression, restore prosperity, and make the federal government responsive to a broad range of issues affecting most Americans. Although the New Deal only partially solved the grave problems of economic depression, Roosevelt and his program achieved a resounding political success. Roosevelt became one of the most powerful and popular leaders in the history of the republic. His overwhelming reelection victory in 1936 demonstrated that the New Deal accorded with the hopes and dreams of most Americans. Before the New Deal ran its course, the basic American approach to governance had been redefined, and the role of the federal government in the lives of most Americans had been enlarged. The American welfare state had been forged and the federal government had committed itself to maintaining minimum living standards for those in need. The New Deal reshaped modern America.

FDR

Franklin Delano Roosevelt was a professional politician from a wealthy background. Born on an estate in Hyde Park, New York, in 1882, Franklin Roosevelt was the son of a middle-aged country gentleman of Dutch descent and a young mother who doted on her only child. He enjoyed all the privileges and luxuries that wealth could command, including extensive travel in Europe with his family. He was tutored by governesses at home until he was 14, then went away to Groton, a distinguished prep school near Boston. At Groton he came under the influence of Headmaster Endicott Peabody, who implanted within young Roosevelt the Christian gentleman's ideal of service to the less fortunate, the conviction that privileged Americans should help solve national and international problems.

Franklin grew up to be an ambitious young man who believed himself destined to achieve distinction, and he already harbored political ambitions. He was much influenced by the achievements of his famous distant cousin, Theodore Roosevelt, whom he affectionately called "Uncle Ted," and Franklin apparently aspired to the presidency from an early age. After Groton he enrolled at Harvard. He was fiercely competitive, trying hard to win distinction in athletics, but he had to settle for managing the baseball team and editing the college newspaper. From Harvard, he went to Columbia Law School. In the spring of 1905 he married his fifth cousin, Eleanor. In 1907 Roosevelt began a law career with a prominent Wall Street firm. Roosevelt at 25 was a well-educated, wealthy, athletic, handsome young man. He was widely traveled, already well acquainted with many men prominent in American life, and moved comfortably in high society. But corporate law could never satisfy his ambitions or his exalted sense of himself as a man of destiny. He yearned for a larger arena and found it in politics.

His political career began in 1910 when he was elected to the New York state senate. He entered politics as a Progressive Democrat and worked for political reform, conservation, and aid for farmers. In 1912 he campaigned energetically for Woodrow Wilson, and President Wilson rewarded his efforts by making him Assistant Secretary of Navy, a position he held for eight years. It was the job he most wanted, for it both advanced his political career and was closely tied to his favorite pastime, sailing. Sailing was Roosevelt's passion; he spent as much time as he could on his family's yacht, and later on his own yacht. Most vacations were spent with upper-class friends who shared his love of ships and the sea.

In 1920 he was the Democratic vice-presidential candidate, running with James Cox on a ticket that got buried by Harding and Coolidge. This experience did no harm to Roosevelt, however, and he emerged from the campaign a nationally known figure and party leader. Then in the summer of 1921 Roosevelt was felled by a severe attack of polio at age 39. His recovery was slow and exceedingly painful and left him a cripple with wasted legs. His wife Eleanor said that his suffering gave him a courage and strength that he never had before.

His illness slowed but did not deter his political career. He was never out of politics; he remained a party leader all through the 1920s. He supported New York Governor Alfred E. "Al" Smith's candidacy at the 1924 Democratic convention and attracted national attention with a brilliant

Mar. 4, 1933 THE Price 15 cents

NEW YORKER

A New Yorker cover featuring a gloomy Hoover and a buoyant Roosevelt en route to the inauguration ceremony on March 4, 1933.

speech endorsing Smith's nomination. Standing before the delegates on crutches, he urged the nomination of Smith, whom he called the "Happy Warrior." He supported Smith again in 1928 and also won election as governor of New York, succeeding Smith, who had lost his bid for the presidency to Republican Herbert Hoover. Roosevelt's gubernatorial victory instantly made him a leading contender for his party's next presidential nomination. Roosevelt's tenure as New York governor coincided with Hoover's presidency. As governor he showed a greater commitment to unemployment relief than did Hoover and a greater willingness to experiment with innovative programs in time of crisis. Looking ahead to a possible presidency, he was also gathering advisers to develop programs that would combat the effects of depression nationally.

Roosevelt's political philosophy was anchored firmly within the progressive tradition, and despite his association with Wilson, he was more of a New Nationalist than a Wilsonian. These views he shared with his leading advisers. Roosevelt favored a vigorous role for the federal government in regulating corporate enterprise and restoring purchasing power to farmers, workers, and hard-pressed middle-class citizens. He favored the application of scarcity economics—that is, of reducing production in order to raise prices and increase profits and wages—as the best way to end the Depression and restore prosperity.

Roosevelt was an experienced, confident political leader, convinced that he could provide both the leadership and the programs to lead his nation out of its greatest economic crisis. As he prepared for his inauguration, he believed he could restore both confidence and prosperity. He was unafraid, prepared to act boldly and to experiment. He once told a friend that the hardest thing he ever tried to do was to wiggle his big toe after polio had destroyed his legs. After that ordeal, he said, all else was easy.

THE NEW DEAL BEGINS

Not since 1861 had a new president taken office amid such ominous circumstances. With Americans' economy mired in its deepest depression, their government paralyzed, and their financial system crumbling, they turned to Roosevelt with desperate expectations. "First of all," declared the new president in his inaugural address, "let me assert my firm belief that the only thing we have to fear is fear itself—nameless, unreasoning, unjustified terror." Speaking firmly, a tinge of anger in his voice, he denounced businessmen and bankers who caused the Depression and could find no cure for it: "Rulers of the exchange of mankind's goods have failed, through their own stubbornness and their own incompetence, have admitted their failure, and have abdicated. . . . The money changers have fled from their high seats in the temple of our civilization. We may now restore that temple to the ancient truths." The heart of his speech was a promise to fight the Depression with a bold program, to do whatever was necessary to restore prosperity. He also proclaimed his faith that "This nation will revive and will prosper."

His words electrified a people yearning for reassurance. He instilled hope and courage in millions of his fellow citizens. In one speech he had accomplished what Hoover had failed to do in four years; he convinced Americans that an effective leader with faith in the future had taken command. That night, instead of attending the inaugural ball, he met with financial advisers to face the nation's imminent financial crisis. The next day he declared a four-day "bank holiday" and summoned Congress to a special emergency session, which began on March 9.

His first measures revealed a streak of fiscal conservatism which characterized the early New Deal. An Emergency Banking Relief bill, drafted with the help of Hoover's treasury officials, who were still on the job, attacked the banking crisis. It outlawed hoarding and exporting of gold. It also arranged for the reopening of solvent banks and the reorganization of failed banks under Treasury Department supervision. However, it left the banking system essentially unchanged and with the same people in charge. Complained one Congressman, "The President drove the money changers out of the Capitol on March 4th—and they were all back on the 9th." Roosevelt then sent Congress an Economy Act to trim federal expenditures by $400 million and balance the budget, mainly by cutting veterans' benefits. Another measure raised federal excise taxes. These deflationary measures made the New Deal initially appear more conservative than Hoover's program.

On Sunday evening, March 12, Roosevelt gave the first of his "Fireside Chats." He spoke informally to an estimated 60 million Americans gathered around their radios across the nation. He talked about the banking crisis and the measures his administration had taken to end it. He assured his fellow Americans that the banks were once again sound and "would take care of all legitimate needs." He told them it was safe to put their money back in the banks, adding that "Hoarding has become an exceedingly unfashionable pastime." The next day long lines once again appeared outside banks, but this time customers were putting their money back in. Roosevelt had told the people the banks were sound and they had believed him. The banking crisis was over. Roosevelt had shown remarkable leadership. Raymond Moley, one of his advisers, observed, "Capitalism was saved in eight days."

During his presidency Roosevelt relied on his wife more than any

Early in his presidency, Roosevelt hit upon one of his most popular devices—the "fireside chat," an informal radio address to the people in which he discussed important issues of the day. He conducted dozens of fireside chats during his long presidency.

previous president had. Eleanor Roosevelt redefined what it meant to be First Lady. She became a political force in her own right, one of the leaders of the liberal wing of the Democratic Party. She made public appearances, gave speeches, held press conferences, and made weekly radio broadcasts. She wrote a newspaper column that was nationally syndicated. She traveled 40,000 miles a year as the eyes and ears of her husband's presidency. More progressive than Franklin, Eleanor functioned as a liberal conscience, a kind of goad to take actions on behalf of the disadvantaged and downtrodden. She was enormously popular with most Americans and often got higher public approval ratings than did the President.

THE HUNDRED DAYS

During the first three months, which became known as "The Hundred Days," the New Deal gathered momentum. Many legislative proposals, dealing with a wide range of Depression problems, were sent to the Hill to the special session of Congress, and Congress quickly enacted relief measures to help unemployed Americans. One measure created the Civilian Conservation Corps (CCC). Young men were taken out of the cities and put to work in camps organized along military lines in national parks and forests. They planted trees, cleared campsites, built bridges, constructed dams, and made fire trails. The CCC was Roosevelt's favorite relief program; its conservation of both human and natural resources appealed to his patrician humanitarian instincts. During its ten-year lifetime the CCC put over 2 million young men to work. Congress also passed the Federal Emergency Relief Act (FERA), a direct relief measure that allocated $500 million for state and local governments to dispense to needy families.

The Agricultural Adjustment Act (AAA), an important early New Deal measure, was enacted in May 1933. Its chief purpose was to raise farm income by raising commodity prices. Defining the farm problem as one of overproduction, the measure reflected Roosevelt's commitment to scarcity economics. A domestic allotment program was established for seven major commodities—cotton, corn, tobacco, rice, wheat, hogs, and dairy products—whereby the government paid farmers to reduce their acreage and produce less. Subsidy payments came from a tax levied on the primary processor for each crop. For example, the wheat subsidy came from a tax on the companies that ground the wheat into flour. The subsidy payments were based on "parity," a system designed to allow farmers to regain the purchasing power they had enjoyed during the 1910–1914 period, a time of general agricultural prosperity.

The 1933 crops had already been planted before the Triple A could be put into effect. To forestall another year of overproduction, Secretary of Agriculture Henry A. Wallace ordered farmers to plow up millions of

The Civilian Conservation Corps (CCC) was one of the most popular early New Deal programs and it was Roosevelt's favorite. Begun in 1933, it took unemployed young men off the streets where there was nothing for them to do and put them to work in the countryside. Here workers check farmland erosion.

acres of cotton, corn, and wheat and to slaughter millions of baby hogs to be eligible for the subsidy payments. These drastic actions taken at a time when many Americans went to bed hungry each night provoked furious criticism. Wallace called the actions he had ordered "a shocking comment on our civilization." It also raised food prices to consumers during a time of massive unemployment and underemployment. Other New Deal programs shared this depression characteristic with the Triple A: The price of helping a particular interest group was higher living costs borne by the general public. But the AAA did benefit those farmers who participated in its subsidy programs. For the first time since World War I farm income rose.

A month after passing the AAA program for agriculture, Congress enacted a comprehensive program for industrial recovery called the National Industrial Recovery Act (NIRA). The NIRA expressed the early New Deal's commitment to economic planning and business–government cooperation to replace the depression-spawned cutthroat competition raging in all industrial sectors. NIRA set up a planning agency called the National Recovery Administration (NRA), which exempted businesses from antitrust laws. Under NRA supervision, competing businesses within a given industry met with union leaders and consumer groups to draft codes of fair competition that limited production, divided it among various companies, and stabilized prices by establishing minimum price levels. Section 7(a) of the NRA charter guaranteed workers the right to join unions and to engage in collective bargaining. It also established minimum wages and maximum hours for workers. The NIRA, like the AAA, was based on the principles of scarcity economics. It was designed to promote industrial recovery by curbing production and raising prices, thereby generating higher profits and wages. The NRA, launched with much hoopla and great expectations, failed to promote much industrial recovery or reduce unemployment. Production increased only slowly and companies did not hire many additional employees.

The New Deal's first large-scale public works program was incorporated into the NIRA. Called the Public Works Administration (PWA), it carried a $3.3 billion price tag for building roads, public buildings, ships, and naval aircraft. Its purpose was to let contracts to idle construction companies, to put unemployed workers to work, and to stimulate local economies by pumping in federal funding for the projects.

Congress also created the Tennessee Valley Authority (TVA). TVA was a multipurpose regional developmental program for the Tennessee River Valley, which ran through Tennessee, North Carolina, Kentucky, Virginia, Mississippi, Alabama, and Georgia—one of the poorest, most depressed areas of the nation. TVA spent billions constructing dams to control flooding and to generate hydroelectric power. Other TVA projects reclaimed and reforested land and fought soil erosion. The TVA widened and deepened a 650-mile stretch of the river, making it navigable to river traffic. TVA also provided thousands of jobs for poor residents of the region, both black and white. This striking example of progressive enterprise was one of eight originally proposed regional development plans for the nation, but effective political opposition by power companies who charged the government with unfair competition killed all the other projects. The TVA still functions today. Like many New Deal programs, it left a mixed legacy. It reclaimed millions of acres and enhanced the regional economy. But it also forced thousands of families from their lands and became one of the worst polluters in the nation.

Other significant early New Deal measures included the Federal Securities Act, which grew out of Senator Pecora's exposures of wrongdoing on Wall Street. This law gave the Federal Trade Commission the power to supervise new securities issues, required each new stock issue to be accompanied by statements disclosing the financial status of the issuing company, and made misrepresentation a federal crime. A Banking Act created the Federal Deposit Insurance Corporation (FDIC), which insured

Tennessee Valley Authority

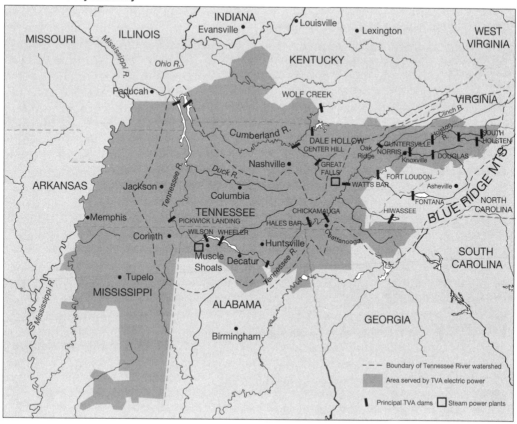

depositor bank accounts through the Federal Reserve System. The Home Owners' Loan Corporation (HOLC) enabled homeowners to refinance their home mortgages at lower rates of interest and with smaller payments. Thousands of families were able to retain ownership of their homes through HOLC mortgages. Roosevelt also took the nation off the international gold standard in order to inflate the currency to complement his efforts to raise domestic price levels through the Triple A and the NRA.

Roosevelt also requested that Congress make good his campaign promise to repeal Prohibition. The lame-duck Congress meeting in February 1933 had proposed a constitutional amendment repealing the Eighteenth Amendment. While the amendment was making its way through the states, the new Congress modified the Volstead Act by legalizing beer and wine with an alcoholic content of 3.2 percent. These beverages went on sale April 7, 1933, marking the first time in over thirteen years that it was legal to drink in America. The new amendment, the Twenty-first, was ratified in December 1933. Booze was back, although eight states remained dry. The Noble Experiment was over. Roosevelt supported repeal of Prohibition mainly because enforcement had failed and also repeal would reactivate a major industry, employ thousands of workers, and generate federal revenue in a time of severe depression.

Congress ended its special session on June 16. The "Hundred Days" were over. During this intensely busy Congressional session Roosevelt and his New Dealers had sent up fifteen major bills, and all were enacted with few changes. Normal partisan rivalries and debate were suspended as both houses responded positively to Roosevelt's energetic assault on a wide range of Depression miseries. During the "Hundred Days" the public mood had been transformed. A nation of pessimists had reclaimed their characteristically American optimism, confident that they could whip the Depression and control their destiny. During the next year many more New Deal measures became law, giving further help to farmers, creating additional relief projects that employed thousands of workers, strengthening trade unions, aiding small businessmen, and helping homeowners refinance their mortgages.

The New Deal of 1933 and 1934 represented interest group democracy at work, not the single interest government characteristic of the 1920s. Government help went to business, agriculture, and labor. Also consumers, homeowners, local governments, and the unemployed benefited. And the New Deal seemed to work. Unemployment fell steadily from 13 million in 1933 to 9 million by 1936. Farm income doubled, from $3 billion in 1933 to $6 billion in 1936. Manufacturing wages rose from $6 billion in 1933 to $13 billion in 1937.

THE 1934 ELECTIONS

The 1934 elections confirmed the immense popularity of Roosevelt and his New Deal. Normally the party in power loses seats in an off-year election, but voters in November elected 322 Democratic Congressmen to only 103 Republicans, a gain of 13 seats for the Democrats. Never in its history had the Republican Party possessed such a low percentage of House seats. In the Senate the rout of the GOP was worse. The Democrats gained 9 seats, bringing their total to 69 and leaving the Republicans with only 37. One of the new Democratic senators was a county judge from Missouri named Harry Truman. Also 41 of the 48 states elected Democratic governors.

The 1934 elections almost erased the Republican Party as a national force. Republicans controlled few governorships, few state legislatures, and fewer than a third of the Congressional seats. They had no program and no national leader with any popular appeal. Arthur Krock of the *New York Times* exclaimed that the New Deal had won "the most overwhelming victory in the history of American politics." William Allen White noted that Roosevelt "has been all but crowned by the people." Whatever its economic shortcomings and failures, the New Deal made good politics.

CRITICS—LEFT, RIGHT, AND POPULIST

Although the 1934 elections demonstrated the immense popularity of Roosevelt and the New Deal, the President and his programs called forth a barrage of criticism. New Deal critics spanned the political spectrum from radical left to far right, and some of them defied political categorizing. As an activist president with a penchant for using demagogic rhetoric in which he attacked the nation's financial and industrial leaders as greedy, socially irresponsible, and incompetent, Roosevelt incurred the hostility of many rich people. Many of the wealthy hated him personally, viewing the Hyde Park patrician as a renegade, as a class enemy and traitor. Many businessmen and conservative politicians attacked the New Deal. They denounced excessive taxation and government regulation of business. Others criticized deficit financing, public works, and federal relief payments to the unemployed. Conservatives denounced the growth in size and power of the federal government and its subversion of individual initiative. They worried that Roosevelt might be assuming dictatorial powers, and they suggested that the New Deal state resembled totalitarian Fascist and Communist regimes.

The most vitriolic criticism of Roosevelt and the New Deal came from the American Liberty League, formed in 1934 by members of the Du Pont family, owners of the nation's largest chemical company. The Du Ponts also provided most of the funding for the League, which served as a vehicle for corporate anti-New Deal critics. Some of Roosevelt's personal enemies, such as former President Hoover and former Democratic presidential candidate Alfred E. Smith, joined the American Liberty League. Both men bitterly attacked the New Deal and its energetic leader. Liberty League spokesmen railed at the whole range of New Deal economic and social legislation. Most speakers made little effort to offer positive alternatives. They insisted that Roosevelt was bent on destroying the American capitalist system and replacing it with a socialist dictatorship. Despite spending over $1 million, Liberty League orators failed to inflict any serious political wounds on Roosevelt or the New Deal. During the depths of the Great Depression most Americans were not terribly concerned about the plight of the wealthy, the fate of big business, or the sensibilities of rich people.

Other critics attacked specific New Deal programs as inadequate and unfair. The National Recovery Administration attracted much criticism; its detractors charged that corporate leaders had written NRA codes that favored big business' interests over the interests of workers, consumers, and small businesses. The AAA also came under attack; people were angry about the wasteful destruction of food crops to start the program at a time when millions were ill fed. Although the Triple A worked for landowners, it neglected tenants and sharecroppers. They rarely got subsidy money for cutting back production. In the South, plantation owners who took land out of production to collect the AAA subsidies often turned their sharecroppers off the land, depriving them of their economic base. Thousands of these uprooted "Okies" and "Arkies" headed for California, victims of both hard times and New Deal politics.

Many people were disappointed by the partial recovery made under the New Deal in 1933 and 1934. In their eyes the New Deal had failed to bring full economic recovery to the nation and Roosevelt had failed to reduce unemployment significantly. Intellectuals with tidy minds who embraced programmatic ideologies viewed the tentative, experimental nature of the New Deal as inadequate. They believed that recovery from economic depression required careful planning and a more thorough reorganization of American society and government than Roosevelt and his advisers were willing to undertake. Even though business was up and unemployment down, the economy remained well below the 1920s pre-Depression standard. Demagogues appealed to the dissatisfactions and frustrations of many Americans.

Father Charles E. Coughlin, a Roman Catholic priest whose parish lay in a suburb of Detroit, developed a following of millions with his weekly radio broadcasts denouncing the New Deal. His doctrines appealed mainly to midwestern farmers and ethnic city dwellers. In 1934 he organized a political movement called the National Union for Social Justice. Coughlin concentrated on reforming the money and banking systems of the country. He resurrected the old Populist nostrum of free and unlimited coinage of silver as the key to restoring national prosperity and to liberating farmers and workers from the clutches of the money changers. As the years went by, Coughlin became more extreme. He vehemently denounced Roosevelt, and a disturbing anti-Semitic strain laced his rhetoric. As he grew shriller, his influence waned, and he was eventually silenced by Church leaders.

Another anti-New Deal movement that called attention to its shortcomings was the Old Age Revolving Pensions plan conceived by Dr. Francis E. Townsend, a retired dentist. Dr. Townsend proposed that everyone over 60 receive $200 per month on the condition that they spend the money during that same month. The money for the pensions would be raised by a "transaction tax," a sales tax levied each time goods were sold. He claimed that his plan would both provide for the elderly and end the Depression by pumping billions of dollars of purchasing power into the economy. New Deal economists quickly demonstrated that the plan was fiscally unsound. The transaction tax would raise only a portion of the billions of dollars required to fund the plan and would have only a small impact on the Depression.

But Dr. Townsend proved to be a good organizer and charismatic leader. He created a national organization that at its peak had millions of followers and more than 5,000 local Townsend Clubs. Millions of elderly, whose savings and investments had been lost during the Depression, joined his movement. The Townsendites indelibly impressed the plight of the elderly poor on the national conscience and also called attention to inadequate pensions and local relief for aged, retired workers. Roosevelt and the New Dealers were forced to respond to the concerns of the Townsendites. Social Security was enacted in part to undercut the appeal of the elderly dentist's pet panacea.

The most significant challenge to the New Deal came from Huey Long, a brilliant, ambitious southern demagogue. Long, a left-wing Populist, became governor of Louisiana in 1929 and U.S. Senator in 1932. Along the way he crafted a corrupt political machine that gave him dictatorial control of Louisiana politics. He also enjoyed an immense popular following among workers and farmers of Louisiana because of his program of public works and public schools that were paid for by taxes on big businesses doing business in the state. He did much to improve the quality of life for ordinary people in one of the poorest regions of the country.

Long had supported Roosevelt's candidacy for the Democratic nomination in 1932; in fact he had been one of the southern politicians that prevented Roosevelt's supporters from abandoning him at the convention before William Randolph Hearst struck the political bargain that saved the nomination for Roosevelt. Long had supported the New Deal when it began, but he turned against it in 1934 because of its fiscal conservatism. He made a bid for national leadership with a program he called "Share the Wealth," and he coined the slogan "Every Man a King." "Share the Wealth" proposed using the tax power to confiscate all incomes over $1 million and all estates over $5 million. The money raised would furnish each family with $5,000 for buying a farm or home, an annual income of $2,000, a free college education for their children, a radio, and other benefits for farmers and industrial workers. Long's plan was also fiscally unsound. The funds raised by confiscatory taxes would not begin to pay for the promised benefits. The Senate twice rejected his tax bills by large majorities.

But Long's scheme appealed to the aspirations of poor people during the Depression, to their resentment of the rich, and to their disappointment with New Deal efforts. Even though he was a corrupt demagogue and his distributionist schemes were fiscally unsound, Long addressed a real problem: the uneven distribution of wealth in America that allowed mass poverty in a rich country. By mid-1935 he had built a national following of millions and was planning a presidential bid in 1936 as an independent candidate challenging Roosevelt. Roosevelt and his advisers considered Long a serious threat; they feared him as Roosevelt's and the New Deal's most powerful rival. They estimated that a Long candidacy

During the mid thirties, Huey P. Long of Louisiana emerged as the most formidable challenger to Roosevelt and the New Deal.

might draw as many as 4 or 5 million votes from the Democrats. Even if he could not beat Roosevelt in 1936, Long would be a prime contender for the Democratic nomination in 1940. An assassin's bullets cut short Long's career on September 8, 1935, and his movement quickly disintegrated. Nevertheless, his proposals for social reform continued to be part of the public dialogue.

There were also many other left-wing critics of the New Deal. Both the Communist and Socialist parties attacked it. William Z. Foster, the American Communist Party (CPUSA) candidate for president in 1932, proposed a Marxist-Leninist program for the reorganization of American society. He proposed nationalizing all private enterprise and eliminating all political parties except, of course, the Communist Party. Foster and his fellow Communists would eliminate not only depression from the land, but also capitalism and democracy.

During the Depression decade, thousands of Americans who were not members of the party joined organizations that were affiliated with and controlled by Communists. College students joined such Communist "front" organizations as the American Youth Congress and Young People's Communist League. The best-known Communist front organization was the American Writers Congress, which met in 1935. It represented Communist efforts to enlist the support of some of the nation's most prominent intellectuals and writers, including John Dos Passos, Theodore Dreiser, Erskine Caldwell, and Ernest Hemingway. These and other literati signed manifestos condemning the New Deal and calling for the overthrow of the capitalist system.

The Socialist Party under the leadership of a former Presbyterian minister turned socialist, Norman Thomas, attracted a sizable following during the Depression decade. Thomas was an indefatigable speaker and kept a Socialist indictment of the New Deal and American capitalism continually before the American public. Thomas particularly criticized Roosevelt and the New Dealers for their lack of concern for poor people and for their failure to promote civil rights for African Americans. Socialist candidates often made respectable showings in state and local elections and sometimes won. Minnesota elected a Socialist governor. In California the Socialist muckraker Upton Sinclair captured the 1934 Democratic Party gubernatorial nomination. He campaigned for governor on a program he called End Poverty in California (EPIC), which included establishing socialist enterprises within the state. Although he lost to a conservative Republican, Sinclair attracted over 800,000 votes.

The New Deal also came under attack from the Supreme Court. Most justices feared that many New Deal measures, which were hastily drawn up and enacted without debate or criticism by Congress, gave the executive branch too much power. From 1934 to 1936 the Court nullified several important New Deal measures. In *Schechter* v. *U.S.* (1935) a unanimous court declared the NRA unconstitutional on the grounds that it gave excessive legislative power to the White House and that the commerce clause of the Constitution did not give the federal government the authority to regulate intrastate commerce. The Schechter decision killed the New Deal's most important program for industrial recovery. In *U.S.* v. *Butler* (1936) the Court also nullified the AAA when it declared the processing tax unconstitutional because it was not a legitimate use of the tax power. This decision killed the New Deal's major program for agricultural recovery.

THE SECOND NEW DEAL

As 1935 dawned, despite its big victory at the polls, the New Deal faced trouble. Critics were attacking particular programs and its failure to bring complete recovery. Demagogues were offering alternatives and luring away supporters, and the Supreme Court was dismantling its major programs. Roosevelt burst forth again in the spring and summer of 1935 with a flurry of legislative initiatives known as the Second New Deal.

The Second New Deal differed from early efforts in several significant ways. The First New Deal had emphasized relief and recovery measures; the second continued these efforts but was more concerned with reform. Earlier Roosevelt had sought to cooperate with business; in 1935 he accused business of putting its interests ahead of the general welfare. He also proposed measures for increasing business taxes and tightening government regulation of some industries. The First New Deal had been most responsive to political pressures from established interests—bankers, large farmers, and big business; the Second New Deal responded to the rising power of organized labor and included measures that reflected Roosevelt's concern about the emergence of demagogic critics of the New Deal. Already looking ahead to the 1936 election, Roosevelt moved to steal the thunder of his most important critics and to soften their most strident demands. He co-opted some of the issues of the Socialists, the Townsendites, the Coughlanites, and intellectuals, and he incorporated them into his legislative proposals. Together these factors combined to move Roosevelt to the left; the Second New Deal was more liberal than the first. FDR abandoned his alliance with the business community and more directly addressed the needs of the disadvantaged and dispossessed.

In April 1935 Congress enacted the first major piece of Second New Deal legislation, the Emergency Relief Appropriation Act (ERAA). This new law empowered President Roosevelt to establish public works programs for millions of jobless Americans; one of these was the Works Progress Administration (WPA). The WPA was the most important of the New Deal work relief programs. Before it was phased out in 1943, more than 8.5 million people were employed on more than a million different projects.

WPA workers built over 650,000 miles of roads, 125,000 public buildings, 8,000 parks, and hundreds of bridges.

In addition to its construction projects, the WPA also funded many cultural efforts. A Federal Theater Project brought dramas, comedies, and variety shows to cities and towns across the nation. John Houseman and Orson Welles were among the young artists who acted and directed in the Federal Theater Project. Artists on WPA payrolls painted murals in post offices and other public buildings. Dance and music projects sponsored ballet companies and symphony orchestras that performed across the country. A Federal Writers' Project hired writers including Richard Wright, John Steinbeck, and John Cheever to write guidebooks and regional histories. The WPA even hired unemployed historians for its writers' project.

In addition to the WPA, the ERAA also funded other relief and public works measures. The Resettlement Administration (RA) moved thousands of impoverished farm families from submarginal land and gave them a fresh start on good soil with adequate farming equipment and guidance from farm experts. Later the Farm Security Administration (FSA), which replaced the RA, granted long-term, low-interest loans to sharecroppers and tenants, enabling them to buy family farms. Another FSA program built chains of sanitary, well-run camps for migrant farm workers. Both the RA and FSA were New Deal relief agencies that attacked the problem of rural poverty.

The ERAA also established the Rural Electrification Administration (REA). No other New Deal measure improved the quality of rural life as

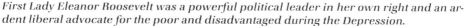

First Lady Eleanor Roosevelt was a powerful political leader in her own right and an ardent liberal advocate for the poor and disadvantaged during the Depression.

much as the REA. Until 1935, rural America lacked electrical power. Kerosene lamps illuminated homes after dark, and farmers' wives lacked washing machines, refrigerators, vacuum cleaners, and radios. The REA subsidized the building of power lines in rural America. Where private power was unavailable or private companies refused to build lines, the REA financed the creation of nonprofit, cooperative electric companies. In 1935 fewer than 10 percent of rural homes had electricity; by 1940, 40 percent were electrified, and by 1950, 90 percent.

The ERAA also authorized the National Youth Administration (NYA), the most important New Deal relief measure for young people. Its director, Aubrey Williams, worked to find part-time employment for more than 600,000 college students and over 1.5 million high school students so that they could continue their studies. It also found employment for over 2 million jobless young people who were not in school.

In June 1935 Roosevelt sent Congress five major bills: a labor bill, a Social Security bill, a banking bill, a public utilities bill, and a tax measure. Congress responded with a "Second Hundred Days" and enacted them all. Out of this remarkable Congressional session came some of the most important and enduring legislation in the history of the republic.

The first bill to pass was the National Labor Relations Act (NLRA), also known as the Wagner Act after its principal sponsor, Senator Robert Wagner of New York. The NLRA reaffirmed the right of workers to unionize and to bargain collectively, a right that had been guaranteed in Section 7(a) of the National Recovery Administration. The Wagner Act was much stronger than the NRA, however, for it required management to bargain with certified union representatives. It also created the National Labor Relations Board to supervise plant elections and to issue "cease and desist" orders against companies that committed unfair labor practices such as refusing to permit union elections, refusing to allow union members to distribute union literature on company property, and firing employees engaged in union activities. The Wagner Act extended the realm of government regulation to include labor–management relations and created a legal framework within which labor–management activities could function. It strengthened the bargaining leverage of unions and reduced the power of companies to resist unionization. Its passage showed the growing political influence of organized labor within New Deal ranks.

After the NLRA came the Social Security Act, which created a series of programs including a partial retirement pension for elderly workers. It also established three joint federal–state systems of unemployment insurance, of disability insurance, and of welfare payments to mothers with dependent children. The pension supplement was a compulsory insurance program funded by a payroll tax paid jointly by employee and employer. Workers who had paid into the system for at least five years would be eligible to receive monthly payments starting in 1940.

Social Security pensions were created in part to deflect the challenge of the Townsendites as well as to meet the pressing needs of the aged. Social Security also reflected the fiscal conservatism of President Roosevelt. It was the only social security system ever established that was self-funding; it was paid for not from general tax revenues, but from a trust fund paid into by workers and their employers. It was also funded by a regressive tax, because the more a worker earned, the less tax he paid proportionally. Furthermore, Social Security was a deflationary measure that took money out of a still depressed economy and did not return any for five years.

Compared to social insurance programs implemented by European nations that were not as rich as the United States, Social Security appeared paltry. Initially it excluded millions of workers—farm workers, domestics, and many categories of industrial workers—and because it excluded many low-wage occupations, it necessarily excluded large numbers of women and minority workers. But for all its limitations, it was a historic measure. It established federal responsibility for helping the elderly, the temporarily unemployed, the disabled, and poor single mothers with dependent children. A new social contract, however narrowly defined, counterbalanced the gospel of self-help. For the first time in the history of the republic the federal government acknowledged the social rights of its citizens and accepted a responsibility to protect them. The American welfare state had arrived.

Next came the Banking Act of 1935, which overhauled the Federal Reserve System, bringing major changes to the nation's banking industry. The new law expanded the size of the Board of Governors of the Federal Reserve to seven members (from five) and lengthened their term of office. It also gave the board greater control over regional banks, interest rates, and the setting of reserve requirements of member banks. Further, it gave the board control over open market operations, and it required that all state banks join the Federal Reserve System before July 1, 1942, if they wished to remain eligible for Federal Deposit Insurance Corporation (FDIC) coverage. The Banking Act of 1935 fulfilled Roosevelt's aim of centralizing the American banking system and giving the federal government much greater control over currency and credit. It was the most important banking measure since the Federal Reserve Act created the system in 1913.

The fourth Second New Deal law was the Public Utility Holding Company Act (PUHCA). This important measure revealed Roosevelt's growing hostility toward big business, and it was the first piece of antitrust legislation enacted since Wilson's first term. Its key provision provided for the elimination of utility holding companies, and within three years of its passage almost all of them had been extinguished.

The fifth of the major Second New Deal measures was a tax measure which proposed to redistribute wealth by "soaking the rich." The bill called for increased inheritance taxes, imposition of gift taxes, graduated income taxes on large incomes, and significantly higher corporate income taxes. Roosevelt also had a political motive for proposing his tax bill: to offset the rising power of Huey Long, who was trumpeting his "Share the Wealth" movement. Roosevelt's "wealth tax," the most radical of all New Deal proposals, provoked a firestorm of criticism from business and the media. William Randolph Hearst, the press baron who had helped Roosevelt get the Democratic nomination in 1932, attacked the measure furiously. Thereafter he always called Roosevelt's reform program the "Raw Deal." Business and other interests lobbied Congress intensively to eliminate or reduce Roosevelt's tax proposals, and Congress proceeded to gut the measure. The tax measure ultimately passed by Congress eliminated the inheritance tax and reduced corporate tax rates sharply. The Wealth Tax Act of 1935 in fact raised little revenue and did not redistribute wealth. Even though this tax had little fiscal effect, no other New Deal measure provoked as much bitter criticism. Roosevelt, despite proposing the wealth tax, remained a fiscal conservative at heart. Most New Deal tax measures were regressive.

The Second New Deal was the culmination of Roosevelt's efforts to impose a welfare state on a capitalistic economic foundation in order to bring the American ideal of equality of opportunity closer to reality. Without challenging the system of private profit or redistributing wealth, New Dealers used the power of the federal government to regulate corporations, strengthen trade unions, provide pensions for the elderly, help the disabled, maintain the poor, and provide relief to the unemployed. The New Deal represented the fullest expression of the progressive social vision to date.

A NEW DEAL FOR THE ENVIRONMENT

Franklin Roosevelt shared his cousin Theodore Roosevelt's love of nature and his desire to promote and develop national conservation policies. New Dealers did more to protect the American ecosystem and to develop national conservation policies than any administration since Theodore Roosevelt's during the first decade of the twentieth century. Conservation was a top New Deal priority from the beginning, with the main environmental concerns being protection of land and water resources.

Both the size of the U.S. Forest Service staff and its budget were increased in 1933 and 1934, and its existing programs were expanded. Perhaps the most spectacular step to enhance ecology taken by New Dealers was the building of a "shelterbelt" on the Great Plains. Over 200 million trees were planted across a 100-mile-wide zone along the 100th meridian. Stretching from the Canadian border south to the state of Texas, the shelterbelt functioned as a giant windbreak and also prevented the disastrous dust storms that had blown away much of the Great Plains topsoil during the early 1930s. In 1935 Congress enacted the Soil Conservation Act, which enabled the federal government to tackle the problem of soil erosion on a national scale. At about the same time, Congress also enacted the Taylor Grazing Act, which set strict requirements for grazing cattle on the vast western rangelands owned by the federal government. CCC and many WPA projects also conserved natural resources as well as providing jobs for the unemployed during the Depression.

President Roosevelt also signed legislation that created the National Resources Planning Board, later known as the National Resources Committee. The board promoted local conservation planning and encouraged the development of regional plans for conserving natural resources. The board's long-range goal, a comprehensive national resource plan, was never fully realized, but the New Deal did much to increase public awareness of and promote resource planning.

REGIONAL NEW DEALS

The New Deal had nationwide effects. It was a national program to promote relief, recovery, and reform in all regions of the nation, but it had especially important impacts on the South and West, the two least developed regions of the country during the depression decade. The South had been especially hard hit by the Great Depression. The region was heavily dependent on agriculture; many southern farmers were poor sharecroppers and tenants. A decade of depression brought these white and black farmers of the South unprecedented misery and poverty.

The impact of the New Deal on the South was far-reaching. The New Deal probably did more for the South and its people than for any other region. President Roosevelt enjoyed a special relationship with southerners. They admired his patrician background and upper-class accent, and they responded positively to his paternalistic style of leadership and his country-squire agrarian romanticism. Roosevelt was also a part-time resident of the South, living part of each year at his retreat in Warm Springs, Georgia. His election gave southerners increased political influence. Further, southern political leaders chaired most of the important committees in the Senate and House of Representatives.

New Deal programs altered the economic structure of the South, hastened the decline of farm tenantry and sharecropping, relieved rural poverty, stimulated industrial development, promoted trade unionism, and gave the South greater influence in national affairs. Several New Deal programs aided southern farmers. The Farm Security Agency set up experimental cooperative farms. The Bankhead-Jones Act provided low-cost, long-term loans to southern sharecroppers to enable them to buy the lands they farmed. The Rural Electrification Administration built cooperative power stations that brought electricity to rural areas. Few southern farms had electricity in 1933; by 1938 more than half did. Rural electrification significantly enhanced the quality of rural southern life. TVA, of course, greatly improved the quality of life for millions living within the seven-state area it served.

New Deal conservation and social programs also affected the South. Over 100 CCC camps were established in southern states, enabling much valuable work to be done in the areas of natural resource and soil conservation. The WPA spent over $2 billion in the South from 1935 to 1942 and put more than 2 million people to work on various projects. The Wagner Act promoted trade union activities in the South, especially CIO (Congress of Industrial Organizations) unions in the steel and coal mining industries. The New Deal also began to shake the foundations of the southern system of segregation, a preliminary to the modern civil rights movement that developed years later.

The New Deal also had a major influence on the West during the 1930s. The West was a vast, undeveloped, sparsely populated region at that time, with little industry and agriculture. It was a land of arid or semi-arid wide-open spaces. Its major industries included mining, oil, livestock, and lumbering. Major New Deal programs of particular value to westerners included vast dam-building and reclamation projects to irrigate the land and promote the development of commercial agriculture. Massive Hoover Dam, spanning the Colorado River between Arizona and Nevada, was completed in 1935, at that time the largest dam ever constructed in the United States. It was the first of many vast construction projects in western states during the ensuing decades. On a per capita basis, more federal money was spent in the West during the New Deal era than in any other region of the nation. During the 1930s western states received $3 in federal funds for every dollar westerners paid to Washington. CCC projects were especially important to the West because of their twin missions of soil conservation and reforestation.

THE 1936 ELECTION

Public opinion polls taken in 1936 showed that Roosevelt and his New Deal programs enjoyed broad popular support in all regions of the nation. Over 100,000 frenzied partisans packed Franklin Field in Philadelphia to hear Roosevelt accept his nomination for a second term. Flashing his famed victory smile, he told the crowd and a national radio audience that "this generation of Americans has a rendezvous with destiny."

The Republicans faced a strong uphill battle in their first campaign to oust the popular incumbent. To oppose the President, the GOP turned to Alfred M. "Alf" Landon, a former follower of Theodore Roosevelt and currently the progressive Republican governor of Kansas. Landon, who had made a fortune in the oil business, was more liberal than most Republican

Party regulars. He had a good civil liberties record and favored regulation of business. He endorsed many New Deal programs, to the dismay of many conservative members of his own party. His support of much of the New Deal forced Landon to run a weak "me too" campaign against the charismatic incumbent.

Landon's campaign against Roosevelt never caught fire, even though the Republicans outspent the Democrats $14 million to $9 million and most of the nation's newspapers and radio stations endorsed Landon. He was a colorless individual and a poor public speaker, with an ineffective radio delivery. He tried to make issues of Roosevelt's deficit spending and the huge increase in the size and power of the presidency, but neither issue carried much beyond the realm of those already converted to his political philosophy. He was hurt by his reactionary supporters, who cost him votes because of their harsh anti-New Deal rhetoric. The American Liberty League was so obviously a front for wealthy critics of New Deal tax and regulatory policies that Landon asked it not to endorse his candidacy. However, the Kansan did attract a number of disaffected Democrats, including two former presidential candidates, Al Smith and John W. Davis.

There was another element in the 1936 election. Roosevelt's political advisers feared that popular demagogues might combine forces to mount a third-party challenge. Huey Long's assassination had eliminated the most dangerous threat. The major challenge came from Father Coughlin and Dr. Townsend. They tried to join with the Reverend Gerald L. K. Smith, an anti-Semitic rabble-rouser who had inherited part of Long's forces, in support of the candidacy of Congressman William Lemke of North Dakota. Lemke was seeking the presidency as the candidate of the newly formed Union Party. He was an outspoken agrarian radical who had sponsored a series of measures in the House to provide low-cost loans to hard-pressed farmers and to prevent foreclosures. Roosevelt had opposed Lemke's proposals, and the prairie populist had turned against the New Deal. Lemke and the other anti-New Dealers allied with him boasted that they represented between 20 and 30 million voters as they made their third-party bid in 1936.

But their efforts came to very little. The extremists feuded among themselves and Father Coughlin went off on his own. Coughlin's radio speeches denounced Roosevelt's New Deal in vicious terms. He sounded anti-Semitic themes, called Roosevelt "anti-God," and also accused him of being a Communist. The challenge posed by the combined demagogues in 1936 proved weak. The Union Party neither hurt Roosevelt's candidacy nor had a major impact on the outcome of the election.

When Roosevelt hit the campaign trail in 1936, he ran hard against the business classes. His opening speech attacked "economic royalists" who took "other people's money" to impose a "new industrial dictatorship." Roosevelt turned his reelection campaign into a great nonpartisan liberal crusade, a clash between the "haves" and "have-nots." For the rest of the campaign he ignored the weak challenge of Landon and ran against former President Hoover and "the interests." Hoover responded with a series of denunciatory speeches, claiming that the New Deal philosophy rested on "coercion and the compulsory organization of men" and that it derived part of its program from Karl Marx.

In his final campaign speech, delivered at Madison Square Garden to a full house cheering his every word, and knowing that he was going to win, Roosevelt taunted his hapless Republican opponents:

> Never before in history have these forces been united against one candidate as they stand today. They are unanimous in their hate for me—and I welcome their hatred! I should like to have it said of my first administration that in it the forces of selfishness and lust for power met their match. I should like to have it said of my second administration that in it these forces met their master.[1]

Roosevelt and the Democrats swept to a landslide victory. Roosevelt got 27.8 million votes to Landon's 16.7 million. Lemke attracted only 882,000 votes, and Socialist Party candidate Norman Thomas received a mere 187,000. Six million more people voted in 1936 than in 1932, and most of these new voters cast ballots for Roosevelt. Most new voters were recruited from the ranks of the poor, people on relief, the unemployed, and the working classes, who expressed their solidarity with the man who had forged the New Deal. They had perceived Roosevelt to be a candidate with a program and a conception of government that favored the common people. The Democrats carried every state in the union except Maine and Vermont, and they rolled up huge majorities in the House and Senate. The people had been given a chance to vote on the performance of Roosevelt and his program, and they had responded with an overwhelming vote of approval. Some analysts thought the Republican Party to be on the verge of extinction, about to go the way of the Federalists after 1801 and the Whigs after 1852. James "Big Jim" Farley, Roosevelt's campaign manager, quipped that the election proved that "as Maine goes, so goes Vermont." Reporter Dorothy Thompson suggested that if the campaign had lasted another week, Roosevelt would have carried Canada too.

THE NEW DEAL COALITION

By 1936 Roosevelt and the Democrats had forged a new political coalition firmly based on the mass of voters living in large northern cities and led in Congress by a new political type, the northern urban liberal. Whereas old-

1. Quoted in William E. Leuchtenburg, *Franklin D. Roosevelt and the New Deal* (New York: Harper & Row, 1963), p. 184.

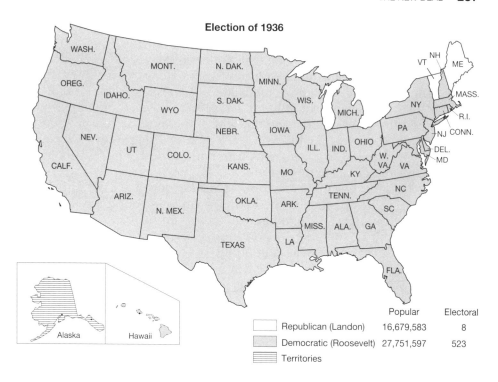

Election of 1936

	Popular	Electoral
Republican (Landon)	16,679,583	8
Democratic (Roosevelt)	27,751,597	523
Territories		

stock Americans in small towns and cities clung to the GOP, the newer ethnic groups in the cities joined the Democrats. These "ethnics" had benefited from New Deal programs and were delighted at the attention given them by New Dealers. Hard times and New Deal programs had also attracted the votes of most farmers and of the elderly. Organized labor was an integral part of the New Deal coalition, especially the new industrial unions being forged by the CIO. These unions fused the interests of millions of workers, both skilled and unskilled, native-born and foreign-born, white and nonwhite, male and female. Black voters in northern cities abandoned their historic allegiance to the Republicans and joined the new coalition. Many former Republican progressive middle-class voters and thousands of former socialists also joined the Roosevelt coalition.

A dramatic political realignment had taken place in America, as important as the one that occurred in 1894 and 1896, which had made the Republicans the dominant party until the Great Depression. Now the Democrats had become the majority coalition and would retain their dominance for more than 30 years. A historic realignment, underway since the election of 1928 and forged in the crucible of the 1932 Depression election, was completed in 1936.

ROOSEVELT ATTACKS THE SUPREME COURT

Roosevelt's Second Inaugural Address, delivered on January 20, 1937, sounded a call for more radical reforms. He spoke feelingly of the plight of the poor: "I see one-third of a nation ill-housed, ill-clad, and ill-nourished." Observers wondered if he had a New Deal war on poverty in mind. Conservatives trembled at the thought of the new tax bills and antitrust measures Roosevelt might propose. The once mighty Republican Party had been reduced to a legislative remnant in both houses of Congress, incapable of effective opposition.

As he began his second term, Roosevelt was at the height of his power and prestige; he was coming off an election in which he, his program, and his party had been given an emphatic endorsement. If he read the result as a mandate to continue on a reformist path, who would resist? If he had in mind an assault on the prerogatives of the rich in favor of the poor, who could prevent it? But when Roosevelt sent a specific legislative proposal to Congress two weeks later, he surprised everyone. He asked not for more social reforms, but for reform of the Supreme Court, an issue that he had never raised in the campaign.

The Supreme Court had already nullified several important New Deal measures, including the Triple A and the NRA. Roosevelt and his advisers were afraid that it would soon invalidate recently enacted Second New Deal measures, particularly the Wagner Act and Social Security Act. Roosevelt was angry with the Court's conservative majority that had thwarted many New Deal efforts to promote recovery and reform American society. He feared that the Court might kill more programs.

To prevent further damage to the New Deal, he proposed a scheme to "pack" the Court, disguised as judicial reform. In February 1937 Roosevelt sent Congress his Judiciary Reorganization Bill in which he requested authority to add a federal judge whenever an incumbent reached age 70 and failed to retire within six months. He proposed adding 50 federal judges, including six Supreme Court justices. He insisted that the current judiciary was understaffed and that additional jurists were required to relieve overworked "elderly, feeble" judges. Six additional judges on the Supreme Court would help the "nine old men." Roosevelt's scheme fooled no one. It was obvious that he would use court reform as a vehicle to liberalize the Supreme Court by appointing younger, more progressive members. At the time Roosevelt proposed packing the Court, its lineup included four reactionaries who opposed the New Deal, three liberals who usually supported it, and two moderates—Chief Justice Charles Evans Hughes and Associate Justice Owen Roberts. Hughes and Roberts were the swingmen; they sometimes upheld New Deal legislation, more often they opposed it.

Roosevelt's controversial proposal generated much opposition. Two polls showed the public divided on the issue. Media editorials almost uni-

Roosevelt's proposal to reform the Supreme Court alarmed many Americans who feared that he was trying to impose one-man rule on the country.

versally condemned it. Most Republicans opposed it, as did many Democrats, including some liberals. Roosevelt had attacked a national symbol that gave Americans a sense of identity and unity. He also had threatened the constitutional principle of checks and balances with his blatant proposal to politicize the Court and bend it to the executive will. There were limits beyond which many people did not want even this most powerful and popular of modern presidents to venture. The debate in Congress lasted for months and divided the Democrats.

As debate over the measure continued, the two swingmen, Hughes and Roberts, voted to sustain a state minimum wage law. In April 1937 in *National Labor Relations Board* v. *Jones and Laughlin Steel Corp.* they voted with the majority in a 5-to-4 decision sustaining the National Labor Relations Act. A month later they joined with another majority in a 5-to-4 decision to uphold Social Security. The conservatives had been eclipsed.

A few days after the Social Security decision Justice Willis Van Devanter, a conservative judge, announced his retirement from the Court. Roosevelt would now have a 6-to-3 majority on the Court willing to approve New Deal legislation. The need for drastic Court reform had vanished.

The conversion of Hughes and Roberts to New Deal liberalism, coupled with Van Devanter's resignation, doomed Roosevelt's bill. But the President refused to yield; he continued to battle stubbornly for what had become a hopeless cause. The Senate adjourned in July without passing his judicial reform proposal, handing Roosevelt his first major political defeat. The Court fight had consumed 168 days, during which no important legislation was enacted.

In later years Roosevelt claimed that he had lost the "battle" but had won the "war" for judicial reform. In a sense he was correct. He appointed a liberal, Alabama Senator Hugo Black, to replace Van Devanter. Within two and a half years after Congress had rejected his Court-packing scheme, Roosevelt had appointed four more liberals to the Supreme Court. The new "Roosevelt Court" greatly expanded the constitutionally permissible areas of government regulation of economic activity. Never again would a major Roosevelt bill be overturned.

But in more important ways Roosevelt lost the "war." The Court fight divided and weakened the Democratic Party, and it greatly strengthened the emerging conservative bipartisan coalition of southern Democratic and northern Republican opponents of the New Deal. The Roosevelt Court might uphold all new laws, but a divided Congress, no longer so responsive to Roosevelt's leadership, passed few measures for the justices to consider. Shortly after the Court fight a major administration bill to reorganize the executive branch was sent to Capitol Hill. Alarmed opponents denounced the measure as an effort to impose dictatorship on the American people. The House of Representatives rejected the bill, handing Roosevelt another stinging political defeat. Although Roosevelt would never acknowledge it, the fight he provoked over the Supreme Court helped kill the New Deal.

THE ROOSEVELT RECESSION

Roosevelt was also largely responsible for triggering a severe economic recession that began in 1937 and persisted until 1939. Never comfortable with deficit financing, the President decided that the economy had recovered to the point where it no longer needed stimulation from government spending and budget deficits. During the first half of 1937 Roosevelt ordered the WPA to cut its enrollment from 3 million to 1.5 million jobs. Other New Deal relief agencies slashed their enrollments drastically. To reduce the inflation rate, which had reached 3.5 percent, the Federal Reserve System tightened reserve requirements and raised interest rates. The weak economy, deprived of billions in federal spending, declined sharply; within a year the unemployment rate had risen 5 percentage points, approaching the 1933 and 1934 levels.

Confronted with the sharp economic downturn, Roosevelt reversed

himself and revived deficit financing. The WPA, CCC, and other work relief agencies all increased their appropriations. But not until the end of
1939 did unemployment return to early 1937 levels. Leaders of both parties criticized Roosevelt for having unnecessarily subjected Americans to
two years of increased hardship. The "Roosevelt recession" quickly erased
gains that had taken four years to achieve and discouraged many people
who had believed that the Depression was behind them. The President's
popularity and prestige sagged to new lows.

The 1938 elections, occurring in the midst of a recession that Republicans could blame on the President, severely damaged the Roosevelt
coalition. Republicans picked up 81 seats in the House and 8 seats in the
Senate, and they gained 13 governorships. Robert Taft from Ohio, son of
the former President and Chief Justice William Howard Taft, was one of
the new Republican senators. Several prominent incumbent liberals went
down to defeat. It was mainly the effects of the "Roosevelt recession" that
hurt the Democrats and allowed the Republican comeback. Roosevelt also
hurt himself politically by entering the 1938 elections. He intervened in
several southern elections, trying to get rid of prominent conservative
Senate opponents of the New Deal. All the incumbents defeated the liberal challengers backed by Roosevelt, dealing him another serious defeat.
By 1938 Roosevelt also was increasingly involved with conflicts in Europe
and Asia. Japanese aggression in China and Germany's forced annexation
of Austria threatened to send the world skidding toward another world
war. Increasingly the outer world claimed the President's attention. Domestic reform became a less urgent Roosevelt priority.

THE END OF THE NEW DEAL

Congress enacted the last two significant New Deal measures in early
1938. One was a new Agricultural Adjustment Act to replace the one nullified by the Supreme Court. Yielding to pressure from the farm bloc, the
new AAA allowed unlimited crop production and larger subsidies. The
government was required to store the inevitable surplus production and
sell some of it overseas at low prices. Agricultural overproduction returned, but farm income was maintained by taxpayers' providing new
Triple A subsidies. The final New Deal reform was the Fair Labor Standards Act (FLSA), enacted in May 1938. It established the first minimum
wage at 40 cents an hour and set the standard workweek at 40 hours. The
FLSA forced immediate pay raises for over 12 million workers who had
been making less than the minimum wage.

The New Deal had ended by the summer of 1938. It was a victim of
recession, growing bipartisan conservative opposition, declining liberal
support, political blunders by President Roosevelt, and the growing
prominence of foreign affairs in a sullen world girding for war.

FDR AND THE NEW DEAL IN PERSPECTIVE

The New Deal was an extension of the commanding personality at its center, Franklin Roosevelt. He began his presidency confident that he could lead the American people out of the morass of depression, that he could provide both the inspiration and the means to restore prosperity and confidence. His leadership proved effective. Feelings of despair, of imminent collapse, vanished. Partial recovery occurred and people regained their optimistic vitality. James MacGregor Burns, a Roosevelt biographer, found in Roosevelt "the lineaments of greatness—courage, joyousness, responsiveness, vitality, faith, and above all, concern for his fellow man." A poll of American historians taken in 1984 rated Roosevelt number 2 among all presidents, behind Lincoln and ahead of Washington. During the New Deal years neither his popularity nor his power were seriously challenged by spokesmen for the Left or Right. His smashing electoral victory in 1936 confirmed his popularity and the political success of New Deal programs.

But Roosevelt and the New Deal were controversial, and he provoked legions of detractors. Most newspaper and radio editorials regularly attacked the man in the White House, often vehemently. Rightist critics called him a dictator, a Socialist, a Communist, and a Fascist. They denounced the New Deal as un-American, subverting the American way of life. They also insisted that deficit spending for New Deal relief programs would bankrupt the nation and that Roosevelt's usurpations of power would destroy democracy. None of these rightist criticisms is valid; they mainly expressed the feelings of intense fear, hostility, and hatred that Roosevelt aroused among corporate executives and the wealthy elite whose prerogatives had been curtailed by New Deal reforms.

More thoughtful critics have faulted Roosevelt for being too pragmatic, too opportunistic. They assert that he failed to formulate a coherent strategy for economic recovery and social reform. The New Deal was not planned; it evolved, a series of *ad hoc* improvisations. Roosevelt's grasp of economics was superficial—he did not understand economic processes or grasp economic theory—and this ignorance of economics hindered his recovery efforts.

Other critics have cited flaws in the personality, character, and intellect of President Roosevelt. He had few close friends and lacked personal warmth. He was not close to his wife Eleanor and was not a particularly good father to his several children. He had a long-term affair with another woman, Lucy Mercer. He was not always truthful, nor was he particularly loyal to many political associates. He seemed to enjoy setting his advisers against one another and having them compete for influence and power within his administrative circle. He had a petty, even vindictive streak and appeared to delight in humiliating his political opponents such as former President Herbert Hoover. He was a man of ordinary, perhaps slightly above average intelligence. He had a lazy, undisciplined mind. He was poorly read and lacked the ability to think systematically or analytically about public policies and problems. He got most of his ideas and policies from picking the brains of his advisers.

During the New Deal the institution of the presidency was transformed. It vastly increased in size, power, and scope. Most New Deal agencies were created as bureaucracies within the executive branch. Government, particularly executive government, became a major growth industry during the 1930s. During this era the federal government became the focal point for civic life. People increasingly turned to Washington for solutions to problems; the importance of local and state governments withered. The New Deal was an ongoing civics lesson educating people in possible uses of federal power to stimulate the economy, change the money and banking system, provide jobs, aid farmers, supervise labor–management relations, and save homes and small businesses. The New Deal created the American welfare state. Many governmental agencies that were created during the New Deal still function today to regulate business, stimulate the economy, and distribute benefits to millions.

Yet capitalism survived under the New Deal. Profits and private property remained fundamental to the American system. The wealthy survived as a class, although the New Deal accomplished a modest redistribution of wealth. In 1929 the top 5 percent of the population received 30 percent of national income; in 1938, at the end of the New Deal, the share of the top 5 percent had dropped to 26 percent. The income lost to the wealthy went mostly to middle- and upper-middle-income families, whose share increased from 33 percent in 1929 to 36 percent in 1938. The income share going to the poorest families rose slightly from 13.2 to 13.7 percent.

The New Deal also altered the distribution of political power. Business remained the single most powerful political interest, but during the New Deal it was forced to share power with other groups. Farmers gained political clout and so did trade unions. The New Deal also responded to consumers and homeowners. Millions of unemployed workers benefited from New Deal relief programs. New Dealers created a broker state during the 1930s. They responded to organizations, to interest groups, to lobbies, and to trade associations. The web of power and influence expanded and diversified. Mediating claims of various groups pressuring the government became a complex art form. However, the millions of Americans who were not organized to make claims upon the broker state were neglected. The reach of the New Deal rarely extended to minorities, to slum dwellers, to sharecroppers, and to other poor, unorganized, and powerless people. Those whose needs were greatest got the least help from the New Deal because they lacked the means to influence New Deal power brokers.

At its core the New Deal was an evolutionary centrist reform program. It drew upon ideologies that had been around for decades, principally the "New Nationalism" of Theodore Roosevelt and Wilsonian progressivism. Roosevelt and most other prominent New Dealers had previously been active progressive reformers. New Dealers rejected socialism and fascism and also eschewed indigenous radicalisms such as the confiscatory tax schemes of the populist demagogue Huey Long. Fundamentally, the New Deal tried to conserve the American capitalistic system by rescuing it from depression and reforming it to make it responsive to a broader range of interest groups. New Dealers were also concerned with reforming the American economy to prevent a recurrence of the Depression and to fend off more radical reforms. Roosevelt, himself a wealthy man, saw himself as saving the American system from both self-destruction and socialism, and he was annoyed at shrill attacks leveled on him by other rich people, which appeared to him both misguided and unfair.

But the New Deal was only a partial economic success. It proved politically invulnerable to the challenges of both radicalism and reaction. Although it succeeded politically, it failed to solve the fundamental economic problem caused by the Great Depression—unemployment. As the New Deal ended in 1938, over 10 million men and women were still without jobs; the unemployment rate hovered near 20 percent. New Dealers failed to eliminate unemployment because they never solved the problem of underconsumption. Consumers and businesses never were able to buy enough to stimulate enough production to approach normal employment patterns. For example, in the pre-Depression year of 1929 new car sales totaled $6.5 billion; in 1938, at the end of the New Deal, the figure was $3.9 billion. Years after the New Deal had ended, massive unemployment persisted.

The most serious failure of the New Deal was its inability to promote economic recovery from depression. New Dealers enjoyed great success with most of their efforts to relieve distress and reform the American system of political economy, but they failed to revive the American economy, restore prosperity, restore full employment, stimulate sufficient capital investment, or promote economic growth. Programs such as the National Recovery Administration (NRA) retarded economic recovery during 1933–1935. It favored stagnating large corporations over small, dynamic companies. Only the gigantic federal spending and deficit financing that were required to pay the costs of World War II restored production, put everyone back to work, and regenerated prosperity. Prosperity returned to America only years after the New Deal was a spent force; prosperity was the adventitious by-product of the exogenous factor of the largest and most destructive war in the history of the world. Long before a world war restored American prosperity, many other nations had shaken off the effects of the worldwide depression. But had war not come, economic stagnation in America would have persisted well into the 1940s, perhaps longer.

BIBLIOGRAPHY

There is a vast historical literature on the New Deal era and the commanding figure at its center. The best one-volume treatment is William E. Leuchtenburg, *Franklin D. Roosevelt and the New Deal, 1932–1940*. A very good recent study is Paul K. Conkin, *The New Deal*. Arthur M. Schlesinger, Jr., *The Age of Roosevelt* has two lively volumes covering the 1933–1936 years. James MacGregor Burns, *Roosevelt: The Lion and the Fox* is the best political biography of the most powerful and popular modern American president. Joseph P. Lash, *Eleanor and Franklin* is a graceful study of the President and his extraordinary First Lady. Lois Scharf, *Eleanor Roosevelt: First Lady of American Liberalism* is a recent first-rate biography of the great First Lady. Walter J. Stein, *California and the Dust Bowl Migration* is the best study of the uprooted "Okies" who left the southern plains states for California during the Depression. Alan Brinkley, *Voices of Protest: Huey Long, Father Coughlin, and the Great Depression* is a fine study of major New Deal critics. William R. Brock, *Welfare, Democracy, and the New Deal* is a good account of the Second New Deal, 1935–1938. James T. Patterson, *Congressional Conservatism and the New Deal* charts the rise of the bipartisan conservative coalition of southern Democrats and northern Republicans that blocked New Deal reforms after 1938. Two valuable studies of important New Deal agencies are Bernard Bellush, *The Failure of the NRA* and John A. Salmond, *The Civilian Conservation Corps, 1933–1942: A New Deal Case Study*. Roy Lubove, *The Struggle for Social Security 1900–1935* tells the story of how Social Security came to be implemented during the New Deal era. Donald S. Howard, *The WPA and Federal Relief Policy* is an account of the most important work relief agency in American history.

CHAPTER
9

Society and Culture during the 1930s

The severe financial and economic crises of the Depression decade powerfully influenced the ways most Americans lived, thought, and felt. The Depression bore powerfully on millions of individuals, who struggled to survive, cope, and advance. For organized labor the Depression posed severe problems but also historic opportunities. Amidst unprecedented economic downturn and massive unemployment, there occurred the greatest upsurge in union organizing drives in American labor history. Women often experienced the Depression differently than did men, and in some ways they coped better with its peculiar mix of threats and opportunities. Most women did not work outside the home during the 1930s and thus experienced the Depression from the home rather than from the workplace. Working women generally experienced a lower rate of unemployment than did men during the Great Depression. Women also took advantage of opportunities to enhance their political status. Minorities, especially African Americans, were often devastated by the impact of the Great Depression, but during the 1930s some African American and Native American families benefited from New Deal programs.

American cultural life was profoundly affected by searing Depression experiences. For many American intellectuals the Depression appeared to prove that the American system of middle-class capitalism and democracy was no longer viable. To these disillusioned American thinkers, the ideological alternatives posed by Communism and Fascism looked like the wave of the future. Other thinkers questioned basic American values and searched for answers to the persistent question: What had gone wrong? But most Americans, the mass of ordinary middle-class and working-class citizens, found in the Depression and the New Dealers' response to it a reaffirmation of American values and a deepened sense of national identity. During the 1930s there occurred a great upsurge in cultural nationalism even as the economic downturn revealed serious problems and inequities. The reaffirmations of American nationhood were reflected in the work of mainstream writers, artists, and popular entertainers.

THE RISE OF ORGANIZED LABOR

At the outset of the Great Depression trade unions in this country were neither strong nor militant. Only about 3 million of the nation's 46 million workers belonged to unions, and most of these unionists were skilled workers who belonged to the American Federation of Labor. AFL membership consisted mainly of members of craft unions. (Craft unions typically represented skilled workers in a particular trade, such as plumbing or typesetting.)

The National Recovery Administration promoted union growth through its Section 7(a), which required that every industrial code grant employees "the right to organize and bargain collectively through representatives of their own choosing." The greatest increase was among industrial unions within the AFL. (Industrial unions represented all workers, skilled and unskilled, in a given industry, such as steelworkers or autoworkers.) The United Mine Workers added 300,000 workers within a few months. After one year of NRA, over 1,700 locals had been formed in the automobile, steel, rubber, aluminum, and other mass production industries, adding one million members to AFL rolls. But many companies resisted unionization through the NRA codes; they prohibited unions or formed company unions. Collective bargaining rarely occurred in these companies, and NRA officials often went along with their efforts to thwart independent unions. Disappointed labor leaders complained about the "National Run Around," and a wave of strikes spread across the country in 1934.

An important strike occurred on the San Francisco waterfront in July 1934, when shipping companies rejected longshoremen's demands for union recognition, control of hiring halls, and higher wages. A violent confrontation occurred when police tried to clear 5,000 pickets from the Embarcadero, the main waterfront street, to let strikebreakers work. Shots were fired from both sides. Scores were injured and two strikers were killed. The governor sent National Guardsmen to occupy the waterfront. Organized labor responded with a general strike that nearly shut the city down for four days. Federal officials intervened to facilitate a settlement granting union recognition and control of hiring halls, a major victory for labor.

In 1935 the Supreme Court nullified the NRA; a few months later Congress enacted the National Labor Relations Act (Wagner Act), which created a more hospitable environment for unionizing activities and strengthened union bargaining leverage with employers. Union organizing efforts increased dramatically. The Wagner Act also spurred the creation of a new labor organization, which originated as a faction within the AFL that was dissatisfied with the Federation's lack of sympathy for industrial unionism. Its leader was John L. Lewis, head of the United Mine Workers, who formed a Committee for Industrial Organizations within the AFL. In 1936 AFL leaders expelled Lewis and his industrial unions, and they later formed their own trade union organization, renamed the Congress of Industrial Organizations (CIO).

The CIO launched major organizing drives in mass-production industries in the late 1930s. One of its first campaigns occurred in the steel industry, which had been a bastion of nonunion shops since the failed strikes of 1919. It created a Steel Workers Organizing Committee (SWOC) under the leadership of Philip Murray and 400 organizers who descended upon the nation's major steel centers. "Big Steel," as the United States Steel Corporation, the nation's largest steel company, was known, gave up without a fight. After secret negotiations, a contract was signed recognizing SWOC as the bargaining agent and granting workers an eight-hour day, a 40-hour week, and a large pay raise. It was an astonishing settlement from a major company that had been an anti-union bastion since its creation in 1901. USS's management cut the deal with SWOC because it did not want a strike disrupting its production schedule during a time of improving business.

"Little Steel," the four companies ranking from second to fifth, refused to surrender. Under the leadership of Republic Steel, the companies prepared to battle SWOC. In May 1937 the union called a strike against the companies and a fierce conflict occurred. "Little Steel" employed a variety of anti-union tactics, including intimidation and violence. The worst violence occurred on May 30 when Chicago police attacked pickets in front of Republic's main plant. They fired into the crowd, killing ten strikers and wounding dozens more. This brutal incident, known as the Memorial Day Massacre, created widespread sympathy for strikers, but "Little Steel" broke the strike and defeated the CIO's organizing effort that year.

In January 1937 another CIO union, the United Automobile Workers (UAW), began a famous strike in Flint, Michigan, against General Motors, the world's largest industrial corporation. The strikers used a novel tactic against the giant automaker—the "sit-down strike." Instead of walking out of the plant at the end of a shift, the workers sat at their stations on the shop floor, shutting down the factory and preventing strikebreakers from working. Caught off guard by the sit-down tactic, company officials tried to dislodge the workers, who were guilty of trespassing. They cut off the heat, letting the temperature drop to zero, but the workers built bonfires and stayed inside the factory. Police charged the plants but were driven off by a barrage of coffee mugs, tools, lunch pails, and auto parts. Police then lobbed in tear gas, but the workers broke windows to let the gas out and again drove the police back, this time using company fire hoses.

General Motors officials then demanded that the state militia be mobilized to remove the strikers, and they got a court order setting February 3 as a deadline for evacuation. The workers, who were risking fines, imprisonment, and possibly violent assaults, refused to yield. They demanded that the company engage in collective bargaining. When February 3 arrived, Michigan Governor Frank Murphy, a liberal Democrat elected with labor support, refused to call out the troops. President Roosevelt, who also sympathized with the strikers, appealed for negotiations. Faced with the prospect of class warfare and powerful political opposition, General Motors capitulated. Negotiations between company representatives and UAW leaders began. Within weeks the UAW was recognized as the autoworkers' bargaining agent. Company and union representatives negotiated a contract that provided substantial pay increases and a 40-hour week. Chrysler signed a similar agreement after a short strike. Ford, bitterly anti-union, held out until 1941, and there were several bloody encounters at Ford's River Rouge plant between UAW forces and company guards.

Membership in labor unions, 1929-1941

Source: Historical Statistics of the United States, Colonial Times to 1970.

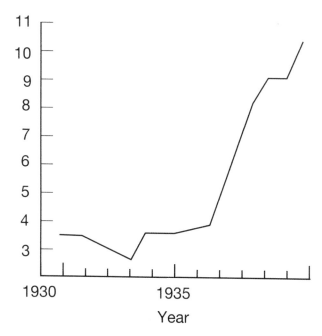

Year

The sit-down strike proved an effective tactic, and all kinds of workers used it in the late 1930s: textile, glass, and rubber workers; dime store clerks, janitors, dressmakers, and bakers. Sometimes workers sat down spontaneously at the job and waited for CIO organizers to come sign them up. No large mass-production or service industry was neglected. The sit-down tactic expressed the rank-and-file militancy that energized the trade union movement in the late 1930s—and it worked. Public opinion, however, generally sympathetic to the CIO union drives of the late 1930s, disapproved of the sit-down strike. It appeared too radical, too disrespectful of employer property rights. A liberal-dominated Supreme Court outlawed the tactic in 1939.

The CIO, aided by legislation, liberal politicians such as Governor Murphy and President Roosevelt, and often favorable public opinion, added millions of union members during its organizing drives of the late 1930s. Hundreds of thousands of autoworkers, coal miners, steelworkers, clothing workers, rubber workers, and others formed strong industrial unions. Most of the nation's major mass-production industries were organized during this time. CIO membership reached 5 million by the end of the decade.

WOMEN DURING THE GREAT DEPRESSION

The Depression severely affected family life. Heads of family feared for the survival of their families and doubted their ability to provide adequate shelter, food, and clothing for their children. The marriage rate dropped sharply. Often marriages were postponed. During the 1930s the number of women aged 25 to 30 who never married increased 30 percent over the previous decade. Young married couples put off having children, and the birth rate fell sharply. Although the divorce rate declined during the early 1930s, the desertion rate increased sharply. Young people dropped out of school or decided not to go to college. Family members, too poor to enjoy recreational pursuits outside the home, spent more time together. People found ways of amusing themselves and passing time without spending money. Church attendance dropped off but public libraries were heavily utilized.

During the fun-loving 1920s the feminine ideal had been the flapper. During the somber 1930s the most popular feminine image became more matronly and serious. Skirts and dresses grew longer, as did hairstyles. Ads during the 1930s pictured women with fuller, more curvaceous figures and larger breasts. In the words of social historian Gary Nash, "The fall of the stock market was accompanied by the fall of hemlines." But women during the 1930s continued to enjoy the greater sexual freedom that had been won during the 1920s. Premarital sex became more widely practiced and the use of condoms greatly increased. In many states condoms could be purchased over the counter in drug stores or from dispensing machines located on the walls of men's restrooms in service stations and bars.

When the Depression struck, most families had one income-earner, almost always the husband. Unemployment usually meant the man lost his job. After a few weeks of fruitless searching for another job, the men often grew discouraged, became lethargic, and began hanging around the home. Many were demoralized by the experience of long-term unemployment. Traditional cultural values had defined them as society's producers and providers for their families. Unemployment deprived them of their accustomed social role and robbed their lives of meaning and purpose. Within a culture that accentuated the traditional values of self-reliance and self-help, millions of unemployed men felt shame; they saw themselves as worthless, as failures. Feeling responsible for their children's having to wear old clothes and to subsist on inadequate diets, they often felt intense guilt and self-hate.

Most of the nation's 30 million homemakers stayed at home during the Depression. Their daily routine was less disrupted than their spouse's. Nevertheless pressures on them mounted, because during hard times the role of homemaker became more important and their resources were often drastically limited. Managing a household on a severely shrunken budget often required enormous resourcefulness. It meant endless little economies and constant anxiety that accident or illness might overwhelm the meager family budget. Often Depression conditions strengthened family cohesion, however. Limited financial resources often required women to labor more hours and sacrifice more than ever before to keep the family together. Women stopped buying canned goods and did their own home canning. They often stopped buying clothes at department stores and made their and their family's clothes. Some families took in boarders, relatives, and in-laws. Some women started home businesses to supplement meager family incomes.

The Depression affected women workers differently from male workers. Female unemployment rates during the Depression were always lower than male rates because "men's jobs" in manufacturing were lost at a greater rate than were "women's jobs" in the service sectors. Assembly line workers were laid off more often than secretaries, teachers, social workers, or nurses. In some formerly two-income families the wife continued to work after the husband had been dismissed. The proportion of women in the work force rose during the 1930s from 20 to 25 percent. Most new entrants were young, single women, but more married and middle-aged women also entered the 1930s work force.

But traditional gender discriminations still dogged women. Over half of women workers were domestic servants or in the garment trades. Pay in these jobs was low; working women earned about 50 cents for every dollar that men earned. Few school districts would hire married women as teachers. During the 1930s government employers prohibited more than one member of a family from working for the civil service, and if a spouse were forced to resign it was the woman who usually gave up her job. During the 1930s, opinion polls consistently showed that most Americans did not approve of women in the work force. There were two prime reasons for this view: fear that women would take jobs away from men, and the belief that the women's proper place was in the home and not the workplace. Children benefited from having a full-time mother at home.

Various New Deal programs designed during the 1930s often helped women less than they did men. The National Recovery Act allowed industries to structure gendered wage differentials into their codes of fair practices; women inevitably received the lower wages. Many New Deal programs resisted hiring women or hired far fewer women than men. Of the myriad of programs established by the WPA, the largest of the New Deal public works programs, perhaps 10 percent of jobs went to women, and these jobs were largely limited to clerical work, libraries, recreational activities, health and nutrition programs, and, most often, sewing projects. The Civilian Conservation Corps excluded women while providing work for over 2 million unemployed young men.

Women continued to improve their political status during the 1930s. Arkansas elected the first woman to serve in the U.S. Senate, Hattie Caraway. Middle- and upper-middle-class women, led by First Lady Eleanor Roosevelt and Secretary of Labor Frances Perkins, the first woman Cabinet member, made significant political gains during the New Deal years. Josephine Roche served as Assistant Secretary of the Treasury and Nellie Taylor Ross became the director of the U.S. Mint. Many women joined the staffs of newly created New Deal agencies. Franklin Roosevelt was the first president to appoint women diplomats. Women also became an important part of the Democratic Party political machinery and the new Democratic Party coalition. There were over 200 women delegates at the 1936 Democratic convention. Under the leadership of Mary W. "Molly" Dewson, a close friend of Eleanor, the Women's Division of the Democratic National Committee played a major role in Franklin Roosevelt's landslide reelection victory in 1936.

During the Depression decade women significantly increased their influence in the nation's cultural life. This increasing influence derived largely from the Depression-generated upsurge of cultural nationalism. Government patronage of the arts was more likely to be gender-neutral than was that of private patrons and it involved a far larger number of women because it was publicly funded. Thousands of talented women participated in WPA artistic and cultural projects. Women writers participated in the Federal Writers Project. Women also made their mark in the popular culture—in aviation, sports, and, above all, the movies. The greatest woman athlete of the 1930s was a young Texan named Babe Didrickson. At the 1932 summer Olympics in Los Angeles she won four gold medals! Later she became the nation's finest woman golfer. Amelia Earhart was the most famous pilot of the 1930s, the first woman to fly solo across the Atlantic, duplicating Charles Lindbergh's famed feat. Determined to prove that women aviators could equal or surpass the achievements of male pilots, Earhart set many new records before she disappeared while on a flight across the Pacific Ocean. It was through the medium of the motion picture that women actresses exercized their greatest cultural influence on the American people, in styles of dress, speech, manners, mores, behavior, sexuality, and appearance. Women movie stars were the highest paid women in the country; in fact salaries of top women film stars equaled or surpassed those of all but a few men. Each week, of the 80 million or more Americans who attended the movies, probably 60 percent were females.

During the 1930s, despite the hard times and widespread suffering of women, they were often able to achieve greater economic independence, enter a wider range of occupations, have more opportunity to join unions, enjoy greater personal and sexual freedom, enhance their political status, achieve greater cultural influence, and achieve a more serious and positive public image than ever before. In the words of Susan Ware, the leading historian of women during the 1930s, women "held their own" and even made modest advances.

THE EMERGENCE OF ETHNIC AMERICANS

During the 1930s millions of ethnic Americans, the sons and daughters of the "new" immigrants who had poured into America during the first fifteen years of the twentieth century, came of age. The large majority of these first-generation Americans identified with Roosevelt and the New Deal. They saw Roosevelt as a liberal leader who acknowledged their claim that they, too, were Americans entitled to all the opportunities and challenges of citizenship. Ethnic Americans also perceived the New Deal as a response to their special concerns and as an effort to preserve the modest social and economic gains that they had made during the 1920s. Roosevelt cemented his hold on the political loyalties of ethnic Americans by appointing their leaders to important public offices in unprecedented numbers. Nearly one-fourth of the federal judicial appointments made during the New Deal era were Catholics.

Most ethnic Americans during the 1930s resided in the large cities of the Northeast and the Midwest, especially New York and Chicago. During his 1936 electoral sweep, Roosevelt carried 104 of the nation's 106 largest cities. By 1936 northern ethnic Americans had acquired enough political clout within the Democratic Party to abolish the rule requiring the Party's presidential candidate to win a two-thirds majority vote at its nominating convention. This rule, in place for more than one hundred years, had been used by southern Democrats to prevent any candidate unacceptable to them from getting the nomination. The anachronistic two-thirds rule had nearly cost Roosevelt the 1932 nomination. Bolstered by the support of northern ethnics, he had gotten rid of it by the 1936 convention.

Most Catholics supported the New Deal and the Democratic Party. In large eastern cities, Irish Americans and Italian Americans flocked to Roosevelt's banner. In the Midwest, Polish Americans and other Slavic groups likewise joined the New Deal coalition. A large majority of American Jews, most of them the sons and daughters of Russian or Polish Jews who had come to America during the first decade of the twentieth century, enthusiastically supported Roosevelt and the New Dealers. Jews perceived the Roosevelt administration as a special protector of Jews that was also determined to extend their educational, economic, and social opportunities.

AFRICAN AMERICANS IN DEPRESSION

Depression brought devastation to millions of African Americans. Black people, many of whom were poor when the Depression began, sank deeper into poverty, disfranchisement, segregation, and deprivation. Most African Americans lived in the South during the 1930s, and most southern blacks resided in rural areas. Depression exacerbated anti-black racism in the South. The Ku Klux Klan reported an upsurge in membership and the number of lynchings tripled between 1932 and 1933.

African Americans continued to migrate north, but during the Depression years they found that opportunities were no better in northern cities. Black unemployment was always far higher than white; both employers and unions discriminated against African American workers. Black industrial unemployment ran between 40 percent and 50 percent in most cities. President Hoover appeared to be relatively unconcerned about the problems African Americans faced during the Depression. Hard times meant a continuing struggle for survival for most African Americans within the confines of second-class citizenship.

Still African Americans benefited from many New Deal programs and rallied to Roosevelt's leadership. New Dealers were more responsive to their concerns than any administration since Reconstruction. Roosevelt invited many African American visitors to the White House and appointed an unofficial black cabinet to advise him on the special needs of African Americans. He asked Secretary of the Interior Harold Ickes to find qualified blacks to fill key government positions. Appointees included a prominent attorney, William R. Hastie, and a college professor, Robert C. Weaver. Both leaders worked in the Department of the Interior. Ira De A. Reid was another top black political appointee; he worked for the Social Security administration, where he became an expert on black poverty. The ablest of Roosevelt's black appointees was a dynamic educator, Mary

Private charities tried to relieve the effects of poverty and unemployment during the 1930s, but were overwhelmed by conditions. Here African American children in Harlem line up to receive food from a Catholic agency.

McLeod Bethune, who became Director of Negro Affairs of the National Youth Administration. Bethune was an indefatigable advocate of education as the chief means of black economic advancement. African American social scientists, such as Dr. Ralph Bunche and Rayford Logan, served as government consultants. African American illiteracy declined and life expectancy for black people jumped about five years during the 1930s.

Several New Dealers were committed to undermining both segregation and African American disfranchisement. Eleanor Roosevelt was the leader of those New Dealers committed to civil rights for African Americans. She worked closely with Walter White, president of the NAACP, supporting its efforts to strike at the legal foundations of Jim Crow laws. In 1939, when the Daughters of the American Revolution refused to allow a gifted African American opera singer, Marian Anderson, to perform in Washington's Constitution Hall, Mrs. Roosevelt arranged for her to sing on Easter Sunday from the steps of the Lincoln Memorial.

But for political reasons President Roosevelt was never committed to black civil rights. He believed that the top New Deal priority was enacting national legislation, and if he antagonized southern white politicians who controlled key committees in both the House and Senate, he risked not getting legislation enacted. Unwilling to risk alienating southern whites, he never endorsed two key African American demands of the 1930s: a federal anti-lynching law and abolition of the poll tax. In 1938 an anti-lynching bill passed the House, only to be killed by a southern filibuster in the

Senate. Roosevelt never tried to overcome the filibuster, and in fact maintained a discreet silence on the entire issue.

Roosevelt also accepted discrimination and segregation against African Americans by many government agencies, as New Dealers acceded to prevailing racist practices. The Federal Housing Authority (FHA) refused to guarantee mortgages purchased by African American families in white neighborhoods. The CCC was racially segregated, as was the TVA, which constructed all-white towns and confined African American workers to low-paying job categories. Since waiters, cooks, janitors, domestics, and farm workers were excluded both from Social Security coverage and from the minimum wage provisions of the Fair Labor Standards Act, millions of African American workers were denied benefits available to most white workers.

One New Deal program even harmed blacks. The first Triple A denied crop subsidies to African American tenants and deprived thousands of black sharecroppers of their livelihoods by forcing them off the land. Perhaps 200,000 poor African American families were victimized by the politics of the first AAA. An NAACP report issued in 1934 charged that the nearly 6 million black Americans dependent on agriculture for their livelihood received no help from the federal government. Even though African Americans were worse off than whites during the Depression and their needs were greater, they received fewer government benefits than whites. When African Americans did benefit from New Deal programs, they did so more because they were economically distressed citizens than because they belonged to an oppressed racial minority.

African American sharecroppers joined the Southern Tenant Farmers Union organized in Arkansas in 1934. The union organized strikes in the field and attracted national support from liberal and radical political leaders. Union spokesmen denounced the AAA and called for direct rental and parity payments to sharecroppers and tenants. In time the New Deal, responding in part to union complaints and the protests of other advocates for the poor, developed programs designed to help poor African American farmers. The Second AAA provided payments to tenants and croppers, and other New Deal agencies made loans to poor black farmers to buy or improve the lands they farmed.

Despite the shortcomings of the New Deal for African Americans, blacks supported it enthusiastically. In thousands of poor black households in the rural South and in northern ghettos, families hung pictures of Franklin Roosevelt on the walls. African American voters abandoned their historical allegiance to the party of Lincoln and moved into the Democratic political camp. Whereas two-thirds of African American voters had voted for Hoover in 1932, in 1936 two-thirds voted for Roosevelt, joining the New Deal coalition. By the 1938 Congressional elections 85 percent of African American voters had joined the Democratic Party. In the 1940 presidential election 97 percent of black voters cast ballots for Roosevelt! During the New Deal era African Americans became a significant force in the urban coalition that provided Roosevelt and New Dealers with much of their support. Since the New Deal era, African American voters have been a loyal Democratic constituency, and the Democratic Party has been much more responsive to black concerns than the Republicans. In recent times African American politicians have formed one of the most powerful blocs within the Democratic Party.

Despite achieving more political influence in Washington than at any time since Reconstruction, black influence on the New Deal, and on all public affairs, remained quite limited. During the 1930s the large majority of America's 13 to 14 million African Americans remained relatively poor and uneducated. They were unorganized politically and could not press their demands effectively on the power brokers in Washington. Their underlying lack of economic power hindered their efforts to achieve greater political power. Internal conflicts within the African American community also hindered their efforts. Within the NAACP, the most influential organization in the black community, conflict arose between its executive secretary, Walter White, and William E. B. Dubois, the militant editor of the organization's journal, *The Crisis*. White, an urbane, liberal integrationist, sought to advance black interests via public relations, legal action, and support for the New Deal, while Dubois promoted militant black nationalism and self-help. Dubois resigned from the NAACP in disgust in 1934.

HISPANIC AMERICANS

Many of the 1.2 million Mexican Americans living in the southwestern United States suffered extreme hardship during the Depression but got no help from the New Deal. Mexican Americans had little political clout and official America was not much concerned about their welfare. Mostly uneducated and unskilled, they toiled at the economic margins, either beyond the reach of or falling through the cracks of many New Deal programs. U.S. government policy during the 1930s discouraged Mexican Americans from living in the United States. The Mexican-born population declined substantially during these years as many families returned to Mexico because of U.S. government pressure and declining economic opportunities.

But despite poverty, hardship, and official indifference or hostility, the members of the Mexican American population who were politically active generally voted Democratic and supported Roosevelt's New Deal. In Texas, Arizona, and California, Mexican Americans enrolled in sizable numbers in the Civilian Conservation Corps and some of the WPA projects. One of the major reasons Hispanic Americans benefited to the extent that they did from social programs, and supported Roosevelt, was the political influence of Senator Dennis Chavez of New Mexico, the only important U.S. political leader of Hispanic descent during the 1930s. Roosevelt frequently sought the advice of Chavez and regarded him as the national spokesman for the Hispanic American community. Chavez proved an effective advocate and he succeeded in channeling millions of New Deal dollars into programs that benefited Hispanic American populations.

During the 1920s hundreds of thousands of Mexicans had moved to California and the Southwest, and when depression struck the Golden State, they composed the bulk of the agricultural work force. They reacted to hard times by engaging in strikes. Mexican American workers in Southern California formed a union that staged about 20 strikes from 1933 to 1936. About 18,000 Mexican American cotton pickers joined a union and struck the cotton fields of the San Joaquin Valley in 1933. Vigilantes fired on their union hall, killing two workers. In addition, the Immigration Service supported grower efforts to break the strike by deporting workers, some of whom were legal residents.

The arrival of dispossessed white tenant farmers and sharecroppers from the southern plains states further undermined the economic position of Mexican American farm workers in California. Between 1935 and 1938 about 300,000 "Okies" came to California's Central Valley to work in the fields, and growers were happy to hire them as strikebreakers and replacements for the Mexicans. By the late 1930s poor whites composed 90 percent of the state's migrant farm workers, and many of the Hispanic workers they had displaced had been forcibly taken or voluntarily returned to Mexico.

During the 1930s a sizable number of Mexicans emigrated to midwestern states such as Illinois, Michigan, and Ohio. Refugees from grinding rural poverty in their native land, they arrived uneducated and unskilled and often found work as migratory farm laborers. Some found their way into the lower ranks of unskilled workers in some of the traditional industries, including railroad gangs, meatpacking, steel, and autos. Many of the *barrios* of midwestern as well as southwestern and western cities were founded or greatly expanded during the Depression decade.

During the 1930s a relatively small immigration from Puerto Rico to the United States mainland continued. These Puerto Ricans, like the Mexicans, mostly refugees from a grinding rural poverty, settled in New York, Philadelphia, and a few other large eastern cities. Most lacked education, had no job skills, and did not speak English. Many Puerto Ricans discovered in the Depression America of the 1930s that they had traded rural poverty in their homeland for urban poverty in America.

During the late 1930s, hundreds of thousands of farm families fled rural poverty in the southern plains states for California. This photo shows a family of "Okies" stalled by car trouble somewhere in New Mexico in 1937.

NATIVE AMERICANS

Federal Indian policy was transformed during the 1930s. Although President Roosevelt had little firsthand knowledge of Native Americans or their problems, he relied on Harold Ickes, who did. Ickes arranged for John S. Collier to become commissioner of the Bureau of Indian Affairs (BIA). Collier, a social scientist who had been a director of the American Indian Defense Association, had long championed Native American causes. He had also edited *American Indian Life*, the most important journal devoted to Native American issues. Collier had become convinced that the federal government's integrationist policy had failed to work and that it was destroying Native American culture and ways of living. He believed that Native Americans required autonomy and self-determination to survive. During his long tenure as commissioner of the BIA from 1933 to 1945, Collier worked to promote cultural pluralism and cultural nationalism among Native Americans.

Collier fought for Indian tribal ownership of land. He championed the Indian Reorganization Act passed by Congress in 1934, which ended the allotment policy established by the Dawes Act nearly fifty years earlier. The allotment system had worked over decades to transfer much Indian land to white ranchers, miners, and farmers. Since 1887 Indian landholdings had dropped from 138 million acres to 48 million. When the Depression struck, Native Americans were the poorest, most deprived, and most depressed of all major ethnic groups in the country. Indian families on reservations earned an average annual income of about $100. Their infant mortality rate was the highest, their life expectancy the shortest, their educational attainment the lowest, and their rate of unemployment the highest of any major ethnic group in the nation.

The Indian Reorganization Act restored lands to tribal ownership. Collier also tried to get additional lands for many of the tribes via government grants, court actions, and private efforts. It also provided for Indian self-government and loans for economic development. Collier promoted efforts by Native Americans to develop their own business enterprises on reservations. Medical and educational services were expanded. Native American religious practices and traditional cultures were protected. Collier, deeply respectful of Indian ways, was committed to democratic pluralism: "The cultural history of Indians is in all respects to be considered equal to that of any non-Indian group. And it is desirable that Indians be bilingual." For the first time in its history, under Collier's leadership the Bureau of Indian Affairs hired many Native Americans for its own staff. Of the approximately 5,000 employees of the BIA in 1938, 1,300 were Native Americans.

Native Americans also benefited from some New Deal relief programs. The Civilian Conservation Corps was especially appealing to young Native American men, who got an opportunity to do important conservation work and earn money desperately needed by their families. Altogether more than 80,000 young Indian men participated in CCC projects in fifteen western states. During the 1930s, for the first time since Columbus "discovered" America, the Native American population showed a net increase.

Under Collier's enlightened leadership, the BIA promoted efforts by various tribes to develop governing councils to administer programs and formulate policies at the local level. At the same time, bureau officials sought to promote Native American cultural awareness and pride. Indians were encouraged to preserve their native religion, arts and crafts, language, rituals, ceremonials, and traditions. Native Americans were urged to respect and celebrate the traditional Indian ways and to speak their native language. Collier hoped that Native Americans would achieve both political and cultural autonomy, protected from the oppressions and depredations of Euro-American society. Collier also worked to end the practice of sending young Native Americans away to boarding school. BIA officials built schools on reservations, where Native American youngsters could learn to cope with mainstream America, learn about their own culture, and develop a strong Indian identity.

SCHOOLS AND COLLEGES

Many public schools suffered serious damage because of Depression conditions. In 1931 and 1932 about 5,000 schools closed across the nation for lack of funds. Thousands of others shortened the instructional day, shortened the school year, fired teachers, increased class size, and eliminated programs. Enrollment in public schools tended to increase at a greater rate than the population of the country, but per capita spending in both elementary and secondary schools dropped during the 1930s. Educational opportunities, especially in the rural Midwest and South, were curtailed. In Chicago teachers worked for months without pay from the bankrupt school district. Across the land thousands of teachers joined the swelling ranks of the unemployed.

It is also true that within America's underfunded, understaffed, and overcrowded Depression school system of the 1930s, students stayed in school longer and a higher percentage both graduated from high school and went to college than ever before. Greater numbers of women also graduated from high school and went to college than ever before. Because many students of the 1930s could attend college only by means of major family sacrifices and many also worked full-time or part-time, Depression era collegians were more serious and career oriented than those during the 1920s. Most college students of the 1930s retained conventional or traditional political values, and most were relatively apolitical, something that has always been the norm among American collegians, but there was a small but highly visible minority of students who were politicized by the Depression and who embraced radical political ideologies. Thousands of students, disillusioned by memories of World War I, embraced pacifism. They signed pledges vowing never to go to war for their country under any circumstances.

Social life on college campuses during the 1930s focused on joining sororities and fraternities, attending football games, drinking alcohol, going to parties, and having sex. Both young women and men dated extensively, and both eschewed going steady or developing a serious, long-term relationship with one person. Depression conditions forced many young men and women with active social lives to do a lot of economical dating, perhaps just meeting at a private spot on the college campus for a few hours—talking, holding hands, maybe necking a little, or just sitting together looking at the stars. Perhaps they shared their hopes and dreams for the future. It might not have been a very exciting date, but it was fun and it cost nothing.

There is probably a distortion built into public memories of collegiate social life of the 1930s compared with that of the 1920s. During the "Roaring Twenties" college students, especially the upper-middle-class party animals, became a staple of the mass media and the stuff of popular fiction, such as F. Scott Fitzgerald's *This Side of Paradise*. But evidence suggests that heavy petting and premarital sex were actually more common in the 1930s than in the 1920s. Most 1930s collegians knew about birth control and they used condoms. They just received less publicity during the Depression decade, when public attention was focused on more serious issues such as unemployment, world trade, and the value of the dollar.

RELIGION

As most Americans became preoccupied with the accumulating problems of the Great Depression, public attention turned away from religious issues. Most religions turned inward during the 1930s; religious leaders appeared more concerned about their particular faith than about politics or public controversies. All major American religious groups concerned themselves with strengthening their institutions and the religious identity of their communicants. The realms of faith and the realms of politics increasingly diverged.

Among Protestant churches, the Fundamentalist churches continued to gain communicants—increasing by nearly 50 percent during the 1930s—while mainline churches suffered a decline in membership. In a time of secular troubles, millions of Americans turned to the emotional otherworldliness of the Fundamentalists. Among Protestant religious thinkers the 1930s was a time of great theological ferment. A profound religious thinker and perhaps the foremost Protestant theologian of the time, Reinhold Niebuhr, developed the doctrines known as Neo-Orthodoxy. Niebuhr challenged the fashionable liberal theologies such as the Social Gospel that had asserted the essential goodness of man, human perfectibility, the need for good works, and social reform. He revived the ancient doctrines that stressed the innate depravity of man, the need for God's grace, and the quest for spiritual salvation.

Norman Vincent Peale, a Methodist minister with training in psychology, became the leading popularizer of Protestant doctrines during the 1930s. In 1933 Peale began a radio program called "The Art of Living," which soon had a following in the millions and continued for over 40 years. He preached a simple, upbeat doctrine that depended on positive thinking: "You can if you think you can." Most Protestant religious leaders eschewed politics, although many were involved in the various peace movements of the 1930s. Many college students active in various peace causes also attended church.

The American Catholic Church by the 1930s had established itself as the largest single denomination in America, and many Catholic laymen had achieved prominence in a wide range of fields. In 1939 Cardinal Francis J. Spellman became the head of the archdiocese of New York, the most influential archdiocese in the American Catholic Church, and soon became the foremost spokesman of American Catholicism. Church leaders were concerned primarily with addressing the faith and morals of their vast constituencies rather than with commenting on Depression conditions or criticizing the New Deal. Father Coughlin's spirited diatribes against Roosevelt and the New Deal acutely embarrassed the Catholic hierarchy at a time when about 80 percent of Catholics supported Roosevelt's administration. Church officials finally silenced the radio priest in 1938.

During the 1930s American Jews tended to move away from traditional orthodoxies and embrace the more liberal forms of Judaism such as the Reform and Conservative movements. There was a generational conflict within the American Jewish community—between the older immigrant generation, who tended to retain the Orthodox faith, and the younger, American-born Jews, who turned to more liberal forms of worship. American Jews were also divided between those of German origin, who had come to America prior to the Civil War, and the much larger and generally poorer numbers of Jews who had emigrated from Eastern Europe between 1890 and 1914.

Jews, regardless of their class or status, country of origin, and whether they were Orthodox, Reform, or Conservative, tended to embrace liberal politics and were strong supporters of Franklin Roosevelt. Public opinion polls taken during the mid-1930s showed over 80 percent of American Jews endorsing the New Deal. Roosevelt responded to this massive support by appointing a number of brilliant young Jews to high positions in his administration. Benjamin Cohen became an influential White House adviser. Henry Morgenthau became Secretary of the Treasury and advised Roosevelt on a wide range of issues. Roosevelt also appointed a distinguished Harvard law school professor, Felix Frankfurter, to the Supreme Court in 1938. Before his appointment to the Court, Frankfurter had recruited scores of Jewish intellectuals for government service in Washington.

AMERICAN LITERATURE AND THE GREAT DEPRESSION

The severe downturn in the American economy and the decade of hard times profoundly influenced nearly all American writers, whether they were serious or popular writers, fiction or nonfiction writers, and whether they wrote for newspapers and magazines or wrote plays, novels, poetry, history, biography, or social science tracts. Most of the fiction writers of the 1930s were distinctly inferior to the great writers of the 1920s. In general, the quality of novel writing in the 1930s suffered by comparison with the 1920s. But nonfiction flowered during the 1930s. The Depression decade was a great age of cultural renewal, a time when intellectuals reaffirmed traditional values and the basic strength and goodness of the mass of ordinary American men and women.

During the 1930s there occurred an unsuccessful effort by writers who embraced Marxist ideologies to create a "proletarian literature" in America. This effort harnessed novel writing to a political ideology, with mostly disastrous literary consequences. Writers were using literature as a political weapon; they endeavored to create a revolutionary consciousness among American industrial workers and farm laborers so that they would rise up and throw off the ruling capitalist elites. These proletarian novels were usually so poorly constructed, so artlessly conceptualized, and so badly written that they did not sell. About the last person to be found reading a proletarian novel during the 1930s would be its intended audience, an unemployed worker.

Some of the nation's best writers, influenced by Marxist ideas, wrote searing novels about depression America. The finest black writer, Richard Wright, wrote *Native Son*, a powerful and frightening condemnation of racism. Erskine Caldwell wrote *God's Little Acre*, a bitterly funny portrayal of the demoralization of poor rural whites and the oppressive system that degraded them. John Steinbeck wrote perhaps the best book about the effects of depression on poor whites; his *Grapes of Wrath* told the story of the "Okies," the uprooted tenant farmers from the south-central plains states who had been driven from their lands by a combination of natural and man-made disasters. The Joad family made its way to California's Central Valley to make a fresh start, but they do not rediscover the American dream; they find only more misery and poverty. They are exploited by growers and brutalized by deputies and vigilantes. But despite their hardships, the Joads retain their basic decency and humanity. Steinbeck's novel probably defined the way most Americans viewed the Depression and its effects on poor whites. But the single most popular novel of the Depression decade by far was a piece of escapist romantic fiction, *Gone with the Wind*. Written by a southerner, Margaret Mitchell, who had never written a book before, *Gone with the Wind* was a melodrama on an epic scale that chronicled the lives of an aristocratic southern family brought low by the dislocations and disruptions of the Civil War and Reconstruction. Millions fled to the make-believe world of Tara, Scarlett O'Hara, and Rhett Butler, to escape grim Depression realities.

History and biography were both popular genres during the 1930s. Their appeal derived from the Depression-induced desire of many Americans to learn about their past and to put the crises of the 1930s in a historical perspective. American readers also sought to derive inspiration and guidance from the lives of great men and women from the American past. Perhaps the finest 1930s biographical study was Carl Sandburg's epic four-volume biography of the greatest American president, Abraham Lincoln.

GAMES AND SPORTS

Popular culture flourished during hard times and also reflected the impact of Depression. Games, hobbies, and fads, many of them carryovers from the 1920s, continued to be popular. Along with stamp collecting, contract bridge, and marathon dancing came a new game, Monopoly, invented by an unemployed Atlantic City real estate salesman. Millions of Americans who had no money to invest in the real world accumulated a tidy fortune in Monopoly properties. In a generally depressed decade, Monopoly permitted vicarious accumulation of real estate and reinforced capitalistic values. Other people took a shot at the Irish Sweepstakes and got involved in chain-letter schemes.

Millions of Americans remained enthusiastic sports fans during the Depression. The most popular sport continued to be baseball, the "national pastime." Each year millions of Americans clustered around their radios to listen to the World Series. College football was also very popular. One of the leading radio sportscasters during the mid-1930s was a young man from a small Illinois town destined for a political career one day, Ronald "Dutch" Reagan. Boxing was also a major attraction during the 1930s, and the most popular fighter was heavyweight champion Joe Louis, the son of an African American sharecropper. Another African American athlete, Jesse Owens, starred in the 1936 Olympic Games in Berlin, winning four gold medals in three days. Professional sports offered determined athletes an opportunity to make good money during the Depression, although professional baseball was closed to African Americans.

MUSIC

Music benefited from improvements in recording technology and from the wider dissemination of songs via jukeboxes, radios, and the sound tracks of film musicals. Pop music in America during the 1930s reached a far larger audience than ever before. Record sales increased. Popular music generally gave expression to cheerful, sentimental, and romantic themes.

In the later 1930s "swing" and "big band" orchestras became enormously popular. A jazz clarinet player, Benny Goodman, became known as the "King of Swing" and his concerts inevitably played to sold-out audiences. Young couples learned an acrobatic dance, the "jitterbug," to keep pace with the fast rhythms produced by Goodman's and other swing orchestras. Other dancers added exotic Latin American imports like the rhumba, the samba, and the beguine to their repertoires.

Many of the nation's leading songwriters and composers came to Hollywood during the 1930s to write movie scores and theme songs for films. Among them were George and Ira Gershwin, Irving Berlin, and Cole Porter. A generation of new young singers, many of them with some of the most prominent big bands, emerged in the late 1930s—Frank Sinatra, Bing Crosby, and Billie Holiday. Some of the hit songs of the era included "I Got

Rhythm," "Smoke Gets in Your Eyes," and "Brother Can You Spare a Dime?"

THE GOLDEN AGE OF RADIO

The 1930s coincided with the golden age of radio. Most middle-class families during the Depression managed to own at least one radio. By the end of the 1930s Americans owned 30 million radios; probably 85 percent of all households had a radio, or at least had access to one. Technological innovations made during the 1930s meant that radios were smaller and no longer required cumbrous outdoor antennae. People were having radios installed in their cars, and many of the more expensive new cars sold during the 1930s came with a radio as standard equipment. Network broadcasting expanded and hundreds of new radio stations come on line. By the end of the Thirties radio programming reached every town and village in the country.

By the 1930s radio was probably the most pervasive cultural influence; it became the mass medium that reached the most Americans in the most compelling way. Music remained the most important genre of radio entertainment, with radio promoting both swing and classical music. Politicians increasingly used radio to promote their ideas and themselves. The amount of air time devoted to broadcast news increased steadily throughout the 1930s. The most popular newscasters, such as Elmer Davis, Lowell Thomas, and the legendary Edward R. Murrow, became prominent radio personalities.

Radio programs occupied a central place in family life during the 1930s. Daytime radio presented soap operas, cooking shows, and programs advising mothers on how to raise their children. Evening programs offered adventure shows such as "The Lone Ranger" and "Buck Rogers," as well as quiz programs such as "Information Please." Radio comedians were popular. Some of the best shows starred Fred Allen, Jack Benny, Bob Hope, Red Skelton, Burns and Allen, and ventriloquist Edgar Bergen and his dummy, Charlie McCarthy. The most popular radio show of the 1930s was "Amos n' Andy." This show was the creation of two white comedians, Freeman Gosden, who played Amos, and Charles Correll, who played Andy. Amos and Andy were two black men who owned a Harlem taxi company that had one taxi. The humor of the show derived from the misadventures of the two principals and the portrayal of comic stereotypes of black people. Week in and week out "Amos n' Andy" attracted the largest radio audiences.

During the 1930s people relied on radio for everything—news, sports, weather, music, drama, comedy, adventure, murder mysteries, soap operas, religious inspiration, and advice. Radio provided some of the strongest cultural bonds holding Depression era Americans together.

Generally this electronic mass medium functioned as a conservator of traditional values in a time of crisis.

THE HEYDAY OF HOLLYWOOD

Hollywood also entered its golden age during the 1930s. Eight large studios churned out most of the hundreds of feature films made each year. Technicolor made its appearance in 1935, although most motion pictures made in the late 1930s continued to be black and white. The major studios tended to serve up low-budget escapist fare that steered clear of Depression realities and avoided raising serious social issues. Horror films such as *Frankenstein* and gangster films such as *The Public Enemy*, both made in 1931, were popular. The prevailing morality required that all gangsters be killed off at the end, usually by other gangsters to reinforce the didactic message that "crime does not pay."

The most successful movie comedians were the Marx brothers, who brought a kind of inspired anarchy to the cinema that entertained millions. Groucho, Harpo, Chico, and Zeppo made several films during the mid-1930s, including two smash hits, *A Night at the Opera* (1935) and *A Day at the Races* (1937). W. C. Fields was another popular film comedian of the 1930s. Fields developed a comic persona that was part con artist and part grumpy old man who hated little children. When asked how he liked children, Fields once responded, "Oh, I prefer them medium well with the skin left on." The most popular female comic movie star of the 1930s was Mae West. West played a sexually aggressive woman and used bawdy Western humor to become a box office star. Her most famous lines included "Why don't you come up and see me some time?" "Is that a gun in your pocket or are you just glad to see me?" and "When a girl goes wrong, men go right after her."

There were many other popular film genres in the 1930s. Frank Capra directed a series of successful "screwball" comedies, of which the best was *It Happened One Night* (1934), starring Clark Gable and Claudette Colbert. Busby Berkeley's choreography and the dancing of Fred Astaire and Ginger Rogers thrilled audiences in the best musicals of the 1930s, which have never been surpassed. In 1939 Hollywood produced an extravagant film version of Margaret Mitchell's blockbuster novel *Gone with the Wind*. Done in spectacular fashion in technicolor, the four-hour-long epic starred Vivien Leigh as the passionate, headstrong Scarlett and Clark Gable as the mysterious and romantic Rhett Butler. The movie broke all box office records, quickly became a classic, and has been seen by more people than any other motion picture. It is revealing both of the film industry and the viewing public that the two most popular movie stars of the Depression years were an animated cartoon character, Walt Disney's Mickey Mouse, and a child actress, Shirley Temple.

America's child sweetheart. Child actress and movie star Shirley Temple was one of Hollywood's biggest box office attractions during the depression decade.

Under pressure from religious groups, Hollywood instituted The Motion Picture Production Code of 1934, which strictly regulated the film industry. The code forbade filmmakers from depicting homosexuality, abortion, drug use, or sex. Actors could not utter profanities, not even a "hell" or a "damn." If couples were shown in bed, they had to be wearing clothes and both partners had to keep one foot on the floor during the scene. In the mid-Thirties about two-thirds of the nation's 135 million inhabitants went to the movies at least once a week. The top movie stars were among the highest paid entertainers in the world. Both the film and radio industries boomed during the Depression decade.

BIBLIOGRAPHY

There is a sizable historical literature covering the social and cultural history of the 1930s. There is also a large and growing literature on the impact of the Depression and the New Deal on particular groups and classes. Walter Galenson, *The CIO Challenge to the AFL* is a good account of the rise of industrial unionism during the late 1930s. Susan Ware, the foremost historian of women during the 1930s, has written two important books. Her *Holding Their Own: American Women in the 1930s* is the best study of the impact of the Depression on American women. Her *Beyond Suffrage: Women in the New Deal* is an account of the growing political influence of American women. Oscar Handlin, *The Americans* is a good survey of ethnic Americans. Raymond Wolters, *Negroes and the New Deal* is a good study of what the New Deal did and did not do for African Americans. For the impact of the Depression on Mexican Americans and how they coped with hard times, see the relevant chapters of Matt S. Meier and Feliciano Rivera, *The Chicanos: A History of Mexican Americans*. Kenneth Philip, *John Collier's Crusade for Indian Reform, 1920–1954* is a fine account of the New Deal and Native Americans. David Tyack et al., *Public Schools in Hard Times: The Great Depression and Recent Years* contains a good account of the impact of the Depression on the nation's public schools. For those readers interested in learning more about religion during the 1930s, see Samuel C. Kincheloe, *Research Memorandum on Relgion in the Depression*. Richard H. Pells, *Radical Visions and American Dreams: Culture and Social Thought in the Depression Years* records the nation's artistic and intellectual life during the 1930s. Andrew Bergman, *We're in the Money: Depression America and Its Films* is an informative account of Hollywood in the 1930s.

CHAPTER
10
Diplomacy between Wars

The United States emerged from World War I an acknowledged world power with the most productive and prosperous economy in the world. American banks dominated the realms of international finance and investment. American products and technology dominated world markets. American exports led the world, and U.S. imports were second only to Great Britain's. American literature, music, and films flooded the world. Thousands of Americans went abroad to work, to teach, to write, and to convert souls to Christianity. In addition to dollars, agricultural commodities, and manufactured goods, America exported culture and people.

American diplomats understood that even had they desired it, America could not be a bystander in world affairs. It is true that during the interwar period Americans tried to avoid foreign entanglements, but it is also true that American diplomats pursued an activist foreign policy appropriate to that of a leading world power. During the 1920s and 1930s American leaders sought a peaceful and prosperous world order through nonmilitary means: treaties, disarmament conferences, and financial arrangements. The United States pursued isolationist policies between the wars only in the sense that it wanted to avoid war, reduce foreign military involvements, and preserve its freedom of action in international affairs. Nationalism, not isolationism, was the driving force behind American foreign policy between the wars. Historian Joan Hoff Wilson has characterized American interwar diplomacy as "independent internationalism," that is, being actively involved in international affairs but preserving independence in actions. With differing degrees of success and sophistication, all the presidents who served between the wars pursued this uniquely American approach to international affairs called independent internationalism.

American presidents, secretaries of state, senior diplomats, and prominent members of Congress responsible for making and implementing U.S. foreign policy during this time tended to react to events rather than anticipate them. None of the presidents or secretaries of state who served between wars achieved the stature of world leader or statesman. Neither Harding nor Coolidge knew much about or had any real interest in the affairs of the larger world beyond American boundaries. Charles Evans Hughes, Frank Kellogg, and Cordell Hull had no prior experience with or any expertise in foreign policy before becoming Secretary of State. U.S. foreign policy during the interwar period focused primarily on maintaining order and stability. Any concessions made to revisionist powers were designed to preserve the status quo.

THE SEARCH FOR PEACE

President Harding came to office in 1921 committed to returning the nation to "normalcy." In foreign policy, "normalcy" meant repudiating Wilsonian internationalism and its commitment to collective security. Harding believed that his landslide victory expressed deeply felt popular yearnings for ending overseas crusades, avoiding foreign entanglements, curtailing huge military expenditures, and healing domestic conflicts.

In November 1921 Harding presided at ceremonies burying the Unknown Soldier in Arlington National Cemetery. In a moving speech, the President resolved that "never again" would the nation be led into another foreign war, and he called for "a new and lasting era of peace." That same month Harding signed separate peace treaties with all Central Power nations that were still technically at war with the United States because of the Senate's rejection of the Treaty of Versailles. He also opened a major international conference in Washington hosted by the United States.

The Washington Conference, which convened in the nation's capital on November 12, 1921, was the first important diplomatic gathering of the postwar era. It was called by the United States to show America's commitment to ensuring peace in the postwar world despite its refusal to join the League of Nations. It was also the first major international conference ever held in America, indicating the new prestige of the United States, which had come out of the war as the world's preeminent power. Eight nations joined with the United States to discuss disarmament and Far Eastern diplomatic problems left by war.

Washington took the lead in calling for the conference because American leaders wanted to avoid a costly arms race with the other major naval powers, a race that would require large expenditures and higher taxes. The British and Japanese responded positively to the call for a conference. Great Britain had an aging fleet that would be expensive to replace, and Japanese leaders knew that they could not match America's wealth and industrial might. Leaders of all the major powers also understood that limiting naval competition required that they settle outstanding political issues in the Pacific Basin and Asia left over from the war.

Secretary of State Charles Evans Hughes seized the initiative at the conference with a bold speech calling for naval disarmament. Public opinion rallied behind Hughes, putting additional pressure on the statesmen gathered in the nation's capital. After intense negotiations, three treaties emerged from the conference, each complementing the others. Concessions made in one were repaid by concessions in others. The major accord was the Five Power Treaty. Each of its signatories agreed not to fortify their Pacific colonies; more important, they accepted Hughes's proposals for naval disarmament. Signed February 6, 1922, by the United States, Great Britain, Japan, France, and Italy, the Five Power Treaty established a ten-year moratorium on new capital ship construction. (Capital ships were battleships and cruisers exceeding 10,000 tons.) The treaty also required that the signatories scrap ships built or being built until their relative strength in capital ships reached a ratio of 5 to 5 to 3 to 1.75 to 1.75, with a 5 equaling 525,000 tons. The Americans and the British would have the highest ratio, 525,000 tons of capital ships each. The Japanese would have a ratio of 3, and the French and Italians would have 1.75 each. To reach treaty limits, the major powers had to scrap 70 warships totaling nearly 2 million tons, with the United States scrapping the most ships. The Five Power Treaty curbed a costly and dangerous postwar naval arms race among the major powers. Yet, although it was a significant disarmament agreement, the treaty had loopholes. There were no limits applied to submarines, destroyers, and cruisers under 10,000 tons.

A second treaty worked out at the Conference, the Four Power Treaty, signed by the United States, Great Britain, Japan, and France, required those four nations to respect each other's rights in the Pacific and to refer any disputes to a joint conference. This agreement bound the four powers to respect one another's island possessions in the Western Pacific. A third agreement, the Nine Power Treaty, tried to limit competition among foreign powers in China. Historically, many nations, exploiting the weakness of Chinese governments, had seized territory and extracted major trading concessions within their spheres of influence. The Nine Power Treaty endeavored to open all areas of China to free trade. The treaty bound all the nations attending the conference to observe the American Open Door policy toward China and to respect the "sovereignty, the independence, and the territorial and administrative integrity of China." The signatories formally affirmed the traditional Open Door policy toward China promulgated by John Hay in 1899 and 1900.

The Washington Conference, although it did not guarantee peace, nevertheless represented a major diplomatic achievement for the United States. The three treaties were the greatest diplomatic achievements of the interwar period. The Five Power Treaty was the first major arms limitation pact in the history of modern diplomacy. Secretary of State Hughes had provided the leadership that halted a naval arms race, saving taxpayers billions of dollars and easing international tensions. In the Far East the Open Door was given a new lease on life, and a new power balance emerged in Asia reflecting postwar realities.

Harding, unlike Wilson, had consulted with Senate leaders during conference negotiations and kept them informed of its proceedings. The Senate promptly ratified all three treaties, although isolationist senators attacked them during debates, especially the Four Power Treaty, which they saw as possibly involving the United States in a future war with Japan. Irreconcilable J. A. Reed of Montana called the Four Power Treaty "treacherous, treasonable, and damnable." As they ratified these agreements, the Senate, reflecting the isolationist sentiments of most Americans, declared "there is no commitment to armed force, no alliance, no obligation to join in any defense."

All three treaties would eventually prove to be toothless because neither the United States nor any other signatories bound themselves to defend the agreements with force or sanctions. Americans wanted peace, but they would not take responsibility for preserving peace. The treaties were gentlemen's agreements; their effectiveness depended on good faith compliance, which proved in time to be a frail prop. Beginning in 1931 the Japanese ultimately violated all the agreements, and for years America and the League of Nations reacted weakly to Japanese aggression, which went unchecked in China and the Pacific.

American peace societies during the 1920s advocated many strategies to preserve order in the world. They proposed cooperating with the League of Nations, joining the World Court, having additional disarmament conferences, signing arbitration treaties, curbing international business activity, and cutting military spending. The National Council for the Prevention of War kept alive ghastly memories of war carnage and reminded Americans of the suicidal folly of trying to settle international conflicts by war. *What Price Glory* (1926) and other antiwar films depicted the slaughter of World War I combat.

President Coolidge issued a call for another naval disarmament conference, which convened in Geneva in 1927. Coolidge wanted to extend the 5 to 5 to 3 to 1.75 to 1.75 ratios to all categories of warships to end a developing naval arms race in cruisers under 10,000 tons, destroyers, and submarines. France and Italy refused to participate and the conferees got bogged down in trying to work out the technical details of an agreement. After six weeks of angry debate the delegates failed to find a formula they could accept. The conference broke up in complete failure.

Following the failure at Geneva, peace advocates shifted their emphasis from abolishing arms to abolishing war under international law. Americans took the initiative in this movement. They approached the French

Foreign Minister, Aristide Briand, who announced in April 1927 that France was prepared to sign a bilateral pact with the United States outlawing war. The drive generated wide popular support in both countries. American Secretary of State Frank Kellogg suggested that the proposed bilateral agreement be expanded to include other powers, and the French agreed. The treaty was worded to permit defensive wars but to outlaw war "as an instrument of national policy." On August 27, 1928, the Pact of Paris was signed by 15 nations, and in succeeding months another 45 nations signed it, including Japan and Germany. The American public overwhelmingly supported the pact, which the Senate ratified by a vote of 85 to 1. Kellogg was awarded the 1929 Nobel Peace Prize.

The Pact of Paris was a feeble document, a mere statement of principle requiring neither sacrifice nor the assumption of any responsibilities for keeping the peace. It reflected the delusions of Americans and others who believed that one could eliminate war by declaring it illegal. But the treaty did not outlaw war, it outlawed only aggressive wars and declared wars. Thereafter nations were to fight only "defensive" wars and were to become involved only in "incidents." Even as they approved the treaty, most U.S. senators understood that the pact was nothing more than a pious gesture. Senator Hiram Johnson made fun of it, calling it "a helmless ship, a houseless street, a wordless book, a swordless sheath." Then he voted for it. On the same day that the Senate ratified the treaty, it also voted funds to build fifteen new cruisers. Proponents of the cause knew that this pact did not guarantee peace, but they reasoned that they had improved the odds against war.

Other disarmament conferences were held during the 1930s. The London Naval Conference (1930) extended the Five Power Treaty ratios to all categories of warships, closing a huge loophole in the previous treaty. But the French and Italians refused to accept these limits, the former because they feared for their security, the latter because they had expansionist ambitions. The conferees then added an "escalator clause" that permitted any member to disregard the ratios if a nation not bound by the ratios, such as Italy, began building ships that threatened the security of a nation that had accepted the ratios. The London conference also extended the moratorium on capital ship construction another five years, to 1936.

Another disarmament conference took place in Geneva in 1932 to try to reduce the size of armies. President Hoover strongly supported this conference, urging it to abolish all offensive weapons, reduce all weapons by 30 percent, and limit the size of armies to 100,000 troops for each 65 million people in its population. The Geneva conference failed completely, mainly because of Japanese aggression in Manchuria and the rise of Hitler to power in Germany. Security-conscious nations did not dare disarm in the face of these threatening developments. Another naval conference met in London in 1935, but no major agreements could be reached because the Italians still refused to accept any more limits on its naval forces and the Japanese, harboring expansionist ambitions in China and Southeast Asia, walked out. In 1936 the Japanese formally renounced all naval limitations. By 1938 all nations had abandoned them. That year, Congress appropriated a billion dollars for U.S. naval construction in all ship categories. Disarmament ultimately failed to prevent World War II.

The League of Nations building in Geneva. The sphere in the foreground was a gift from the Woodrow Wilson Foundation, donated in 1939.

The League of Nations also failed to keep the peace, not only because the United States refused to join, but because its members usually chose not to use it to settle international disputes. Although the United States was not a member, Americans participated in League activities during the 1920s and 1930s, attending meetings about public health, drug trafficking, and other affairs not connected with international security. Eminent American jurists such as Charles Evans Hughes served on the World Court, even though America had never joined that either. But the League of Nations, the World Court, the Pact of Paris, and the disarmament conferences could not maintain world peace once the Great Depression of the 1930s and its disastrous economic effects upset the fragile world order.

FOREIGN ECONOMIC POLICY

During the early 1920s the Harding administration and Congress both promoted American business activity overseas. Secretary of State Charles Evans Hughes believed that a prosperous world would be a peaceful world, free of political extremism, aggression, revolution, and war. He understood that in the modern world American international commercial and financial interests blended with traditional diplomatic concerns in the conduct of foreign affairs. The chief governmental agency actively promoting overseas business during the 1920s was the Department of Commerce, headed by Herbert Hoover, who had had a career as an international businessman.

Americans assumed a dominant role in international economic activity during the 1920s. The gigantic U.S. economy produced nearly half of the world's manufactured goods. American traders had become the world's leading exporters and American bankers the world's foremost lenders. Between 1920 and 1929 American investments abroad increased from $6 billion to almost $16 billion, most of them made in Europe and Latin America. U.S. corporate investors led the way: General Electric invested heavily in various German enterprises, Standard Oil of New Jersey bought into Venezuela's rich oil resources, United Fruit Company was a huge landowner in several Central American countries, and International Telephone and Telegraph built Cuba's communication network.

As American companies expanded their overseas activities, the government moved energetically to collect war debts owed by European nations, thereby incurring their resentment. When war had begun in 1914, the United States was the world's largest net debtor; Americans owed foreigners $3 billion more than foreigners owed them. Huge European expenditures for war quickly transformed America into the world's leading creditor. By 1920, Europeans owed the U.S. Treasury $10.4 billion, of which the British owed $4.3 billion, the French $3.4 billion, and the Italians $1.6 billion. The smaller nations together owed another $1 billion to the United States.

These nations had borrowed the money mostly to buy war matériel, principally ammunition, from American suppliers. The money American citizens paid to buy Liberty Bonds was credited by the government to European accounts in American banks; the banks in turn paid it to businesses who sold ammunition to the Europeans. These loan funds never left the United States and, being spent in the United States, contributed significantly to the wartime prosperity that most Americans enjoyed.

During the 1920s Europeans tried to persuade Americans to cancel these debts. They used a variety of arguments to claim the loans were subsidies: They pointed out that American losses in property and lives were modest relative to Allied losses. While Europeans had fought and died, neutral Americans had prospered. The Allies had paid in blood, and Americans should pay in dollars by canceling the loans. The war had been fought for common objectives. Had the Germans won, the United States would have had to spend far more than $10 billion building up its defenses. The Europeans also insisted that they could not repay the loans. They had no gold. American tourism did not begin to provide enough funds, and American tariff barriers prevented Europeans from earning export credits to apply against their loans.

Americans rejected all the European arguments and demanded repayment. They insisted that the funds were loans made in good faith with money borrowed from the American people. President Coolidge put the matter tersely: "Well, they hired the money didn't they?" Americans also noted that despite their pleas of poverty, the Europeans, especially the French, were quickly rearming after the war.

Congress established a World War Foreign Debt Commission to set up repayment schedules with each of the debtor nations. The British were the first to sign up, agreeing to repay their $4.3 billion obligation in full over 62 years at 3.3 percent interest, a mortgage on the wealth of the next two British generations. An embittered Briton observed that for the next 60 years "the American flag is going to look like the $tars and $tripes." Other Europeans grumbled about selfish "Uncle Shylock" profiting from war and demanding his pound of flesh.

Several European nations refused to pay their war debts unless they could be assured of collecting reparations from Germany with which to pay them. The Allied Reparations Commission, meeting in 1921, had saddled the hapless Germans with an absurdly inflated $33 billion reparations bill. Germany could not begin to pay that amount and soon defaulted. In response to the default, French troops occupied Germany's Ruhr Valley, its industrial heartland, and prepared to extract reparations in kind. The Germans foiled the French efforts by mounting a campaign of passive disobedience. Reparations dried up. Angry American officials denied any connection between German reparations payments to the Allies and Allied war debt payments to the United States, and they demanded that the French and others pay up.

Even though the United States officially rejected any tie-in between reparations and war debts, Washington demonstrated flexibility. An American banker, Charles Dawes, headed a League of Nations commission that worked out an arrangement, with Secretary Hughes's unofficial approval, to ease the payments crunch in 1924. The Dawes Plan permitted U.S. bankers to lend the Germans $200 million, and it scaled down the size of German reparations payments to one billion marks ($250 million) per year, an amount the Germans could pay. Assured of reparations, the French and the other debtors all negotiated repayment plans similar to that of the British. In 1929 the Dawes Plan gave way to a plan devised by another commission, headed by Owen Young, Chairman of the Board of General Electric, which was a major investor in German companies. The Young Plan called for Germany to pay reparations annually for 59 years, at the end of which the Germans would have paid about $9 billion plus interest, a drastic reduction of the $33 billion originally demanded by the Allies.

With repayment of the Allied war debts to the United States chained to German reparations to the Allies, a financial merry-go-round evolved. American investors loaned the Germans money; the Germans paid the Allies reparations; and the Allies in turn paid war debts to the United States. But the debt and reparations payments depended on the continuing flow of loan money from Americans. After the stock market collapsed in the United States in October 1929, American loans to Germany dried up, German reparations ceased, and Allied payments to the United States stopped. The financial merry-go-round ground to a halt.

President Hoover and Congress contributed to the spreading depression by enacting the Smoot-Hawley Tariff Act (1930), which raised U.S. tariffs to historic high levels and triggered a chain reaction of economic miseries at home and abroad. Foreign traders, no longer able to sell their goods in the United States, stopped buying American exports. Twenty-six nations retaliated against the Smoot-Hawley tax schedules by raising their tariff rates, thereby closing their markets to American goods. Great Britain abandoned its historic free-trade policy and bound its empire more closely to its home market through an imperial preference system.

Worldwide depression wrecked international trade and finance. From 1929 to 1933 world trade declined 40 percent, and American exports shrank 60 percent. As the Great Depression deepened, economic nationalism intensified. Nations increasingly sought to insulate themselves from the virus of economic depression at the expense of other countries. Efforts at international cooperation failed. Autarky, a kind of international anarchy, became the rule of the day.

President Hoover tried to salvage the system of international debt payments before it collapsed completely. He declared a general moratorium for one year on all intergovernmental debts and reparations transactions, beginning in June 1931. Congress approved Hoover's proposal and the public applauded his efforts. During the one-year holiday, efforts were made to reduce further the size of both reparations and war debt payments, but these efforts proved unsuccessful. Just before the moratorium expired in July 1932, Germany's creditors met in Lausanne, Switzerland; they agreed to cancel 90 percent of the debts owed them if the United States would cancel the war debts. Washington abruptly refused. When the first war debt payments came due in December 1932, six nations, led by France, defaulted. More nations defaulted in 1933, and all except Finland were in default by 1934. Payments were never resumed. The Allied war debts owed to America joined the ranks of history's bad debts.

Resentment and disunity lingered on both sides of the Atlantic during the 1930s, facilitating Hitler's rise to power. The collapse of debt payments, the decline in trade, and the rise of economic nationalism were major causes of World War II. American efforts to use its vast economic and financial resources to promote international prosperity and peace failed in the face of international depression and anarchy.

LATIN AMERICA

By 1920 the Caribbean Sea had become a "Yankee lake." An informal American empire, including many countries within the sea and along its Central American coast, flourished. The United States maintained control of its client nations in this region through military occupation and economic domination, which American officials justified by evoking the Roosevelt Corollary to the Monroe Doctrine. In 1920 American troops occupied Cuba, the Dominican Republic, Haiti, Panama, and Nicaragua. There were also many benign effects of American imperialism evident in these countries—more schools and roads, improved public health, communication systems, irrigation networks, and higher national incomes.

During the 1920s American military occupation of Latin American countries came under fire both at home and abroad. Domestic progressive critics such as Senator William Borah asserted that Latin Americans should have the right of self-determination; he also accused President Coolidge of violating the U.S. Constitution by ordering troops into Nicaragua in 1927 without a Congressional declaration of war. Nationalistic Latin Americans claimed that U.S. military intervention in the Caribbean area violated both American democratic traditions and the spirit of Pan-Americanism. American businessmen worried that resentful Hispanic terrorists might attack Americans or their property.

President Hoover came to office in 1929 determined to improve U.S. relations with Latin America. As President-elect, he had gone on a goodwill tour of many Latin American nations, the first ever by an American leader. Many Latin Americans were delighted by Hoover's visit, especially when he stated that relations between Western Hemisphere nations should be governed by the principle of the "Good Neighbor." In his inaugural address the new President made clear his determination to accelerate a "retreat from imperialism" in Latin America and to remove American troops. Hoover embraced a memorandum prepared in 1928 by Undersecretary of State Reuben Clark that repudiated the Roosevelt Corollary, arguing that the many American interventions in the Caribbean had not been justified by the Monroe Doctrine, which had aimed at keeping European nations out of the Western Hemisphere, not promoting U.S. intervention in Latin America. President Franklin Roosevelt, who succeeded Hoover, embraced and enlarged the Good Neighbor policy during the 1930s.

The Great Depression severely tested Hoover's Good Neighbor policy during the early 1930s. Economic hardship weakened governments and provoked rebellions in many Latin American nations. Hoover refrained from sending in the Marines in all these uprisings, even when revolutionaries triumphed. The Depression also caused large reductions in U.S. investments and trade in Latin America, "dollar diplomacy in reverse." Congress pressured Hoover to withdraw troops stationed in Latin American as an economy measure, and before he left office in March 1933, all U.S. military forces were out of Latin America.

In small, poor countries such as the Dominican Republic, Nicaragua, and Haiti the withdrawal of American troops did not bring democratic governments to power. The departing Americans had trained national guards to maintain order, and from the ranks of these national guards dictators emerged and seized control of the government. In the Dominican Republic a guard commander, Rafael T. M. Trujillo, became head of state in 1930 and ruled his country with an iron fist until he was assassinated in 1961. In Nicaragua the head of the national guard, General Anastasio Somoza, became dictator in 1936. With American backing, he (and then his son) ruled Nicaragua like a medieval fiefdom for over 40 years. In Haiti the government was in the hands of a series of military strongmen following U.S. troop withdrawal.

In Cuba the scenario was somewhat different, but military dictatorships backed by the United States ruled Cuban affairs most of the time. By 1929 U.S. investments in Cuba had reached $1.5 billion; Americans owned about two-thirds of the Cuban sugar industry, the mainstay of its economy. With American troops withdrawn, Cuban rebels overthrew a military dictator, General Gerardo Machado. They installed a radical intellectual as president, Ramón Grau San Martín, in 1933. San Martín cancelled the Platt Amendment and nationalized some American properties. Roosevelt, unhappy with San Martín, refrained from military intervention, honoring the Good Neighbor spirit. However, he supported a coup led by an army sergeant, Fulgencio Batista, that overthrew San Martín in 1934.

Batista ruled Cuba, sometimes as president and sometimes from behind the scenes, with American backing for 25 years. The Batista era in Cuba ended in 1959 when the aging dictator was overthrown by Fidel Castro.

U.S. relations with Mexico during the Depression years took a different turn. At the time of the Mexican revolution, from 1910 to 1917, American investments in Mexico were extensive—railroads, silver mines, timber, cattle, farmland, and oil. Over 40 percent of the capital wealth of Mexico belonged to American companies. Then the Mexican Constitution, proclaimed in 1917, stated in Article 27 that all land and subsoil raw materials belonged to the Mexican nation, placing in jeopardy about $300 million of U.S. investments in land and oil. In 1923 the two nations signed an agreement that permitted American companies holding subsoil rights before 1917 to keep them, and it required payment to Americans whose holdings were expropriated by the Mexican government.

In 1938 American business interests collided with Mexican nationalism when Mexican President Lázaro Cárdenas nationalized all foreign oil properties, including extensive U.S. holdings. Secretary of State Cordell Hull angrily denounced the Mexican takeover. President Roosevelt suspended U.S. purchases of Mexican silver, and American oil companies refused to transport Mexican oil. Standard Oil of New Jersey, whose Mexican subsidiary was the largest company to be nationalized, mounted a propaganda campaign in the United States depicting Cárdenas as a Bolshevik bent on socializing Mexico's entire economy.

Roosevelt ruled out military intervention, opting for negotiations to gain compensation for expropriated U.S. oil properties. Roosevelt's restraint was caused partly by his desire to observe the Good Neighbor policy and partly by Mexico's threat to sell its oil to Japan and the European Fascist powers if the American companies continued to boycott Mexican oil. After lengthy negotiations, the two nations reached an agreement. Mexico would retain ownership of its oil but would pay the foreign companies for their nationalized properties. Mexico remained a major trading partner of the United States and joined the fight against the Axis powers in World War II.

Pan-Americanism also flourished during the era of the Good Neighbor. Pan-Americanism had originated with Secretary of State James G. Blaine in 1889 to promote trade and political stability among Western Hemisphere nations. It later was broadened to include cultural exchanges and to encourage inter-American unity and friendship. At a Pan-American conference held in Montevideo, Uruguay, in 1933 Secretary of State Cordell Hull supported a resolution that stated: "No state has the right to intervene in the internal or external affairs of another." At the 1936 conference held in Buenos Aires, Argentina, Hull again endorsed a nonintervention statement, which he understood to bar military intervention but not political or economic pressure.

By the late 1930s the United States was clearly worried about possible Axis inroads in Latin America. Nazi activists were present in Argentina, Uruguay, Chile, and Brazil. At the 1938 Pan-American conference held in Lima, Peru, the United States stressed continental solidarity and hemispheric security. All nations attending the conference signed the Declaration of Lima, which committed them to cooperate with one another in resisting any foreign activity that might threaten them. In 1939 these nations formed a security belt around the Western Hemisphere to prevent Axis intrusions. With the outbreak of World War II the United States led a united band of Western Hemisphere nations against the Axis powers. The U.S. Latin American policy of the Good Neighbor paid off: It increased hemispheric friendship, promoted American trade and investment, curtailed revolution, allowed the United States to retain its hegemony by nonmilitary means, and promoted regional solidarity in wartime.

THE TRIUMPH OF ISOLATIONISM

Franklin Roosevelt took office in March 1933, determined to concentrate his energies on rescuing the American economy from depression. When an economic conference convened in London in the summer of 1933 to grapple with urgent international economic problems, including war debts, tariff barriers, and monetary stabilization, Roosevelt opposed any changes in tariff policy and refused to discuss war debts. When the conference tried to commit the United States to a currency-stabilization system, Roosevelt, who had recently devalued the American dollar to promote American exports, rebuked the conferees for ignoring "fundamental economic ills." Roosevelt, the leader of the world's preeminent economic and financial power, refused to commit the dollar to any stabilization program that threatened to harm the weak American economy. His actions undermined the London Economic Conference, which collapsed shortly thereafter, its participants unable to reach an agreement on any important issues and also bitterly critical of the economic nationalism displayed by the new American leader.

Roosevelt also sought to undo the damage done to American trade by the Smoot-Hawley tariff. His Secretary of State, Cordell Hull, was a longtime advocate of lower tariffs. In June 1934, Congress enacted the Reciprocal Trade Agreements Act, which empowered the President to negotiate bilateral arrangements to reduce tariffs up to 50 percent with each nation that was willing to make reciprocal concessions. The act also granted "most favored nation" status with the United States to any nation that joined her in negotiating a trading arrangement, entitling both nations to the lowest tariff rates on the commodities they sold each other. Hull actively sought reciprocal agreements in Latin America and Europe during his long tenure as Secretary of State from 1933 to 1944. He negotiated agreements with over twenty nations, which reduced domestic tariffs covering nearly 70 percent of American imports. Smoot-Hawley tariff rates were reduced and American exports, particularly to Latin American countries, increased.

The American peace movement, active in the 1920s, increased in strength during the 1930s. Led by women, clergy, and college students disillusioned by World War I, it claimed 12 million members and reached an audience of 50 million. As depression and international tension increased, and as disarmament conferences failed, peace advocates pushed for an arms embargo to be applied by the President in time of war against aggressors. Roosevelt supported this discretionary arms embargo, but opposition from arms manufacturers and isolationist Congressmen killed it.

The lobbying of munitions makers who opposed arms embargoes provoked a Senate investigation of the arms industry. The chairman of the committee was a progressive isolationist, Gerald P. Nye of North Dakota. Nye believed that America had been pressured into entering World War I by a conspiracy of American business interests protecting their investments in an Allied victory. Committee hearings, held between 1934 and 1936, investigated the activities of bankers and munitions makers. Staff members found many instances of business profiteering and lobbying, which made headline news. They found that the Du Pont Company had made huge profits from the war, a revelation that angered millions of Americans who were suffering from the deprivations of the Great Depression.

Senator Nye claimed his committee investigations proved that the bankers who had lent the Allies money, and the "merchants of death" who sold them ammunition, had conspired with President Wilson to take the country to war in 1917. In reality his committee found no evidence to sustain his charge; committee findings showed that munitions makers profited more during neutrality than during American participation in World War I. Nye also found no evidence that industry spokesmen had pressured President Wilson into a declaration of war, and committee investigators ignored the German submarine threat. But many Americans were willing to believe the worst about big business during the 1930s, and they accepted Nye's sensational charges. The Nye Committee hearings reinforced the popular conviction that American involvement in World War I had been a mistake or, worse, had been promoted by a sinister conspiracy of business interests. It also strengthened many people's determination never again to participate in a foreign war.

As the Nye Committee was going after the munitions makers, journalists and popular historians were writing accounts of the American entry into World War I. The best of these books, Walter Millis's best-selling *Road to War* (1935), claimed that British propaganda, business and financial ties to the Allies, and President Wilson's pro-Allied bias combined to draw the United States into a war that it should have avoided. Charles Warren, a prominent authority on international law, asserted that the United States should never enter another foreign war "to preserve and protect . . . profits to be made out of war trading by some of its citizens." An isolationist historian, Carl Becker, argued that although the United States had gone to war in 1917 to defend its property and to make the world safe for democracy, it lost billions of dollars in bad debts and helped make the world safe for dictators. A 1937 public opinion poll found that 60 percent of Americans believed that U.S. involvement in World War I had been a mistake.

The activities of peace groups, the Nye Committee investigations, and the writings of antiwar scholars and journalists, all reinforcing the idea that American participation in World War I had been mistaken, led to the triumph of isolationism in the mid-1930s. As the threat of another war increased steadily in the world because Japan, Italy, and Germany were using force to achieve their expansionist aims, isolationist attitudes intensified. Americans tried to withdraw from world affairs and immunize themselves from the contagion of war. If, as many Americans believed, U.S. entry into World War I had been a mistake, they vowed not to blunder into another foreign war in the 1930s.

Isolationist sentiment was strongest in the Midwest, particularly among German Americans and Irish Americans, but isolationism cut across all regional, class, and ethnic lines, appealing to most Americans during the mid-1930s. It spanned the American political spectrum from left-wing New Dealers to right-wing Republicans and it also included Socialists such as Norman Thomas, Communists, and neo-Fascists. Businessmen, scholars, scientists, ministers, publishers, and many other professionals could be found within isolationist ranks. What united these disparate groups was the shared conviction that involvement in another world war would be ruinous to America and must be avoided. They believed that the nation could pursue diplomatic and economic policies that would both avoid war and preserve American security and freedom. Although he remained a Wilsonian internationalist at heart, President Roosevelt too expressed isolationist attitudes during the mid-1930s, as did most senators and Congressmen. It was not until the late 1930s that Roosevelt and many other Americans, at last perceiving the danger of Axis aggression, cautiously distanced themselves from the noninterventionists.

EUROPE DISINTEGRATES

In 1933 Adolph Hitler came to power in Germany by promising to solve Germany's severe economic and security problems. Like Benito Mussolini, who had gained power in Italy in 1922, Hitler was the leader of a Fascist movement. He headed the National Socialist Party, nicknamed the Nazis. Hitler vowed to revive German economic and military power, to crush the Bolshevik threat, and to purify the German "race" from the "contamination" of Jewish influence, whom he blamed for all of Germany's many severe problems.

In 1933 and 1934 Hitler withdrew from the Geneva disarmament conference, pulled Germany out of the League of Nations, and began to rearm his nation in violation of the Versailles Treaty. He began secret planning for the conquest of Europe. Neither Western leaders nor Roosevelt perceived initially the mortal danger Hitler would pose to their interests. His fanatical doctrines and ambitions were not taken seriously for several years.

Hitler watched approvingly as Mussolini prepared to invade the African country of Ethiopia in 1935. This Italian threat of war caused American isolationists to impose a strict neutrality policy on the U.S. government. In August Congress passed the Neutrality Act of 1935 which prohibited arms sales to either side in a war. President Roosevelt had wanted a law that allowed him to embargo arms sales only to aggressors, but the legislators, who recalled what they believed were President Wilson's unneutral maneuverings that had led America into World War I, wanted a law that strictly limited presidential action. Roosevelt signed the measure and kept his misgivings to himself.

In October 1935 Italy invaded Ethiopia. Roosevelt invoked the Neutrality Act. Most Americans sympathized with the Ethiopians, who fought with spears against a modern, mechanized army using planes, tanks, and poison gas. The League of Nations imposed a limited embargo against Italy, which did not curtail its war effort. Roosevelt, who wanted to curb Italian aggression if he could, called for an American "moral embargo" that would deny shipment of important raw materials to feed Italy's war machine. The moral embargo failed; American companies increased their shipments of strategic raw materials, especially oil, to the Italians. Italy conquered Ethiopia and turned it into an Italian colony. In February 1936 Congress enacted another Neutrality Law, which tightened America's neutrality policy, adding a loan embargo to the arms embargo.

In the summer of 1936 civil war began in Spain when Francisco Franco, an army officer holding Fascist beliefs, led a revolt of Spanish army units against Spain's center-left republican government. Roosevelt adopted a policy of neutrality toward the Spanish Civil War and supported French and British efforts to confine the war to Spain, even if doing so resulted in a Fascist victory. Congress responded with a third Neutrality Law in 1937, applying the arms and loan embargoes to the Spanish Civil War.

Most Americans were indifferent to the outcome of the Spanish Civil War, but some Americans passionately took sides, especially when the Fascist powers, Italy and Germany, intervened to aid Franco's Nationalist forces and the Soviet Union aided the Spanish Republicans. American volunteers, many of them Communists, calling themselves the Abraham Lincoln Battalion, went to Spain to fight for the Republican cause. Franco's forces, with German and Italian help, eventually prevailed. General Franco took power in early 1939 and established in Spain an authoritarian government with Fascistic characteristics that lasted until his death in 1976.

As the Spanish Civil War raged, the aggressors became bolder. In 1936 Hitler sent his troops into the Rhineland, a region demilitarized by the Versailles Treaty. France, responsible for enforcing the treaty, accepted the German action. Later that year Germany and Italy signed an agreement called the Rome-Berlin Axis. In addition, Germany and Japan united against the Soviet Union, forming the Anti-Comintern Pact. Great Britain and France responded to these moves by adopting a timid policy of appeasement, hoping to satisfy Germany's and Italy's expansionist appetites with territorial concessions that would avoid war.

In 1938 Hitler pressed Europe to the brink of war. In March he forcibly annexed Austria. The democracies, pursuing appeasement, again did nothing. In the fall Hitler continued his "war of nerves" by threatening to invade Czechoslovakia when it refused to give him its Sudetenland, a mountainous region bordering the two countries whose inhabitants were mostly ethnic Germans. The Czechs mobilized their small but well-fortified army and turned to their allies, France and the Soviet Union, for help. But both the French and the Soviets refused to honor their treaties with the only democracy in Eastern Europe. Britain and France both pressed the Czechs to give Hitler what he wanted in exchange for his pledge: "This is the last territorial claim I have to make in Europe."

To a hastily called conference at Munich on September 29, 1938, came Prime Minister Neville Chamberlain of England and Premier Edouard Daladier of France. There they met with the Fascist leaders, Hitler and Mussolini, to sacrifice Czechoslovakia upon the altar of appeasement. The hapless Czechs, isolated and vulnerable, surrendered. They demobilized their army and Germany sheared off the Sudetenland for annexation.

Although he had doubts about the effectiveness of the British and French appeasement policies, President Roosevelt hailed the Munich agreement as an act of statesmanship that had averted war. Upon his return to England, Chamberlain proclaimed, "I believe it is peace for our time." In Parliament Winston Churchill rose to dissent: "England and France had to choose between war and dishonor. They chose dishonor; they will have war." Churchill perceived the folly and moral bankruptcy of appeasement embodied in the Munich agreement; it was merely surrender on the installment plan. Six months after Hitler solemnly promised to seek no more territory, German columns erased the Czech remnant from the map. A month after the rape of Czechoslovakia, Mussolini's legions conquered defenseless Albania. Two more dominoes had fallen to the Fascists. The Munich agreement could only postpone war, not prevent it.

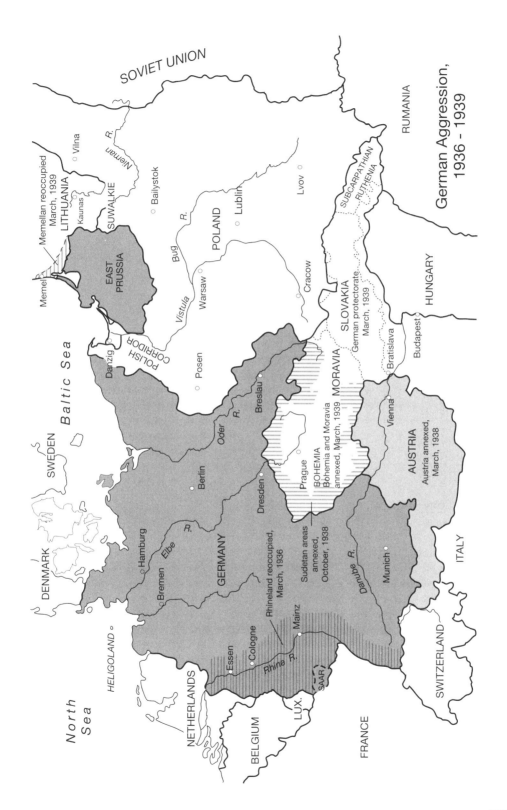

German Aggression, 1936 - 1939

SOVIET UNION

RUMANIA

HUNGARY

SUBCARPATHIAN RUTHENIA

SLOVAKIA

Bratislava

Budapest

German protectorate, March, 1939

MORAVIA

Bohemia and Moravia annexed, March, 1939

BOHEMIA

Prague

Vienna

AUSTRIA

Austria annexed, March, 1938

ITALY

SWITZERLAND

FRANCE

SAAR

LUX.

BELGIUM

NETHERLANDS

Munich

Danube R.

Mainz

Rhine R.

Cologne

Essen

Rhineland reoccupied, March, 1936

Sudetan areas annexed, October, 1938

Dresden

Berlin

GERMANY

Elbe R.

Bremen

Hamburg

DENMARK

SWEDEN

HELIGOLAND

North Sea

Baltic Sea

Breslau

Oder R.

Posen

Danzig

POLISH CORRIDOR

EAST PRUSSIA

Memel

Memelland reoccupied March, 1939

LITHUANIA

Kaunas

SUWALKIE

Vilna

Nieman R.

Bailystok

Bug R.

Warsaw

Vistula

POLAND

Lublin

Cracow

Lvov

287

THE GATHERING STORM

At last awakened to the Nazi peril, Britain and France abandoned appeasement. They quickly concluded security treaties with Poland, the next target on Hitler's list of intended victims. But the decisive factor in the European political equation that tense summer of 1939 was the Soviet Union. When the Western leaders rebuffed Stalin's offer of alliance against Germany, he turned to Hitler. On August 23 the Germans and the Soviets stunned the West by concluding a nonaggression pact that publicly proclaimed peace between them while secretly divided the spoils in Eastern Europe. With his eastern flank secured by this adroit agreement with the Soviets, Hitler unleashed his torrents of fire and steel on the Polish people on September 1, 1939. Two days later, honoring their commitments to Poland, Britain and France declared war on Germany. World War II in Europe had begun. It was 3:00 A.M. in Washington when Ambassador William Bullitt, calling from Paris, awakened the President to tell him war had broken out. Roosevelt replied softly, "Well, Bill, it has come at last, God help us all."

The United States, as it had done when World War I began, promptly declared itself neutral. Unlike President Wilson in August 1914, however, Roosevelt did not ask the American people to be neutral in thought: "Even a neutral cannot be asked to close his mind or his conscience." He made clear that his sympathies lay with the victims of German aggression, as did those of nearly all Americans. Roosevelt also told the American people: "I hope that the United States will keep out of this war. I believe that it will." Most Americans shared the President's views.

Following his speech, he called Congress into special session to amend the neutrality legislation to permit British and French arms purchases. Isolationists loudly opposed his request and vowed to resist "from hell to breakfast." But the public supported Roosevelt. They wanted to stay clear of the war, but they also wanted to help the Allies. After six weeks of heated debate, Congress modified the neutrality laws to permit "cash and carry"; the Allies could buy American arms if they paid cash and hauled them in their own ships. Roosevelt was determined to help the Allies and to challenge the isolationists.

The Soviet Union posed a special problem for American foreign relations during the years when Europe lurched toward war. Starting with Woodrow Wilson in 1917, four consecutive administrations had refused to recognize the Moscow regime, because in 1917 the Bolsheviks had repudiated wartime alliances and concluded a separate peace with Germany, thus imperiling the Allies. The Communist leaders had also repudiated Czarist debts to Washington and expropriated American properties in Russia without compensation. Furthermore, from the time of their accession to power in 1917 the Bolsheviks had sought the overthrow of the American government through propaganda and subversion. By

1933, however, most other nations had recognized the Soviet Union and so America's policy of nonrecognition had neither isolated nor weakened the Soviets.

The Great Depression changed American attitudes toward the Soviets. American businessmen hoped that normalizing relations with the Soviet Union would open new markets in that vast country and reduce unemployment in the United States. Japan was threatening China, and Hitler was on the rise in Germany; Roosevelt hoped that recognition of the Soviet Union might serve to restrain those two expansionist powers.

After negotiations with Soviet representatives, the United States formally recognized the Soviet Union in November 1933. In exchange for U.S. recognition, the Soviets agreed to permit religious freedom in the Soviet Union and to stop spreading Soviet propaganda within the United States. The debt payment question and other claims were deferred.

U.S. recognition of the Soviet Union proved to be a great disappointment. The expected increase in trade did not materialize. The Soviets continued their anti-American propaganda and their denial of freedom of worship. The two nations did not coordinate their foreign policies to curtail Japanese or German expansionism but continued to pursue independent policies. Relations between the two countries were not notably friendlier following recognition—but now they could officially denounce each other. Relations with the USSR deteriorated further after the Nazi-Soviet Pact of 1939 and a Soviet attack upon its small neighbor, Finland, in 1940. As World War II began, many Americans could see little difference between the Nazis and the Communists: Both appeared to be aggressive totalitarian dictatorships bent on military conquest, and they were partners in aggression.

THE RISING SUN

U.S.–Japanese relations in the twentieth century were seldom cordial. U.S. officials viewed the Japanese as a potential threat to American Far Eastern possessions, which included the Philippines, Guam, and other Pacific islands. The United States also retained a variety of interests in China—missionaries, trade, investments, and maintenance of the Open Door policy. The Japanese suspected that the United States wanted to restrain Japanese expansionism and deprive Japan of the fruits of empire that America and many European powers enjoyed. They resented U.S. criticism of Japanese imperialism, criticism they regarded as hypocritical and self-serving. The Japanese were also deeply insulted by the National Origins Act (1924), which excluded Japanese immigrants from the United States. During the 1920s, despite the Washington treaties, naval competition continued between the two nations. Naval war planners in both countries conducted mock wars against the other's forces, preparing for a possible real war in the future. Trade rivalries also strained relations between the two nations.

In 1931 Japanese army units took control of Manchuria, a semi-autonomous northern province of China. The Japanese had been in Manchuria since they defeated the Russians in 1905; by 1930, 90 percent of Japan's foreign investments were in Manchuria. The region was valuable to them as a buffer against the Soviet Union and as a source of food, timber, coal, and iron. The Japanese army took control of Manchuria because they feared that the Nationalist leader of China, Jiang Jieshi, was about to add the province to his possessions. In 1932 Japan renamed Manchuria Manchukuo and declared it to be an independent nation ruled by the heir to the Manchu dynasty, whom the Japanese controlled. In reality, Manchuria had become a Japanese colony.

Japanese aggression violated the League of Nations covenant. According to its terms, the League of Nations was obligated to defend China against Japan. Rather than send troops or impose economic sanctions against the Japanese, however, the League sent an investigative team led by Great Britain's Earl of Lytton. After about a year of investigating, the Lytton Commission reported the obvious to Geneva: the Japanese were guilty of aggression in Manchuria. After debating the matter, the League formally proclaimed Japan an aggressor, but it took no further action. The Japanese response was to withdraw from the League of Nations and remain in Manchuria. The international organization established after World War I to keep peace in the world had failed its first major test to thwart aggression. League failure established an ominous precedent; potential aggressors in Europe took note.

The American response to Japanese aggression in northern China was equally ineffectual. The seizure of Manchuria also violated the Nine Power Treaty, but that treaty was toothless; it had no binding enforcement provisions. President Hoover and Secretary of State Henry Stimson hesitated for months before responding to Japanese aggression while debating what to do. No one seriously considered military intervention. U.S. forces were inadequate and public opinion would not have supported it. The *Philadelphia Record* editorialized: "The American people don't give a hoot in a rain barrel who controls North China." Stimson favored imposing economic sanctions against the Japanese, but Hoover refused to implement them because he feared doing so might cause a war. Instead, Hoover adopted a policy of nonrecognition of the Japanese conquest. Stimson sent notes to both the Chinese and Japanese government informing them that the United States would not recognize the Japanese takeover of Manchuria because it violated international law. Nonrecognition was a weak policy that merely annoyed the Japanese without deterring them.

In July 1937, following a clash between Japanese and Chinese troops at the Marco Polo Bridge near Beijing, Japanese forces invaded northern

China, and full-scale fighting erupted between Japanese and Chinese troops. World War II in Asia had begun. Japanese planes bombed Chinese cities, killing thousands of civilians. Japanese armies occupied many urban areas. Americans angrily denounced Japanese aggression and atrocities. In an effort to help the Chinese, President Roosevelt refused to declare the existence of war in Asia so that China could buy American arms. Roosevelt also spoke to the American people on October 5, 1937, from Chicago, the isolationist heartland. He tried to rally the Western nations to act against aggressors:

> The peace-loving nations must make a concerted effort in opposition to those violations of treaties and those ignorings of humane instincts which today are creating a state of international anarchy and instability from which there is no escape through mere isolation or neutrality.[1]

1. Quoted in James MacGregor Burns, *Roosevelt: The Lion and the Fox* (New York: Harcourt, Brace, 1956), p. 318.

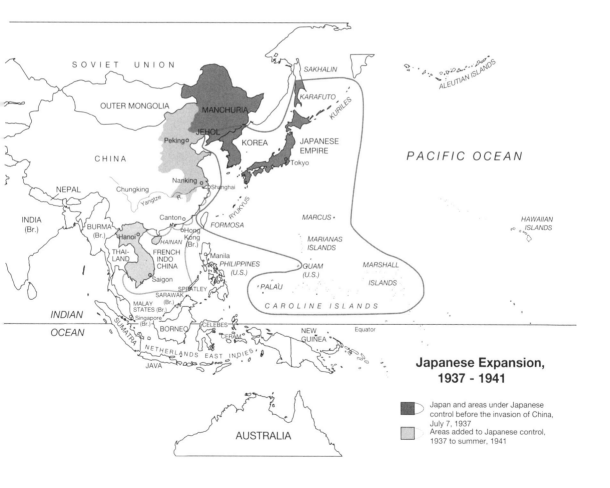

Japanese Expansion, 1937 - 1941

Japan and areas under Japanese control before the invasion of China, July 7, 1937

Areas added to Japanese control, 1937 to summer, 1941

He called for a "quarantine" to curb "the epidemic of world lawlessness." Most Americans responded sympathetically to the President's words, but isolationist leaders such as Senator Nye warned that the President was edging toward war. Europeans ignored the President's call, viewing America as a minor player in world affairs. Roosevelt later confessed that he had no specific plan of action in mind to halt Japanese or Fascist aggression; he was only giving expression to an attitude.

Japan continued its war in China in 1938 and 1939. The United States sent military equipment to the Chinese and loaned them money, but it also continued its extensive trade with Japan, which involved strategic raw materials. Roosevelt did not want to impose economic sanctions on Japan lest they provoke a war at a time when the President saw the more serious threats to U.S. interests coming from Europe. When war broke out in Europe in September 1939, U.S.–Japanese relations were strained further.

BIBLIOGRAPHY

The best account of U.S. foreign policy during the 1920s is Warren I. Cohen, *Empire without Tears: American Foreign Relations, 1921–1933*. Two other good general studies of American foreign policy during the 1920s are L. Ethan Ellis, *Republican Foreign Policy, 1921–1933* and Joan Hoff Wilson, *American Business and Foreign Policy, 1920–1933*. Charles DeBenedetti, *The Peace Reform Movement in American History* has good accounts of American peace activities during the 1920s and 1930s. Dana Munro, *United States and the Caribbean Republics, 1921–1933* and Irwin F. Gellman, *Good Neighbor Diplomacy: United States Policies in Latin America, 1933–1945* are good accounts of U.S. Latin American policies between the wars. Walter LaFeber, *Inevitable Revolutions: The United States in Central America* is a fine recent study of American foreign policy in Central America and its consequences. Robert H. Ferrell, *American Diplomacy in the Great Depression: Hoover Foreign Policy, 1929–1933* is a good account. Robert Dallek, *Franklin D. Roosevelt and American Foreign Policy, 1932–1945* is the best and most comprehensive treatment of Roosevelt's foreign policy that we have. Robert A. Divine, *The Illusion of Neutrality* is a good study of 1930s isolationism. Arnold Offner, *The Origins of the Second World War* is excellent. John Wiltz, *From Isolation to War, 1931–1941* is a good short account of U.S. entry into World War II. See also James V. Compton, *The Swastika and the Eagle: Hitler, the United States, and the Origins of World War II*. Akira Iriye, *After Imperialism: The Search for a New Order in the Far East, 1921–1931* is a good analysis of American foreign policy in the Pacific Basin. Also see Richard D. Burns and Edward M. Bennett, eds., *Diplomats in Crisis: United States–Chinese–Japanese Relations, 1919–1941*.

CHAPTER
11
The Road to War

World War II began in Europe on September 1, 1939, with the German invasion of Poland immediately following the signing of the Nazi–Soviet Pact. Roosevelt's prompt response to the outbreak of war in Europe was to declare American neutrality. Legally, the United States retained the status of a neutral until December 7, 1941, when the Japanese staged surprise air attacks on American military installations in Hawaii. Despite more than two years of official neutrality, Roosevelt made no effort to craft a genuinely neutral foreign policy. His sympathies—and the sympathies of most Americans—were enlisted on the side of the Allies and the victims of Axis aggression. Roosevelt also recognized that supporting the Allied cause clearly served American security needs.

American preparedness efforts during the neutrality period were piecemeal and inadequate until after the fall of France in June 1940. Prior to then Roosevelt had hesitated to undertake a comprehensive mobilization program or to harness American industry to military production because of the huge costs involved and because of strong isolationist opposition. After the fall of France, however, the American rearmament campaign accelerated and Roosevelt, with strong support from public opinion, developed an obviously unneutral foreign policy based on "all aid to the Allies short of war." Still, fear of isolationist criticism compelled the President to proceed slowly and often deviously as he implemented the U.S. policy of gradually stepping up aid to the Allies short of actually entering the war.

Reelected to an unprecedented third term in November 1940, and responding to Great Britain's plea for help, Roosevelt proposed the Lend-Lease program, which Congress, after a bitter debate, adopted in March 1941. Lend-Lease amounted to a declaration of economic warfare against the Axis. In the summer and fall of 1941 Roosevelt gradually involved the U.S. Navy in anti-submarine patrols and escort missions accompanying the cargo ships hauling Lend-Lease supplies to Great Britain and the Soviet Union. Clashes between American destroyers and German submarines became inevitable. By fall of 1941 an undeclared naval war raged in the North Atlantic between the United States and Germany. Roosevelt, convinced that only full-scale U.S. involvement in the European war would enable the Soviets and the British to defeat the Axis powers, hoped to use the clashes between American and German ships to bring Congress and the public to support a declaration of war. But he failed. Both Congress and American public opinion remained divided between isolationists and interventionists. German reactions to clashes with U.S. ships was mild; Hitler was not seeking a war with the United States while the German campaign in the Soviet Union remained in doubt. In November 1941 American policy was drifting. Washington had lost the initiative in the North Atlantic.

Meanwhile, on the other side of the world, relations between the United States and Japan had deteriorated. The ultimate cause of the war that came between Japan and the United States was a diplomatic impasse over China. The United States tried to force the Japanese to cancel their war of aggression against China and withdraw their forces from the Asian mainland. Washington also tried to deter the Japanese from their expansionist objectives in Southeast Asia. To achieve its goals, the United States used economic weapons: the threat of boycott, and then eventually embargoing strategic raw materials vital to Japanese industry and its war machine. The Americans also resorted to traditional diplomacy and negotiations, but all such efforts were ultimately futile. They failed because the Japanese militarists in power had too much invested in the ongoing Chinese war to seriously consider abandoning it. American trade embargoes forced the Japanese to turn to Southeast Asia to find new sources of strategic commodities, particularly oil, rather than accede to American demands.

In the summer and fall of 1941 Roosevelt, focused on the European war, which he saw as much more threatening to American interests than the crisis in Japanese relations, pursued a strategy of stalling in the Pacific. He tried to buy time for the United States and its allies, the British and the Dutch, to build up the defenses of their colonial possessions and territories in the South Pacific. The Japanese leaders finally grew weary of the stalling tactics and set a deadline for a resolution of the conflicts with the United States. They demanded a free hand in China and a quick resumption of trade with the United States, concessions the United States was unwilling to make. The Japanese response to the failure of the negotiations was the surprise air attacks at Pearl Harbor. American isolation had ended with dramatic suddenness. Within a few days the United States went from neutrality and peace to fighting major wars against Japan in the Pacific and Germany and Italy in Europe. The United States had become fully engaged in the largest, costliest, and most destructive wars in world history.

BLITZKRIEG

Poland fell within a month to German forces invading from the west and Soviet forces invading from the east. Following their conquests, the Nazis and the Communists partitioned Poland in accordance with their previous pact and settled in for a joint occupation.

Following Poland's destruction, an eerie silence descended upon Europe. German and French armies faced each other from behind their fortified Siegfried and Maginot lines; neither moved. Isolationist Senator William Borah sniffed, "There's something phony about this war." Soon Americans talked of a "phony war" in Europe. Three thousand miles away, they viewed events in Europe with considerable detachment. Once war erupted, they believed, the British navy would strangle the Germany economy, and the French army, the largest in the world, would whip its upstart foe. Europe's latest conflagration could not reach America.

The American false confidence was shattered by a brilliant series of German offensives launched in April 1940. Hitler's "blitzkrieg" (lightning war) quickly subdued Denmark and Norway. Within weeks of the Scandinavian operations, Germany also overran the Netherlands, Luxembourg, and Belgium. Germany then attacked France. Hitler sent his Panzers (armored divisions) crashing through the Ardennes Forest. Using tanks, armored columns, and Stuka dive bombers in close tactical coordination, the German forces quickly pierced the French defenses. Within two weeks they swept behind the Maginot line. Paris fell on June 16 and Germany soon occupied the northern two-thirds of the country. The unoccupied southern third of France was permitted a rump government at Vichy. Wherever the Nazis extended what they called their New Order, they established a barbaric reign of terror. Concentration camps, slave labor, extreme repression and brutality, mass executions of civilians, and wholesale looting became all too common aspects of Nazi occupations.

The fall of France stunned and alarmed most Americans. Hitler had required only six weeks to achieve what Germany had failed to accomplish in four years of attrition warfare during World War I. The fall of France erased a lot of American illusions; a majority of Americans now understood that the Axis powers posed a potential long-term threat to the United States and the Western Hemisphere. Only the British survived to carry on the struggle against the Germans. If England fell, Germany might gain control of the British navy and the Atlantic Ocean would no longer be a barrier shielding America from Europe's power struggles; it would become a watery highway for Nazi penetration of the New World.

The British, who viewed the fall of France with dismay, prepared to battle the Nazis. Prime Minister Neville Chamberlain resigned in disgrace in May 1940 and was replaced by Winston Churchill. Following the Allied rout on the continent, the British managed to retrieve their army, which had been fighting in France and was cut off from land retreat, by evacuating 330,000 men from the beaches at Dunkirk in the north of France. The British also possessed a formidable fleet, a modern air force, and an indomitable leader who rallied his people to face the German war machine. Churchill offered the British people not only "blood, toil, tears, and sweat," but ultimate victory over the Nazi menace.

THE BATTLE OF BRITAIN

In the summer of 1940 Hitler hurled his Luftwaffe (air force) at the British. His goal was to achieve air superiority over England preparatory to launching an amphibious invasion of the islands. Night after night waves of German bombers attacked British air bases. The Germans were on the verge of winning the Battle of Britain; they had destroyed or shut down almost all the Royal Air Force interceptor bases. One more raid would have given Hitler control of the English skies. At that moment Hitler, impatient for victory, wanting to cut German aircraft losses, and anxious to retaliate for a British air raid on Berlin, suddenly switched tactics. He turned his bombers on British cities. He planned to bring England to its knees by terror bombing civilians.

Hitler's tactical switch saved England. The British people, though badly battered by months of relentless bombing, refused to break. They retained high morale and stubbornly defied the German aerial onslaught. Meanwhile British air defenders used this time as a reprieve to repair their damaged bases and planes. Gradually the tide turned in Britain's direction. Within three months the battle was over. The Royal Air Force had won and Germany had lost the cream of its air force.

Hitler cancelled his planned invasion of Britain and turned his attention to the Balkans and North Africa, where his ally Italy was engaged. German troops came to the aid of the Italians, who were losing battles to Greek forces and Albanian guerrillas. During the spring of 1941 German armies conquered Yugoslavia, Greece, Hungary, Rumania, and Bulgaria. In North Africa, German armies put tremendous pressures on British forces protecting approaches to the Suez Canal. These campaigns in the Balkans and North Africa preceded the German war to destroy Hitler's most hated foe, the Soviet Union, which began in late June of 1941.

"ALL AID TO THE ALLIES SHORT OF WAR"

Following the fall of France, and with the outcome of the Battle of Britain hanging in the balance, President Roosevelt had committed the United States to a policy of "all aid to the Allies short of war," abandoning any pretense of neutrality. The American military buildup accelerated. In July Congress appropriated $8 billion for rearming the nation, an unprecedented sum for a peacetime mobilization. Bidding to form a bipartisan coalition in support of his policy, Roosevelt appointed Republicans Henry L. Stimson Secretary of War and Frank Knox Secretary of the Navy. At the President's request, Congress enacted the first peacetime conscription in American history. American industry, spurred by defense contracts, began to hum. The industrial economy showed signs of life not seen since the late 1920s. By the end of the year U.S. factories had produced 17,000 planes, 9,000 tanks, and 17,000 heavy artillery. Even though isolationists and peace groups denounced the military spending and draft bills, Roosevelt had committed the United States to pro-Allied nonbelligerency. U.S. neutrality was merely a legal sham. A Gallup poll taken at the time showed that more than half of Americans favored all these measures; isolationism was losing some of its hold on the public in the face of the Nazi conquest of Western Europe.

With the Battle of Britain raging, Churchill wrote Roosevelt requesting that the United States transfer a portion of its destroyer fleet to the Royal Navy to protect the British home islands and to escort arms convoys across the Atlantic. Roosevelt, linking American security to the survival of Britain, responded promptly. On his executive authority, he offered the British 50 World War I-vintage destroyers in exchange for leases to eight British military bases stretching from Newfoundland to British Guiana. Giving warships to a nation at war was clearly a violation of America's ostensible neutrality policy, but Roosevelt stressed the importance of guarding the Atlantic approaches to American territory. The President insisted that acquiring the bases from the British made an important contribution to the strategic defense of the United States. Churchill, needing the ships desperately, quickly accepted Roosevelt's proposal. Before making his proposal, Roosevelt consulted with a battery of constitutional lawyers, who assured him that he did not need Congressional approval to transfer the destroyers. Public reaction to the transaction was mostly favorable.

THE 1940 ELECTION

Amidst the U.S. military buildup, the deteriorating world situation, and the destroyer-for-bases deal, the 1940 election occurred. The Republicans held their nominating convention first. It was an emotional and divided gathering that pitted staunch isolationists led by Senators Robert Taft of Ohio, Burton J. Wheeler of Montana, and Hiram Johnson of California against internationalists led by Senator Arthur Vandenberg of Michigan and Governor Thomas E. Dewey of New York. The internationalists outmaneuvered the isolationists, took control of the convention, and pushed through the nomination of Wendell Willkie on the eighth ballot. Willkie was a political unknown and had been a Democrat most of his life. He was a businessman, not a professional politican; at the time he received the presidential nomination he was the CEO of Commonwealth and South-ern, a giant public utilities company that had had some run-ins with New Dealers over TVA and the issue of public power. Willkie, as a spokesman for private power interests, had charged the federal government with un-fair competition. Willkie was an internationalist and sympathetic to the Al-lied cause. At the time of his nomination he strongly supported Roosevelt's foreign policy and military buildup.

Roosevelt, busy in Washington in a time of growing crisis, had said lit-tle about whether he would seek an unprecedented third term. However, he did not encourage other candidates nor did he restrain his supporters who were promoting a third-term bid for the man in the White House. When the Democrats met in July to pick a candidate, Roosevelt made a dramatic announcement by telephone from Washington to the assembled delegates, indicating that he would accept a third-term nomination if it were offered. His message galvanized the convention, and a Roosevelt bandwagon quickly carried the convention.

The election contest was a bitter campaign in time of national crisis when the American people could reach no consensus on what role the United States should play in a troubled world. Willkie proved to be an en-ergetic campaigner. He attacked Roosevelt and his policies fiercely. He de-nounced Roosevelt's failure to clear the destroyer transaction with Congress as "the most dictatorial action ever taken by an American presi-dent." He attacked the New Deal for failing to lift the country out of eco-nomic depression. He attacked Roosevelt's bid for a third term as contrary to the spirit of American democracy and a bold bid to become dictator of America. He attacked Roosevelt's defense buildup as too slow and haphaz-ard, one that put the national security at risk.

While Willkie hammered away at Roosevelt and the New Deal, the President remained in Washington, did not campaign, and did not re-spond to Willkie's attacks. In late September the polls showed Willkie trail-ing Roosevelt badly. His attacks on Roosevelt for failing to end the Depression and to provide a proper defense had been ineffective. Desper-ate to find an issue that would enable him to gain ground, he abandoned his bipartisan approach to foreign policy and attacked Roosevelt as a war-monger whose policies would take the country to war. He struck a re-sponsive chord among anxious voters in both parties. Polls taken in mid-October showed Willkie cutting into FDR's lead.

Willkie's charges that the President was a warmonger flushed Roo-sevelt out of the White House. He responded forcibly to Willkie's charges, but Willkie continued to gain. As election day approached, Democratic Party officials nervously watched the polls. On October 30 a poll showed that Willkie had closed to within 4 percentage points of the President. On the same day, the Republican challenger charged that reelection of Roo-sevelt would mean American entry into the war by April 1941. That night Roosevelt, speaking in Boston, offered unqualified assurances of peace.

Answering what he termed his opponent's "verbal blitzkrieg," he told the mothers of America:

> I have said this before, but I shall say it again and again; your boys are not going to be sent into any foreign wars.[1]

FDR's reassurances worked. Roosevelt fended off Willkie's late surge and won reelection handily, receiving 27 million votes to Willkie's 22 million and with a decisive 449 to 82 margin in the electoral votes. But Willkie had gotten 5 million more votes than Landon had in 1936, and he had given Roosevelt his toughest election campaign to date. The Democrats retained large majorities in both houses of Congress, but the bipartisan conservative coalition of northern Republicans and southern Democrats gained strength.

But neither candidate had leveled with the voters during the campaign. After it was over, Willkie confessed that his warmongering charges had been "just politics," and he returned to supporting Roosevelt's policy of giving all-out aid to the Allies short of war. Roosevelt, bowing to political pressures, had given the American people false assurance of peace, knowing that his policies risked eventual entry into the European war. The 1940 election was neither the first nor the last in which presidential candidates dealt dishonestly with the crucial issues of war and peace. A young New Dealer congressman from Texas, Lyndon Johnson, observed Roosevelt's 1940 election tactics and remembered them. When Johnson ran for President in 1964, he too would give voters false assurances of peace in order to ensure electoral victory.

LEND-LEASE

While Americans were going to the polls to reelect Franklin Delano Roosevelt to an unprecedented third term, the English people huddled in their bomb shelters and worried about their nearly bankrupt government. As the year approached its end, it was evident that the British government had spent nearly all of its dollar reserves and could no longer pay for U.S. war matériel that it so desperately needed to stay in the war against Germany. The Germans, having failed to subdue England by air, had turned to its submarines to try to sever Britain's oceanic lifeline and starve its people into submission. Prime Minister Churchill wrote a personal letter to Roosevelt in which he urged the American president to continue to provide the supplies the British so urgently needed but for which they could no longer pay.

---

1. Quoted in *James* MacGregor Burns, *Roosevelt: The Lion and the Fox* (New York: Harcourt, Brace, 1956), p. 449.

When the British had depleted their dollar reserves during World War I, American bankers had advanced credits to the British, but in this war U.S. neutrality legislation prohibited bank loans to nations at war. Roosevelt himself devised a clever program to circumvent the Neutrality Act: Lend or lease to the British the guns, tanks, planes, ammunition, whatever they needed to win the war, and they would repay or replace these materials after the war ended. In a December 29, 1940, fireside chat, he explained Lend-Lease to the American people, stating that aiding the British was the best way to keep America out of the war:

> There is far less chance of the United States getting into war if we do all we can now to support the nations defending themselves against attack by the Axis than if we acquiesce in their defeat, submit tamely to an Axis victory, and wait our turn to be the object of attack in another war later on.[2]

He also urged the United States to "be the great arsenal of democracy." It was one of his most successful speeches; over 60 percent of the public approved the Lend-Lease proposal. Churchill pleaded, "Give us the tools and we will finish the job."

Roosevelt asked Congress for the authority to send war supplies to England in return for goods and services rather than dollars. His request fell upon responsive ears, although isolationists in Congress battled to defeat Lend-Lease, convinced that its passage would lead into a war whose consequences would be ruinous to the United States. Senator Burton K. Wheeler compared Lend-Lease to the Agricultural Adjustment Administration's crop plough-up of 1933, calling it "the New Deal's triple A foreign policy: it will plough under every fourth American boy." But the isolationists did not have the votes. Lend-Lease passed easily, 60 to 31 in the Senate and 317 to 71 in the House. Public opinion polls showed that a broad national consensus favored the legislation. Roosevelt signed the measure, formally titled "An Act to Promote the Defense of the United States," into law on March 11, 1941, and Congress appropriated $7 billion to fund the program. In return for war supplies, the British also made available to the United States additional air and naval bases off the Canadian coast and in the British West Indies. An elated Churchill hailed Lend-Lease as "a new Magna Carta."

Passage of Lend-Lease marked a point of no return for America. The United States had committed itself to the survival of Great Britain with an economic aid program that amounted to a declaration of economic warfare on Germany. Lend-Lease committed more than American economic resources to the British. During the first half of 1941 American public opinion increasingly accepted America's pro-Allied nonbelligerency sta-

---

2. Quoted in Robert Dallek, *Franklin D. Roosevelt and American Foreign Policy, 1932–1945* (New York, Oxford University Press, 1979), p. 256.

tus. They understood that only the British navy stood between Germany and strategic threats to American and Western Hemisphere interests.

Polls showed growing public support for U.S. military intervention. Roosevelt, who followed the polls closely, inched America closer to war. He authorized U.S. shipyards to repair British warships. He transferred U.S. Coast Guard cutters to the Royal Navy for convoy duty. In April 1941, American Marines occupied the Danish colony of Greenland, and in August the Marines also took over Iceland. President Roosevelt extended American nonbelligerency further when he approved limited action by American naval forces. Fleets of German submarines were roaming the North Atlantic shipping lanes and were sinking cargo ships hauling Lend-Lease supplies at the rate of one or two a day. England's lifeline was endangered. On Roosevelt's orders, U.S. destroyers began patrolling for German submarines, with orders to locate the submarines but not to attack them. In August Roosevelt also authorized U.S. destroyers to convoy British ships hauling Lend-Lease supplies as far as Iceland.

Roosevelt was determined to do everything necessary to ensure Germany's defeat even though it risked American entry into the war. At some point, probably by the spring of 1941, the President had concluded that American military intervention would be necessary to achieve victory over the Axis powers. He seized Axis shipping in American ports; he froze German and Italian assets in the United States. When Germany invaded the Soviet Union on June 21, 1941, Roosevelt promptly offered support to the embattled Soviets.

For four days in August Roosevelt met with the British prime minister for the first time at a conference held off the Newfoundland coast aboard USS *Augusta*. Churchill hoped to get a commitment from Roosevelt to join the war against Germany, but Roosevelt refused to be bound in that fashion. Instead, their discussions focused on the means necessary to defeat Germany and contain Japan. The meeting also produced the Atlantic Charter, a joint declaration of war aims, which also reiterated Anglo-American adherence to the Four Freedoms, espoused by Roosevelt during a speech to Congress earlier that year: freedom from want, freedom from fear, freedom of speech, and freedom of religion. The charter also reaffirmed the principles of self-determination, free trade, and freedom of the seas and called for the creation of a new postwar international organization to keep the peace. Roosevelt hoped that the charter would educate Americans to what was at stake in the European war and would make them more willing to intervene if conflicts with Germany escalated.

The Atlantic Charter embodied an Anglo-American vision for organizing the postwar world: a stable, unified international order based on self-determination of nations; a world in which all nations could enjoy freedom and prosperity; a world in which American power and wealth would dominate. Henry Luce, an influential publisher, in a 1941 editorial in *Life* magazine, wrote of the "American century" that was dawning, ex-

Roosevelt and Churchill first met in August 1941 off the Newfoundland coast during the Atlantic Charter meeting.

horting his fellow citizens "to assume the leadership of the world" for the good of people in every land. The Atlantic Charter gave ideological shape to the American century.

UNDECLARED NAVAL WAR

With American destroyers convoying British ships as far as Iceland, clashes between U.S. warships and German submarines became inevitable. On September 4, 1941, a German U-boat, after being chased for hours by a destroyer, USS *Greer*, turned and attacked the destroyer, but the fired torpedo missed. Roosevelt used the *Greer* incident to announce an undeclared naval war in the North Atlantic. He ordered all ships engaged in escort duty to "shoot on sight" any German submarines appearing in waters west of Iceland. He called German submarines "the rattlesnakes of the Atlantic" and denounced their "piratical acts." He also misled Americans by reporting the *Greer* incident as if it had been an unprovoked German attack on a peaceful American ship. Isolationists accused the President of professing peace while plotting war, but polls showed that most Americans supported the "shoot on sight" policy and believed that Hitler must be defeated "at all costs."

Nevertheless, most Americans were clinging to the hope of staying out of the war. They hoped that all the aid, short of war, would prevent American entry. Roosevelt faced a dilemma, given the public's contradictory attitudes. Seventy percent wished to avoid the war, and 70 percent also wanted Hitler defeated at all cost even if that meant entering the war. President Roosevelt believed that if he asked Congress for a declaration of war, he would not get it and would lose popular support. The request would also trigger an angry, divisive debate between isolationists and interventionists. He decided to build a consensus for war incrementally by devious means, believing that it was essential to national security that America defeat Germany. He would wage an undeclared war and look for incidents that would unify the country behind a war in Europe.

Having committed the country to undeclared naval war by the fall of 1941, President Roosevelt then asked Congress to repeal the remaining neutrality legislation in order to permit the arming of American merchant ships and allow them to sail into war zones. On October 17 a U-boat torpedoed a U.S. destroyer, USS *Kearny*, inflicting severe damage and killing eleven crewmen. Two weeks after the attack on the *Kearny* a submarine sank an American destroyer, USS *Reuben James*, killing 115 sailors. These two incidents strengthened public opinion in support of Roosevelt's request. Polls taken in October showed a large majority favoring repeal of the neutrality laws, and Congress repealed the Neutrality Acts on November 13, 1941, although the votes were close. Armed American merchant ships were permitted to sail through war zones to British and Soviet ports. The last remaining restrictions on American actions had been removed. Now American merchant ships as well as destroyers would become targets of German U-boats. It appeared that it was only a matter of time, perhaps a few weeks or months at the most, before repeated sinkings of American ships would lead to a formal declaration of war against the Axis powers.

While Roosevelt was taking these fateful measures in November 1941, his foreign policy of pro-Allied nonbelligerency with a drift toward military intervention continued to draw fire from various isolationist groups and individuals. Senator Wheeler belittled the Nazi threat and denounced Roosevelt as a warmonger. The All-American hero Charles Lindbergh believed Roosevelt "could make a deal with Hitler" if he had to. An odd assortment of ethnic isolationists, religious pacifists, liberal intellectuals, Socialists, Communists, and Fascists opposed Roosevelt's foreign policies. The most prominent isolationist organization called itself the American First Committee and was chaired by Robert E. Wood, CEO of Sears, Roebuck, and Co., the world's largest retailer. America First spokes-

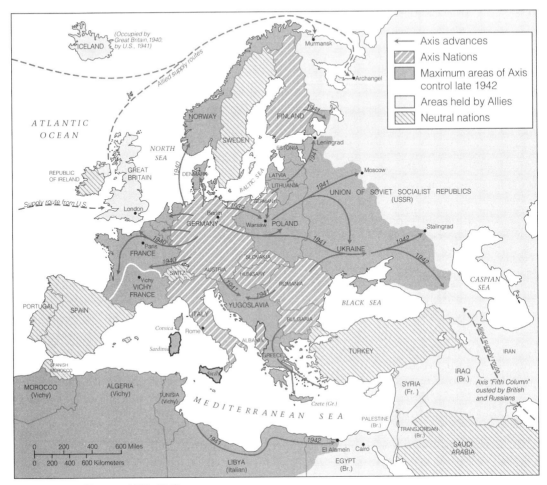

The European Theater, 1939–1942

men kept their views constantly before the public, and their agents formed a powerful lobby in Washington. Committee spokesmen espoused a concept of "Fortress America" and denied that Germany posed any significant threat to American or Western Hemisphere security. They claimed that the United States had sufficient military strength to defend itself regardless of who controlled Europe.

At the same time that isolationists accused Roosevelt of secretly plotting to take the country to war, interventionists believed that the President was moving too slowly and too cautiously in extending aid to the Allies and preparing for possible military intervention. Interventionists were recruited from the ranks of Eastern Anglophiles, moderate New Dealers, and liberal Republicans such as Thomas Dewey and Wendell Willkie. The most influential interventionist organization was the Committee to Defend America by Aiding the Allies, chaired by a prominent journalist from Kansas, William Allen White. White and his organization worked to increase the amount of military aid going to the Allies. They also tried to influence public opinion, to move the American people in the direction of supporting Roosevelt's foreign policy. Above all, interventionists rejected the isolationist premise that an aggressive Germany posed no threat to the security of the United States. White stated, "The future of Western civilization is being decided upon the battlefield of Europe."

Neither the America First Committee nor the Committee to Defend America by Aiding the Allies had much influence on public opinion. It was the events themselves, the rapidly deteriorating military situations in Europe and the Far East, that swayed growing numbers of Americans to support Roosevelt's foreign policy even while clinging to the hope of avoiding war.

As November 1941 ended, the United States was at war unofficially with Germany. But Roosevelt could only wait upon events, hoping that German submarines would provide him with incidents that would allow a declaration of war and full-scale involvement against the Fascist powers. The initiative lay with Hitler and his submarine forces. Ironically, with all eyes upon the European conflict, Japanese military actions on the other side of the world rescued the United States from the uncertain drift of its European policy. American entry into World War II came first in the Pacific following the surprise Japanese attack on Pearl Harbor on December 7, 1941.

Many Americans have found it difficult to understand why the Japanese caught the Americans in Hawaii by complete surprise. Revisionist historians have resorted to conspiracy theories to solve the riddle: President Roosevelt, wanting badly to get into war in Europe but unable to generate popular support for a formal declaration, put economic pressure on the Japanese and forced them to fight. He then lured them to Pearl Harbor by exposing the U.S. fleet and let the raid come without alerting American commanders in Hawaii. The surprise attack angered and united Americans in support of war. Revisionists, in effect, have accused Roosevelt of forcing America into the European war via the "back door" of Asia.

The case for conspiracy at Pearl Harbor is flimsy. It rests entirely on circumstantial evidence, a kind of simplistic plausibility, and on the willingness of Roosevelt's accusers to believe that the President was a Machiavellian leader capable of sacrificing the American Pacific fleet and thousands of lives to achieve his goal. No documentary proof of conspiracy has ever been found. No professional historian of World War II takes this devil theory seriously. It is easily refuted by knowledgeable scholars who can explain Japanese success at Pearl Harbor in nonconspiratorial terms.

IMPASSE OVER CHINA

The fundamental cause of the war in the Pacific between the United States and Japan was an impasse over China. Taking advantage of the war in Europe, Japan since 1937 had been extending its control over that country. But the Japanese, although able to conquer the populous coastal areas of China, had been unable to defeat Jiang Jieshi's Nationalist forces, who had retreated into China's vast interior regions. The United States supported the Chinese Nationalists and condemned Japanese aggression. The German defeat of the Netherlands and France in 1940 left these two nations' colonial possessions in Southeast Asia defenseless. Japan set out to incorporate these territories, rich in oil, rubber, tin, and rice, into their imperial orbit. President Roosevelt tried to use American economic pressure to pry the Japanese out of China and contain its expansion into Southeast Asia. American efforts at economic coercion ultimately failed and the Japanese struck first at Pearl Harbor.

Knowing that the Japanese were heavily dependent upon the United States for shipments of petroleum as well as scrap iron and steel, on July 26, 1939, Roosevelt renounced the major commercial treaty between the two countries as of January 1, 1940. This action would allow the United States to curb or halt Japan's access to American iron, oil, and other strategic goods. The President hoped that Japan would ease its pressure on China instead of risking an American embargo of essential raw materials. The threatened embargo did not deter the Japanese, however. They were determined to conquer China and to forge an empire they called the Greater East Asia Co-prosperity Sphere. Still they did not want a rupture of relations with the United States, which would dry up sources of needed commodities. Roosevelt also applied economic sanctions against them cautiously. His first priority was the European war, where he perceived the threat to American interests to be much greater than Japanese imperialism in Asia. Also he had to be careful lest economic sanctions provoke the Japanese to a war for which the United States was completely unprepared.

Japanese–American relations deteriorated further during the summer and fall of 1940. A more militant government came to power in Japan headed by Prince Fumimaro Konoye. A key official in his new government was war minister General Hideki Tojo. Konoye and Tojo were determined to defeat China and end the drain on Japanese men and matériel. The Japanese also intended to ally with the European Fascist powers and expand into Southeast Asia. They planned to take advantage of German victories in Europe by seizing the lightly protected European Southeast Asian colonies and expropriating their rich resources.

In July 1940 the Japanese moved into northern Indochina, a lightly defended French colony in Southeast Asia. In September Japan concluded a Tripartite Pact with Germany and Italy, creating the

Rome–Berlin–Tokyo Axis. The treaty bound the three nations to help one another if any was attacked by a power not currently involved in fighting in Europe or Asia. The treaty clearly aimed to prevent the United States either from joining the British against the Germans or from directly opposing Japan's efforts to carve out an empire in China and Southeast Asia.

The United States responded to Japan's signing the Tripartite Pact by embargoing all shipments of scrap iron and steel to Japan. Roosevelt also began coordinating American Far Eastern policy with the British and increased U.S. economic and military aid to China. He sent the Chinese 50 fighter planes and arranged for American volunteers to go to China to fly them. These volunteers, all military pilots, formed the nucleus of the famed "Flying Tigers," commanded by Claire Chennault. Roosevelt believed that aiding China was the most effective way of restraining Japanese expansion, keeping them tied down in that vast country. He also sent additional forces to Guam, the Philippines, and other American territories in the Pacific.

THE STRATEGY OF STALL

In February 1941 Japan sent a new ambassador to the United States, Admiral Kichisaburo Nomura. He and Secretary of State Cordell Hull held a series of talks that continued off and on until the Japanese attack at Pearl Harbor. Nomura urged the United States to restore trade with Japan and to stop supporting Jiang Jieshi, the Chinese Nationalist leader. These proposals were unacceptable to the United States, but Roosevelt told Hull to avoid outright rejection of them and to leave open the possibility of American concessions. Roosevelt hoped to encourage moderate elements within the Japanese government to restrain the militant expansionists. He was also following a strategy of stalling the Japanese. He wanted to restrain Japan yet avoid a showdown with them because of the increasing danger of American entry into the European war. Roosevelt and Hull hoped that a combination of limited economic sanctions, the threat of additional sanctions, and aid to the Chinese might eventually force Japan to withdraw from China and refrain from further aggression in Southeast Asia.

These negotiations between Japanese and American officials did not have a realistic possibility of success; the two sides were too far apart and neither was willing to compromise. The Japanese wanted a free hand to continue their war of conquest against China and an end to American economic sanctions. The United States demanded that the Japanese withdraw from China and not attack the Southeast Asian territories belonging to European colonial powers.

Relations between the two countries worsened in July 1941, when the Japanese forced the French to let them take over eight air and two naval bases in southern Indochina. Roosevelt, interpreting the action as the opening move in a campaign of conquest in Southeast Asia, froze all Japanese assets in the United States, a major step down the road to war. The freeze order became the American instrument for ending trade between the United States and Japan. A few days after it went into effect, America embargoed all oil and steel shipments to Japan. All trade between the United States and Japan came to a halt.

The Dutch government-in-exile quickly followed the U.S. oil embargo with one of its own. These oil embargoes pushed the Japanese into a corner. Without petroleum, their industrial economy and war machine would grind to a halt within a few months. The only feasible means to oil would be for Japanese military forces to seize the oil wells located in the Dutch East Indies, an action that would probably mean war with the United States and the British. Either the Japanese had to find a way quickly to restore trade with America, or else Japan would have to get these necessary goods elsewhere and probably provoke a war.

Since all but the most extreme Japanese leaders opposed war with the American colossus at this date, Japanese diplomats sought to negotiate an arrangement with Washington that would restore the lost strategic trade. Nomura met several times with Hull. He also met with the President, who told him that the United States wanted improved relations with Japan. Roosevelt indicated that he was interested in meeting with Prince Konoye if Japan were ready "to suspend its expansionist activities" and the two countries could resolve their "fundamental differences." Even as he made these statements, Roosevelt was skeptical that a meaningful rapprochement was possible. He was mainly continuing to stall the Japanese in order to allow more time for the American military buildup in the Pacific and to avoid a war in Asia while preparing to enter one in Europe.

High-level Japanese meetings held in early September proved that American–Japanese differences were irreconcilable. Convinced that they must move before American economic sanctions hindered their ability to fight, army militants insisted that Konoye settle differences with the Americans by mid-October. If no agreement was made, Japan would prepare for war with the United States. The conditions for a settlement, agreed to by an Imperial Conference on September 6, set Japan firmly on the road to war: The United States was not to interfere with Japanese efforts in China, was not to increase its forces in the Pacific, and was to restore trade with Japan. In return, Japan pledged no further moves into Southeast Asia and guaranteed the neutrality of the Philippines. In late September Nomura conveyed these terms to Roosevelt and Hull.

Roosevelt found them unacceptable, a confirmation of his sense that irreconcilable differences separated the two nations, especially regarding China, and that a meeting with Konoye would be pointless. He also read public opinion polls showing Americans to be firmly opposed to any ap-

peasement of Japanese aggression in China. He and Hull continued negotiations but made no concessions on China or agreements to restore
trade. They continued the strategy of stalling, trying to buy time in the Pacific to allow the United States to build up its air force in the Philippines,
hoping the added striking power might deter Japanese expansion into
Southeast Asia. Roosevelt's top military advisers, General George Marshall
and Admiral Harold Stark, cautioned the President against taking any actions that might provoke the Japanese to war, since the American forces in
the Pacific were not ready and the United States could soon be at war in
Europe.

In early October 1941, when it became evident that Prince Konoye
could not achieve a diplomatic agreement with the United States, he and
his cabinet resigned. General Tojo headed the new government, a military
dictatorship committed to ending what Tojo called the "deadlock of inde-
cision." On November 5, Japanese leaders, meeting in the presence of Emperor Hirohito, reached a crucial decision: They would continue
diplomacy for three more weeks, but if no agreement was reached by November 26, Japan would go to war. The date for the attack was set for December 8, Tokyo time (December 7, Washington time).

Japan's final proposals offered no prospect of avoiding war. The proposals were divided into Plan A and Plan B, with B to be offered only if
Plan A failed. On November 10 Admiral Nomura presented to Roosevelt
Plan A, which made clear Japan's continuing refusal to get out of China
and its refusal to leave the Tripartite Pact. Roosevelt rejected these terms.
Tokyo sent another envoy to join Nomura, Saburo Kurusu, and together
they presented Plan B to Secretary of State Hull on November 20. It was a
more complex proposal but it still left Japan a free hand in China and
called for a full restoration of American trade with Japan. Roosevelt and
Hull both understood that diplomacy had failed. The United States rejected Plan B on November 26 and told Japan to "withdraw all military,
naval, air, and police forces" from China and Indochina. The Japanese
prepared to assault the Dutch East Indies, Malaya, and the American territory of the Philippines. They also planned a surprise attack on Pearl Harbor to destroy the American Pacific fleet, the only military force that
posed a serious threat to the Japanese imperial ambitions in the Far East.

PEARL HARBOR ATTACKED!

Because a brilliant Army cryptanalyst, Colonel Lawrence Friedman, had
cracked the principal Japanese diplomatic code, which the analysts called
code "Purple," President Roosevelt knew that the Tojo government had
set a November 26 deadline for a diplomatic solution and that now war
would soon follow. The decoding machines enabling Americans to read

the coded Japanese messages were named "Magic." But "Magic" intercepts never contained specific information pinpointing where and when any attacks would occur.

On November 27, the day after the Tojo government's deadline for diplomacy, Washington sent a final alert to American military commanders in the Pacific. The message sent to Admiral Husband E. Kimmel at Pearl Harbor read in part as follows:

> This dispatch is to be considered a war warning. . . . an aggressive move by Japan is expected within the next few days.[3]

On November 29 Tokyo learned that the European Axis powers promised to declare war on the United States if new Japanese actions in the Pacific provoked war. The Japanese now knew they would not be fighting America alone. That same day Emperor Hirohito gave his assent for war.

In Washington American leaders waited grimly for the Japanese blow, wherever it might come. "Why not attack first?" Roosevelt's top aide, Harry Hopkins, asked the President. "No," said Roosevelt, "we would have to wait until it came." Secretary of War Stimson, concerned about divisions of public opinion within the country and the continuing isolationist assault on Roosevelt's foreign policy, explained that the United States had to let Japan fire the first shot, "so there should remain no doubt in anyone's mind as to who were the aggressors." Where would the Japanese strike? Roosevelt's guess, based on his analysis of information available from "Magic" intercepts and many other intelligence sources, was that Japan would strike somewhere in Southeast Asia, maybe British Malaya or the Dutch East Indies. Neither Roosevelt nor any of his senior military or civilian advisers anticipated an attack on American military installations in Hawaii.

The evening of December 6 "Magic" began decoding a long message from Tokyo to Nomura. Its final section announced that there was no chance of reaching a diplomatic settlement with the United States "because of American attitudes." Reading the intercept, Roosevelt said, "This means war." Another intercept received early Sunday morning, December 7, indicated that an attack could occur any time. Another alert was sent to the commanders at Pearl Harbor; tragically, that message did not arrive until after the Japanese attack had begun.

The Japanese naval task force assigned to attack Pearl Harbor had set sail from its home port in the Kurile Islands on November 26. To avoid detection while sailing across more than 3,000 miles of ocean, all ships observed radio silence and sailed in lanes unused by commercial vessels. On

---

3.   Quoted in John E. Wiltz, *From Isolation to War, 1931–1941* (New York: Thomas Y. Crowell, 1968), pp. 126–27.

December 2 the task force received final clearance to attack from imperial headquarters. Early morning on December 7 the task force reached the point from which it would launch air strikes. Shortly after 6:00 A.M. local time the planes began taking off from four carriers. They were launched in two waves, 360 planes in all. Pearl Harbor lay 275 miles southwest, 105 minutes flying time.

Conditions for the attack were ideal. Visibility was perfect. The Americans were caught by complete surprise. The attackers encountered no anti-aircraft fire, and no interceptors rose to challenge them. Spread out before them in neat alignment was the American Pacific fleet. At 7:55 A.M. Hawaiian time the first wave of dive bombers screamed to the attack. Their primary targets were the American battleships and the airfields. The assaults lasted about two hours. At 9:45 the planes withdrew and headed back to their carriers.

Although caught off guard, the Americans recovered quickly and fought courageously. Some pilots found undestroyed planes on the ground and took to the air after the swarming enemy. Many acts of valor and sacrifice were performed that day by the outgunned Americans, but the odds were hopeless and American losses were severe. The Japanese sank or crippled 18 warships, destroyed or damaged 204 planes on the ground, extensively damaged 5 airfields, and killed 2,403 Americans—over 1,000 of whom were entombed in USS *Arizona* when it exploded and sank. Japanese losses were light: 29 planes, 45 pilots and air crewmen, 1 regular submarine, and 5 midget subs.

The Japanese exceeded even their most optimistic expectations. Their carrier task force escaped detection and returned to its home waters undamaged and with no casualties. On the same day that they attacked Pearl Harbor, other Japanese forces attacked U.S. bases on Guam and Midway Island. Japanese planes also destroyed the American air forces in the Philippines, catching the planes on the ground. December 7, 1941, was the worst day in American military history.

American military blunders contributed to the smashing Japanese successes at Pearl Harbor and elsewhere in the Pacific. Intelligence analysts seriously underestimated Japanese military capabilities. The costliest error was the failure of the American commanders in Hawaii, Admiral Kimmel and General Short, to respond properly to the war alert from Washington that they had received on November 27. Expecting the Japanese attack to come elsewhere, they had taken precautions only against sabotage.

The Japanese made serious errors when carrying out their attacks at Pearl Harbor. They failed to destroy oil storage and ship repair facilities, which the Americans soon put to good use. Most of the eighteen ships left battered and helpless that day were restored, and they later got into the battles that would destroy Japanese sea power. The attackers also failed to seek out and destroy the two American aircraft carriers that were, as luck would have it, operating at sea that fateful December morning. One car-

The Japanese surprise attack on Pearl Harbor on December 7, 1941, severely damaged the U.S. Pacific Fleet.

rier was at sea on a training exercise, the other had been sent to Midway Island to ferry some aircraft back to Pearl Harbor. The war in the Pacific was principally a naval war, and naval aviation played a far more important role than battleships in determining the eventual American victory.

In a larger military context, although the Japanese achieved a decisive tactical victory, they committed a colossal strategic blunder by attacking Pearl Harbor. Had they attacked European colonial possessions in Southeast Asia as expected, Roosevelt would have had difficulty bringing America promptly into the war. Isolationists were still vocal on the eve of Pearl Harbor, and a sizable number of American senators and Congressmen would have strongly opposed a declaration of war against Japan following an attack on Borneo or Malaya. At the least, Roosevelt would have taken a badly divided nation to war. Roosevelt later told Churchill that if "it had not been for the Japanese attack, he would have had great difficulty in getting the American people into the war."

DAY OF INFAMY

Thus the Japanese solved Roosevelt's dilemma. Eager to destroy the American fleet at Pearl, the only military force in the Pacific capable of blocking their planned Pacific conquests, they directly attacked American soil and shed American blood. The surprise attack, and the death and destruction it caused, enraged and united nearly all Americans in support of an immediate declaration of war against Japan. Admiral Isoruku Yamamoto, the brilliant strategist who conceived the Pearl Harbor attack, upon learning that it had been a great success, felt no joy. Instead he somberly told his colleagues, "I fear all we have done is to awaken a sleeping giant and fill him with a terrible resolve."

The next day an angry President Roosevelt appeared before a tense joint session of Congress to ask for a declaration of war against Japan:

> Yesterday, December 7, 1941—a date which will live in infamy—the United States of America was suddenly and deliberately attacked by naval and air forces of the empire of Japan. . . .
>
> The attack yesterday on the Hawaiian Islands has caused severe damage to American naval and military forces. I regret to tell you that very many American lives have been lost. . . .
>
> As Commander-in-Chief of the Army and Navy, I have directed that all measures be taken for our defense. Always will our whole nation remember the character of the onslaught against us.
>
> No matter how long it may take us to overcome this premeditated invasion, the American people, in their righteous might, will win through to absolute victory. . . .
>
> With confidence in our armed forces, with the unbounding determination of our people, we will gain the inevitable triumph, so help us God.
>
> I ask that Congress declare that since the unprovoked and dastardly attack by Japan on Sunday, December 7, 1941, a state of war has existed between the United States and the Japanese empire.[4]

All across the land 60 million Americans gathered by their radios to listen intently to their president's speech. Within hours Congress complied, with only one dissenting vote. Three days later Germany and Italy declared war on the United States, honoring their commitments under the terms of the Tripartite Pact. America replied in kind on the same day. In four days Americans had gone from peace to war in both Europe and the Pacific. The United States was now a full participant in history's largest war. Isolation had ended, forever.

---

4.   Richard, Hofstadter, ed., *Great Issues in American History: From Reconstruction to the Present Day, 1864–1969* (New York: Vintage Books, 1969), pp. 409–11.

BIBLIOGRAPHY

There is a large and generally excellent body of historical studies of the fateful period 1939–1941, during which the United States traveled down the road from neutrality to war. Waldo Heinrichs, *Threshold of War: Franklin D. Roosevelt and American Entry into World War II* is an excellent recent study. William L. Langer and S. E. Gleason, *The Undeclared War, 1940–1941* is a detailed account of the deteriorating relations between the United States and Germany. See also Basil Rauch, *Roosevelt: From Munich to Pearl Harbor.* The best study of the isolationists who were attacking Roosevelt's foreign policy in 1940 and 1941 is Wayne S. Cole, *America First: The Battle against Intervention, 1940–1941.* Warren F. Kimball, *The Most Unsordid Act: Lend-Lease, 1939–1941* is a good study. David Reynolds, *The Creation of the Anglo-American Alliance, 1937–1941* is an important work. The attack on Pearl Harbor is the subject of many books. By far the best of these is Gordon W. Prange, *At Dawn We Slept*, the finest account of the Japanese surprise attack on U.S. military installations in Hawaii which plunged America into the vortex of war. Roberta Wohlstetter, *Pearl Harbor: Warning and Decision* is a brilliant study of intelligence information and misinformation and the best refutation of the Pearl Harbor conspiracy theories. Walter Lord, *Day of Infamy* is a popular account that vividly recreates the events of the day Pearl Harbor was attacked. There is a body of work that accuses Roosevelt of complicity in the attack. One of these is John Toland, *Infamy.*

CHAPTER
12
World War II

When the United States entered World War II immediately following the Japanese surprise attack on U.S. military installations in Hawaii, the vast conflict became history's first global war. The struggle constituted two wars waged simultaneously. In Europe, North Africa, and the Middle East, the United States, Great Britain, and the Soviet Union battled Germany and Italy, with both sides aided by minor allies. In the vast Pacific Basin and along the East Asian perimeter, America, with help from the British, Dutch, Australians, New Zealanders, Indians, and Chinese, fought the Japanese, who had no allies in Asia. World War II was also history's largest, costliest, and most destructive war. About 50 million people perished between 1939 and 1945, half of them civilians. The war also claimed about $2 trillion of the world's wealth.

From its entry into World War II, American armed forces played a crucial role in winning both the European and Pacific conflicts. In addition to supporting its own far-flung forces fighting around the world, the United States furnished its major allies with substantial amounts of food, equipment, ammunition, and weapons. The war revitalized the American economy. Lingering vestiges of the Great Depression were erased and an economic boom that was to last for 30 years began in 1942. When World War II ended in the summer of 1945 in total victory for the Allied cause, the United States strode the world as a new colossus. America emerged from the ashes of war as the richest, freest, and most powerful nation in the history of the planet.

AMERICA AT WAR

President Roosevelt quickly demonstrated that he could be an inspiring war leader as well as an effective leader in time of domestic economic crisis. FDR continually reminded his fellow citizens of the great task at hand and the evil nature of the enemy that must be destroyed. He exhorted Americans to make sacrifices, to subordinate their personal desires to the great cause. He radiated confidence that the Allies would ultimately achieve victory over their hateful foes, and he projected an inspiring vision of the peaceful and prosperous postwar world to come after the enemies of democracy had been vanquished. He also assumed leadership of the powerful wartime coalition. Roosevelt became the biggest leader of the Big Three—Churchill, Stalin, and himself. He proved adept as a diplomat and he was the chief organizer of the greatest mobilization of economic and military power ever seen on the planet.

Roosevelt, although serving ably as commander-in-chief of the armed forces, made no effort to plot grand strategy or make operational decisions. He allowed his senior military advisers, the Joint Chiefs of Staff (JCS), a free hand to plan all strategy and tactics. Admiral William D. Leahy chaired the Joint Chiefs and often advised the president on military matters. Serving with Leahy on the JCS were Admiral Ernest J. King, General of the Army General George C. Marshall, and General Henry H. Arnold, head of the Army Air Corps. Marshall selected the eventual supreme allied commander of the European war, General Dwight D. Eisenhower. The Pacific war was divided into two commands as a political concession to the fierce interservice rivalry between the Army and Navy. Admiral Chester W. Nimitz commanded the Central Pacific and reported to Admiral King. General Douglas MacArthur headed the forces in the Southwest Pacific and reported to General Marshall.

America had been gradually rearming during the neutrality period of 1939–1941 as the country slowly drifted toward war. The Navy had been modernized and expanded, the nucleus of a modern air force had been formed, and a peacetime draft had been implemented. But when war came on December 7, 1941, neither the armed forces, American industries, or the American people were prepared to wage fully history's largest war.

During the next four years nearly 16 million men, 95 percent of whom were draftees, served in the armed forces. In September 1944, when the U.S. military forces peaked in size, there were over 12 million Americans in uniform. These vast forces scattered around the globe reflected a rough cross-section of the society they served. About 900,000 African Americans were on active duty, the vast majority of them in the Army. All served in segregated units. Nearly 12 percent of the American Jewish population, over 500,000 persons, served in the military during World War II. Nearly one-third of all Jewish dentists and doctors volun-

Three Native American Marine Corps Woman Reservists at Camp Lejuene, North Carolina, October 1943. They are (from left to right) Minnie Spotted Wolf (Blackfoot), Celia Mix (Potawatomi), and Viola Eastman (Chippewa).

teered for military duty. Nearly 300,000 Hispanic Americans, mostly Mexican Americans, served. Native Americans volunteered in large numbers and more than 25,000 of them served in the armed forces, mostly in the Army.

Some 250,000 women served in the armed forces during World War II. These forces included 140,000 in the Women's Army Corps (WAC), 44,000 in the Women Accepted for Volunteer Emergency Service (WAVES), 23,000 in the Marine Corps Women's Reserve, and 13,000 in the Coast Guard. About 4,000 African American women served in the armed forces. In addition to these women serving in all the auxiliary forces, there were 60,000 women in the Army Nurse Corps and another 14,000 women who served as Navy nurses.

At the war's outset American and British leaders agreed on a "beat Hitler first" strategy, for compelling reasons: Germany posed a potential threat to the Western Hemisphere, its military technology was more likely than Japanese technology to achieve a breakthrough weapon that might enable them to win the war, and Germany in late 1941 was putting tremendous pressure on the Soviet Union. Because the Allies had determined that defeating Hitler took priority over beating the Japanese, most American human resources, weaponry, and supplies were committed to the European war. Two-thirds of U.S. Army and Army Air Corps personnel fought in the European war until Germany's defeat in the spring of 1945. Most of the U.S. Navy forces and all of the Marine Corps, however, were committed to the Pacific war.

THE BATTLE OF THE ATLANTIC

The Joint Chiefs understood that control of the shipping lanes of the North Atlantic were a prerequisite for Allied victory in Europe; hence the first major fighting between Americans and Germans occurred in the Battle of the Atlantic. The German surface fleet was not a major factor in the naval war; it was no match for the British fleet and risked destruction whenever it left its ports. The principal German naval weapon in the North Atlantic was their submarines. In the the spring of 1942, when the Battle of the Atlantic raged at its fiercest, the Germans had more than 150 U-boats engaged. At the time, the Germans possessed much the finest submarine fleet in the world. During the first six months of 1942, German submarines, often hunting in teams called wolfpacks, sunk 360 Allied merchant ships. German subs were sinking ships faster than the Allied shipyards could build them.

Gradually, from July 1942 until the end of 1943, the Allies gained the upper hand and eventually destroyed the German submarine threat. Allied convoy tactics enabled destroyers and destroyer escorts to protect cargo ships from the wolfpacks. Also escort carriers accompanying the convoys allowed aircraft specially configured for anti-submarine warfare to locate, attack quickly, and destroy the marauding U-boats. The Allies also perfected sonar, an acoustical technology used to detect submarines. By 1943 U.S. shipyards were constructing merchant ships at a far faster rate than the Germans could sink them.

The Battle of the Atlantic was costly to both sides. The Allies lost nearly 3,000 merchant ships, 187 warships, and about 40,000 sailors. German losses were catastrophic. Germany lost most of its submarine fleet and crews and was forced to call off the submarine campaign in the North Atlantic by the end of 1943. After the submarine menace had been destroyed, huge amounts of Lend-Lease supplies poured into England and the Soviet Union and hundreds of American troop ships carrying tens of thousands of soldiers arrived safely in Europe during 1944–1945.

THE NORTH AFRICAN CAMPAIGNS

Determined to engage the Germans in decisive battle, American war planners proposed an invasion of France scheduled for fall 1942. The embattled Soviets, fighting for their lives against the best German armies, pleaded with their allies to open a "second front" in the west as soon as possible to ease the pressure on their forces. The British rejected the American invasion proposal; they preferred to strike initially at the periphery of Axis power and to delay a frontal assault until after German resistance had weakened. The British proposed an alternative campaign, a joint Anglo-American invasion of North Africa. President Roosevelt accepted the British offer with the understanding that the North African assault would be followed soon by an invasion of France.

On November 8, 1942, Anglo-American forces, under the command of a rising American star, General Dwight Eisenhower, stormed ashore at points along the coast of the French North African colonies of Morocco and Algeria. The invasion, code-named Operation TORCH, succeeded tactically, but political complications soon developed. The invaded territories were controlled by the collaborationist French regime at Vichy, and its forces resisted the Allied invaders. General Eisenhower negotiated an armistice agreement with Admiral Darlan, the Vichy leader in North Africa, in exchange for Allied recognition of Darlan's authority. The arrangement outraged Charles De Gaulle's Free French government, backed by the British, which claimed authority in North Africa.

Hitler, surprised by the Allied thrust into French North Africa, rushed German troops to neighboring Tunisia. Eisenhower responded by sending his forces into Tunisia from the west. British forces from Egypt, under the command of General Bernard Montgomery, invaded Tunisia from the east, catching the German and Italian forces in giant pincers. Tunisia proved a hard campaign. Its terrain was rugged and arid, vast deserts punctured by sheer cliffs. The Allies also came up against one of Hitler's best generals, Field Marshall Erwin Rommel, whose veteran Afrika Korps defeated inexperienced American forces in early encounters.

One of America's ablest generals made his debut as a field commander during the Tunisian campaign—General George S. Patton, Jr., whose flamboyant attire and severe discipline earned him the nickname "Old Blood and Guts." After months of heavy fighting, the Axis forces surrendered. The North African campaign ended May 11, 1943. Almost a million German and Italian soldiers had been either killed or captured. Although the North African diversion delayed opening a second front in France, it proved a significant victory. The Mediterranean was reopened to Allied shipping, the British lifeline through Suez was secured, and the Middle Eastern oil fields were saved. Victory in North Africa also opened up what Churchill called the "soft underbelly" of the Axis—Italy and the Balkans—to Allied attacks.

As the Allies were winning the North African campaign, Soviet forces began driving the Germans back from the gates of Moscow. Soviet armies also surrounded a large German force at Stalingrad, in the south of the Soviet Union. Both armies fought ferociously in the depths of winter. In January 1943 the Germans, having lost 300,000 men, surrendered. The Battle of Stalingrad was a turning point in the European war. Bolstered by Lend-Lease aid from the United States, by 1943 the Soviets had forged the largest army in the world. The Red Army totaled 6 million troops, more than twice the size of the Wehrmacht. In summer offensives across a thousand-mile front, Soviet armies drove the Germans back. In July, near Kursk, occurred the greatest tank battle in history, in which Russian armor destroyed the once dreaded German Panzers.

THE ITALIAN CAMPAIGNS

As fighting raged in North Africa, President Roosevelt met with the British Prime Minister at Casablanca to plot the next campaign. Roosevelt wanted to attack France; the absent Soviets pointedly endorsed his proposal. Churchill proposed instead a move into Sicily and southern Italy to maintain the Mediterranean initiative. Roosevelt reluctantly accepted Churchill's suggestion, and the French invasion was put off until after 1943. General Eisenhower also commanded the Sicilian operation, codenamed Operation HUSKY.

On July 10, 1943, the U.S. Seventh Army, commanded by Patton, and the British Eighth Army, under Montgomery, invaded Sicily. Montgomery's forces were supposed to advance up the southeast coast and capture Messina, while Patton's forces were supposed to advance from

General George S. Patton, Jr.

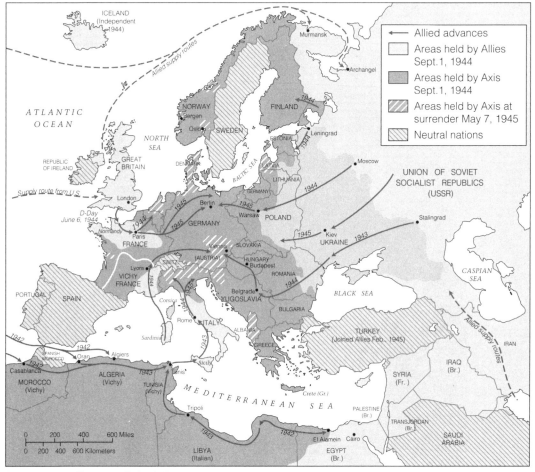

The European Theater, 1942–1945

the southwest and support Montgomery's operation. But Patton decided to beat Montgomery to Messina, and he did, by one day. The Sicilian campaign was costly: 30,000 Allied men were killed or wounded. The Axis lost 164,000 troops, but most Axis soldiers were able to escape across the Strait of Messina to southern Italy.

The Allied conquest of Sicily brought about the downfall of the Italian dictator, Benito Mussolini, and the collapse of the Italian war effort. The Fascist Grand Council brought in a "no confidence" vote against Mussolini, and King Victor Emmanuel III promptly ordered his arrest. General Eisenhower recognized a new Italian government that had been formed by Field Marshall Pietro Badoglio, who surrendered to the Allies on September 3. But Hitler immediately rushed additional German forces to

Italy, disarmed the Italian army, and rescued Mussolini from prison. Hitler installed Mussolini as the head of a puppet regime in northern Italy, and the German forces in Italy took over the war. They threw up a formidable resistance to the Allied invaders. Fighting continued in Italy almost to the end of the European war.

Soon after the Sicilian campaign, Allied forces invaded Italy. On September 9, 1943, the American Fifth Army, commanded by General Mark Clark, landed at Salerno. Naples fell to the Allies on October 1. Although the Allied forces initially met little resistance; the war quickly got tougher as they advanced north up the Italian peninsula, or "up the boot," as the soldiers called it. The Italian campaigns proved to be among the toughest and bloodiest of the entire war. Ground combat operations were extremely difficult, progress was often painfully slow, and Allied casualties were often high. Italy is a mountainous peninsula, traversed by rivers and streams and dominated by rugged terrain.

The Allied offensive stalled at Monte Cassino, site of an ancient Benedictine monastery. There the German defenders turned back wave after wave of Allied assaults, inflicting heavy casualties. Unable to storm Monte Cassino, the Allies tried to outflank it with an amphibious landing at Anzio. But because the American commander of the landing forces was too cautious in attempting to break out of the beachhead, the Germans were able to mount a powerful counterattack that nearly drove the Allies into the sea. Meanwhile, a siege at Monte Cassino had turned into a bloody stalemate. Months later the Allied forces eventually broke the German lines and pushed on toward Rome, which fell to the Allies on June 4, 1944.

Many critics of the Allies' European war strategy have questioned the necessity of the Italian campaign. It had small impact on the overall war effort. While it tied down many German divisions, it also diverted Allied forces from the major invasions of France. The war in Italy was a bloody sideshow that unnecessarily cost the lives of thousands of brave American and Allied soldiers.

AIR WAR OVER EUROPE

World War II was the first major war in which air power played a crucial part, although strategic analysts have differed in regard to just what missions aircraft could perform in war and how well they performed them. The Royal Air Force, which carried the main burden, early in the war, preferred night bombing. The British also had a preference for saturation bombing, to try to destroy everything within a given target area. The Americans, with better aircraft and more accurate bombsights, preferred daylight precision bombing of specific targets such as munitions factories, oil fields, and railroad yards. By the summer of 1943 the Allied air war fea-

tured around-the-clock bombing of Germany and its East European allies—the Brits by night and the Americans by day. The American aircraft
were flying out of bases located in England and, beginning in the summer
of 1943, from bases in North Africa and Italy. By year's end Allied planes
controlled the air over Germany. American and British bombs destroyed
German factories, railroads, and military installations. Air raids also severely damaged many German cities including Hamburg, Berlin, and
Dresden, killing thousands of civilians.

The air war also forced the Germans to devote significant assets to
combat the Allied air offensive and to repair the damage bombing inflicted. Early in the air war the Luftwaffe shot down numerous Allied aircraft, especially American planes flying daylight bombing missions.
Accurate German anti-aircraft batteries also claimed many casualties. By
1944, however, U.S. long-range fighter escorts, especially the P-51 Mus-
tang, which accompanied the bombers over their target sites, eliminated
the Luftwaffe threat.

Air power made many significant contributions to the eventual Allied
victory in Europe. It enabled the British to win the Battle of Britain and to
avert a German invasion of their home islands. It also ensured the success
of the famed landings at Normandy in June 1944. Aircraft also played a decisive role in the Battle of the Atlantic; planes sank more German submarines than either the destroyers or destroyer escorts could sink.

WARTIME DIPLOMACY

During the war the Axis powers failed to coordinate their military and
diplomatic strategies. The Allies, despite much tension and disagreement,
maintained a wartime harmony of interests. The Americans and British
forged a partnership even before the United States entered the war. Then
in December 1941 the two nations created a Combined Chiefs of Staff to coordinate grand strategy in both Europe and Asia. Although they agreed on
war aims, American and British leaders disagreed on the timing and loca-
tion of a second front in Europe. Churchill also refused to apply the principle of self-determination, embodied in the Atlantic Charter, to the British
Empire. The Soviet Union, the third member of the Allied coalition, endorsed the Atlantic Charter but with reservations about its applicability to
Eastern Europe. Generally, the Soviets were willing to mute their strategic,
political, and ideological differences with Western powers as long as military necessity bound them together. But Stalin protested bitterly the con-
tinual delays by the Western nations in opening a second front in France.
The Grand Alliance remained a shotgun wedding; only the necessity of defeating Germany kept the unnatural marriage together. In these wartime
tensions and conflicts of the Allies lay the origins of the Cold War.

Wartime coalition required periodic meetings among the Allied leaders. Early in 1943 Roosevelt and Churchill met at Casablanca to plot strategy following the successful North African landings. Here they adopted the doctrine of "unconditional surrender," meaning they would press the war until the Axis leaders gave up without any assurances that they would remain in power. The Big Three (Roosevelt, Churchill, and Stalin) met for the first time at Teheran in November 1943. Before the Teheran conference, Roosevelt, Churchill, and Jiang Jieshi had met in Cairo and discussed the Asian war, in which the Soviet Union was not engaged at the time; they agreed that Manchuria and Formosa would be returned to China after the war. The Teheran conference focused primarily on military strategy. Stalin got his long-sought commitment from the Western powers that a second front would be opened in France within six months. The Soviet dictator also agreed to time an offensive to complement the Normandy invasion. The three leaders also discussed postwar political questions involving Germany and eastern European countries. President Roosevelt, in his meetings with Stalin, used his talents at personal diplomacy to try to win the trust and cooperation of the Soviet dictator. Teheran was the last of the wartime summit meetings devoted mainly to wartime strategies.

D-DAY!

In the late spring of 1944 the Allies, under the supreme command of General Eisenhower, prepared to launch their long-delayed second front. The Allies had gone to great lengths and employed elaborate deceptions to disguise their points of attack along the French coastline. They convinced the Germans that they would land near Calais, north of Normandy, their real target. The Germans were inclined to believe that the Allies would make their landing at Calais because the English Channel was narrower and the waters calmer at that site. They positioned most of their forces to stop the Allied assault that they believed would come at Calais.

A large part of the Allies' ability to deceive the Germans came from their ability to read some of the German radio codes. The Germans believed that they had the most secure military communications in the world. Their radio messages were encoded by a complex enciphering machine which the British called Enigma; the Germans believed that only someone with an Enigma machine could decipher the codes, and they carefully controlled access to these machines. But British cryptanalysts were able to build an Enigma machine of their own, and with practice they could decipher most German radio messages within hours. Without these deciphered messages, which the British called Ultra, the Allies could not have carried off the Normandy deception.

D-Day, June 6, 1944. American troops wade ashore at Omaha Beach in the face of fierce resistance from German gunners.

At dawn on the morning of June 6, 1944, "D-Day," German sentries scanning the approaches to the Normandy coast were shocked to discover the horizon filled with an armada of 3,000 ships, which launched an intense bombardment preceding the invasion. Troops then pushed ashore at beaches that on Allied maps bore the code names Utah, Omaha, Gold, Juno, and Sword. Utah and Omaha beaches were the sectors assigned to the American forces. The U.S. invaders met stiff resistance at Omaha beach the first day and sustained heavy casualties.

The Normandy landings constituted the largest amphibious operation in history: an armada of landing craft spilling more than 60,000 men and 7,000 vehicles onto the French beaches. German defenses kept the invaders pinned to the coast until July 3, when the U.S. First Army broke through toward St. Lo. By the end of July German defenses in Normandy were collapsing. The Allies began a rapid advance and streaked across western France. Triumphant Allied forces liberated Paris on August 25, 1944.

During the fall of 1944 Eisenhower sent Montgomery's Eighth Army group sweeping north toward the Ruhr valley, Germany's principal indus-

The Supreme Allied commander General Dwight D. Eisenhower, flanked by General Omar Bradley (right) and British General Bernard Montgomery.

trial region. He sent General Omar Bradley's army group, which included Patton's Third Army, sweeping south toward the Saar region. As the winter of 1944 arrived, with the Allied forces everywhere advancing rapidly, Allied commanders did not believe the Germans were still capable of mounting a major counteroffensive. But Hitler ordered his Panzers to mount an offensive in the Ardennes Forest area. His move caught the Allies by surprise. German forces penetrated 60 miles in a few days, opening a bulge in the Allied lines. On December 22 the Germans surrounded Bastogne, a crucial junction that blocked the German's westward progress. On December 26, Allied forces relieved Bastogne and gradually extinguished the German salient.

The Battle of the Bulge involved over 600,000 U.S. troops; it was the largest land engagement in the history of American warfare. Nearly 20,000 Americans died in the Battle of the Bulge. This German counteroffensive delayed the Allied advance for a few weeks. It was also the last major German offensive military operation of the war. They could not replace their losses of men and matériel; the fighting ability of Wehrmacht forces in Western Europe deteriorated rapidly in the months following the Battle of the Bulge.

YALTA

As the European war turned rapidly in favor of the Allies during 1944 and 1945, they held a series of summit conferences to plan the shape of the postwar world. In July 1944 the Allies met at Bretton Woods, New Hampshire, to create the financial and economic foundations of the new postwar order. Guided by the chairman of the conference, American Secretary of the Treasury Henry Morgenthau, the delegates recommended the creation of an International Monetary Fund and a World Bank. Two months later representatives from the United States, the Soviet Union, Great Britain, and China met at Dumbarton Oaks, an estate near Washington, D.C., to plan for a new international organization to keep the peace in the postwar world. It would be called the United Nations. The American delegates took the lead at the conference, proposing a charter that bore a strong resemblance to that of the defunct League of Nations.

As the end of 1944 approached, the Allies were winning both the European and Asian wars, although much bloody fighting remained. The approaching victory generated a host of strategic and political questions that required the personal attention of the Big Three. They had to chart the final drives of the European war, discuss the Pacific war, talk about the postwar political status of Eastern European countries, plan for occupying Germany, and arrange for the creation of a proposed United Nations. The three leaders met at Yalta, a Crimean resort on the Black Sea coast, February 4 through 11, 1945.

The first important matter discussed at Yalta was the occupation policy for postwar Germany. Roosevelt and Churchill rejected a Soviet request to to strip Germany of $20 billion worth of reparations. To prevent this dispute from dividing the conference, all parties accepted the principle of reparations and referred the matter to an appointed commission to determine specific amounts. The Big Three agreed to divide Germany into four occupation zones, with France assigned the fourth zone. They also agreed to a joint occupation of Berlin, which lay deep within the Soviet zone in eastern Germany, an arrangement both sides deeply regretted after the rise of the Cold War.

Roosevelt initiated discussions at Yalta on the pending formation of the United Nations. His chief concern was vigorous American participation in an international organization that would be armed with power to maintain peace through economic sanctions or military force. He wanted Stalin, without whose cooperation it could not succeed, to commit himself to full support for the new agency to be created at San Francisco in April 1945. To ensure Soviet cooperation, he accepted Stalin's demand for three votes in the General Assembly; he also accepted veto power for all permanent members of the Security Council designed to protect great power prerogatives within the UN.

The postwar political status of Poland caused the most controversy at the conference, particularly the composition of its new government. There were at the time two governments claiming to represent all Poles, one headquartered in London and championed by the British, and one in Lublin, backed by the Soviets. Stalin, making it clear that Poland was a vital Soviet interest, proposed that the Communist-controlled government at Lublin become the government of a new Poland. Roosevelt proposed a government comprising representatives of Poland's five major political parties. The Soviets rejected that proposal, but Stalin agreed to add "democratic elements" to the Lublin regime. To maintain conference harmony, the Allies worked out an agreement that papered over significant differences over Poland with vague, elastic language. Stalin agreed to "free and unfettered elections" at an unspecified time in the future. Roosevelt settled for a reorganized Lublin regime that included "other" political leaders, language susceptible to many differing interpretations. The compromise favored Soviet interests.

Roosevelt understood that the presence of Soviet troops in Poland, and elsewhere in Eastern Europe, gave them controlling influence over the political future of these countries. He did not expect to achieve genuine democracy for Poland, but he hoped to convince American public opinion that he had succeeded in doing so. The best he privately hoped for was that the United Nations might be able to restrain Soviet actions in Poland in the future. Roosevelt also got Churchill and Stalin to sign a Declaration of Liberated Europe, which committed the Big Three to help the liberated people of Eastern Europe form democratic governments through free elections. Here again the declaration was worded in such a fashion that it was susceptible to different interpretations.

Roosevelt also wanted to commit the Soviets to entering the Asian war against Japan as soon as possible. On February 10 Stalin and Roosevelt signed a secret treaty in which the Soviet Union agreed to enter the war within three months following Germany's surrender. In return the Soviets were given several concessions: a Soviet-controlled satellite in Outer Mongolia; guaranteed return to the Soviets of the southern portion of Sakhalin Island; internationalization of the port of Darien; a lease to the Russians for the use of Port Arthur as a naval base; a joint Chinese-Soviet consortium to operate the Manchurian railways; and the ceding of the Kurile Islands by the Japanese to the Soviets.

President Roosevelt and his advisers considered the price of Soviet entry into the Asian war reasonable at the time. The expectation that an atomic bomb would be ready in August did not alter Roosevelt's goal of getting the Russians into the war. His military advisers told him that Soviet participation at the earliest possible moment would ensure the defeat of Japanese forces in Manchuria and that Soviet air raids on Japan flown from Siberia would ensure the disruption of Japanese shipping from the Asian mainland. Most important, Soviet intervention would shorten the war and save thousands of American lives. However, Roosevelt did not consult with Jiang Jieshi before granting the Soviets the concessions affecting China.

The atmosphere at Yalta was cordial, as befitted members of a wartime coalition who still needed one another to achieve victory over their enemies. Both sides made compromises and concessions. Roosevelt left the conference believing that he had attained Soviet cooperation in winning the war and building a postwar structure of peace. On March 1 he told Congress that Yalta had been "a great success" and he asked the American people to support it. A Gallup poll showed 87 percent of the people approved the Yalta arrangements.

But the Soviets achieved more important diplomatic victories at Yalta than the United States. Stalin used the military situation favoring the Soviet Union at the time to achieve his objectives. The role of the Allied mili-

The Big Three—Prime Minister Winston Churchill of Great Britain, President Franklin Roosevelt of the United States, and Premier Joseph Stalin of the Soviet Union—held several wartime conferences. At Yalta, a Black Sea resort in the Crimea, they met for the last time in February 1945.

tary in the ultimate defeat of the Germans was minor compared to the So- viet effort. Hundreds of Soviet divisions fighting the best Wehrmacht armies in the Soviet Union and Eastern Europe eventually broke the spine of German power. As Red forces overran eastern and southern Europe, Stalin used military occupation to gain political control of countries within these strategic regions. Stalin also used the American desire for So- viet entry into the war against Japan to exact major diplomatic conces- sions in the Far East. Roosevelt did not "sell out" China to the Soviets at Yalta as Republican critics later charged, but the Yalta agreements amounted to a significant diplomatic victory for the Soviet Union.

VICTORY IN EUROPE

Shortly after Yalta, advancing American forces reached the Rhine River. With the Nazi regime approaching extinction, the Soviets installed the Lublin Communists in power in Poland, violating the Yalta agreement. Roosevelt warned Stalin that his actions jeopardized "future world coop- eration." The President also warned Churchill on April 6 that they would have to be firm in their dealings with the Soviets about Poland's political future. But on April 12 Roosevelt died of a cerebral hemorrhage.

Harry Truman, an unknown professional politician with an undistin- guished record, succeeded Roosevelt. Truman initially doubted if he could handle the responsibilities of the world's most demanding job. Af- ter taking the oath of office, a shaken Truman told reporters that he felt as if "the moon, the stars, and all the planets had suddenly fallen on me." Fate had thrust Truman into the presidency, an office he had never sought and for which he was ill-prepared. He had no background in foreign policy. During Truman's brief vice-presidency, Roosevelt had never involved him in policy decisions, nor had he even kept him informed of the issues. Yet the new president was assuming office at a time when momentous strate- gic and political decisions had to be made.

As Truman struggled to take hold of the reins of office, the European war ground toward its inevitable conclusion. Churchill, reacting to Soviet political moves in Poland, advised Roosevelt just before his death that An- glo-American forces should "beat the Russians to Berlin" to stretch West- ern postwar political leverage as far east as possible. Roosevelt died before he could make a decision, and he was replaced by the uninformed and inexperienced Truman. The Supreme Allied Commander in Europe, General Eisenhower, rejected Churchill's proposal and permitted the So- viets to capture Berlin. Eisenhower did not consider the German capital an important strategic objective. He ordered American advance forces to halt at the Elbe river, 50 miles from the German capital. In the final days of the European war Eisenhower directed the American forces to the region of the Danube River to isolate and destroy remaining pockets of German resistance. The Joint Chiefs and President Truman both accepted Eisenhower's decision to let the Soviets take Berlin.

Some historians believe that Anglo-American forces could have beaten the Soviets to Berlin, and had they done so, they would have gained advantage over the Soviets in postwar conflicts over Germany that were among the major causes of the Cold War. They argue that Berlin would have been a Western city, and there would have been no Berlin blockade and no Berlin wall. Further, they believe that Germany would never have been divided and would have always remained within the Western orbit. In their view, General Eisenhower, guided by short-term military considerations, made a grave political error by rejecting Churchill's advice, and the Soviets, guided by long-term political goals serving their interests, took advantage of American shortsightedness. Such views are historically untenable. Had American forces taken Berlin and other territory in eastern Germany, they would have been withdrawn beyond the Elbe after the war to be in accord with the Yalta agreement. The Soviets would have then occupied their zone in East Germany and their sector of Berlin just as they did. After these arrangements were in place, events would have unfolded exactly as they did.

Eisenhower made his decision to stop at the Elbe because all his efforts were aimed at defeating Germany and ending the war as fast as possible. He feared that a Berlin campaign would enable remaining German forces in southern Germany to regroup into guerrilla units that could prolong the war and increase American casualties. Further, he knew that a U.S. drive on Berlin could result in military conflicts with the Soviets. American public opinion would have exploded at the prospect of substituting Soviets for Germans as enemies. His most important consideration was that America still had another war to win in the Pacific. Washington wanted to end the European war as quickly as possible so troops fighting in Europe could be sent to the Far East. It was also crucially important that the Soviets honor their commitment to enter the Asian war.

It is unlikely that American forces could have beaten the Soviets to Berlin had they tried. On April 11 General William Simpson had 50,000 troops within 50 miles of the city. A weak German army and some water barriers stood between them and the capital. On that same date the Soviets were 15 miles closer, had 1,250,000 men, and faced two weak German armies. The terrain was flat, dry land. It cost the Soviets over 100,000 casualties to take Berlin, more than America had suffered in fighting on German soil during the final months of war. After war's end the Soviets had to give up half the city they had captured at a fearsome price. The Western forces got their Berlin sectors without losing a single man. As the Soviets took Berlin, Eisenhower's forces crushed remaining pockets of German resistance. Fighting ended May 5, and Germany surrendered on May 7.

Hitler did not live to see the German surrender. He committed suicide the evening of April 30. The Third Reich, which he had predicted would last a thousand years, perished after having survived for only 12. But Hitler had fulfilled his demonic promise that either he would make Germany the greatest nation in the history of the world or he would destroy it.

As Allied armies liberated Poland and conquered Germany, they discovered the death camps that revealed the radical evil in the heart of the Nazi regime. On April 4, 1945, advance units of Patton's army liberated the Ohrdruf Nord concentration camp. On April 11 elements of the U.S. Third Army liberated the camp at Buchenwald, where the wife of the camp commandant had collected the skins of tattooed prisoners to make lamp shades. Battle-hardened soldiers stared in horrified disbelief at open mass graves filled with skeletons, and at still-living, emaciated victims of Nazi savagery. Some soldiers collapsed in uncontrollable anguish; other vomited at the sickening sights. Early in the war Hitler had approved a plan for "a final solution to the Jewish question": their systematic destruction. The Nazis built five extermination centers, the most infamous one located near the Polish village of Auschwitz. For three years trains of cattle cars from all German-occupied areas of Europe hauled doomed human cargoes to their final destination.

Jews were not the only Holocaust victims. Slavs, gypsies, criminals, homosexuals, mentally retarded people, resistance fighters, and even some Germans opposing Hitler's regime—all were liquidated, all victims of Germany's ferocious racism, viciousness, and heartless technical efficiency. But Jews remained the primary targets, and before the victorious Allies halted the horrid process, an estimated 5 to 6 million of the 7 million European Jews were murdered or died from starvation, disease, abuse, and overwork. The non-Jewish victims totaled about 6 million. Thus as many as 12 million human beings were killed by a self-styled master race who had decreed whole races of people unfit to live. In a brutal war that featured many barbaric acts by both sides, the enormity of Nazi genocide overwhelmed all others. The Holocaust was the ultimate atrocity.

WAR IN THE PACIFIC

At the outset of the Pacific war the Americans faced a daunting task against a formidable foe. Victory at Pearl Harbor had marked the beginning of a period of rapid Japanese expansion in the Far East. One after another, the bastions of Western imperialism fell to their advancing forces: Guam, Hong Kong, Singapore, Java, and the Philippine archipelago. Japanese propagandists portrayed themselves as liberators, liberating Asians from the clutches of European colonialism. They welcomed the people of their newly acquired territories into a new imperial order that they called The Greater East Asia Co-Prosperity Sphere. In reality the Japanese proved themselves to be exploitative and brutal conquerors, who subjected the people under their control to harsh military rule and immediately proceeded to expropriate their resources.

For six months after Pearl Harbor the Japanese ruled the Pacific. The Japanese navy was the most powerful fleet in the world. American forces trying to stem the Japanese tide were hampered by the damage done at Pearl Harbor, and by the priorities of war planners in Washington who gave the European war preference in men and weapons. The logistics were formidable challenges; the United States had to transport men, weapons, and supplies vast distances to faraway battle sites. On land U.S. soldiers had to face a ruthless and determined enemy who fought tenaciously amidst the rugged terrain and steamy jungles of South Pacific islands. Japanese soldiers believed that to surrender to their enemies was to disgrace themselves and their homeland. Often they adopted suicide tactics, refused to surrender even when beaten, and always suffered far higher casualties than they inflicted on their American enemies.

Naval air power proved to be the decisive factor in the Pacific war. The U.S. Pacific fleet was organized around aircraft carrier task forces. These carriers were accompanied by protective screens of cruisers and destroyers and were trailed by fleets of supporting vessels. Submarines were used for scouting missions, but their primary assignment was to destroy the enemy merchant fleet and attack its warships.

The Japanese grand strategy, implemented in the aftermath of the Pearl Harbor attack, involved seizing and fortifying an empire of Pacific islands and archipelagos thousands of miles from the Japanese home islands. The Japanese leaders hoped that the Americans, when confronted with the apparently impregnable barrier of fortified islands, would consider the costs of retaking them by military force too high; therefore, rather than fight a costly war of attrition, the United States would concede the Japanese a sphere of influence encompassing the vast Pacific Basin. The Japanese strategy was based upon a fundamental misreading of American intentions in the aftermath of the surprise attack at Pearl Harbor. Americans were determined to fight a war until Japanese power in the Pacific and along the eastern perimeter of Asia was destroyed.

During the first six months of the Pacific war, during which the Japanese seized the islands that comprised their new empire, the longest and hardest of their campaigns was the conquest of the U.S. territory of the Philippine Islands. The main invading Japanese forces landed on the large northern island of Luzon on December 22, 1941. Amidst intense fighting, U.S. and Philippine forces under the command of General Douglas MacArthur retreated south to the jungle-covered ridges of the Bataan Peninsula. MacArthur's troops were poorly supplied; they were short of food, medicine, and ammunition. More of his troops died from malnutrition and disease than from Japanese bullets. MacArthur set up his command post on the fortified island of Corregidor, guarding the entrance to

orld War II: Japanese advances, 1941-1942

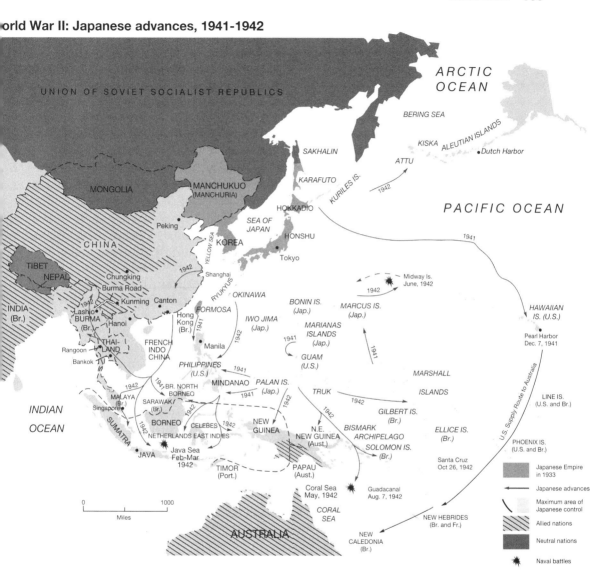

ARCTIC
OCEAN

BERING SEA

UNION OF SOVIET SOCIALIST REPUBLICS

KISKA
ALEUTIAN ISLANDS

SAKHALIN

ATTU

•Dutch Harbor

PACIFIC OCEAN

MONGOLIA

MANCHUKUO
(MANCHURIA)

KARAFUTO

1942

KURILES IS.

HOKKAIDO

SEA OF
JAPAN

Peking

HONSHU

1941

CHINA

KOREA

Tokyo

TIBET
NEPAL

Chungking

Shanghai

1942

YELLOW SEA

Midway Is.
June, 1942

Burma Road

Kunming Canton

1942

RYUKYUS

OKINAWA

BONIN IS.
(Jap.)

MARCUS IS.
(Jap.)

HAWAIIAN
IS. (U.S.)

INDIA
(Br.)

Lashio
BURMA
(Br.)

Hanoi

FORMOSA

Hong
Kong
(Br.)

1941

IWO JIMA
(Jap.)

MARIANAS
ISLANDS
(Jap.)

1941

Pearl Harbor
Dec. 7, 1941

Rangoon

THAI-
LAND

FRENCH
INDO
CHINA

1942

Manila

1941

GUAM
(U.S.)

Bankok

PHILIPPINES
(U.S.)

1941

MARSHALL

MALAYA
(Br.)

MINDANAO

PALAN IS.
(Jap.)

1941

TRUK

ISLANDS

LINE IS.
(U.S. and Br.)

INDIAN
OCEAN

Singapore

BR. NORTH
BORNEO

SARAWAK
(Br.)

1942

1942

1942

1942

GILBERT IS.
(Br.)

U.S. Supply Route to Australia

SUMATRA

BORNEO

CELEBES

1942

NEW
GUINEA

N.E.
NEW GUINEA
(Aust.)

BISMARK
ARCHIPELAGO

SOLOMON IS.
(Br.)

ELLICE IS.
(Br.)

PHOENIX IS.
(U.S. and Br.)

NETHERLANDS EAST INDIES

JAVA

Java Sea
Feb-Mar
1942

TIMOR
(Port.)

PAPAU
(Aust.)

Santa Cruz
Oct 26, 1942

Coral Sea
May, 1942

Guadacanal
Aug. 7, 1942

Japanese Empire
in 1933

Japanese advances

Maximum area of
Japanese control

AUSTRALIA

CORAL
SEA

NEW HEBRIDES
(Br. and Fr.)

NEW
CALEDONIA
(Br.)

Allied nations

Neutral nations

Naval battles

0   1000
Miles

Manila Bay. In February, as the Japanese put intense pressure on the embattled defenders, General Marshall ordered MacArthur to leave Corregidor and assume command of Allied forces in Australia. MacArthur fled
through the Japanese lines aboard a PT boat and made his way to Australia.

Major General Edward P. King, the field commander of the Bataan
forces, fearful that his ill and starving forces would be annihilated by the
advancing Japanese, surrendered on April 9, 1942. Corregidor fell on May
6. The Japanese had conquered America's most important territory in the
South Pacific. The victorious Japanese forced the captured American and

Filipino soldiers to go on a forced march of over 60 miles to prison camps, through jungle terrain in blazing hot and humid weather without food or water. This infamous event has become known in American and Filipino annals as the Bataan Death March. Nearly 10,000 soldiers died en route. After the war the Japanese commanders who ordered the death march were tried as war criminals and hanged.

MIRACLE AT MIDWAY

About the time the Battle of the Philippines was coming to a miserable end, a powerful Japanese fleet embarked for Port Moresby, located on the island of Papua New Guinea. If the Japanese succeeded in occupying Port Moresby, Japanese bombers flying out of airfields in its vicinity could reach targets in Australia. An American fleet intercepted the Japanese fleet as it steamed toward New Guinea. From May 5 to May 8, in the Battle of the Coral Sea northeast of Australia, American and Japanese aircraft carrier task forces fought a series of engagements. Each side suffered the loss of an aircraft carrier. The Battle of the Coral Sea was history's first sea battle in which surface ships never made visual contact nor fired a shot at each other. The battle was fought entirely by carrier-based aircraft. The battle was a tactical draw, but it was a major strategic victory for the U.S. forces because they prevented Japanese control of the Coral Sea region and ended any possibility of Japanese attacks on northern Australia. The Japanese expansionist thrust southward had been halted.

The most important naval battle of the Pacific war, the Battle of Midway, occurred a month after Coral Sea. The Japanese objective was to capture Midway Island, located a thousand miles west of Hawaii, and to take islands in the Aleutian chain southwest of Alaska. These islands would then serve the Japanese navy as anchor points for an expanded defense perimeter for their island empire in the Pacific Basin. Japanese control of Midway would also allow them to launch further attacks on Hawaii. The Japanese also intended to force American forces to defend Midway in order to finish what the attack at Pearl Harbor had begun, the destruction of American sea power in the Pacific.

For the Midway campaign the Japanese assigned four aircraft carriers; the Americans had three, one of which had sustained severe damage during the Battle of the Coral Sea. Japanese naval aircraft, particularly their "Zeroes," were superior to American planes. The Japanese had hundreds of the finest navy pilots in the world while American naval aviators were mostly young, inexperienced pilots, fresh out of flight training in the states. It appeared that only a miracle could give the United States victory over vastly superior Japanese forces.

American code breakers scored an intelligence coup when they decoded a Japanese message which enabled them to learn the exact date, time, and place of the Japanese attack as well as the composition of their forces. Using this valuable information, Admiral Chester Nimitz, Commander of the Pacific Fleet, prepared a battle plan to surprise the Japanese attackers by attacking them early.

The crucial encounters during the Battle of Midway occurred on June 4, 1942, the most important single day's fighting of the entire Pacific war. Admiral Richard Spruance, commander of Task Force 16, boldly executed the American battle plan. His planes caught the Japanese carriers before they could launch their aircraft. American dive bombers sank all four Japanese aircraft carriers, destroying the heart of their mighty task force. The Japanese lost 250 planes and many experienced pilots. American losses included a carrier, a destroyer, and dozens of planes and pilots, but the United States scored a magnificent and critical victory at Midway. Victory at Midway halted the westward thrust of the Japanese forces; it also turned the Pacific war around. In the months following the Battle of Midway, American forces went on the offensive in the South Pacific.

SOUTH PACIFIC

Following the victories in the Coral Sea and at Midway, American Marines and Army infantry invaded Japanese strongholds in the South Pacific. Guadalcanal, an island in the Solomon chain, was one of the most important campaigns of the Pacific war. After Marines had invaded the island on August 7, there ensued a series of naval and air battles between Japanese and American forces as both sides attempted many times to land reinforcements. The battle for Guadalcanal raged for months. In February 1943, after six months of air and sea battles and grueling combat in steamy jungles and rugged mountainous terrain, the Japanese abandoned the strategic island to American forces. After their loss of Guadalcanal, the Japanese forces in the South Pacific went on the defensive. American forces in the Pacific never lost a major battle for the rest of the war.

By mid-1943 the American offensives in the Pacific war were gathering momentum. U.S. war planners had developed a strategy that would bring victory in the Pacific. It comprised two parallel offensives. Forces commanded by General Douglas MacArthur would advance from the South Pacific through New Guinea to the Philippines, and then to Japan. Other forces, commanded by Admiral Nimitz, would advance through the Central Pacific via a line of islands that included the Gilberts, the Marshalls, and the Marianas Islands to Formosa (Taiwan), along the China coast, and then to Japan. In the fall of 1943 forces under Nimitz's command captured Tarawa in the Gilbert chain after a bloody campaign. U.S. forces then proceeded to the Marshalls, a cluster of small island atolls. These islands fell to the Americans in February 1944.

As these two forces battled toward Japan during the ensuing two years, Army Air Corps planes bombed and strafed Japanese shipping and their island garrisons. Battles at sea continued as carrier task forces encountered Japanese fleets. Under the sea American submarines attacked both Japanese naval and merchant shipping. As the American campaigns progressed, strategists discovered that they could bypass heavily fortified Japanese-held islands because American air and sea power could prevent the enemy from reinforcing them. Isolated and impotent, these bases posed no threat to American forces. This bypass technique, called "leap-frogging," saved thousands of American lives and accelerated the war effort across the Pacific toward Japan.

During 1944 the Pacific war turned decisively against Japan. Admiral Nimitz's forces advanced into the Marianas, an island chain located within 1,500 miles of Tokyo. The Japanese defenders were determined to destroy the American fleet and beat back the invaders. During the Battle of the Philippine Sea, June 19, 1944, waves of Japanese planes attacked the American task force off the coast of Saipan. U.S. Navy pilots massacred the Japanese aviators. At day's end, fewer than 100 of the 373 Japanese planes returned to their carriers; America lost 29 planes. One of the American navy pilots labeled the day's action "the Great Marianas Turkey Shoot." The air arm of the Japanese navy, once the finest in the world, was annihilated. The American victory in the Philippine Sea isolated the Marianas. Saipan fell after a bloody struggle on July 9. The battle for Saipan cost over 30,000 Japanese lives, and the Americans sustained 14,000 casualties. U.S. forces liberated Guam on August 10 and regained control of its important port facilities. In both these campaigns Japanese defenders resorted to wild "banzai" charges, trying to frighten and overwhelm American invaders. U.S. Marines and Army infantrymen cut them down with deadly machine gun and automatic rifle fire.

Conquest of the Marianas provided forward bases for American submarines, which cut off Japanese shipments of men and matériel going to and from the home islands and the South Pacific. The Air Force got bases from which its new bomber, the B-29 "Superfortress," could strike Japan directly. On November 24, 1944, 144 Superfortresses left Saipan for a raid on Tokyo. The size and frequency of air raids steadily increased through the remaining months of war, devastating most of Japan's cities. A B-29, flying out of Tinian, another Marianas island, would one day carry an atomic bomb to Hiroshima.

Following the occupation of the Marianas, President Roosevelt approved a campaign to liberate the Philippines, which had been seized by the Japanese in 1942. A gigantic combined force of air, sea, and land units assembled, while the Japanese gathered their still formidable forces for an all-out defense of the vital archipelago linking Japan to Malaya and the East Indies.

Leyte, one of the central islands, would be the point of attack by the most powerful strike force in military history. The Battle of Leyte Gulf, the largest naval battle in history, a series of engagements occurring over several days among various units of both navies, preceded the invasion. During one of these battles the increasingly desperate Japanese first used a suicide attack unit known as the Kamikaze. Kamikazes were trained to crash-dive their planes on enemy aircraft carrier decks. This unorthodox military tactic inflicted heavy losses on U.S. naval forces before the war's end. But Kamikazes could not prevent a crushing Japanese defeat in the battle for Leyte Gulf. In the last great sea battle of the war the Japanese navy was decimated. The Japanese lost their last four aircraft carriers, three battleships, six cruisers, and twelve destroyers.

General MacArthur, when forced to flee the Philippines in early 1942, had vowed to return, and he insisted on redeeming his promise. On October 20, 1944, he waded ashore on a Leyte beach and made his dramatic pronouncement: "People of the Philippines: I have returned!" Between October 25 and 27 the American fleets completed their destruction of the world's once mightiest navy. American sea power now controlled the Pacific. Leyte was liberated on Christmas Day of 1944.

The invasion of Luzon, the largest and most important Philippine island, began January 9, 1945. Japanese defenders numbered 250,000. The battle for Luzon proved to be a long, fierce campaign. Japanese troops occupying Manila, its capital, refused to surrender, and much of that beautiful city was destroyed by weeks of house-by-house fighting. Over 100,000 Filipino civilians perished during the fighting to liberate Manila. It took six months to pacify Luzon, during which most of the Japanese soldiers were killed. Filipino guerrillas furnished valuable help to the American forces during the long, hard campaign. On June 30, 1945, all Japanese resistance on Luzon island ceased. But fighting continued in the outlying islands until the end of the war.

President Roosevelt had hoped China could play a major role in the war against Japan, but Jiang Jieshi's Nationalist regime, exhausted from years of warfare, could not take effective action against the Japanese, even with extensive American aid and support. In 1941 and 1942 American pilots, flying from India "over the hump" of the Himalayas, ferried supplies to the Chinese government at Chungking. In 1943 Allied forces under General Joseph "Vinegar Joe" Stilwell constructed the Burma Road across northern Burma to the Chinese city of Kungming. Roosevelt then assigned General Stilwell to Chungking with orders to maximize the Chinese war effort against Japan. But Stilwell discovered that Jiang was more concerned about fighting an enemy within China, the spreading Communist movement led by Mao Zedong. Frustrated, Stilwell fired off a report to Washington accusing Jiang of preventing the fulfillment of his mission to China. A furious Jiang then demanded that Roosevelt recall General Stilwell. Roosevelt complied with Jiang's request. China's military potential went down the drain of internal political conflict.

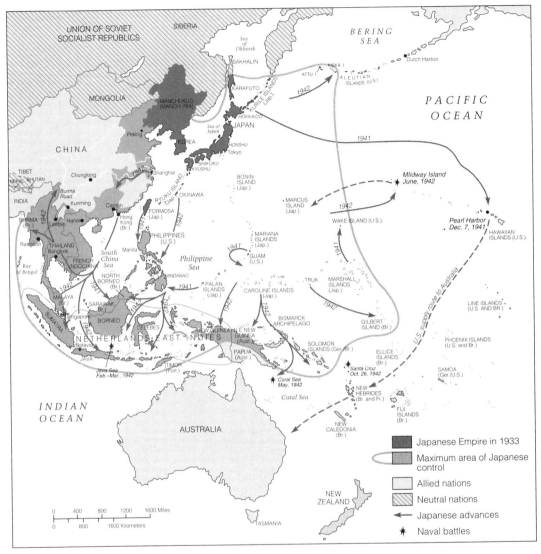

The War in the Pacific

IWO JIMA AND OKINAWA

As the war ended in Europe, Japanese resistance in the Pacific stiffened. The Japanese made last-ditch stands at Iwo Jima and Okinawa. Iwo Jima, a tiny volcanic atoll situated midway between the Marianas and Japan, had to be taken because Japanese interceptors based on this island were attacking B-29 bombers flying to and from Japan. Also U.S. pilots needed the atoll as a haven for crippled planes unable to reach their bases at Tinian and Saipan. Japanese defenders on the island had constructed what they believed were impregnable defenses: a maze of caves and tunnels beneath the island. Mount Suribachi, which dominated the small island, had been honeycombed with caves, pillboxes, and bunkers. The Japanese were prepared to defend their fortified island to the death.

It cost the lives of over 6,000 U.S. Marines to take Iwo Jima in March 1945. Of the 23,000 Japanese defenders, 21,000 were killed. The most famous photograph of the Pacific war came out of the Battle for Iwo Jima. On the third day of fighting, four Marines and a sailor were photographed proudly raising the American flag atop Mount Suribachi in the midst of battle.

The last American objective before invasion of the Japanese home islands was Okinawa, a 60-mile-long island located about 325 miles from southern Japan. Control of Okinawa would give the U.S. forces a staging area from which to launch amphibious attacks against the China coast and Japan. The largest amphibious assault of the Asian war occurred at Okinawa. Over 180,000 troops hit its beaches at various landing sites, and 77,000 Japanese troops mounted a fierce defense that forced the American invaders to fight a protracted and bloody war of attrition. Nearly all of the Japanese forces died in the last-ditch defense of Okinawa.

During the campaign the Japanese made extensive use of Kamikazes, who inflicted severe damage on the huge American fleet supporting the Okinawa invasions. U.S. casualties exceeded 50,000, including over 12,000 killed during a three-month war of annihilation ending June 22. The capture of Okinawa secured the final stepping-stone for the invasion of Japan, scheduled to begin in November 1945. The fanatic Japanese resistance at Iwo Jima and Okinawa foretold that the impending invasions of their home islands would be long, bloody campaigns. War planners estimated that the conquest of Japan could take a year and cost as many as 500,000 casualties.

THE BOMB

But an extraordinary new weapon radically altered the course of the Pacific war. In 1939 the noted scientist Dr. Albert Einstein had informed President Roosevelt that it might be possible to build "extremely powerful [atomic] bombs." Einstein also warned the President that German scientists might already be developing a nuclear bomb. Roosevelt, after conferences with scientific advisers, ordered work to begin on developing nuclear weapons.

Between 1941 and 1945 American and British scientists, engineers, and technicians labored intensively to build the atomic bomb. General Leslie Groves of the Army Corps of Engineers headed the secret, top-priority program, code-named the "Manhattan District Project." A brilliant scientific team, gathered under the leadership of Dr. J. Robert Oppenheimer and working at Los Alamos, New Mexico, eventually solved the complex theoretical and technical problems involved in creating the immensely powerful new weapons.

The Manhattan District Project was so secret that Congressmen who appropriated the vast sums of money for the bomb had no idea what the money was for. Harry Truman came to the presidency ignorant of the project. He was astonished to learn in April 1945 from Secretary of War Stimson that the United States would soon have "the most terrible weapon ever known in human history, one bomb of which could destroy a whole city." In July the world's first atomic device was exploded in the desert near Los Alamos. An awed Dr. Oppenheimer, witnessing the enormous fireball created by the explosion, was reminded of a passage from Hindu scriptures, "I am become Death, destroyer of worlds."

Before the weapon was completed, Stimson convened an Interim Committee, which recommended unanimously to the President that the atomic bomb, when ready, be used without warning against Japan. Truman concurred. Some scientists who had worked on the project had opposed this recommendation and proposed instead that the United States invite Japanese observers to witness a harmless demonstration of the bomb's power, which would perhaps induce their surrender. Committee members unanimously rejected their recommendation and Truman never learned of their proposal. Other high-ranking officials also urged holding back and trying to get Japan to surrender without having to use atomic weapons, perhaps by offering them better surrender terms. Truman consistently rejected such advice.

Meanwhile a new government took power in Japan. Its civilian faction sought a way to end the hopeless war. Unaware of the secret Yalta agreements, which would soon bring the Soviet Union into the war against Japan, a member of the peace faction sought Soviet mediation to get a modification of the unconditional surrender terms so that the Japanese could keep their emperor. The Soviets rebuffed the Japanese approach and informed Washington. U.S. officials already knew of the Japanese peace feeler from reading "Magic" intercepts. They also knew that Japanese army officers, controlling the government, meant to fight on.

After discussions with advisers, Truman issued a final warning to Japan before dropping the bombs. The message urged Japan to surrender unconditionally or else face "the utter devastation of the Japanese homeland." It made no mention of atomic weapons. The divided Japanese government, rejecting the ultimatum as "unworthy of public notice," ignored it.

Interpreting their silence as rejection, Truman saw no need to rescind an order given July 30 to proceed with the atomic bomb attack. Early on the morning of August 6, 1945, three B-29s lifted off the runway at Tinian bound for Hiroshima, Japan's eighth largest city. The lead aircraft, the *Enola Gay*, carried a ten-ton atomic bomb in its specially configured bomb bay. The other two planes were escorts, carrying cameras and assemblages of scientific recording instruments.

At 8:45 A.M. local time the sky exploded over Hiroshima: The world's first atomic bomb struck with the force of 12,000 tons of TNT. It killed about 100,000 people instantly and thousands more died later of burns, shock, or radiation poisoning. A city of 250,000 inhabitants was reduced to instant rubble. A few hours after the bombing, U.S. government officials announced the existence and first use of the bomb. They warned the Japanese that unless they surrendered unconditionally immediately,

The Atomic Age began August 6, 1945, when a lone American bomber dropped the world's first atomic bomb on Hiroshima, a city of 250,000 people in southern Japan. Tens of thousands of people died, and much of the city was turned into instant rubble.

"they may expect a rain of ruin from the air, the like of which has never before been seen on earth."

Bad weather delayed the dropping of the second bomb for a few days. On August 8 Red army units invaded Manchuria and Korea. The day after the Soviet Union entered the war, a second atomic bomb was dropped, on Nagasaki, as previously planned. It yielded 20,000 tons of TNT, destroying large sections of the city and killing 35,000 people. Had it not fallen a mile off target, it would have done far greater damage and killed thousands more people.

Even after the atomic bombings and the Soviet entry into the war, Japanese military leaders wanted to fight on. It was only the personal intercession of Emperor Hirohito that induced them to surrender. On August 10 the Japanese offered to surrender if they could keep their emperor. Truman accepted unconditional surrender on August 14, although he did offer veiled assurances that the Japanese could retain their emperor, provided Hirohito was stripped of his status as a divinity and subordinated to Allied occupation authorities. Surrender ceremonies occurred September 2 aboard the battleship USS *Missouri*, anchored in Tokyo Bay, with General Douglas MacArthur presiding.

Most Americans have accepted President Truman's justification for using the atomic bomb: "We have used it in order to shorten the agony of war, in order to save the lives of thousands and thousands of young Americans." But some critics have contended that the Japanese, perceiving their cause to be hopeless, would have surrendered soon without the atomic bombings. They argue that Truman had other, more important, motives for using nuclear weapons: to enhance American postwar diplomatic leverage against the Soviet Union. They accuse him of using the bombs on the already beaten Japanese to hasten their surrender in order to keep the Soviets from sharing in the postwar occupation of Japan and to make the Soviets more amenable to U.S. solutions to a myriad of difficult postwar political problems.

Truman hoped that American use of the powerful new weapon would make the Soviets more cooperative, that it would give the United States additional bargaining leverage with them. He also hoped that use of the bombs might induce Japanese surrender before the Soviet Union entered the war, but the Soviets intervened before the dropping of the second bomb. Truman was also disappointed to discover that U.S. possession of atomic bombs did not soften Soviet diplomacy. The Soviet response to the bombings was to become more intractable, not less.

American willingness to use the atomic bomb in war coupled with Washington's failure to keep Stalin informed of the progress of the Manhattan Project, as well as American refusal to share any broad scientific information about nuclear weaponry with the Soviets, contributed to the development of the Cold War. At a meeting of the Big Three held at Potsdam, Truman told Stalin informally that the United States had recently tested an extremely powerful new weapon, but he did not tell the Soviet dictator that it was a nuclear device. Stalin merely smiled and said he hoped that it would soon be used on Japan. But when Truman walked away, Stalin hastily conferred with his aides and decided on the spot to speed up a Soviet atomic weapons project that had been curtailed in wartime. The nuclear arms race began at that moment. Spies working for the Soviet Union had penetrated the Manhattan Project and by the time the bombs were dropped on Japanese cities, Soviet scientists already knew much of the technology required to process fissionable materials. They would build their own bombs within four years.

Truman decided to use nuclear weapons on the Japanese without much forethought, relying heavily on the advice of Henry Stimson and James F. Byrnes in making that fateful decision. Truman, like Roosevelt before him, never questioned that the bomb would be used when ready, on the Germans, the Japanese, or both. Scientists who built the bombs did not know how powerful they would be, nor did they anticipate the grave health problems posed by radiation poisoning.

Perhaps the Japanese should have been forewarned. Perhaps a demonstration explosion should have been made. Perhaps the unconditional surrender terms should have been modified before the bombs were used in order to strengthen the peace party within the Japanese government. Any or all these measures might have induced Japanese surrender before the bombs were used, although no one can know for sure how the Japanese would have responded to any of these initiatives.

It is also important to remember that even if Japan could have been induced to surrender without having to endure the horrors of two atomic bombings, the conceivable alternative scenarios would have in all probability been worse. Had the war gone on even for a few weeks more, the continuing fire bomb raids over Japanese cities would have killed more people and destroyed more property than did the two atomic bombs. Had invasions by American forces been necessary, there would have been devastating losses on both sides, including millions of Japanese civilians. Hand-to-hand combat in Japan might have destroyed the country. And while fighting was going on in Japan between Americans and Japanese, Soviet soldiers would have annihilated the Japanese armies in Korea, Manchuria, and northern China.

VICTORY

So victory came to the United States and its allies. They had prevailed in the costliest, most destructive war in the planet's history. For the United States, war costs came to about $350 billion. The war also claimed over a million American casualties, including 292,000 battle deaths. American casualties were light in comparison to those of the Soviets, who lost 30 million people, and of the Chinese, who lost about 15 million. The Germans lost 4 million people and the Japanese another 3 million. That summer of 1945, Americans could gaze into a future bright with hope because the Axis menace had been destroyed and democracy appeared to have no enemies in the world. They also gazed at a world darkened by the nuclear shadow that they had allowed to be cast over its future. The future beckoned, bright with opportunity and dark with danger.

BIBLIOGRAPHY

There is a vast literature on all facets of American involvement in World War II. The following books are recommended for those who want to know more about the war experience in general or wish to explore a particular aspect. Two good short surveys of World War II are Martha Byrd Hoyle, *A World in Flames: A History of World War II* and Mark Arnold-Foster, *The World at War*. Basil Collier, *The Second World War: A Military History* is a good short account of the U.S. military role in World War II. A longer general history is A. Russell Buchanan, *The United States and World War II*, 2 vols. A recent book on the Pacific war is Ronald H. Spector, *Eagle against the Sun*. Samuel Eliot Morison, *The Two Ocean War* (2 vols.) is a naval history of World War II. An English scholar, John Costello, has written an encylopedic account of the war in the Pacific: *The Pacific War, 1941-1945*. A recent study that highlights the racial antagonisms that undergirded the war between the United States and Japan is John Dower, *War without Mercy: Race and Power in the Pacific War*. The best war journalism can be found in Ernie Pyle's classic *Brave Men*. Bill Mauldin, *Up Front* is a book of "Willie and Joe" cartoons. The best account of the decision to build and use atomic bombs on Japan is Martin J. Sherwin, *A World Destroyed*. John Hersey, *Hiroshima* is an eyewitness account of the tragedy that launched the atomic age. The horrors of the Jewish Holocaust have been recorded by Arthur D. Morse, *Six Million Died*. For American diplomacy during World War II, the best short study is Gaddis Smith, *American Diplomacy during the Second World War*. For the best study of President Roosevelt's conduct of diplomacy during the war read Robert Dallek, *Franklin Roosevelt and American Foreign Policy, 1932-1945*, pp. 171-538. The best novels about the war experience are James Jones, *From Here to Eternity*, which is about enlisted life in the Army on the eve of Pearl Harbor; Norman Mailer, *The Naked and the Dead*, a powerful novel which uses a platoon of infantrymen to symbolize American society, its class structure, and its social values; and Herman Wouk, *The Caine Mutiny*, the dramatic story of a ship's officers rebelling against a mentally ill, tyrannical ship commander.

CHAPTER
13
Home Front USA

PEOPLE AT WAR

Americans in the late fall of 1941 drifted into history's largest war. As they faced and eventually defeated dangerous threats to the American way of life and democratic values, they got caught up in the greatest collective experience of their lives. Sharing a sense of common purpose under the inspired leadership of President Franklin D. Roosevelt, Americans enjoyed greater national unity than at any time in their history. Citizens who remained behind on the home front contributed in many ways large and small to the war effort. They gave blood, bought war bonds, planted victory gardens, and collected scrap metal, used tires, oil and grease, newspapers, and tin cans. People worked as volunteers on civil defense, as school aides, in hospitals, in first aid programs, as volunteer fire-fighters and police, and as airplane spotters.

The war effort involved many home front sacrifices. Between the attack at Pearl Harbor and V-J Day (December 7, 1941, and August 14, 1945) about 300,000 workers died in industrial accidents and one million workers were permanently disabled. More workers were killed or crippled in home front accidents than soldiers were killed or crippled in battle! It was safer to be a soldier during World War II than it was to be a war worker. Consumers had to do without many of the civilian goods and services normally churned out by the gigantic American economy. The nation's automakers ceased making new cars early in 1942; for the duration of the war they turned out trucks, jeeps, tanks, and planes. Major consumer items were rationed. People traveled less, dressed more informally, entertained more at home, and went to bed earlier. Hunting and fishing were banned for the duration of the war.

DEMOGRAPHIC CHANGE

World War II had a dramatic impact on the lives of nearly all Americans—on where they lived and what kind of work they did. It also affected family life and patterns of leisure and recreation. The war experience set demographic patterns that would persist for the next half-century. Military bases and war industries transformed cities and revitalized entire regions of the country. The West Coast, especially California, which had been a relatively isolated and underdeveloped area of the nation, became the most dynamic region in the country. The western coastal states, with perhaps 10 percent of the nation's population, accounted for 20 percent of total wartime production. An economist estimated that the coastal states' economies did about 50 years of growing in less than 4 years.

Between 1941 and 1945 approximately 16 million men (about 95 percent of whom were drafted) and 250,000 women served in the armed forces. About half of those who went into the military during the war never left the continental United States, but many who never left the states were assigned to bases in parts of the country that they had never seen before. After the war ended and they were discharged, some returned with their families to become permanent residents of the locales where they had done military service. In addition to service personnel, millions of civilian war workers moved from rural areas to the cities where jobs in war industries could be found. In many cases those transplanted civilian war workers, refugees from rural poverty and isolation, did not go home after the war. They and their families joined the burgeoning postwar urban and suburban populations.

Several important population shifts occurred in wartime that would shape the demographic contours of postwar America for decades. Population flowed from the rural interior outward toward the cities along the Pacific, Atlantic, and Gulf coasts, and from the inland farms and villages to the cities of the Upper Midwest. People moved to these coastal and midwestern cities because the major military installations, shipyards, aircraft assembly plants, and other war industries were located there. Population also made a major shift westward, particularly to California, where it increased by 40 percent between 1940 and 1945. Millions of the military personnel and war workers who came to California in wartime remained or returned after the war to become permanent residents of the Golden State. The Sunbelt, that southern rim of states stretching from South Carolina to California, also began to grow rapidly during the war years. The Sunbelt states, especially Florida, Texas, and Southern California, would become the nation's most dynamic centers of population growth and economic expansion in the postwar decades.

Another important demographic trend induced by World War II was that over a million African Americans, lured by good-paying jobs in war industries, moved out of the Old South to New York, Chicago, Philadelphia,

Detroit, and the rapidly growing cities along the West Coast. They and their families also remained in these new locales after the war, becaming permanent residents of New York, Pennsylvania, Illinois, Michigan, and California. The geographic mobility induced by the war in fact resulted in permanent relocations for millions of American families. Rural America declined. Regional differences among Americans diminished, and the demographic foundations for the postwar surge of urban and suburban communities were lain.

Despite the mobilization of America's vast human and economic resources for the war effort, there occurred more social reform affecting the quality of American lives during the war than had occurred during the previous years of New Deal reforms. Medical and dental care improved dramatically. Prepaid health insurance for working people became available for the first time. Some progressive employers such as Kaiser Shipyards offered medical care as a fringe benefit. Millions of young men from disadvantaged backgrounds drafted into the armed forces enjoyed a nutritious diet and adequate medical and dental care for the first time in their lives. Even with the nation at war and even with the dangers of war work, the overall health of the American people improved dramatically during the war years. The birth rates rose rapidly; the death rate sharply diminished. Median life expectancy increased by five years!

A huge increase in the size of the American middle class was the most significant demographic transformation of the war years. The United States became for the first time in its history a middle-class nation in the sense that more than half of its families enjoyed a middle-class income and lifestyle. Personal income more than doubled during the war, and national income was more equitably distributed than ever before. Perhaps one-third of the nation's families remained poor, but most of these enjoyed relative improvements in their living standard. It was during the early 1940s that prosperity levels that had been reached in the late 1920s before the Great Crash were finally eclipsed.

ECONOMIC TRANSFORMATIONS

It was American industrial output that largely determined the eventual Allied victory over the Axis. According to historian Glen Jeansonne, "The war was won as much on the assembly lines as on the front lines." Hitler fatally underestimated U.S. economic power when he sneered that Americans "only know how to make refrigerators and razor blades." During 45 months of war America's factories built 86,000 tanks, 300,000 planes, 15 million rifles, 5,500 merchant ships, and 6,000 naval ships. American military production more than doubled the Axis output, winning a war of attrition.

In addition to raising a vast military force, the United States had to gear its economy for global war. America's factories had to produce arms for ourselves and for our major allies, the British, the Soviets, and the Chinese. During the first half of 1942 the federal government placed orders for over $100 billion in war contracts, more goods than the economy had ever produced in a year. Federal spending surged in wartime—$35 billion in 1942, $75 billion in 1943, and $98 billion in 1945. These gigantic expenditures dwarfed New Deal spending, which had never exceeded $10 billion for any year. The unprecedented federal spending, 90 percent of which was for war or war-related enterprises, fueled the economic and social transformations that had created a new American society by the summer of 1945.

Converting the economy to a war footing challenged American industrialists and government bureaucrats. To manage the gigantic wartime effort, Roosevelt created a central planning agency, the Office of Economic Stabilization, headed by James F. Byrnes. To spur industrial production, the Justice Department suspended antitrust laws and the Pentagon awarded lucrative cost-plus contracts to manufacturers whereby the government paid all research and development costs and then purchased the products at a price that guaranteed companies a substantial profit. Because of such incentives, America's corporate industrialists not only accomplished the "miracle of production" that defeated the Axis, they also earned historic high profits for their shareholders.

Fueled by vast federal expenditures, total productivity increased at

American industry made a major contribution to eventual military victory. This ship was completed in ten days, a remarkable feat that brought FDR (in the foreground, left) to the Portland, Oregon shipyard where it was accomplished.

the remarkable rate of 25 percent per annum, a growth rate never approached before or since World War II. The gross domestic product more than doubled, from $95 billion in 1940 to more than $211 billion by 1946. Economic expansion added 10 million new jobs. The federal government during World War II spent more than twice as much money than all previous governments combined had spent since the creation of the republic!

To help pay for these prodigious expenditures, Congress broadened and deepened the tax structure. The Revenue Acts of 1942 and 1943 created the modern federal income tax system. Most Americans had never filed an income tax return before World War II because the income tax, on the books since 1913, had been a small tax on upper-income families and corporations. In 1939 only 4 million people had paid income taxes. Starting with 1942, anyone earning $600 or more annually had to file an income tax return. A withholding tax went into effect in 1943, making employers the nation's principal tax collectors. Income tax revenues rose from $5 billion in 1940 to $49 billion in 1945, a tenfold increase. In 1945 over 40 million people paid income taxes. These wartime tax increases were by far the largest in the nation's history.

Although the government presented the new income tax system to the American people as a temporary wartime necessity, it remained a permanent feature in the postwar era. Even with the significant increase, tax revenues paid only 41 percent of the cost of the war. Government paid the rest of the war bills by borrowing. War bonds, peddled by movie stars, war heroes, and professional athletes, added $135 billion. But ordinary citizens bought only about a third of these bonds; large institutional investors purchased the bulk of them. By war's end the national debt had climbed to $280 billion, up from $40 billion when it began. The national debt was now larger than the economy, that is, the debt exceeded the gross domestic product.

Vast federal spending for war ended the lingering depression that had afflicted Americans for a decade. The New Deal had failed to find a cure for economic depression. On the eve of war, over 7 million Americans were out of work, 14 percent of the labor force. Real wages in 1941 were below 1929 levels. By New Year's day 1943, however, unemployment in the United States had vanished. Wartime economic expansion, fueled by unprecedented levels of government spending, combined with mass conscription to create severe labor shortages. At war's end the nation's workers still enjoyed full employment at the highest wages in history.

The discovery that government spending could banish the specter of depression confirmed the claims of the world's foremost economist, England's John Maynard Keynes. Keynes contended that if private sector investment proved inadequate, government could cut taxes and begin large-scale spending programs to stimulate demand and restore the business cycle. During the New Deal of the mid-1930s government spending was not large enough and taxes were generally regressive, so Keynes's theories could not be confirmed until the war. The wartime success at eliminating the Depression also gave American political leaders a confidence that they could regulate the economy—a confidence that lasted for the next 30 years. They believed they now possessed fiscal tools to monitor spending levels in order to maintain prosperity, keep unemployment low, and prevent the recurrence of recession, all the while controlling inflation. Citizens too looked to government after the war to maintain and promote prosperity.

Farmers and industrial workers, two classes devastated by the Depression, prospered during the war years. Farm output rose 28 percent even though the farm population declined more than 50 percent, and farmers struggled with chronic labor shortages. Wartime proved to be a bonanza for many farmers. Farm income more than doubled during the war years. Food consumption on the Home Front soared to historic highs and the armed forces siphoned off a fourth of all agricultural production. Sharecropping and farm tenantry declined rapidly. Farming became a much more efficient industry because of mechanization, the development of improved crops, and wider use of pesticides and fertilizers. The government also aided agriculture by exempting farm workers from the draft and by providing price supports for many staple crops.

Big labor prospered along with big business. In 1942 Congress created the National War Labor Board (NWLB), which set guidelines for wages, hours, and collective bargaining. Employers, unions, and government officials generally cooperated during the war. Union membership grew from 10.5 million in 1941 to over 15 million in 1945, a third of the non-farm work force. Proportionally, this growth represented the high watermark of union membership in American history. During the war trade union leaders consolidated their new status as members of the nation's political and economic establishment.

There were some labor problems the NWLB could not resolve. The American Federation of Labor and the Congress of Industrial Organizations engaged in bitter, sometimes violent, jurisdictional disputes. Although organized labor had given a no-strike pledge for the duration of the war, it could not be enforced. The United Mine Workers, led by crusty John L. Lewis, went on strike in 1943, causing major disruptions in the nation's economic life. When a national railroad strike threatened in 1944, the government took over the railroads and operated them for three weeks until federal mediators could work out a settlement that averted the strike. Most work stoppages during the war years lasted only a few days and didn't cause serious production delays in the industries that cranked out the huge amounts of war materials required by the armed forces.

Vastly increased federal spending, full employment, and shortages of consumer items sent powerful inflationary forces surging through the

economy. The shift from peacetime to wartime production sharply reduced the amount of consumer goods available just when people had
more money to spend. By early 1942 the production of new cars and
other durable goods had stopped. A giant inflationary gap generated by
too much money chasing too few goods threatened to drive prices way up
and to rob Americans of their wartime economic gains. To clamp a lid on
inflation, the government imposed price controls, joining them to a rationing system by which coupons were alloted to consumers for scarce
items such as sugar, butter, coffee, beef, tires, and gasoline.

Roosevelt created the Office of Price Administration (OPA) to administer the control apparatus nationally. The OPA had a daunting task. Economic interests accepted controls on the other fellow's prices but
regarded controls on their own prices as subversive. Business lobbyists,
farm bloc politicians, and union leaders waged unceasing "guerrilla warfare" against the OPA for the duration of the war. Consumers chafed under rationing restrictions, particularly those on beef and gasoline. A ban
on all "pleasure driving" and a 35-mph speed limit accompanied gasoline
rationing. The average motorist got 3 gallons of gas per week. Most people
walked to work or took public transportation. Auto touring all but vanished. The black market in gasoline flourished; racketeers had not had it
so good since Prohibition. Nevertheless, at times motorists could get no
gas, legal or illegal. Service stations often closed, stranding motorists and
truckers. When a station could get gas, customers lined their cars up for
miles waiting to buy it. Beef rationing caused the worst problems. Butcher
display cases frequently emptied. Butchers sometimes favored old customers, infuriating new ones. Frustrated shoppers often abused butchers
and occasionally rioted. Horsemeat and muskrat meat appeared in several
places as beef substitutes. But despite grievances and injustices, the uni-
versally unpopular OPA maintained price stability and distributed scarce
goods equitably. Most people complied with the system of controls, con-
sidering it to be both a wartime necessity and to their economic advantage. The OPA controls, along with rationing, did effectively contain
wartime inflation; the cost of living rose only 3 per cent in 1944 and 1945.

Even as ordinary citizens chafed under the restrictions of rationing
and price controls, a quite remarkable redistribution of income occurred
during the war years. Real wages for workers employed in manufacturing
rose over 50 percent, from $24 to $37 per week. The share of national
wealth owned by the richest 5 percent of American families dropped
from 23.7 to 16.8 percent. The number of families earning less than
$2,000 annually declined by 50 percent from 1941 to 1945, and the num-
ber of families earning $5,000 or more quadrupled during that time.
World War II was the most successful war on poverty in American history;
it also created the social foundations for the affluent society that flowered
during the postwar era.

Despite shortages and rationing, people in wartime with money to

spend found ways to enjoy it. Wartime prosperity strengthened materialistic values and revived consumerism, which had been largely suspended
during the Depression decade. Americans spent money on entertainment, going to movies, and going out to dinner. They resorted to the black
market when rationed goods could not be found. Many saved their money
for the new cars, homes, appliances, and radios they would buy after the
war. Advertisers promised consumers new and better goods when civilian production patterns were restored following victory over the Axis.
Consumerism, reborn amid war, would become a powerful engine driving the postwar affluent economy.

WOMEN IN WARTIME

Between 1941 and 1945 over 6 million women entered the labor force,
about half of them working in the manufacturing sector. The female labor
force increased by more than 50 percent. More than one million women

*Over 6 million women entered the labor force during World War II. Many of them
worked in industries such as these two "Rosie the Riveters" helping to build military aircraft.*

were hired by the federal government. Married women, many with children, made up three-quarters of the working women. Before the war the typical working woman had been young and single; only about 15 percent of married women worked outside the home. By 1945 more than half of working women had married and their median age was 37. Most women in the prewar labor force had been confined to low-paying, low-status jobs in the service, clerical, and light manufacturing fields, but during the war years their wages rose both absolutely and in relation to men's. In 1942 the NLRB ordered equal pay for women who performed the same jobs as men; however, there was no ruling that women should get equal pay for comparable work.

Employers had considered women unsuitable for heavy labor amidst the masculine atmosphere prevailing in factories, but acute wartime labor shortages quickly changed those attitudes. Women learned skilled trades, joined unions, and earned high wages. Whereas before the war they made up less than 10 percent of union membership, by 1944 they comprised 22 percent. Women performed certain jobs better than men, such as those requiring close attention to detail and manual dexterity. Women worked in munitions factories and foundries. They became riveters, welders, crane operators, tool and die makers, and iron workers. They operated heavy equipment, drove trucks, and became train engineers. Women increased their geographic and occupational mobility tremendously in wartime. Thousands of black women quit work as domestics to join the factory labor force. Millions of women moved from the rural South and Midwest to coastal cities where the war-generated jobs were located. In southern California hundreds of thousands of women went to work in aircraft assembly plants.

Opinion polls showed that the general public favored wartime work by women. Corporate public relations campaigns encouraged women to get jobs in war industries. A government propaganda agency, the Office of War Information (OWI), mounted publicity campaigns to persuade women to join the war labor force. These media campaigns portrayed women's work in shops and factories as both noble and absolutely necessary to the war effort. A fictional "Rosie the Riveter" became a popular wartime symbol of women working in war industries. She was celebrated in an eponymous hit tune of the era, and her picture appeared on posters and magazine covers. "Do the job HE left behind," exhorted the billboards.

Yet patterns of gender discrimination persisted in wartime. Surveys showed that women in manufacturing earned about 60 percent of what men got for comparable work. Factories offered them limited opportunities for promotions and supervisory positions. Even though the war emergency opened up hitherto closed occupations to women, most jobs in the sex-segregated labor market remained classified as "male" or "female" work. Where women worked in factories, they often worked on all-female shop floors, under male supervisors and managers. Women resented the unequal pay and working conditions as well as the occasional sexual harassment from chauvinistic males. But they loved the opportunity to do important work that contributed to the war effort and they also enjoyed the camaraderie and support of their female co-workers.

The most serious problem faced by working mothers in wartime was the almost complete absence of child-care centers. During the war juvenile delinquency, venereal disease, and teenage pregnancies rose sharply. "Latchkey children," children left alone while their mothers worked their factory shifts, became a national scandal. Children roamed the streets, were put in all-day or all-night movie houses, or were locked in cars outside defense plants. Police arrested many teenage girls for prostitution and apprehended boys for theft and vandalism.

Because so many men went to war, millions of women found themselves the *de facto* head of a single-parent household. They had a much greater range of responsibilities than just working full-time. They were the center of family life. Many also found time for neighborhood volunteer work. They served on Civil Defense committees. They attended club meetings and went to PTA meetings. They gave blood and worked as hostesses at USO centers. Many women simply never found enough hours in a day to do their jobs, fulfill all their family obligations, attend union meetings, and meet the myriad of other demands on their time and energy.

Increased numbers of women got married at the same time that they went to work in war industries. Marriage rates rose sharply in 1942. A higher percentage of women were marrying than ever before. Many young couples got married to spend time together before the man got shipped overseas. The birth rate climbed sharply also. Many of the births enabled the fathers to qualify for military deferments. Some women conceived "goodbye babies" to perpetuate the family even if the father got killed in war. The main reason for the increase in marriages and births was the returning prosperity. A parent, often two parents with good jobs in a war industry, headed the new families. The population, which had grown by only 3 million during the entire decade of the 1930s, added 6.5 million people during the war years. The baby boom that would be one of the most significant demographic trends of the postwar years had begun. Because a lot of these wartime marriages were hastily arranged, the divorce rate was higher than ever before. Contraception was more widely practiced than ever before. Even so, the rate of children born to unmarried women also rose to historic highs in wartime.

Women's wartime factory work was considered only a temporary response to a national emergency. Once victory was achieved and the soldiers returned, women were supposed to surrender their jobs to a returning GI. The president of the National Association of Manufacturers intoned, "Too many women should not stay in the labor force. The home is the basic American institution." However, surveys showed most women wanted to continue working after the war. Seventy-five percent of Detroit's female factory workers wanted to keep working. When company war contracts were cancelled or phased out after the war, women employees were fired. Others were pressured by their husbands to quit and return to the kitchen. Single working women continued to work, but often they could find only low-paying jobs in domestic service, restaurants, and department stores. Many of these women felt a keen sense of personal defeat at having to resume work in the low-status fields from which they had temporarily escaped during the war.

The roots of the modern feminist movement can be found in the work experience, financial independence, and attitudinal changes achieved by millions of women during World War II. They had found new opportunities and met new challenges that traditionally had been denied women. They acquired job skills and developed talents that they did not realize they could until the war came along. Many of them reared their daughters to have greater self-esteem and to demand more from life than their own mothers had taught them to expect. When their children were grown in the 1960s and 1970s, many of these middle-aged Rosie the Riveters rejoined the work force.

AFRICAN AMERICANS AT WAR

World War II proved a mixed blessing for African Americans: It provided both unprecedented economic opportunities and continuing encounters with the hardships of segregation and racism. About a million black men and women, nearly all of the men draftees, served in all branches of military service. Even though the American military was segregated then, African Americans attained far more opportunities in World War II than had been available in World War I. The Army Air Corps trained black pilots, who flew in all-black squadrons. African American Marines, fighting in all-black units, fought heroically in savage island battles in the Pacific war.

Black–white race relations within the military reflected the racist society it served. Many race riots occurred on military bases. White civilians often attacked African American soldiers stationed in the South. The morale and motivation of black soldiers often suffered from encounters with racist whites. African American soldiers often found themselves serving in menial positions. Black troops were sometimes commanded by white southern officers who subjected them to harsh and humiliating treatment. African American soldiers sometimes found enemy prisoners of war treated better than they were. But most black soldiers found reasons to fight the Axis, even if at times they could see little difference between German racism and the homegrown kind. They also kept up steady pressures for better assignments, fairer treatment, and improved status. African Americans planned to trade their

African Americans made a major contribution to American victories during World War II. Here the Army Air Force's all-black 99th Fighter Group assembles at the beachhead of Anzio, Italy, in 1944.

wartime military service for improved educational and job opportunities after the war. A NAACP spokesman asserted that the war gave African Americans the chance "to . . . compel and shame our nation . . . into a more enlightened attitude toward a tenth of its people." African Americans fought for a double victory: over the Axis abroad and Jim Crow at home. Many returning black veterans could not celebrate the victorious end of the war as enthusiastically as white Americans could because they knew that they were coming home to face a segregated society and the racist attitudes that sustained it.

The war also opened many new employment opportunities for African Americans. In January 1941 a black union leader, A. Philip Randolph, angered because employers with war contracts refused to hire African American workers, threatened to stage a march on Washington to protest both employer discrimination and segregation in the armed forces. President Roosevelt, wanting to avoid the embarrassment of a protest march and possible violence, persuaded Randolph to call off the proposed march in return for an executive order establishing a President's Fair Employment Practices Committee (FEPC). On June 25, 1942, Roosevelt issued such an order. The FEPC ordered employers in defense industries to make jobs available "without discrimination because of race, creed, color, or national origin." The FEPC was understaffed, was underfunded, and had limited enforcement powers. It was merely a symbolic gesture that proved to be of little use during the war. It was acute labor shortages more than government policy that opened war employment opportunities for African Americans.

Over 2 million African American men and women left the South to find work in the industrial cities of the North and West. Many joined CIO unions. The number of African Americans holding government jobs increased dramatically in wartime, from 50,000 to over 200,000. Black voters in northern cities became an important constituency in local and state elections. Most of the families who left the South remained a permanent part of the northern urban population. Southern black migrants often encountered racist hostility as they struggled to adapt to their new lives in the North. They discovered there was little difference between northern and southern white racial attitudes. Many whites hated their new African American competitors for housing, jobs, and schools. They resented coming into contact with African Americans at parks, beaches, and other public facilities.

These racial antagonisms flared violently during the summer of 1943. About 250 race riots occurred in nearly 50 northern cities, the largest ones happening in Detroit and Harlem. The worst violence occurred in Detroit. It had been building for years. The immediate provocation was an angry struggle for access to a public housing project demanded by both African American and white workers during a time of acute housing shortages. One hot night in June things got out of control, and a full-scale race riot exploded, lasting several days during which 25 African Americans and 9 whites died.

Despite these outbreaks of home front racial violence, World War II proved to be a watershed for African Americans; the war experience aided the black struggle for civil rights and full citizenship. Military service gave most African American veterans greater self-esteem and a sense of empowerment. It raised their expectations. Many black veterans did not return to the rural South after the war but chose to settle in the North or West, perhaps in one of the states in which they had been stationed in the military. Others took advantage of the GI Bill to go to college or learn a skilled trade. These educated black professionals and technicians formed a new and much larger African American middle class. The National Association for the Advancement of Colored People (NAACP) increased its membership from 50,000 members at the time of the Pearl Harbor attack to ten times that number at war's end. A new, more militant civil rights organization was created in wartime: the Congress of Racial Equality (CORE) was founded in 1942 in Chicago. In 1944, for the first time, President Roosevelt admitted black journalists to his press conferences. A combination of vastly improved economic opportunities and continuing encounters with racism generated a new militancy among black people. They were determined not to accept second-class citizenship after the war. These

African American veterans and their children took the lead in challenging Jim Crow and racism in the postwar era. The roots of the modern civil rights movement can be found in World War II.

HISPANIC AMERICANS IN WARTIME

According to the 1940 census about 2.7 million Hispanic people lived among the American population. Most were of Mexican descent living in California, Texas, and the Southwest. Much of this predominantly rural population endured poverty, discrimination, and segregation. They lacked decent jobs, housing, and educational opportunities, and they had no political influence. Many of the Mexican Americans moved to urban areas to find work in war industries. World War II created opportunities for Hispanics. About 350,000 went into the armed forces, nearly all of them draftees. Although the military never segregated Hispanics in the thorough way they did African Americans, many served in predominantly Hispanic units. Mexican American warriors joined elite units such as the airborne rangers and often volunteered for dangerous missions. Eleven Mexican Americans won the nation's highest military award, the Congressional Medal of Honor.

At the same time, the war created acute shortages of agricultural workers, so American growers persuaded the U.S. government to make arrangements with Mexico to import farm workers from there. Under a program established in 1942, nearly 2 million Mexican *braceros* (laborers) entered the United States. Because of lax government supervision, employers often ruthlessly exploited these contract laborers. Many *braceros* worked for 50 cents a day, had no fringe benefits, and were housed in shacks and converted chicken coops.

Hispanics in the war labor force often suffered discriminations similar to those encountered by African Americans and women. They sometimes got paid less than Anglo employees for doing the same work. They found their problems most acute in the crowded cities. Many young Mexican Americans belonged to neighborhood gangs. They called themselves *pachucos* and favored a distinctive style of dress, called a "zoot suit," which consisted of baggy trousers flared at the knees and fitted tightly around the ankles complemented by a wide-brimmed felt hat. These costumes were an assertion of a distinct cultural identity and a defiance of Anglo values.

In June 1943, at a time when black–white racial tensions were erupting in cities, ethnic relations in Los Angeles were also strained. Hundreds of sailors and Marines on leave in southern California assaulted Mexican Americans on the streets of Los Angeles and tore off their zoot suits. Police either looked the other way or arrested only Mexican-American youths during these encounters, and the local media supported the attacks on the *pachucos.* Only after the president of Mexico threatened to cancel the *bracero* program did President Roosevelt intervene to stop the violence.

Despite the zoot suit incidents, Hispanic American wartime experiences brought some advances. As was the case for African Americans, military service gave thousands of Mexican Americans an enhanced sense of self-worth. They returned from the war with greater expectations and enlarged views of life's possibilities. Many Hispanic veterans took advantage of the GI Bill. In the postwar years Mexican American veterans and their sons assumed leadership roles in organizations that challenged discrimination against Hispanic people in southwestern states.

NATIVE AMERICANS IN WARTIME

In addition to the 25,000 Native Americans who served in the armed forces during World War II, many thousands more left their reservations to work in war industries around the country. Most of these mobile people did not return to their reservations and tribal life after the war; they remained in the cities and became part of the rapidly growing postwar urban and suburban population. Some of those who did return to the reservations brought with them new ideas and technologies.

In 1944 in California lawyers representing a group of Native Americans filed suit in federal court for $100 million as compensation for lands taken illegally from their ancestors during the 1850s. Congress enacted legislation to pay them for their lands, but President Roosevelt vetoed the bill. Litigation on this matter continued off and on for the next 35 years until finally both parties reached a compromise agreement. The Native Americans accepted a settlement that brought them about 47 cents per acre.

ASIAN AMERICANS IN WARTIME

The war to save democracy featured many home front violations of democracy. In some ways civil liberties violations during World War II were not as severe as during World War I. For example, most conscientious objectors were permitted to serve in noncombatant roles in the military or else perform essential civilian work. (Of the more than 5,500 conscientious objectors jailed for refusing to serve in the military, most were Jehovah's Witnesses. They refused to cooperate with the Selective Service authorities, insisting that they were all ministers. Further, they did not oppose all wars, only secular wars for political objectives.) Some Fascist publications were banned from the mails. In July 1942 a federal grand jury brought indictments against 28 Fascists for sedition. The cases continued off and on for the duration of the war, but no one was convicted and all charges against the 28 defendants were dropped after the war ended. German Americans were not harassed or persecuted, as in World War I, nor were Italian American citizens. Congress never enacted repressive measures like the Espionage Act or the Sedition Act.

However, during the spring and summer of 1942 about 120,000 Japanese Americans, two-thirds of them native-born American citizens, were uprooted from their homes along the Pacific coast and taken to internment centers located in remote interior regions of the country. There they lived in tarpaper barracks behind barbed wire for three years. The internment of Japanese Americans during World War II represented the worst violation of civil liberties in wartime in American history.

The initiative was taken by the military commander in charge of security along the West Coast, General John Dewitt. Dewitt and other officials claimed that relocation of Japanese Americans was necessary to guarantee military security along the West Coast. They argued that if the Japanese Americans were not relocated, some of them would aid the enemy in case of attack. Since the "disloyals" could not be separated from the "loyals," all would have to go. Their accusations were demonstrably false. FBI agents admitted that they never discovered a single proven act of disloyalty by any Japanese American. The real reasons for their removal were anti-Japanese race prejudice, wartime hysteria, and greed. The claim of military necessity was based on unfounded suspicion, not evidence. Relocation of Japanese Americans in wartime was also the culminating act of a half-century of anti-Japanese agitation and assaults in California, Oregon, and Washington.

Japanese American spokesmen asserted their loyalty to no avail. No political leaders or newspaper editors defended the Japanese Americans nor did any of them question the need for relocation. Earl Warren, California's Attorney General in 1942, strongly advocated removal. The removal order, Executive Order No. 9066, came from President Roosevelt and could not be challenged. In 1944 the Supreme Court placed the constitutional seal of approval upon relocation of Japanese Americans. In the case of *Fred Korematsu* v. *the United States*, the Court accepted the claim of Army lawyers that relocation was a wartime military necessity. A 5-to-3 majority ruled that in time of war, individual rights could be sacrificed to military necessity. Associate Justice Frank Murphy filed a powerful dissenting opinion, stating that relocation of Japanese Americans fell "into the ugly abyss of racism."

Following the advice of their leaders, virtually the entire Japanese American population complied with the relocation order without resistance or protest. They submitted in accordance with the spirit of *Shikata Ga Nai* (realistic resignation). Because they were given little time to gather at assembly centers and allowed to take only what they could carry to the camps, families lost homes, businesses, farms, and personal property worth an estimated $400 million. They arrived at the camps to find hastily

U.S. soldiers uprooted about 110,000 Japanese Americans, most of them U.S. citizens, from their homes in early 1942 and imprisoned them in various internment centers. The move, spawned by panic and prejudice, was both unnecessary and wrong. Here, a family awaits a bus to haul them away.

built tarpaper barracks amidst bleak desert landscapes that would be their homes for three years. The internment centers were *de facto* prisons. People were not free to come and go. The camps were under continuous surveillance by armed guards and enclosed by barbed wire fencing. During the course of the war some internees were allowed to leave the camps provided they agreed to settle in eastern states. By the summer of 1945 all were allowed to leave. A fortunate few families had friends who had saved their homes or businesses for them while they were incarcerated, but many internees had no homes or businesses to return to. They found that interlopers now resided in their former residences and owned their former businesses.

Even though their families were imprisoned in camps, thousands of young Japanese American men volunteered for military service. They were determined to prove their loyalty to a government that had betrayed them. Japanese American soldiers contributed much to the war effort.

They fought in the European theater, and many served in the Pacific war as translators, interpreters, and intelligence officers. They proved themselves to be brave warriors, winning medals and suffering severe casualties. One Japanese American unit, the 442nd Regimental Combat Engineers, was the most decorated unit in American military history.

It is revealing that the government refused to relocate Japanese Americans living in Hawaii. Thousands of them continued to work for the American military at Pearl Harbor and other installations following the Japanese attacks. Ironically, the reason they were not removed was military necessity. They made up one-fifth of the Hawaiian population, their labor was essential, and there was no place to put them nor ships to transport them.

In truth, loyal Americans were the victims of an egregious injustice, a vicious example of the tyranny of the white majority in wartime. In 1948 Congress authorized token restitution for Japanese Americans, and a total of about $38 million was paid to claimants during the 1950s—payments representing about 10 cents for each dollar of loss. Years later, after much litigation and quiet political pressure, Japanese Americans belatedly received vindication and additional restitution. In 1983 U.S. District Court Judge Marilyn Hall Patel vacated Fred Korematsu's conviction. Judge Patel's action came after Korematsu's attorneys discovered secret government documents proving that government officials knew that Japanese Americans posed no dangers to national security in wartime but withheld this evidence from the Supreme Court. In 1988 President Ronald Reagan, speaking for all Americans, acknowledged that wartime relocation had been unnecessary and wrong and apologized to the Japanese American community. In 1989 Congress agreed to pay each of the estimated 60,000 survivors of the wartime relocation experience $25,000. Although some embittered victims dismissed the money as "too little, too late," others were grateful and appreciated the symbolic significance of the gesture.

After the war Japanese Americans did not protest the gross injustices they had been forced to endure. They internalized the anger, hurt, and shame associated with the relocation experience. They rarely talked about those experiences even among close friends and family. Instead they vowed to put their wartime experiences behind them and go forward—to prove to the government and white majority that had abused them that they were good citizens and productive members of society. Their postwar record of achievement was astonishing. Japanese Americans, by any measure, are among the most successful and prosperous groups in the country. They have integrated themselves into the larger society. They have achieved distinction in the sciences, the arts, medicine, the law, engineering, academic life, business, finance, athletics, and politics. They are among the leaders in amount of education attained and annual per capita income. In the half-century following their harrowing wartime experiences, Japanese Americans and their descendants have emphatically demonstrated that they are good Americans, in fact better citizens than those who deprived them of their civil liberties during World War II.

In contrast to the brutal mistreatment of Japanese Americans in wartime, Chinese Americans fared comparatively well. Chinese Americans enjoyed the sympathy and goodwill of most Americans because China was a wartime ally of the United States. Americans also felt much sympathy for the Chinese who were suffering terribly at the hands of the Japanese soldiers during the war years. Because of their status as allies and because of acute labor shortages in war industries, unprecedented opportunities for Chinese workers suddenly opened up. By the thousands Chinese families streamed out of the Chinatown ghettos into the mainstream of American life. Most of these mobile families never returned to the Chinatowns, and after the war they headed for the suburbs.

In 1943 Congress at long lost repealed the Chinese Exclusion Act, that embarrassing artifact of anti-Asian racism that had been in place since 1882. For the first time in over 60 years it was now possible for people to emigrate from China to the United States. In addition the government finally extended citizenship to thousands of Chinese, many of them now quite elderly, who were long-time residents of the United States but had hitherto been ineligible for citizenship.

THE POLITICS OF WAR

War moved the country toward the Right. As prosperity returned, many Americans, with something to conserve, became increasingly conservative. In the 1942 midterm elections resurgent Republicans gained 77 seats in the House of Representatives and 10 in the Senate. The Democratic majority in the House was shaved to 218 to 208. Democrats were hurt by a low voter turnout. A conservative coalition of northern Republicans and southern Democrats, which had emerged following the 1938 elections, consolidated its control of Congress. Roosevelt, sensing the political drift and preoccupied with the immense task of running history's largest war, put social reform on the back burner. The conservative coalition snuffed out many New Deal agencies in 1942 and 1943 on the grounds that wartime economic revival had rendered them obsolete. Among their most prominent victims were the Works Progress Administration (WPA), the Civilian Conservation Corps (CCC), and the National Youth Administration (NYA). Federal spending for social programs declined sharply in wartime.

Antitrust activity also ceased. Businessmen poured into Washington to run new wartime bureaucracies, and they regained much of the popularity and prestige they had lost during the 1930s. Depression-bred popular resentment of business greed and social irresponsibility gave way to a new image of businessmen as patriotic partners providing the tools needed to win the war. Roosevelt, needing business cooperation for the war effort, cultivated a cordial relationship among his former adversaries. Populistic, anti-business rhetoric vanished from public discourse. Secretary of War Henry Stimson observed, "If you are going to go to war . . . in a capitalist country, you have got to let business make money out of the process or business won't work." Many corporate leaders abandoned their bitter criticisms of Roosevelt and New Deal policies, having discovered that they could profit from the policies of the welfare state turned warfare state. Businessmen switched their political strategy from one of trying to dismantle big government to trying to use it to their advantage. Corporate executives would continue these new political strategies in the postwar era.

The war effort further centralized the corporate economy because 90 percent of the billions of dollars the government spent on war contracts went to 100 large corporations. Big business got bigger in wartime and most companies enjoyed profits surpassing anything earned during the best years of the 1920s. Wartime politics showed that the positive state, erected by liberals to fight the Great Depression and promote social reform, could be manned by conservatives who would use its power to promote business interests, curtail reform, and attack trade unions—while winning a war. Conservatives continued to apply what they learned in wartime during the postwar era.

In the 1944 election President Roosevelt did not hesitate to seek a fourth term, and no Democrat dared challenge him. FDR, to keep his party unified in wartime, dumped his vice president, Henry Wallace. Wallace, a fervent New Dealer, had alienated powerful big city bosses and conservative southerners within the Democratic Party, so Roosevelt replaced him with a candidate acceptable to all factions within the party, Missouri Senator Harry Truman. Truman had rendered valuable service to the country in wartime, heading a watchdog committee which had investigated government war contracts. Senator Truman's energetic, scrupulous efforts saved taxpayers billions of dollars and expedited delivery of crucial war materials. Despite his wartime service, though, Truman was still a relative unknown in 1944, an undistinguished political journeyman but acceptable to all powerful factions within the Democratic Party.

Several candidates sought the Republican nomination in 1944, including the 1940 nominee Wendell Willkie, Minnesota Governor Harold Stassen, Ohio Governor John Bricker, Senator Robert Taft of Ohio, and Governor Thomas E. Dewey of New York. Willkie flamed out early in the primaries and the 42-year-old Dewey went on to an easy first-ballot nomination. Dewey chose Bricker to be his vice-presidential running mate after California Governor Earl Warren, Dewey's first choice, declined.

The contest between Roosevelt and Dewey was a rather dull and one-sided affair. In the eyes of many observers, Dewey did not appear presidential. He was a short, neat little man who came across as rather aloof, cold, and stiff. He also did not cultivate a good relation with the press. Alice Roosevelt Longworth asked, "How can we be expected to vote for a man who looks like the bridegroom on a wedding cake?"

Newly empowered, organized labor played a major role in the 1944 campaign. The CIO, through its Political Action Committee, circumvented laws restricting union activities and funneled millions of dollars into the campaign for the Roosevelt ticket and many liberal congressional candidates. It also registered voters, circulated campaign literature, and got out the vote on election day.

Dewey's campaign strategy differed from previous Republican efforts. He accepted the New Deal welfare state but accused New Dealers of waste and inefficiency. He endorsed U.S. membership in a postwar United Nations. He also refused to make Roosevelt's foreign policy a campaign issue, not wishing to revive isolationist issues during the war. By embracing the welfare state and internationalism, Dewey placed both the New Deal and the war beyond partisan debate. His campaign proved to be ineffective.

Roosevelt, who did not campaign much, exploited his prestige as wartime Commander-in-Chief of a vast military effort that was winning everywhere. He attacked the Republicans for their isolationism and reminded the electorate that they had been responsible for the Depression. He called attention to legislation benefiting veterans, including the "G.I. Bill of Rights." Ominously, Roosevelt had aged dramatically by 1944. Friends and political associates noticed that he had grown thin and frail. His hands trembled and there were dark circles under his eyes. His doctors knew that he was suffering from heart disease and hypertension. Most Americans, however, were not informed or apparently took no notice of Roosevelt's failing health and happily voted for him one more time.

Roosevelt easily won his fourth presidential election victory in November, carrying 36 states to Dewey's 12. His electoral vote count was 432 to 99, but his popular vote tally was only 25.6 million to 22 million for Dewey. Roosevelt's 53.4 percent of the popular vote was his lowest margin ever. The Democrats gained 22 seats in the House but lost one in the Senate. The conservative coalition retained its control of Congress. The 1944 vote revealed an important demographic change that was occurring. The Democratic Party was becoming more urban as a result of the wartime migration that had lured millions of workers into the cities.

The huge increase in the size and scope of the federal government, particularly the executive branch, represented the most important wartime political development. As government spent more and more money, it became far more centralized than ever before. Federal bureaucracies assumed many economic functions previously performed by the private sector. The number of federal employees rose from 1 million in 1940 to 3.8 million in 1945, the most ever in the nation's history. Wartime agencies proliferated, generating an alphabetical avalanche that dwarfed the New Deal. President Roosevelt issued more executive orders during World War II than all previous presidents had during the entire history of the nation. The most powerful politicians in the country, after Roosevelt, were the men he appointed to run the war agencies. The President recruited most of these "war lords" of Washington from the ranks of business.

As the executive branch made a quantum leap in size and power, Congress suffered a relative decline in power and prestige. Through his active participation in foreign conferences and various domestic agencies coordinating the gigantic war effort, Roosevelt significantly enhanced the powers of the presidency and set an example followed by all postwar presidents. The "imperial" presidency had its origins in World War II.

The Supreme Court, dominated by Roosevelt's eight liberal appointees, refused to review any cases involving wartime extensions of federal power into economic affairs, an arena in which the Court had been especially active during the New Deal years. The Court also refused to intervene in cases involving wartime violations of civil liberties, except to affirm the relocation of Japanese Americans from the Pacific Coast. The FBI acquired enhanced authority to spy on Americans and to tap telephones in national security cases.

The war multiplied the points of contact between the federal government and its citizens. Millions of names were added to the Social Security rolls and everyone who worked had to pay federal income taxes. War experiences strengthened the tendency of people to look to Washington for solutions to their problems. This trend weakened social bonds and undermined local governments. People traded some of their personal freedom for greater government control and an enhanced sense of social security. This tradeoff of liberty for security carried into the postwar era.

Washington became the biggest of all war boomtowns. In 1942 the Pentagon, the world's largest office building, opened. It housed over 35,000 bureaucrats and its offices consumed 30 tons of paper annually. Lobbyists stalked the corridors of political power seeking ever-larger shares of the vast wartime expenditures flowing from Washington into corporate coffers. The broker-state, a creation of New Dealers, was much refined and significantly expanded. The government also subsidized the creation of new industries that were necessitated by the war. For example, with supplies of natural rubber from Southeast Asia cut, Washington spent nearly a billion dollars to create a synthetic rubber industry.

Much basic research for new weaponry and war industries had come from universities and colleges, which committed themselves to meeting the needs of military research. Most colleges and universities suffered no loss of enrollment during the war despite massive conscription, because the government utilized their campuses for training enlisted men and officers. In addition, the number of women enrolled increased dramatically. After the war the GI Bill, which paid for millions of veterans' college educations, ensured continuing expansion of higher education.

World War II created a wartime partnership among business, universities, Congress, and the Pentagon. This "military-industrial complex" (as President Eisenhower would later call it during his famed farewell address), nurtured during the war, came of age during the Cold War and became a powerful lobby for creating the permanent war economy in the postwar decades. The military-industrial complex guaranteed that the vastly enhanced authority of government in American economic and scientific affairs would continue after the war.

WAR AND CULTURE

During the war television had not yet come of age. Print journalism (newspapers and magazines), radio, and movies flourished in vigorous variety. The three major mass media enjoyed a rough equality. People spent hours each week listening to the radio in their homes or while driving their cars, but they also read one or two daily newspapers, subscribed to several magazines, and went to the movies on the average of twice a week.

Sales of both fiction and nonfiction books increased sharply in wartime. People had more money to spend on books and more time available for reading. Writers generally were less alienated than they had been during the 1920s and 1930s. In 1943 Ayn Rand wrote *The Fountainhead*, a best seller that praised individualism over collectivism. Friedrich Hayek, an expatriate Austrian economist living in the United States, wrote *The Road to Serfdom*, a conservative tract that argued that modern liberalism was the path to tyranny. Although a difficult book to read, *The Road to Serfdom* enjoyed wide sales. It is important to point out that by no means did most Americans read serious fiction or nonfiction in wartime. By far the most popular literary genre was comic books. One-third of young adults read comic books regularly. Special editions of the most popular comic books were made available to soldiers. Some adults read only comic books.

A rising generation of young writers found in the war the central experience of their lives, among them Saul Bellow, Irwin Shaw, and John Hersey. Many war novels and journalistic accounts of the war made the best-seller lists. The best and most popular war correspondent was Ernie Pyle, a quiet midwesterner who wrote with great insight and accuracy about ordinary soldiers in combat. His *Brave Men*, published in 1945 after he had been killed covering the Okinawa campaign, remains the finest account of GI life ever written.

Ballroom dancing also flourished during the war. The popularity of jitterbugging, a carryover from the late 1930s, continued unabated, especially among young people, for whom it offered a distinctive world with its own clothes, language, and ritual behaviors. Energetic, athletic youngsters spun, whirled, and tossed their partners to the pulsing rhythms of hot jazz. Other couples enjoyed the more sedate pleasures of fox-trots and waltzes. Nightlife, particularly New York City nightlife, sparkled. Patrons at the Copacabana or the Latin Quarter could spend $100 in an evening of drinking, dancing, and enjoying the singing of young crooners like Frank Sinatra and Perry Como, or the sounds of Big Bands like Tommy Dorsey's or Frankie Carle's.

Professional spectator sports drew large crowds, and racetracks enjoyed historic high attendance in wartime. With most of the outstanding major league baseball players in military service, pennant races and World Series continued with mostly teenagers, castoffs, and overage players. World series games were broadcast overseas to the troops to maintain morale. Minor league baseball was suspended for the duration, spring training was cancelled, and night games were discontinued. A women's professional baseball league started up and, after a rugged start, flourished in wartime. Many of the women were fine athletes who played a spirited and highly skilled brand of baseball. The women's league continued its run into the 1950s before disbanding, mainly because of a lack of fan interest.

HOLLYWOOD GOES TO WAR

Hollywood prospered in wartime even though the major studios produced far fewer movies a year than in the late 1930s. Before-tax profits increased from $42 million in 1939 to $239 million in 1945, and attendance at the nation's 18,000 movie houses tripled between 1941 and 1945. Surveys showed that about 75 percent of Americans went to movies. The typical moviegoer patronized a neighborhood theater at least twice a week. Millions of them also avidly read Hollywood fan magazines and newspaper stories about movie stars. Two Hollywood gossip columnists, Hedda Hopper and Louella Parsons, were syndicated and had millions of devoted readers nationwide. The film industry was dominated by five major studios—Metro-Goldwyn-Mayer (MGM), Paramount, Warner Brothers, RKO, and Twentieth Century Fox—and each employed a small army of actors, directors, writers, technicians, and production personnel who turned out hundreds of pictures each year to slake the great American thirst for celluloid entertainment. In 1945 the Big Five enjoyed vertical control over both the creation and distribution of their films; they made the pictures and then distributed them through their own theater chains. In 1945 studio-owned theater chains earned over 70 percent of total box office receipts.

Hollywood had to adapt to wartime conditions. Most top male stars either got drafted or enlisted, and thousands of technicians and production personnel went off to war. Jimmy Stewart flew bombing missions over Germany. Henry Fonda joined the Navy and served in the South Pacific. Clark Gable, "The King," joined the Army Air Corps. A lesser star from Warner Brothers, Ronald Reagan, was assigned to an Army Air Corps motion picture unit in Hollywood that made documentary and propaganda films. Many actors not in the armed forces, along with top women stars like Dorothy Lamour, Rita Hayworth, and Betty Grable, entertained the troops both in the states and around the world.

Even though the major studios continued to turn out the standard genres—westerns, detective thrillers, adventure films, romances, gangster pictures, and musicals—wartime Hollywood made mostly war movies. The studios churned out a flood of war and spy stories. Many Chinese actors got work in Hollywood films for the first time, playing Japanese villains. John Wayne starred in a series of war epics glorifying various branches of the military service—*Flying Tigers, Fighting Seabees*, and *The Sands of Iwo Jima*, the last about the Marine Corps. A 1944 war film starring Bing Crosby who played a Catholic priest, *Going My Way*, was the biggest box-office hit since *Gone with the Wind*. The best war film was *The Story of GI Joe*, adapted from Ernie Pyle's reporting. It contained no preaching, no propaganda, no hateful enemy stereotypes, and no heroes. It depicted American soldiers as skilled professionals doing a dirty job, trying mainly to survive and return home after the war. Hollywood also made several excellent war documentaries, the best a series produced by Frank Capra and John Huston. Another wartime film genre was the "canteen film." This was a celluloid USO show, hosted by a big name star and featuring celebrity guests who sang, danced, and told jokes—all promoting the war effort.

Hollywood films in wartime continued to project cultural stereotypes onto the silver screen. African American soldiers occasionally appeared in war films, usually as "happy Negroes," jiving, dancing, grinning, and laughing. Jewish soldiers were portrayed as guys named "Brooklyn" who looked forward to returning to Ebbets Field after the war and jeering at the Giants. Women were usually portrayed as the "weaker sex," dependent upon men and totally involved with their homes, children, and marriage. Native Americans continued to be depicted as primitive and duplicitous savages. The Japanese were portrayed as depraved, cruel, and vicious, with many references to "slant-eyed rats," "little yellow monkeys," and "beasts." Responding to government pressure applied through the Office of War Information, war films portrayed American allies such as the Chinese, the British, and the French as heroic. Wartime movie Russians were hearty, simple people and gallant fighters. In *Mission to Moscow* an American diplomat goes off to Moscow to meet the Russians. There he is tailed by two jolly KGB agents who cheerfully inform the American star that the infamous purge trials of the 1930s were necessary to save the Soviet Union from a Fascist coup.

Wartime Hollywood had to continue to conform to strict moral codes and observe political limits as well. Churches functioned as moral watchdogs for the movie industry. The major studies were scrupulous in placating these powerful censors, especially the Catholic Church's Legion of Decency, which purportedly spoke for the 20 percent of the national movie audience that was Catholic. The studios tried to anticipate Legion objections and pre-censor their movies. The major film factories also resorted to considerable self-regulation to placate the self-appointed guardians of movie morality. Criminals could never escape unpunished in a Hollywood film. Sexual contact was carefully limited to gentle kissing between fully clothed adults. Homosexuality was never mentioned, much less displayed. Profanity was forbidden. Characters were statically portrayed either as total villains with no redeeming features or else as heroic figures with no faults or weaknesses. Ideas were censored as well as morality. Films had to stay within mainstream ideological boundaries. Radical ideas or serious social criticism was excised from Hollywood pictures. Serious political discourse rarely found its way into Hollywood films, and when it did it usually parroted the bland liberalism emanating from Franklin Roosevelt's wartime White House.

Most wartime films were mediocre, but a few qualified as serious art. In 1945 Billy Wilder directed *Lost Weekend*, starring Ray Milland and Jane Wyman, a serious, sensitive treatment of alcoholism and its ruinous effects upon the lives of people. *Lost Weekend* won an Academy Award for best picture, and both Milland and Wilder also received "Oscars." One World War II film has become a classic. In 1942 Warner Brothers brought out a low-budget melodrama set in Morocco, a tale of an American nightclub owner, Rick Blaine, who hides patriotic idealism beneath a hard-boiled surface. In the end Rick sacrifices both his business and the woman he loves to rescue an anti-Nazi resistance fighter. The picture was *Casablanca*, and Humphrey Bogart played Rick Blaine, becoming a cult hero to millions of moviegoers in the postwar era.

WARTIME RADIO

In the pre-television wartime years the electronic medium of radio became more popular than ever. Just as the film industry was dominated by five major studios, the radio industry was controlled by four major national networks. The National Broadcasting Company (NBC) was the oldest and largest. Columbia Broadcasting System (CBS) was second, followed by the American Broadcasting Company (ABC), which began as a spinoff from NBC in 1941, and the Mutual Broadcasting System. More than half of the country's 75,000 radio stations were affiliated with one of the major networks, and all the networks had affiliates in the large metropolitan centers of the nation.

Radio programming fell into different categories or genres. The most popular in 1945 were musical shows, and one of the top ones was the "Lucky Strike Hit Parade." Other popular musicals featured well-known singers such as Kate Smith and Bing Crosby. For aficionados of serious music there was the NBC symphony orchestra sponsored by Standard Oil and the New York Metropolitan Opera sponsored by Texaco. The second most popular type of program was drama, including the daytime dramas or "soap operas," whose large audiences consisted mostly of women. Prime-time programming at night featured a variety of action-adventure dramas with a cast of heroic detectives, cowboys, and space warriors who overcame villains and upheld law and order. Other genres included quiz programs and situation comedies. The longest-running and one of the most popular of these weekly comedies in 1945 was "Amos 'n Andy." The show highlighted the usually hilarious adventures of two African Americans from the South now living in Harlem, but the characters of Amos and Andy were played by two white actors.

Radio was also a prime source of news about the war. World War II was the first war given live media coverage. War correspondent Edward R. Murrow described the Battle of Britain for American radio audiences in the summer of 1940. People listened to his deep, solemn voice and heard shrill air raid sirens and the roar of exploding bombs in the background, as Murrow vividly described the "blitz" of London. He brought the European war into American living rooms. Throughout the war, foreign correspondents in Europe and Asia often risked their lives to go everywhere the soldiers went and transmit first-hand accounts of battles to the folks back home. Radio correspondents hit the beaches at Normandy with the invading forces. Many of them were killed or wounded in action. Never had war journalism been so direct or authentic.

But censors often edited the news. Broadcasters often sacrificed factual accuracy for dramatic effect. War news had entertainment as well as informational value. Wartime radio remained essentially an entertainment medium, always accompanied by incessant commercial messages urging listeners to buy cigarettes, soap, and chewing gum. Radio often appeared to be little more than a conduit through which advertisers poured their commercials for the myriad products they manufactured. Advertisers also had great influence on the content of the shows that they sponsored, including news and news commentaries. Sponsors favored the largest possible audiences and frowned upon any programming that was artistically or politically controversial, because they feared it might alienate viewers. The biggest single purchaser of airtime, Procter and Gamble, the giant cleaning products company, had a policy of never offending a single listener. In 1945 good radio often was subordinated to good salesmanship.

BIBLIOGRAPHY

The best general studies of the home front are Richard Polenberg, *War and Society: The United States, 1941–1945* and John Morton Blum, *"V" Was for Victory: Politics and American Culture during World War II.* The best social history of the United States at war is Geoffrey Perrett, *Days of Sadness, Years of Triumph: The American People, 1939–1945.* Susan M. Hartmann, *The Homefront and Beyond: American Women in the 1940s* is an account of women and the war. See also Sherna B. Gluck, *Rosie the Riveter Revisited: Women, the War, and Social Change.* Neil A. Wynn, in *The Afro-American and the Second World War,* has recorded the crucial experiences of black people in wartime. There is a large amount of literature on the relocation of Japanese Americans. The best account of this atrocity is Edward Spencer, *Impounded People: Japanese Americans and World War II.* See also Roger Daniels, *Concentration Camps U.S.A.: Japanese Americans and World War II* and Allan R. Bosworth, *America's Concentration Camps.* Jeanne Wakatsuki Houston and James D. Houston, *Farewell to Manzanar* is a compelling story of a Japanese family interned for the duration of the war. Roland Young, *Congressional Politics in the Second World War* is a good political history. Richard R. Lingeman, *Don't You Know There's a War On?* is a general account of popular culture in wartime. Joel Greenberg, *Hollywood in the Forties* is an account of wartime movies and their effects on the populace. John Brooks, *The Great Leap: The Past Twenty-Five Years in America* (1966) is an important book highlighting the immense changes brought about in this country by World War II which shaped the postwar era. The finest novel about the home front experience is Harriet Arnow, *The Dollmaker,* which movingly describes the disruptions and dislocations of war.

CHAPTER
14
Epilogue:
The American People
in 1945

On August 14, 1945, the Japanese government announced Japan's unconditional surrender, bringing history's largest war to a triumphant conclusion for the United States and its allies. Across America people erupted in frenzied victory celebrations. There were gigantic parades in New York, Chicago, San Francisco, and other large cities. In the American countryside, in small towns and villages, citizens joined in spontaneous victory parades. All rejoiced at the final destruction of the Axis menace and the advent of peace throughout a battered world.

In 1945 approximately 140 million Americans were inhabiting the nation, its territories or serving overseas in the armed forces. World War II had had a dramatic impact on the lives of nearly all Americans—on where they lived and what kind of work they did. It also affected family life and patterns of leisure and recreation. The war experience set demographic patterns that would persist for the next half-century.

At war's end the United States was vastly changed from the nation that had been thrust suddenly into the cauldron of war by the Japanese surprise attack on Pearl Harbor on December 7, 1941. During the intervening three years and nine months it had undergone profound transformations that forever changed the social landscape and created new possibilities for its people.

During the war years huge military forces were raised and sent to fight on land, sea, and air around the globe. The world's most productive economy sustained America's large civilian population and simultaneously supplied its own and its allies' military forces fighting the Axis powers. The war revitalized the American economy, lifted the American people out of the Great Depression, and inaugurated a cycle of affluence that stretched into the 1970s. War also enhanced the power and reach of

August 14, 1945, at 7:00 P.M. Washington, D.C. time, President Truman formally an-
nounces the end of World War II. Seated to his left: Cordell Hull. To his right sit James F.
Byrnes & Admiral William Leahy.

the federal government. It thrust the United States irrevocably into the center of world affairs and destroyed forever isolationist tendencies that had
lingered tenaciously until the morning that Japanese aircraft bombed Pearl
Harbor. War transformed the nation's social structure as well. Well-paying
jobs in war industries located in coastal cities triggered a vast migration that
depopulated the countryside. War opened up unprecedented economic
opportunities for women, African Americans, and Hispanic Americans. At
the same time, war, hysteria, and race prejudice combined to harm gravely
the Japanese American population who lived along the West Coast; Army
troops uprooted 120,000 people from their homes and interned them in
desolate camps in isolated desert regions for the duration.

WORLD WAR AND ITS LEGACIES

World War II was an intense, transforming experience for most Americans. The war fundamentally changed American society in many ways,
and these changes were more profound and permanent than any since
the industrial revolution of the late nineteenth century. On the eve of war
Americans suffered from lingering effects of the Great Depression—high
unemployment, low productivity, massive poverty, and lurking doubts

about the vitality of American institutions and the purpose of national life. Americans looked out at a threatening world engulfed in war, a world in which their nation played only a peripheral role. They quarreled bitterly among themselves over President Roosevelt's conduct of foreign policy, until the bombing of Pearl Harbor abruptly ended the debate.

Four years later a unified, proud, and powerful nation emerged victoriously from war. Its armed forces and industrial might had played decisive roles in destroying Fascism, militarism, and imperialism around the globe. The United States had won the largest war in human history. This war revitalized the American economy, which emerged far more productive and prosperous than ever. More Americans were living better than they ever had before, and the proportion of poor Americans had been reduced to historic lows. American faith in capitalism and democratic institutions had also been restored. Compared with those of other nations at war, American casualties had been light. American civilians had been spared the devastations and terrors of a war that was fought outside its continental boundaries. Fewer than 12 percent of the nation's population had served in the armed forces; over half of those who did never left the states, and the majority of those who were sent overseas never experienced a moment's combat.

The day the war against Japan ended, the United States reached its apogee as a global power. It strode the world as an international colossus; its armed forces, linked to its nuclear monopoly, made it the most powerful nation-state in the history of the planet. Its statesmen took the lead in creating a new international agency to preserve peace in the postwar era. Fittingly, the United Nation's permanent home would be New York, the financial and cultural capital of the new imperium.

The war was a watershed from which emerged the dominant patterns of postwar life. The war forced Americans to accept involvement with the world beyond national boundaries; there could be no reversion to isolationism after 1945. Their war experiences gave Americans new confidence that they could solve all serious problems, both internal and external. They had proved that they had both the will and the means to lick depression at home and aggression abroad.

The major contours of post-1945 American history originated in the war experience. The 40-year Cold War with the Soviet Union that dominated international affairs for decades after the war stemmed from the tensions and conflicts that strained the Grand Alliance. The Soviet leader, Joseph Stalin, distrusted the Western leaders, whom he suspected of deliberately delaying the opening of a second front against the Germans. Even before the war's end Truman and Churchill were alarmed by Stalin's violation of the Yalta accords in Poland. At Potsdam the Big Three quarreled over the issue of Soviet reparations from Germany and other looming postwar political problems. The American willingness to use atomic bombs on the Japanese coupled with our unwillingness to share nuclear technology with the Soviets or even keep them informed of the progress of the atomic bomb project frightened the Soviets and aroused their suspicions.

The war experience significantly influenced the political life of the nation and established patterns that would prevail in the postwar era. American politics shifted to the Right. Americans generally became more conservative fundamentally because the return of prosperity gave them more to conserve. The Republican Party made a significant comeback during the war, and the informal conservative coalition of southern Democrats and northern Republicans consolidated its control of the legislative process. Leviathan was the most important political legacy of the war. Big government became the foundation of the modern social welfare/warfare state that was to dominate American politics in the decades following the war. Washington also regulated the economy and was the conservator of the natural environment. In addition, during the war the federal government became by far the nation's largest employer. In the postwar era the huge federal bureaucracies became a fourth branch of the national government; most of the actions taken by the federal government directly affecting the lives and wealth of its citizens were taken by government bureaucrats. The organizational society, a society dominated by large public and private bureaucracies, that has characterized the postwar era came of age during World War II.

World World II left a mixed environmental legacy. On the one hand it heightened awareness that the American economy was becoming less self-sufficient and increasingly dependent on foreign sources for strategic minerals and oil. On the other hand, the crash production programs of wartime to outproduce the enemy accelerated the depletion of natural resources. During the war energy sources, technology, and industrial capacity were all maximally utilized. Trees were cut down. Air and water were polluted. Farmers made far greater use of chemical fertilizers and pesticides to enhance output. Ecological awareness and conservation issues were neglected in wartime; these were luxuries a nation engaged in a total war for national survival could not afford. These trends established in wartime continued in the postwar era. Deteriorating environmental conditions finally forced a surge of environmental concerns that surfaced during the 1960s.

Postwar economic policies derived from the awareness that federal spending in wartime had finally ended economic depression. Government officials assumed responsibility for managing the postwar American economy to ensure full employment and economic stability. Public opinion polls indicated that a majority of American voters accepted the new role of the federal government as manager of the national economy. They had abandoned their traditional belief that economic affairs were the responsibility primarily of individuals and the private sector. Congress, by a large bipartisan majority, enacted the Employment Act of 1946, which institutionalized the notion of government responsibility for full employment and which created a new agency, the Council of Economic Advisers, to advise the President on economic policy. Political leaders during the postwar era assumed that government fiscal practices could stabilize the business cycle and promote economic growth. New understanding of the role of consumerism in sustaining economic growth meant the government would promote spending instead of saving after the war. The Federal Reserve Board would often use its power to raise or lower interest rates in order to influence the pace of economic activity.

In the course of fighting the Great Depression and World War II, Americans evolved a unique form of political economy. It conformed to neither classic *laissez-faire* capitalist nor socialist models. Americans opted for a middle way, a "mixed economy," a uniquely American blend of public and private incentives. Private enterprise—corporate capitalism, small business, and farming—continued to flourish, but it co-existed within an intricate framework of local, state, and federal regulation. Despite continuing antitrust laws and government intervention to curtail the power of monopoly and oligopoly, the postwar economy continued the centralizing trends that accelerated during World War II. The pattern of a mixed economy increasingly dominated by giant corporations that had come of age during the war characterized American economic life in the postwar era.

The struggles and achievements of women and various minorities in wartime planted the seeds of their postwar drives for equal access to the American dream. Wartime work for millions of American women represented a crucial breakthrough, for both economic independence and an enlarged sense of self-worth. Even though most women were forced out of their good jobs at war's end and in time the memories of war work faded, these experiences were not forgotten. A precedent was established, key attitudinal changes had occurred, and in time these breakthroughs would bear fruit.

For African Americans the enactment of the Fair Employment Practices in wartime established the precedent of using the power of the federal government to strike down racist barriers to economic opportunity. Wartime service gave African Americans a greater sense of worth and entitlement. Black veterans believed that they deserved equal treatment, the right to vote, and economic opportunity, and they refused to resume the status of second-class citizens. They were prepared to lead the fight to obtain all the benefits of American citizenship and to assume all its responsibilities.

The war also afforded Hispanic Americans, predominantly Mexican Americans, opportunities for military service and for good jobs in war industries. In the years after the war Hispanic Americans became increasingly an urban population, the large majority of them inhabiting *barrios* in Los Angeles, San Diego, Phoenix, El Paso, San Antonio, Denver, Kansas

City, Chicago, and New York. It was in the cities that Mexican Americans made their postwar drive for economic opportunity, political involvement, and civil rights.

War service for thousands of Native Americans fostered ethnic pride, provided job training, and expanded their horizons. Thousands of Native Americans went to college on the G.I. Bill. Most of the leaders in the Native American community were World War II veterans. These leaders, most of whom had left the reservation during the war and settled in cities after returning to the states, led the postwar fight for civil rights and political empowerment.

The war restored America's philosophic birthright, an optimistic sense of individual and national potential that would shape the national

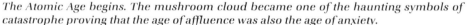

The Atomic Age begins. The mushroom cloud became one of the haunting symbols of catastrophe proving that the age of affluence was also the age of anxiety.

experience for the next three decades. The Axis powers were destroyed, the Soviet Union exhausted, and Western Europe depleted, but America was strong, prosperous, and free. Its people felt ready for the "American Century" they knew lay ahead. America's economy was powerful, its resources were abundant, and it had the scientific and technological talent to use them. Success in wartime gave Americans confidence and great expectations for a future that appeared to stretch limitlessly before them.

Americans also soberly confronted a future that they feared could bring a recurrence of the Great Depression. Could prosperity, growth, and full employment be sustained in a postwar era without the stimulus of the war economy? Could jobs be found for the millions of returning veterans and displaced war workers? Americans also worried about threats to their peace and security posed by the expanding Communist power, the Soviet Union. Perhaps the war had not made the world safe for democracy. Perhaps there was not going to be an American century after all, or at least not an uncontested American century. Most of all, Americans were alarmed by the nuclear shadow they had cast over the postwar era.

And so Americans in the summer of 1945 faced the future with mixed feelings: feelings of pride, confidence, and hope, but also feelings of fear—of the return of depression, of expanding Soviet power, and of a nuclear Armageddon.

BIBLIOGRAPHY

Students wishing to read about American history and culture during the mid-1940s are referred to the books listed in the bibliography for Chapter 13, "Home Front USA." General accounts that carry the story of America forward from World War II include Robert Wiebe, *The Segmented Society: An Introduction to the Meaning of America*; Richard S. Polenberg, *One Nation Divisible: Class, Race, and Ethnicity in the United States since 1938*; William E. Leuchtenburg, *In the Shadow of FDR: From Harry Truman to Ronald Reagan*; and Alonzo Hamby, *Liberalism and Its Challengers: Roosevelt to Reagan*. For two fine regional studies of the impact of World War II see Gerald D. Nash, *World War II and the West: Reshaping the Economy* and Avram Mezerick, *The Revolt of the South and West*.

APPENDIX

A

The Declaration of Independence

When in the Course of human events, it becomes necessary for one people to dissolve the political bands which have connected them with another, and to assume among the Powers of the earth, the separate and equal station to which the Laws of Nature and of Nature's God entitle them, a decent respect to the opinions of mankind requires that they should declare the causes which impel them to the separation.

We hold these truths to be self-evident, that all men are created equal, that they are endowed by their Creator with certain unalienable Rights, that among these are Life, Liberty and the pursuit of Happiness. That to secure these rights, Governments are instituted among Men, deriving their just powers from the consent of the governed, That whenever any Form of Government becomes destructive of these ends, it is the Right of the people to alter or to abolish it, and to institute new Government, laying its foundation on such principles and organizing its powers in such form, as to them shall seem most likely to effect their Safety and Happiness. Prudence, indeed, will dictate that Governments long established should not be changed for light and transient causes; and accordingly all experience hath shown, that mankind are more disposed to suffer, while evils are sufferable, than to right themselves by abolishing the forms to

which they are accustomed. But when a long train of abuses and usurpations, pursuing invariably the same Object evinces a design to reduce them under absolute Despotism, it is their right, it is their duty, to throw off such Government, and to provide new Guards for their future security.—Such has been the patient sufferance of these Colonies; and such is now the necessity which constrains them to alter their former Systems of Government. The history of the present King of Great Britain is a history of repeated injuries and usurpations, all having in direct object the establishment of an absolute Tyranny over these States. To prove this, let Facts be submitted to a candid world.

He has refused his Assent to Laws, the most wholesome and necessary for the public good.

He has forbidden his Governors to pass Laws of immediate and pressing importance, unless suspended in their operation till his Assent should be obtained; and when so suspended, he has utterly neglected to attend to them.

He has refused to pass other Laws for the accommodation of large districts of people, unless those people would relinquish the right of Representation in the Legislature, a right inestimable to them and formidable to tyrants only.

He has called together legislative bodies

at places unusual, uncomfortable, and distant from the depository of their public Records, for the sole purpose of fatiguing them into compliance with his measures.

He has dissolved Representative Houses repeatedly, for opposing with manly firmness his invasions on the rights of the people.

He has refused for a long time, after such dissolutions, to cause others to be elected; whereby the Legislative Powers, incapable of Annihilation, have returned to the People at large for their exercise; the State remaining in the mean time exposed to all the dangers of invasion from without, and convulsions within.

He has endeavoured to prevent the population of these States; for that purpose obstructing the Laws of Naturalization of Foreigners; refusing to pass others to encourage their migration hither, and raising the conditions of new Appropriations of Lands.

He has obstructed the Administration of Justice, by refusing his Assent to Laws for establishing Judiciary powers.

He has made Judges dependent on his Will alone, for the tenure of their offices, and the amount and payment of their salaries.

He has erected a multitude of New Offices, and sent hither swarms of Officers to harass our People, and eat out their substance.

He has kept among us in times of peace, Standing Armies without the Consent of our legislature.

He has affected to render the Military independent of and superior to the Civil power.

He has combined with others to subject us to a jurisdiction foreign to our constitution, and unacknowledged by our laws; giving his Assent to their acts of pretended Legislation:

For quartering large bodies of armed troops among us:

For protecting them, by a mock Trial, from punishment for any Murders which they should commit on the Inhabitants of these States:

For cutting off our Trade with all parts of the world:

For imposing taxes on us without our Consent:

For depriving us in many cases, of the benefits of Trial by Jury:

For transporting us beyond Seas to be tried for pretended offences:

For abolishing the free System of English Laws in a neighbouring Province, establishing therein an Arbitrary government, and enlarging its Boundaries so as to render it at once an example and fit instrument for introducing the same absolute rule into these Colonies:

For taking away our Charters, abolishing our most valuable Laws, and altering fundamentally the Forms of our Governments:

For suspending our own Legislature, and declaring themselves invested with Power to legislate for us in all cases whatsoever.

He has abdicated Government here, by declaring us out of his Protection and waging War against us.

He has plundered our seas, ravaged our Coasts, burnt our towns, and destroyed the lives of our people.

He is at this time transporting large Armies of foreign Mercenaries to compleat the works of death, desolation and tyranny, already begun with circumstances of Cruelty & perfidy scarcely paralleled in the most barbarous ages, and totally unworthy the Head of a civilized nation.

He has constrained our fellow Citizens taken Captive on the high Seas to bear Arms against their Country, to become the executioners of their friends and Brethren, or to fall themselves by their Hands.

He has excited domestic insurrections amongst us, and has endeavoured to bring on the inhabitants of our frontiers, the merciless Indian Savages, whose known rule of warfare, is an undistinguished destruction of all ages, sexes and conditions.

In every stage of these Oppressions We have Petitioned for Redress in the most humble terms: Our repeated Petitions have been answered only by repeated injury. A Prince, whose character is thus marked by every act which may define a Tyrant, is unfit to be the ruler of a free People.

Nor have We been wanting in attention to our British brethren. We have warned them from time to time of attempts by their legislature to extend an unwarrantable jurisdiction over us. We have reminded them of the circumstances of our emigration and settlement here. We have appealed to their native justice and magnanimity, and we have conjured them by the ties of our common kindred to disavow these usurpations, which, would inevitably interrupt our connections and correspondence. They too have been deaf to the voice of justice and of consanguinity. We must, therefore, acquiesce in the necessity, which denounces our Separation, and hold them, as we hold the rest of mankind, Enemies in War, in Peace Friends.

We, therefore, the Representatives of the United States of America, in General Congress, Assembled, appealing to the Supreme Judge of the world for the rectitude of our intentions, do, in the Name, and by Authority of the good People of these Colonies, solemnly publish and declare, That these United Colonies are, and of Right ought to be Free and Independent States; that they are Absolved from all Allegiance to the British Crown, and that all political connection between them and the State of Great Britain, is and ought to be totally dissolved; and that as Free and Independent States, they have full Power to levy War, conclude Peace, contract Alliances, establish Commerce, and to do all other Acts and Things which Independent States may of right do. And for the support of this Declaration, with a firm reliance on the protection of divine Providence, we mutually pledge to each other our Lives, our Fortunes and our sacred Honor.

APPENDIX
B

The Constitution of The United States (And What It Means Today)

The Preamble. Chief Justice John Marshall pointed out in 1803 that the Preamble begins "We the people," and not "We the states." Thus the federal government derives its authority directly from the people and not from the states.

We the people of the United States, in Order to form a more perfect Union, establish Justice, insure domestic Tranquility, provide for the common defense, promote the general Welfare, and secure the Blessings of Liberty to ourselves and our Posterity, do ordain and establish this CONSTITUTION for the United States of America.

ARTICLE I

Section 1. All legislative powers herein granted shall be vested in a Congress of the United States, which shall consist of a Senate and House of Representatives.

Section 2. The House of Representatives shall be composed of Members chosen every second Year by the People of the several States, and the Electors in each State shall have the Qualifications requisite for Electors of the most numerous Branch of the State Legislature.

No Person shall be a Representative who shall not have attained to the Age of twenty-five Years, and been seven Years a Citizen of the United States, and who shall not, when elected, be an Inhabitant of that State in which he shall be chosen.

Direct taxes. This provision was altered by the Sixteenth Amendment, which allows the federal government to levy an income tax directly on the people.

Representatives and direct Taxes shall be apportioned among the several States which may be included within this Union, according to their respective Numbers, which shall be determined by adding to the whole Number of Free Persons, including those

Apportionment of representation. In 1929 Congress limited the House of Representatives to 435 members, who are allotted among the states on the basis of population. Each ten-year census thus requires a rearrangement of the House of Representatives. "Three fifths of all other persons" referred to slaves, and it was among the several sectional compromises in the Constitution.

Selection by senators. By the provisions of the Seventeenth Amendment, senators are chosen by the voters rather than by the state legislatures.

The vice president's "casting vote." John Adams cast the first tie-breaking vote in 1789 on a rule that allowed the President to remove important executive officers without the "advice and consent" of the Senate.

Impeachments. The persons subject to impeachment are "civil officers of the United States," which does not include

bound to Service for a Term of Years, and excluding Indians not taxed, three fifths of all other Persons. The actual Enumeration shall be made within three Years after the first Meeting of the Congress of the United States, and within every subsequent Term of ten Years, in such Manner as they shall by Law direct. The number of Representatives shall not exceed one for every thirty Thousand, but each State shall have at Least one Representative; and until such enumeration shall be made, the State of New Hampshire shall be entitled to chuse three, Massachusetts eight, Rhode Island and Providence Plantations one, Connecticut five, New York six, New Jersey four, Pennsylvania eight, Delaware one, Maryland six, Virginia ten, North Carolina five, South Carolina five, and Georgia three.

When vacancies happen in the Representation from any State, the Executive Authority thereof shall issue Writs of Election to fill such Vacancies.

The House of Representatives shall chuse their Speaker and other Officers; and shall have the sole Power of Impeachment.

Section 3.   The Senate of the United States shall be composed of two Senators from each State, chosen by the Legislature thereof, for six Years; and each Senator shall have one Vote.

Immediately after they shall be assembled in Consequence of the first Election, they shall be divided as equally as may be into three Classes. The Seats of the Senators of the first Class shall be vacated at the Expiration of the second Year, of the second Class at the Expiration of the fourth Year, and of the third Class at the Expiration of the sixth Year, so that one-third may be chosen every second Year; and if Vacancies happen by Resignation, or otherwise during the Recess of the Legislature of any State, the Executive thereof may make temporary Appointments until the next Meeting of the Legislature, which shall then fill such Vacancies.

No Person shall be a Senator who shall not have attained to the Age of thirty Years, and been nine Years a Citizen of the United States, and who shall not, when elected, be an Inhabitant of that State in which he shall be chosen.

The Vice President of the United States shall be President of the Senate, but shall have no vote, unless they be equally divided.

The Senate shall choose their Officers, and also a President pro tempore, in the absence of the Vice President, or when he shall exercise the Office of the President of the United States.

The Senate shall have the sole Power to try all Impeachments. When sitting for that purpose, they shall be on Oath or Affirmation. When the President of the members of Congress. *Impeachment* means an accusation of misconduct, which must first be voted by the House of Representatives. The misconduct must amount to a charge of "treason, bribery, or other high crimes and misdemeanors" (Article II, Section 4). The Senate tries all impeachments, with members of the House serving as the prosecution. A two-thirds majority is required for conviction. It has never been determined whether a person has to be convicted of a crime or simply of "misbehavior." Judges are appointed for life during good behavior (Article III, Section I), but they can be removed only by impeachment. In all, three persons, all judges, have been convicted and removed under this article.

Qualifications of members. Control over seating was one of the early privileges claimed by the English Parliament, and American legislatures have uniformly claimed the same power. Congress has usually used the power to purge itself of undesirable elements. In 1900 the House refused to seat a representative from Utah because he was guilty of polygamy. In 1919 it refused to seat a Wisconsin congressman because he was a Socialist.

Journal of proceedings. The requirement that each house keep a journal and record roll-call votes was intended to ensure that the voters could keep track of the conduct of their representatives and senators.

Immunity. Immunity from arrest while attending sessions and freedom of speech in debate were rights claimed by the English Parliament to protect itself against interference from the Crown. In America they have served little purpose other than to protect legislators from libel suits.

United States is tried, the Chief Justice shall preside: And no person shall be convicted without the Concurrence of two thirds of the Members present.

Judgment in Cases of Impeachment shall not extend further than to removal from Office, and disqualification to hold and enjoy any Office of honor, Trust, or Profit under the United States: but the Party convicted shall nevertheless be liable and subject to Indictment, Trial, Judgment, and Punishment, according to Law.

Section 4. The Times, Places and Manner of holding Elections for Senators and Representatives, shall be prescribed in each state by the Legislature thereof; but the Congress may at any time by Law make or alter such Regulations, except as to the Places of Chusing Senators.

The Congress shall assemble at least once in every Year, and such Meeting shall be on the first Monday in December, unless they shall by Law appoint a different Day.

Section 5. Each House shall be the Judge of the Elections, Returns and Qualifications of its own Members, and a Majority of each shall constitute a Quorum to do Business; but a smaller number may adjourn from day to day, and may be authorized to compel the Attendance of absent Members, in such Manner, and under such Penalties, as each House may provide.

Each House may determine the Rules of its Proceedings, punish its Members for disorderly Behaviour, and, with the Concurrence of two thirds, expel a Member.

Each House shall keep a Journal of its Proceedings, and from time to time publish the same, excepting such Parts as may in their Judgment require Secrecy; and the Yeas and Nays of the Members of either House on any question shall, at the Desire of one fifth of those Present, be entered on the Journal.

Neither House, during the Session of Congress, shall, without the Consent of the other, adjourn for more than three days, nor to any other Place than that in which the two Houses shall be sitting.

Section 6. The Senators and Representatives shall receive a Compensation for their Services, to be ascertained by Law, and paid out of the Treasury of the United States. They shall in all Cases, except Treason, Felony, and Breach of the Peace, be privileged from Arrest during their Attendance at the Session of their respective Houses, and in going to and returning from the same; and for any Speech or Debate in either House, they shall not be questioned in any other Place.

No Senator or Representative shall, during the Time for which he was elected, be appointed to any civil Office under the Authority of the United States,

Revenue bills. The provision that taxation measures must originate in the House of Representatives was intended to make that house more important. It was part of the large state–small state compromise that based representation in the House by population and in the Senate by states.

The veto. The requirement that the President must sign a bill before it becomes law, and the requirement that each house of Congress must muster a two-thirds vote to override a president's veto, are among the "checks and balances" of the Constitution. The ten-day rule allows a president to give a bill a "pocket veto" simply by withholding his signature until Congress adjourns, if the bill has been sent to him within ten days of the end of the session.

The powers of Congress. The phrase "general welfare" in the first paragraph of Section 8 is a limitation on what Congress can do with tax revenue; it does not add to the powers of Congress. The framers of the Constitution intended the powers of Congress to be specific, not general. However, the courts over the years have found within these specifically enumerated powers various "implied powers." For instance, the power to regulate interstate commerce has been interpreted to include Social Security, Medicare, labor legislation, and civil rights acts. The power to "raise

which shall have been created, or the Emoluments whereof shall have been increased, during such time; and no Person holding any Office under the United States shall be a Member of either House during his continuance in Office.

Section 7. All Bills for raising Revenue shall originate in the House of Representatives; but the Senate may propose or concur with Amendments as on other Bills.

Every Bill which shall have passed the House of Representatives and the Senate, shall, before it become a Law, be presented to the President of the United States; If he approve he shall sign it, but if not he shall return it, with his Objections, to that House in which it shall have originated, who shall enter the Objections at large on their Journal, and proceed to reconsider it. If after such Reconsideration two thirds of that House shall agree to pass the Bill, it shall be sent, together with the Objections, to the other House, by which it shall likewise be reconsidered, and if approved by two thirds of that House, it shall become a Law. But in all such Cases the Votes of both Houses shall be determined by Yeas and Nays, and the Names of the Persons voting for and against the Bill shall be entered on the Journal of each House respectively. If any Bill shall not be returned by the President within ten Days (Sundays excepted) after it shall have been represented to him, the Same shall be a Law, in like Manner as if he had signed it, unless the Congress by their Adjournment prevent its Return, in which Case it shall not be a Law.

Every Order, Resolution, or Vote to which the Concurrence of the Senate and House of Representatives may be necessary (except on a question of Adjournment) shall be presented to the President of the United States; and before the Same shall take Effect, shall be approved by him, or being disapproved by him, shall be repassed by two thirds of the Senate and House of Representatives, according to the Rules and Limitations prescribed in the Case of a Bill.

Section 8. The Congress shall have Power To lay and collect Taxes, Duties, Imposts and Excises, to pay the Debts and provide for the common Defense and general Welfare of the United States; but all Duties, Imposts and Excises shall be uniform throughout the United States;

To borrow money on the credit of the United States;

To regulate Commerce with foreign Nations, and among the several States, and with the Indian Tribes;

To establish an uniform Rule of Naturalization, and uniform Laws on the subject of Bankruptcies throughout the United States;

and support armies" includes the power to build interstate highways to facilitate army movements.

Necessary and proper. The advocates of "implied powers," beginning with Alexander Hamilton, have always pointed to the final clause of Article 1, Section 8, as a catchall intended to give Congress broad legislative authority. John Marshall interpreted the clause thus in 1819: "Let the end be legitimate, let it be within the scope of the Constitution, and all means which are appropriate, which are plainly adapted to that end, which are not prohibited, but consist with the letter and spirit of the Constitution, are constitutional."

To coin Money, regulate the Value thereof, and of foreign Coin, and fix the Standard of Weights and Measures;

To provide for the Punishment of counterfeiting the Securities and current Coin of the United States;

To establish Post Offices and post Roads;

To promote the Progress of Science and useful Arts, by securing for limited Times to Authors and Inventors the exclusive Right to their respective Writings and Discoveries;

To constitute Tribunals inferior to the Supreme Court;

To define and punish Piracies and Felonies committed on the high Seas, and Offenses against the Law of Nations;

To declare War, grant Letters of Marque and Reprisal, and make Rules concerning Captures on Land and Water;

To raise and support Armies, but no Appropriation of Money to that Use shall be for a longer Term than two Years;

To provide and maintain a Navy;

To make Rules for the Government and Regulation of the land and naval forces;

To provide for calling forth the Militia to execute the Laws of the Union, suppress Insurrections and repel Invasions;

To provide for organizing, arming, and disciplining the Militia, and for governing such Part of them as may be employed in the Service of the United States, reserving to the States respectively, the Appointment of the Officers, and the Authority of training the Militia according to the discipline prescribed by Congress;

To exercise exclusive Legislation in all Cases whatsoever, over such District (not exceeding ten Miles square) as may, by Cession of particular States, and the acceptance of Congress, become the Seat of Government of the United States, and to exercise like Authority over all Places purchased by the Consent of the Legislature of the State in which the Same shall be, for the Erection of Forts, Magazines, Arsenals, dock-Yards, and other needful Buildings;—And

To make all Laws which shall be necessary and proper for carrying into Execution the foregoing Powers, and all other Powers vested by this Constitution in the Government of the United States, or in any Department or Officer thereof.

Section 9. The Migration or Importation of such Persons as any of the States now existing shall think proper to admit, shall not be prohibited by the Congress prior to the Year one thousand eight hundred and eight, but a tax or duty may be imposed on such Importation, not exceeding ten dollars for each Person.

Importation of persons. This phrase referred to the importing of slaves from Africa. The requirement that Congress could not prohibit the import until 1808 was one of the sectional compromises in the Constitution. Congress did prohibit the import in 1808, although the government did not seriously enforce the law until the 1840s.

Habeas corpus. This has been called "the most important single safeguard of personal liberty known to Anglo-American law." It means that a person who has been arrested is entitled to have a court inquiry into the cause of his or her detention, and if she or he is not detained for good cause, is entitled to be freed.

Limits on the states. No state shall. . . . This list of restrictions on state powers was intended by the framers to rectify some of the problems that had arisen during and after the Revolution. The stricture on bills of credit or making anything but gold or silver legal tender was designed to prevent the states from printing paper money and to prevent them from making tobacco, whiskey, or deerskins a medium of exchange. The stricture on laws "impairing the obligations of contracts" was intended to prevent the states from enacting debtor-relief laws. In 1933, however, the Supreme Court held that a state could, in time of depression, enable debtors to postpone meeting their obligations for a "reasonable" period of time.

The privilege of the Writ of Habeas Corpus shall not be suspended, unless when in Cases of Rebellion or Invasion the public Safety may require it.

No Bill of Attainder or ex post facto Law shall be passed.

No Capitation, or other direct, Tax shall be laid unless in Proportion to the Census or Enumeration herein before directed to be taken.

No Tax or Duty shall be laid on Articles exported from any State.

No Preference shall be given by any Regulation of Revenue to the Ports of one State over those of another: nor shall Vessels bound to, or from, one State, be obliged to enter, clear, or pay Duties in another.

No Money shall be drawn from the Treasury, but in Consequence of Appropriations made by Law; and a regular Statement and Account of the Receipts and Expenditures of all public Money shall be published from time to time.

No title of Nobility shall be granted by the United States: And no Person holding any Office of Profit or Trust under them, shall, without the Consent of the Congress, accept of any present, Emolument, Office, or Title, of any kind whatever, from any King, Prince, or foreign State.

Section 10.   No State shall enter into any Treaty Alliance, or Confederation; grant Letters of Marque and Reprisal; coin Money; emit Bills of Credit; make any Thing but gold and silver Coin a Tender in Payment of Debts; pass any Bill of Attainder, ex post facto Law, or Law impairing the Obligation of Contracts, or grant any Title of Nobility.

No State shall, without the Consent of the Congress, lay any Imposts or Duties on Imports or Exports, except what may be absolutely necessary for exercising its inspection Laws: and the net Produce of all Duties and Imposts, laid by any State on Imports or Exports, shall be for the Use of the Treasury of the United States; and all such Laws shall be subject to the Revision and Control of the Congress.

No State shall, without the Consent of Congress, lay any duty of Tonnage, keep Troops, or Ships of War in time of Peace, enter into any Agreement or Compact with another State, or with a foreign Power, or engage in War, unless actually invaded, or in such imminent Danger as will not admit of delay.

ARTICLE II

Section 1.   The executive Power shall be vested in a President of the United States of America. He shall hold his Office during the Term of four Years, and, together with the Vice President, chosen for the same term, be elected, as follows:

Each State shall appoint, in such Manner as the Legislature thereof may direct, a Number of Electors, equal to the whole Number of Senators and Representatives to which the State may be entitled in the Congress: but no Senator or Representative, or Person holding an Office of Trust or Profit under the United States, shall be appointed an Elector.

The Electors shall meet in their respective States, and vote by Ballot for two Persons, of whom one at least shall not be an Inhabitant of the same State with themselves. And they shall make a list of all the Persons voted for, and of the Number of Votes for each; which List they shall sign and certify, and transmit sealed to the Seat of the Government of the United States, directed to the President of the Senate. The President of the Senate shall, in the Presence of the Senate and House of Representatives, open all the Certificates, and the Votes shall then be counted. The Person having the greatest Number of Votes shall be the President, if such Number be a Majority of the whole Number of Electors appointed; and if there be more than one who have such Majority, and have an equal Number of Votes, then the House of Representatives shall immediately chuse by Ballot one of them for President; and if no Person have a Majority, then from the five highest on the List the said House shall in like Manner chuse the President. But in chusing the President, the Votes shall be taken by States, the Representation from each State having one Vote; a quorum for this Purpose shall consist of a Member or Members from two-thirds of the States, and a Majority of all the States shall be necessary to a Choice. In every Case, after the Choice of the President, the Person having the greatest Number of Votes of the Electors shall be the Vice President. But if there should remain two or more who have equal votes, the Senate shall chuse from them by Ballot the Vice President.

The Congress may determine the Time of chusing the Electors, and the Day on which they shall give their Votes; which Day shall be the same throughout the United States.

No person except a natural-born citizen, or a Citizen of the United States, at the time of the adoption of this Constitution, shall be eligible to the Office of President; neither shall any Person be eligible to that Office who shall not have attained to the Age of thirty-five Years, and been fourteen Years a Resident within the United States.

In case of the Removal of the President from Office, or of his Death, Resignation, or Inability to dis-

The electoral college. This cumbersome method of selecting an executive is unique to the American system of government. The only model of it available at the time the Constitution was drafted was in Maryland, where the upper house was indirectly elected. The original purpose of the electoral college was to ensure qualified leadership (since electors experienced in government were assumed to be better judges of a candidate's qualifications than the voters) and to insulate the executive from popular pressures.

The arrangement that the person with the most electoral votes would be president and the one who came in second would be vice president was altered by the Twelfth Amendment (1804), which established the procedure of nomination by ticket.

The Constitution originally made no provision regarding the reelection of a president. George Washington established a tradition of serving no more than two terms. After Franklin Roosevelt violated the tradition by running for office four times, Congress passed the Twenty-second Amendment, which limits a president to two terms.

Removal, death, resignation of the president. The first vice president to suc ceed to the presidency was John Tyler (1841), who established the precedent, since followed, that he was president in fact, rather than merely an "acting president."

Gerald Ford was the only president who was never elected to the office, having been appointed by Richard Nixon as vice president (after Spiro Agnew resigned under criminal indictment) and having succeeded to the presidency on Nixon's resignation.

Congress has established the presidential succession in the event of the death or resignation of both president and vice president as follows: Speaker of the House, president pro-tem of the Senate, and then the members of the Cabinet, beginning with the Secretary of State.

The powers of the President. The powers given to the executive are fewer than those granted to Congress, but they are less specific. The President is made commander-in-chief of the armed forces, thereby ensuring civilian control of the military. He conducts foreign relations, appoints officials (both with the advice and consent of the Senate), executes the laws, and that's it.

Executive power was much feared at the time the Constitution was drafted, and the framers had no desire to make enemies for their document by endowing the President with visible authority to affect the lives of citizens. Yet in the Constitution's vagueness alone lies enough expandable power to create what has been called the "imperial presidency." The rubbery injunction to "take care that the laws be faithfully executed" alone includes the power to spend money, create bureaus, appoint task forces, mediate labor disputes, set aside forest reserves, ban pesticides, and eavesdrop on suspected subversives.

charge the Powers and Duties of the said Office, the same shall devolve on the Vice President, and the Congress may by Law provide for the Case of Removal, Death, Resignation, or Inability, both of the President and Vice President, declaring what Officer shall then act as President, and such Officer shall act accordingly, until the Disability be removed, or a President shall be elected.

The President shall, at stated Times, receive for his Services a Compensation, which shall neither be increased nor diminished during the Period for which he shall have been elected, and he shall not receive within that Period any other Emolument from the United States, or any of them.

Before he enters on the Execution of his Office, he shall take the following Oath or Affirmation:— "I do solemnly swear (or affirm) that I will faithfully execute the Office of President of the United States, and will, to the best of my Ability, preserve, protect, and defend the Constitution of the United States."

Section 2. The President shall be Commander in Chief of the Army and Navy of the United States, and of the Militia of the several States, when called into the actual Service of the United States; he may require the Opinion, in writing, of the principal Officer in each of the executive Departments, upon any subject relating to the Duties of their respective Offices, and he shall have Power to Grant Reprieves and Pardons for Offenses against the United States, except in Cases of Impeachment.

He shall have Power, by and with the Advice and Consent of the Senate, to make Treaties, provided two thirds of the Senators present concur; and he shall nominate, and by and with the Advice and Consent of the Senate, shall appoint Ambassadors, other public Ministers and Consuls, Judges of the supreme Court, and all other Officers of the United States, whose Appointments are not herein otherwise provided for, and which shall be established by Law: but the Congress may by Law vest the Appointment of such inferior Officers, as they think proper, in the President alone, in the Courts of Law, or in the Heads of Departments.

The President shall have Power to fill up all Vacancies that may happen during the Recess of the Senate, by granting Commissions which shall expire at the end of their next Session.

Section 3. He shall from time to time give to the Congress Information of the State of the Union, and recommend to their Consideration such Measures as he shall judge necessary and expedient; he may, on extraordinary occasions, convene both Houses, or either of them, and in Case of Disagreement between them, with respect to the Time of Adjournment, he may adjourn them to such Time as he shall think proper; he shall receive Ambassadors and other public Ministers; he shall take Care that the Laws be faithfully executed, and shall Commission all the Officers of the United States.

Section 4. The President, Vice President and all civil Officers of the United States, shall be removed from Office on Impeachment for, and Conviction of, Treason, Bribery, or other high Crimes and Misdemeanors.

ARTICLE III

The judicial power. Courts, judges, and lawyers were as suspect in the United States of the 1780s as kings and ministers. The poor looked upon law courts as agents of the rich, using the power of the state to collect debts and enforce contracts. Article III, which establishes the third branch of government— "the judicial power of the United States" —is therefore deliberately vague. The framers had no desire to stir up a hornet's nest of controversy by outlining a hierarchy of courts staffed by learned judges. Article III specifies only a Supreme Court, and it leaves to Congress the thorny questions concerning the number of "inferior courts" and the extent of their powers.

Congress in 1789 did establish a hierarchy of circuit and district courts— which, expanded in number, remain today—but it cautiously confined their jurisdiction to the "Constitution, laws, and treaties of the United States." Ordinary civil and criminal jurisdiction is left to the state courts. A federal court can take jurisdiction only when a suit involves a federal issue, such as the interpretation of an act of Congress, or when the parties to the suit reside in different states ("diversity of citizenship"). Even then, the Supreme Court declared in 1938 in the case of *Erie Railroad v. Tompkins*, federal courts are obliged to apply the law of the forum state. There is no federal common law.

Section 1. The judicial Power of the United States, shall be vested in one supreme Court, and in such inferior Courts as the Congress may from time to time ordain and establish. The Judges, both of the supreme and inferior Courts shall hold their Offices during good Behaviour, and shall, at stated Times, receive for their Services, a Compensation, which shall not be diminished during their Continuance in Office.

Section 2. The judicial Power shall extend to all Cases, in Law and Equity, arising under this Constitution, the Laws of the United States, and Treaties made, or which shall be made, under their Authority;—to all Cases affecting Ambassadors, other public Ministers and Consuls;—to all Cases of admiralty and maritime Jurisdiction;—to Controversies to which the United States shall be a Party;—to Controversies between two or more States;—between a State and Citizens of another State;—between Citizens of the same State claiming Lands under Grants of different States, and between a State, or the Citizens thereof, and foreign States, Citizens or Subjects.

In all Cases affecting Ambassadors, other public Ministers and Consuls, and those in which a State shall be Party, the supreme Court shall have original Jurisdiction. In all the other Cases before mentioned, the supreme Court shall have appellate Jurisdiction, both as to Law and Fact, with such Exceptions, and under such Regulations as the Congress shall make.

The trial of all Crimes, except in Cases of Impeachment, shall be by Jury; and such Trial shall be held in the State where the said Crimes shall have been committed; but when not committed within any State, the Trial shall be at such Place or Places as the Congress may by Law have directed.

Section 3. Treason against the United States, shall consist only in levying War against them, or in adhering to their Enemies, giving them Aid and Comfort. No Person shall be convicted of Treason unless on the Testimony of two Witnesses to the same overt Act, or on Confession in open Court.

The Congress shall have power to declare the Punishment of Treason, but no Attainder of Treason shall work Corruption of Blood, or Forfeiture except during the Life of the Person attained.

ARTICLE IV

Section 1.   Full Faith and Credit shall be given in each State to the public Acts, Records, and judicial Proceedings of every other State. And the Congress may by general Laws prescribe the Manner in which such Acts, Records and Proceedings shall be proved, and the Effect thereof.

Section 2.   The Citizens of each State shall be entitled to all Privileges and Immunities of Citizens in the several States.

A Person charged in any State with Treason, Felony, or other Crime, who shall flee from Justice, and be found in another State, shall on demand of the executive Authority of the State from which he fled, be delivered up, to be removed to the State having Jurisdiction of the crime.

No Person held to Service or Labour in one State, under the Laws thereof, escaping into another, shall, in Consequence of any Law or Regulation therein, be discharged from such Service or Labour, but shall be delivered up on Claim of the Party to whom such Service or Labour may be due.

Section 3.   New States may be admitted by the Congress into this Union; but no new State shall be formed or erected within the Jurisdiction of any other State; nor any State be formed by the Junction of two or more States, or parts of States, without the Consent of the Legislatures of the States concerned as well as of the Congress.

The Congress shall have Power to dispose of and make all needful Rules and Regulations respecting the Territory or other Property belonging to the United States; and nothing in this Constitution shall be so construed as to Prejudice any Claims of the United States, or of any particular State.

Section 4.   The United States shall guarantee to every State in this Union a Republican Form of Government, and shall protect each of them against Invasion; and on Application of the Legislature, or of the Executive (when the Legislature cannot be convened) against domestic Violence.

Full faith and credit.   The intent of this provision is to ensure cooperation and mutual respect among the states. In the twentieth century it has been commonly invoked by people who travel to another state, such as Nevada or Florida, in order to obtain a quick divorce.

New states.   The framers of the Constitution contemplated the indefinite expansion of the American union. The organism they created was both a republic and an empire, but it was a unique empire in that the colonies (territories) were expected, upon maturity, to join the Union on a par with the original thirteen states.

Amendments. The framers of the Constitution, with commendable foresight and humility, anticipated that posterity might want to make some changes in their handiwork. But they deliberately made the amendment procedure cumbersome, so that the Constitution would not be subject to popular whim. Amendments must be approved by a two-thirds vote in each house of Congress, and then they have to be ratified by legislatures or conventions in three-fourths of the states. The only amendment ratified by specially summoned conventions was the Twenty-first, which repealed prohibition. The first ten amendments (the Bill of Rights) were drafted and approved only four years after the Constitution was written. Since then, only sixteen have been added.

ARTICLE V

The Congress, whenever two thirds of both Houses shall deem it necessary, shall propose Amendments to this Constitution, or, on the Application of the Legislatures of two thirds of the several States, shall call a Convention for proposing Amendments, which, in either Case, shall be valid to all Intents and Purposes, as part of this Constitution, when ratified by the Legislatures of three fourths of the several States, or by Conventions in three fourths thereof, as the one or the other Mode of Ratification may be proposed by the Congress; Provided that no Amendment which may be made prior to the Year One thousand eight hundred and eight shall in any Manner affect the first and fourth Clauses in the Ninth Section of the first Article; and that no State, without its Consent, shall be deprived of its equal Suffrage in the Senate.

ARTICLE VI

All Debts contracted and Engagements entered into, before the Adoption of this Constitution, shall be as valid against the United States under this Constitution, as under the Confederation.

This Constitution, and the Laws of the United States which shall be made in Pursuance thereof: and all Treaties made, or which shall be made, under the Authority of the United States, shall be the supreme Law of the Land; and the Judges in every State shall be bound thereby, any Thing in the Constitution or laws of any State to the Contrary notwithstanding.

The Senators and Representatives before mentioned, and the Members of the several State Legislatures, and all executive and judicial Officers, both of the United States and of the several States, shall be bound by Oath or Affirmation to support this Constitution; but no religious Test shall ever be required as a qualification to any Office or public Trust under the United States.

Ratification. Mindful of the difficulties that had attended efforts to alter the Articles of Confederation in the 1780s, the framers of the Constitution provided that the document would go into effect when only nine of the thirteen states gave their approval. They also bypassed potentially jealous and divided state legislatures by providing that the Constitution was to be approved by specially elected conventions.

ARTICLE VII

The Ratification of the Conventions of nine States shall be sufficient for the Establishment of this Constitution between the States so ratifying the same.

Done in Convention by the Unanimous Consent of the States present the Seventeenth Day of September in the Year of our Lord one thousand seven hundred and Eighty seven and of the Independence of the

United States of America the Twelfth. In Witness whereof We have hereunto subscribed our Names.

Articles in Addition to, and Amendment of, the Constitution of the United States of America, Proposed by Congress, and Ratified by the Legislatures of the Several States, Pursuant to the Fifth Article of the Original Constitution.

The Bill of Rights. The first ten amendments were intended as restraints on the power of the federal government. Since 1931, the Supreme Court has progressively applied them to the States under the theory that they are embodied in the "due process" clause of the Fourteenth Amendment.

The First Amendment, which protects the freedom of speech, press, and belief, is clearly the most important. In recognition of this, the Supreme Court places the burden of proof on the government where freedom of speech is in question: that is, the government must demonstrate, when a citizen complains, that its action does *not* inhibit freedom of speech, press, or religion.

The Second and Third amendments are the product of English tradition and American colonial experience. The Fourth through the Eighth amendments are judicial safeguards intended to ensure fair court procedure. The Ninth Amendment is a catchall intended to overcome the misgivings, expressed by James Madison among others, that a listing of human rights would be restrictive—that is, imply that these are the *only* rights people have. The Ninth Amendment has been invoked by the Supreme Court most recently in a decision that overturned a state law restricting the use of contraceptives.

The Tenth Amendment, though drafted and approved with the rest of the Bill of Rights, addresses itself to power, not rights. It is a reminder that the government established by the Constitution is one of specifically delegated powers and that all other powers reside in the states. This residual power is usually described as the "police power": the power to legislate for the health, safety, welfare, and morals of the people. The Tenth Amendment was long relied on by the advocates of states' right, but in 1941 the Supreme Court declared the amendment a mere truism that expressed the distribution of power between the federal government and the states without, of itself, restricting the authority of either.

AMENDMENT I [1791]

Congress shall make no law respecting an establishment of religion, or prohibiting the free exercise thereof; or abridging the freedom of speech, or of the press; or the right of the people peaceably to assemble, and to petition the Government for a redress of grievances.

AMENDMENT II [1791]

A well regulated Militia, being necessary to the security of a free State, the right of the people to keep and bear Arms, shall not be infringed.

AMENDMENT III [1791]

No Soldier shall, in time of peace, be quartered in any house, without the consent of the Owner, nor in time of war, but in a manner to be prescribed by law.

AMENDMENT IV [1791]

The right of the people to be secure in their persons, houses, papers, and effects, against unreasonable searches and seizures, shall not be violated, and no Warrants shall issue, but upon probable cause, supported by Oath or affirmation, and particularly describing the place to be searched, and the persons or things to be seized.

AMENDMENT V [1791]

No person shall be held to answer for a capital or otherwise infamous crime, unless on a presentment or indictment of a Grand Jury, except in cases

The Eleventh Amendment was the product of a fleeting political controversy involving the efforts of Loyalists to recover property that states had confiscated during the revolution.

The Twelfth Amendment resulted from the tie in the electoral college between Thomas Jefferson and Aaron Burr in 1800. By requiring a "distinct list" of persons running as president and another for those running as vice president, the amendment, to be workable, requires a nominating procedure. It is therefore an indirect recognition of the function of political parties.

arising in the land or naval forces, or in the Militia, when in actual service in time of War or public danger; nor shall any person be subject for the same offence to be twice put in jeopardy of life or limb; nor shall be compelled in any criminal case to be a witness against himself, nor be deprived of life, liberty, or property, without due process of law; nor shall private property be taken for public use, without just compensation.

AMENDMENT VI [1791]

In all criminal prosecutions, the accused shall enjoy the right to a speedy and public trial, by an impartial jury of the State and district wherein the crime shall have been committed, which district shall have been previously ascertained by law, and to be informed of the nature and cause of the accusation, to be confronted with the witnesses against him; to have compulsory process for obtaining witnesses in his favor, and to have the Assistance of Counsel for his defence.

AMENDMENT VII [1791]

In Suits at common law, where the value in controversy shall exceed twenty dollars, the right of trial by jury shall be preserved, and no fact tried by a jury, shall be otherwise re-examined in any Court of the United States, than according to the rules of the common law.

AMENDMENT VIII [1791]

Excessive bail shall not be required, nor excessive fines imposed, nor cruel and unusual punishments inflicted.

AMENDMENT IX [1791]

The enumeration in the Constitution, of certain rights, shall not be construed to deny or disparage others retained by the people.

AMENDMENT X [1791]

The powers not delegated to the United States by the Constitution, nor prohibited by it to the States, are reserved to the States respectively, or to the people.

AMENDMENT XI [1798]

The Judicial power of the United States shall not be construed to extend to any suit in law or equity, commenced or prosecuted against one of the United States by Citizens of another State, or by citizens or Subjects of any Foreign State.

AMENDMENT XII [1804]

The Electors shall meet in their respective States and vote by ballot for President and Vice President, one of whom, at least, shall not be an inhabitant of the same State with themselves; they shall name in their ballots the person voted for as President, and in distinct ballots the person voted for as Vice-President, and they shall make distinct lists of all persons voted for as President, and of all persons voted for as Vice-President, and of the number of votes for each, which lists they shall sign and certify, and transmit sealed to the seat of the government of the United States, directed to the President of the Senate;—The President of the Senate shall, in the presence of the Senate and House of Representatives, open all the certificates and the votes shall then be counted;—The person having the greatest number of votes for President, shall be the President, if such number be a majority of the whole number of Electors appointed; and if no person have such majority, then from the persons having the highest numbers not exceeding three on the list of those voted for as President, the House of Representatives shall choose immediately, by ballot, the President. But in choosing the President, the votes shall be taken by states, the representation from each state having one vote; a quorum for this purpose shall consist of a member or members from two-thirds of the states, and a majority of all the states shall be necessary to a choice. And if the House of Representatives shall not choose a President whenever the right of choice shall devolve upon them, before the fourth day of March next following, then the Vice-President shall act as President, as in the case of the death or other constitutional disability of the President.—The person having the greatest number of votes as Vice-President, shall be the Vice-President, if such number be a majority of the whole number of Electors appointed, and if no person have a majority, then from the two highest numbers on the list, the Senate shall choose the Vice-President; a quorum for the purpose shall consist of two-thirds of the whole number of Senators, and a majority of the whole number shall be necessary to a choice. But no person constitutionally ineligible to the office of the President shall be eligible to that of Vice-President of the United States.

AMENDMENT XIII [1865]

Section 1. Neither slavery nor involuntary servitude, except as a punishment for crime wherof the party shall have been duly convicted, shall exist within the United States, or any place subject to their jurisdiction.

Section 2. Congress shall have the power to enforce this article by appropriate legislation.

AMENDMENT XIV [1868]

Section 1. All persons born or naturalized in the United States, and subject to the jurisdiction thereof, are citizens of the United States and of the State wherein they reside. No state shall make or enforce any law which shall abridge the privileges or immunities of citizens of the United States; nor shall any State deprive any person of life, liberty, or property, without due process of law; nor deny to any person within its jurisdiction the equal protection of the laws.

Section 2. Representatives shall be apportioned among the several States according to their respective numbers, counting the whole number of persons in each State, excluding Indians not taxed. But when the right to vote at any election for the choice of electors for President and Vice President of the United States, Representatives in Congress, the Executive and Judicial officers of a State, or the members of the Legislature thereof, is denied to any of the male inhabitants of such State, being twenty-one years of age, and citizens of the United States, or in any way abridged, except for participation in rebellion, or other crime, the basis of representation therein shall be reduced in the proportion which the number of such male citizens shall bear to the whole number of male citizens twenty-one years of age in such State.

Section 3. No person shall be a Senator or Representative in Congress, or elector of President and Vice President, or hold any office, civil or military, under the United States, or under any State, who, having previously taken an oath, as a member of Congress, or as an officer of the United States, or as a member of any State legislature, or as an executive or judicial officer of any State, to support the Constitution of the United States, shall have engaged in insurrection or re-

The war amendments. Adopted after the Civil War, the Thirteenth Amendment freed the slaves, the Fourteenth sought to protect their civil rights, and the Fifteenth prevented the states from denying the right to vote on the basis of race.

Due process. The Fourteenth Amendment has, through the years, been the most controversial of the war amendments. The phrase "due process" has been held to include the whole panoply of rights outlined in the first ten amendments. The phrase "equal protection of the laws" has been held to exclude racially segregated facilities and to require periodic reapportionment of state legislatures to ensure that all ballots are of equal weight.

bellion against the same, or given aid or comfort to the enemies thereof. But Congress may by a vote of two-thirds of each House, remove such disability.

Section 4. The validity of the public debt of the United States, authorized by law, including debts incurred for payment of pensions and bounties for services in suppressing insurrection or rebellion, shall not be questioned. But neither the United States nor any State shall assume or pay any debt or obligation incurred in aid of insurrection or rebellion against the United States, or any claim for the loss or emancipation of any slave; but all such debts, obligations, and claims shall be held illegal and void.

Section 5. The Congress shall have the power to enforce, by appropriate legislation, the provisions of this article.

AMENDMENT XV [1870]

Section 1. The right of citizens of the United States to vote shall not be denied or abridged by the United States or by any State on account of race, color, or previous condition of servitude—

Section 2. The Congress shall have the power to enforce this article by appropriate legislation.

AMENDMENT XVI [1913]

The Congress shall have power to lay and collect taxes on incomes, from whatever source derived, without apportionment among the several States, and without regard to any census or enumeration.

AMENDMENT XVII [1916]

The Senate of the United States shall be composed of two Senators from each State, elected by the people thereof, for six years; and each Senator shall have one vote. The electors in each State shall have the qualifications requisite for electors of the most numerous branch of the State legislatures.

When vacancies happen in the representation of any State in the Senate, the executive authority of such State shall issue writs of election to fill such vacancies: *Provided*, That the legislature of any State may empower the executive thereof to make temporary appointments until the people fill the vacancies by election as the legislature may direct.

Civil rights. Section 5 of the Fourteenth Amendment was clearly intended to give Congress power to pass laws for the protection of civil rights. This Congress attempted to do in 1875 by passing a law forbidding inns, railroads, and theaters from discriminating among persons on the grounds of race. In 1883 the Supreme Court struck down the law on the grounds that the Fourteenth Amendment prohibited only official discrimination, not the private acts of individuals. As a result, modern civil rights legislation, notably the Equal Opportunity Act of 1964, rests on Congress's power to regulate interstate commerce, rather than on the Fourteenth Amendment.

The Fifteenth Amendment. For nearly a century after it was drafted, the Fifteenth Amendment was evaded by various devices that hindered blacks from registering and voting. The Voting Rights Act of 1965 is the most recent attempt to enforce the amendment by providing federal supervision of voter registration in localities with a history of discrimination.

The Progressive amendments. The Sixteenth through Nineteenth amendments were the product of the Progressive movement. The Sixteenth was necessitated by a Supreme Court decision in the 1890s that a federal income tax violated the constitutional requirement that direct taxes (as opposed to excises) had to be apportioned among the states, which in turn would collect from the people. The Seventeenth Amendment was intended to democratize the "millionaires' club," the U.S. Senate, by requiring that its members be elected directly by the people. The Eighteenth Amendment authorized prohibition, and the Nineteenth women's suffrage.

This amendment shall not be so construed as to affect the election or term of any Senator chosen before it becomes valid as part of the Constitution.

AMENDMENT XVIII [1919]

Section 1. After one year from the ratification of this article the manufacture, sale, or transportation of intoxicating liquors within, the importation thereof into, or the exportation thereof from the United States and all territory subject to the jurisdiction thereof for beverage purposes is hereby prohibited.
Section 2. The Congress and the several States shall have concurrent power to enforce this article by appropriate legislation.
Section 3. This article shall be inoperative unless it shall have been ratified as an amendment to the Constitution by the legislatures of the several States, as provided in the Constitution, within seven years from the date of the submission hereof to the States by the Congress.

AMENDMENT XIX [1920]

The right of citizens of the United States to vote shall not be denied or abridged by the United States or by any State on account of sex.

Congress shall have power to enforce this article by appropriate legislation.

AMENDMENT XX [1933]

Section 1. The terms of the President and Vice President shall end at noon on the 20th day of January, and the terms of Senators and Representatives at noon on the 3rd day of January, of the years in which such terms would have ended if this article had not been ratified; and the terms of their successors shall then begin.
Section 2. The Congress shall assemble at least once in every year, and such meeting shall begin at noon on the 3d day of January, unless they shall by law appoint a different day.
Section 3. If, at the time fixed for the beginning of the term of the President, the President elect shall have died, the Vice President elect shall become President. If a President shall not have been chosen before the time fixed for the beginning of his term, or if the

The lame duck amendment. The Twentieth Amendment did away with an anomaly created by Article I of the Constitution, the requirement that elections would be held in November but inaugurations delayed until March. This resulted in a "lame duck" session of Congress, lasting from December until March in even-numbered years, when members, many of whom had failed to be reelected and were on their way to private life, were voting on matters of national importance. By moving inauguration day back from March 4 to January 20, the amendment shortens the interval between popular selection and the exercise of presidential and legislative power.

President elect shall have failed to qualify, then the Vice President elect shall act as President until a President shall have qualified; and the Congress may by law provide for the case wherein neither a President elect nor a Vice President elect shall have qualified, declaring who shall then act as President, or the manner in which one who is to act shall be selected, and such person shall act accordingly until a President or Vice President shall have qualified.

Section 4. The Congress may by law provide for the case of the death of any of the persons from whom the House of Representatives may choose a President whenever the right of choice shall have devolved upon them, and for the case of the death of any of the persons from whom the Senate may choose a Vice President whenever the right of choice shall have devolved upon them.

Section 5. Sections 1 and 2 shall take effect on the 15th day of October following the ratification of this article.

Section 6. The article shall be inoperative unless it shall have been ratified as an amendment to the Constitution by the legislatures of three-fourths of the several States within seven years from the date of its submission.

The Twenty-first Amendment. The Twenty-first Amendment repealed the Eighteenth and thereby repealed prohibition. It is the only amendment that provides for its ratification by specially selected conventions, and it is the only one that has been approved in this way.

AMENDMENT XXI [1933]

Section 1. The eighteenth article of amendment to the Constitution of the United States is hereby repealed.

Section 2. The transportation or importation into any State, Territory, or possession of the United States for delivery or use therein of intoxicating liquors, in violation of the laws thereof, is hereby prohibited.

Section 3. This article shall be inoperative unless it shall have been ratified as an amendment to the Constitution by conventions in the several States, as provided in the Constitution, within seven years from the date of the submission hereof to the States by the Congress.

The Twenty-second Amendment. The Twenty-second Amendment, a belated slap at Roosevelt by a Republican-dominated Congress, limits the president to two terms in office. Ironically, the first president to which it applied was a Republican, Dwight D. Eisenhower.

AMENDMENT XXII [1951]

No person shall be elected to the office of the President more than twice, and no person who has held the office of President, or acted as President, for more than two years of a term to which some other person was elected President shall be elected to the office of the President more than once.

But this Article shall not apply to any person holding the office of President when this Article was proposed by the Congress, and shall not prevent any person who may be holding the office of President, or acting as President, during the term within which this Article becomes operative from holding the office of President or acting as President during the remainder of such term.

AMENDMENT XXIII [1961]

Section 1. The District constituting the seat of Government of the United States shall appoint in such manner as the Congress may direct:
A number of electors of President and Vice President equal to the whole number of Senators and Representatives in Congress to which the District would be entitled if it were a State, but in no event more than the least populous State; they shall be in addition to those appointed by the States, but they shall be considered, for the purposes of the election of President and Vice President, to be electors appointed by a State; and they shall meet in the District and perform such duties as provided by the twelfth article of amendment.
Section 2. The Congress shall have the power to enforce this article by appropriate legislation.

The Twenty-third Amendment. The Twenty-third Amendment allows residents of the District of Columbia to vote in presidential elections.

AMENDMENT XXIV [1964]

Section 1. The right of citizens of the United States to vote in any primary or other election for President or Vice President, for electors for President or Vice President, or for Senator or Representative in Congress, shall not be denied or abridged by the United States or any State by reason of failure to pay any poll tax or other tax.
Section 2. The Congress shall have the power to enforce this article by appropriate legislation.

The poll tax amendment. The Twenty-fourth Amendment prevents the states from making payment of a poll tax a condition for voting. Common at the time among southern states, the poll tax was a capitation (poll, or head) tax on individuals. A poll tax receipt was often required in order to vote. It was designed to prevent uneducated people, especially blacks, who were unaccustomed

AMENDMENT XXV [1967]

Section 1. In case of the removal of the President from office or his death or resignation, the Vice President shall become President.
Section 2. Whenever there is a vacancy in the office of the Vice President, the President shall nominate a Vice President who shall take the office upon

The Twenty-fifth Amendment. The Twenty-fifth Amendment, inspired by President Eisenhower's heart attack and President Johnson's abdominal surgery, provides for the temporary replacement of a president who is unable to discharge the duties of the office.

confirmation by a majority vote of both houses of Congress.

Section 3.   Whenever the President transmits to the President pro tempore of the Senate and the Speaker of the House of Representatives his written declaration that he is unable to discharge the powers and duties of his office, and until he transmits to them a written declaration to the contrary, such powers and duties shall be discharged by the Vice President as Acting President.

Section 4.   Whenever the Vice President and a majority of either the principal officers of the executive departments, or of such other body as Congress may by law provide, transmit to the President pro tempore of the Senate and the Speaker of the House of Representatives their written declaration that the President is unable to discharge the powers and duties of his office, the Vice President shall immediately assume the powers and duties of the office as Acting President.

Thereafter, when the President transmits to the President pro tempore of the Senate and the Speaker of the House of Representatives his written declaration that no inability exists, he shall resume the powers and duties of his office unless the Vice President and a majority of either the principal officers of the executive departments, or of such other body as Congress may by law provide, transmit within four days to the President pro tempore of the Senate and the speaker of the House of Representatives their written declaration that the President is unable to discharge the powers and duties of his office. Thereupon Congress shall decide the issue, assembling within 48 hours for that purpose if not in session. If the Congress, within 21 days after receipt of the latter written declaration, or, if Congress is not in session, within 21 days after Congress is required to assemble, determines by two-thirds vote of both houses that the President is unable to discharge the powers and duties of his office, the Vice President shall continue to discharge the same as Acting President; otherwise, the President shall resume the powers and duties of his office.

The Twenty-sixth Amendment. The Twenty-sixth Amendment corrected the anomaly that young men could be drafted and sent to war at the age of eighteen but they were not allowed to participate in the nation's democratic processes until they were twenty-one. It extended the vote to eighteen-year-olds.

AMENDMENT XXVI [1971]

Section 1.   The rights of citizens of the United States, who are 18 years of age or older, to vote shall not be denied or abridged by the United States or any state on account of age.

Section 2.   The Congress shall have the power to enforce this article by appropriate legislation.

The Twenty-seventh Amendment. Originally proposed by Congress in 1789, it was not ratified by the states until 1992. It was rapidly enacted in the wake of public outrage against members of Congress who had voted themselves a substantial pay raise.

AMENDMENT XXVII [1992]

No law, varying the compensation for the services of the Senators and Representatives, shall take effect, until an election of Representatives shall have intervened.

APPENDIX

C

Presidential Elections, 1888 to 1944

1888	**Harrison**	Republican	5,444,337	233
	Grover Cleveland	Democratic	5,540,050	168
1892	**Grover Cleveland**	Democratic	5,544,414	277
	Benjamin Harrison	Republican	5,190,802	145
	James B. Weaver	People's	1,027,329	22
1896	**William McKinley**	Republican	7,104,779	271
	William J. Bryan	Democratic; Populist	6,502,925	176
1900	**William McKinley**	Republican	7,219,530	292
	William J. Bryan	Democratic; Populist	6,356,734	155
1904	**Theodore Roosevelt**	Republican	7,628,834	336
	Alton B. Parker	Democratic	5,084,401	140
	Eugene V. Debs	Socialist	402,460	
1908	**William H. Taft**	Republican	7,679,006	321
	William J. Bryan	Democratic	6,409,106	162
	Eugene V. Debs	Socialist	420,820	
1912	**Woodrow Wilson**	Democratic	6,293,454	435
	Theodore Roosevelt	Progressive	4,119,538	88
	William H. Taft	Republican	3,484,980	8
	Eugene V. Debs	Socialist	897,011	
1916	**Woodrow Wilson**	Democratic	9,129,606	277
	Charles E. Hughes	Republican	8,538,221	254
1920	**Warren G. Harding**	Republican	16,152,200	404
	James M. Cox	Democratic	9,147,353	127
	Eugene V. Debs	Socialist	919,799	
1924	**Calvin Coolidge**	Republican	15,725,016	382
	John W. Davis	Democratic	8,385,586	136
	Robert M. LaFollette	Progressive	4,822,856	13

1928	Herbert C. Hoover	Republican	21,392,190	444
	Alfred E. Smith	Democratic	15,016,443	87
1932	Franklin D. Roosevelt	Democratic	22,809,638	472
	Herbert C. Hoover	Republican	15,758,901	59
	Norman Thomas	Socialist	881,951	
1936	Franklin D. Roosevelt	Democratic	27,751,612	523
	Alfred M. Landon	Republican	16,618,913	8
	William Lemke	Union	891,858	
1940	Franklin D. Roosevelt	Democratic	27,243,466	449
	Wendell L. Willkie	Republican	22,304,755	82
1944	Franklin D. Roosevelt	Democratic	25,602,505	432
	Thomas E. Dewey	Republican	22,006,278	99

APPENDIX D

Cabinet Officers, 1889 to 1945

Secretary of Interior	Cornelius N. Bliss	1897–1899
	Ethan A. Hitchcock	1899–1901
Secretary of Agriculture	James Wilson	1897–1901

The Theodore Roosevelt Administration

Secretary of State	John Hay	1901–1905
	Elihu Root	1905–1909
	Robert Bacon	1909
Secretary of Treasury	Lyman J. Gage	1901–1902
	Leslie M. Shaw	1902–1907
	George B. Cortelyou	1907–1909
Secretary of War	Elihu Root	1901–1904
	William H. Taft	1904–1908
	Luke E. Wright	1908–1909
Attorney General	Philander C. Knox	1901–1904
	William H. Moody	1904–1906
	Charles J. Bonaparte	1906–1909
Postmaster General	Charles E. Smith	1901–1902
	Henry C. Payne	1902–1904
	Robert J. Wynne	1904–1905
	George B. Cortelyou	1905–1907
	George von L. Meyer	1907–1909
Secretary of Navy	John D. Long	1901–1902
	William H. Moody	1902–1904
	Paul Morton	1904–1905
	Charles J. Bonaparte	1905–1906
	Victor H. Metcalf	1906–1908
	Truman H. Newberry	1908–1909
Secretary of Interior	Ethan A. Hitchcock	1901–1907
	James R. Garfield	1907–1909
Secretary of Agriculture	James Wilson	1901–1909
Secretary of Labor and Commerce	George B. Cortelyou	1903–1904
	Victor H. Metcalf	1904–1906
	Oscar S. Straus	1906-1909
	Charles Nagel	1909

The Taft Administration

Secretary of State	Philander C. Knox	1909–1913
Secretary of Treasury	Franklin MacVeagh	1909–1913
Secretary of War	Jacob M. Dickinson	1909–1911
	Henry L. Stimson	1911–1913

Attorney General	George W. Wickersham	1909–1913
Postmaster General	Frank H. Hitchcock	1909–1913
Secretary of Navy	George von L. Meyer	1909–1913
Secretary of Interior	Richard A. Ballinger	1909–1911
	Walter L. Fisher	1911–1913
Secretary of Agriculture	James Wilson	1909–1913
Secretary of Labor and Commerce	Charles Nagel	1909–1913

The Wilson Administration

Secretary of State	William J. Bryan	1913–1915
	Robert Lansing	1915–1920
	Bainbridge Colby	1920–1921
Secretary of Treasury	William G. McAdoo	1913–1918
	Carter Glass	1918–1920
	David F. Houston	1920–1921
Secretary of War	Lindley M. Garrison	1913–1916
	Newton D. Baker	1916–1921
Attorney General	James C. McReynolds	1913–1914
	Thomas W. Gregory	1914–1919
	A. Mitchell Palmer	1919–1921
Postmaster General	Albert S. Burleson	1913–1921
Secretary of Navy	Josephus Daniels	1913–1921
Secretary of Interior	Franklin K. Lane	1913–1920
	John B. Payne	1920–1921
Secretary of Agriculture	David F. Houston	1913–1920
	Edwin T. Meredith	1920–1921
Secretary of Commerce	William C. Redfield	1913–1919
	Joshua W. Alexander	1919–1921
Secretary of Labor	William B. Wilson	1913–1921

The Harding Administration

| Secretary of State | Charles E. Hughes | 1921–1923 |
| Secretary of Treasury | Andrew Mellon | 1921–1923 |

Secretary of War	John W. Weeks	1921–1923
Attorney General	Harry M. Daugherty	1921–1923
Postmaster General	Will H. Hays	1921–1922
	Hubert Work	1922–1923
	Harry S. New	1923
Secretary of Navy	Edwin Denby	1921–1923
Secretary of Interior	Albert B. Fall	1921–1923
	Hubert Work	1923
Secretary of Agriculture	Henry C. Wallace	1921–1923
Secretary of Commerce	Herbert C. Hoover	1921–1923
Secretary of Labor	James J. Davis	1921–1923

The Coolidge Administration

Secretary of State	Charles E. Hughes	1923–1925
	Frank B. Kellogg	1925–1929
Secretary of Treasury	Andrew Mellon	1923–1929
Secretary of War	John W. Weeks	1923–1925
	Dwight F. Davis	1925–1929
Attorney General	Henry M. Daugherty	1923–1924
	Harlan F. Stone	1924–1925
	John G. Sargent	1925–1929
Postmaster General	Harry S. New	1923–1929
Secretary of Navy	Edwin Denby	1923–1924
	Curtis D. Wilbur	1924–1929
Secretary of Interior	Hubert Work	1923–1928
	Roy O. West	1928–1929
Secretary of Agriculture	Henry C. Wallace	1923–1924
	Howard M. Gore	1924–1925
	William M. Jardine	1925–1929
Secretary of Commerce	Herbert C. Hoover	1923–1928
	William F. Whiting	1928–1929
Secretary of Labor	James J. Davis	1923–1929

The Hoover Administration

Secretary of State	Henry L. Stimson	1929–1933
Secretary of Treasury	Andrew Mellon	1929–1932
	Ogden L. Mills	1932–1933
Secretary of War	James W. Good	1929
	Patrick J. Hurley	1929–1933
Attorney General	William D. Mitchell	1929–1933
Postmaster General	Walter F. Brown	1929–1933
Secretary of Navy	Charles F. Adams	1929–1933
Secretary of Interior	Ray L. Wilbur	1929–1933
Secretary of Agriculture	Arthur M. Hyde	1929–1933
Secretary of Commerce	Robert P. Lamont	1929–1932
	Roy D. Chapin	1932–1933
Secretary of Labor	James J. Davis	1929–1930
	William N. Doak	1930–1933

The Franklin D. Roosevelt Administration

Secretary of State	Cordell Hull	1933–1944
	E. R. Stettinius, Jr.	1944–1945
Secretary of Treasury	William H. Woodin	1933–1934
	Henry Morgenthau, Jr.	1934–1945
Secretary of War	George H. Dern	1933–1936
	Henry A. Woodring	1936–1940
	Henry L. Stimson	1940–1945
Attorney General	Homer S. Cummings	1933–1939
	Frank Murphy	1939–1940
	Robert H. Jackson	1940–1941
	Francis Biddle	1941–1945
Postmaster General	James A. Farley	1933–1940
	Frank C. Walker	1940–1945
Secretary of Navy	Claude A. Swanson	1933–1940
	Charles Edison	1940
	Frank Knox	1940–1944
	James V. Forrestal	1944–1945
Secretary of Interior	Harold L. Ickes	1933–1945
Secretary of Agriculture	Henry A. Wallace	1933–1940
	Claude R. Wickard	1940–1945
Secretary of Commerce	Daniel C. Roper	1933–1939
	Harry L. Hopkins	1939–1940
	Jesse Jones	1940–1945
	Henry A. Wallace	1945
Secretary of Labor	Frances Perkins	1933–1945

APPENDIX
E

Population of the United States, 1890 to 1945 (estimated)

1890	62,500,000
1900	76,200,000
1910	92,200,000
1920	106,000,000
1930	123,200,000
1940	132,200,000
1945 (est.)	141,000,000

APPENDIX F

Immigration to the United States by Region and Selected Countries of Last Residence, 1891 to 1950

Region and Country of Last Residence	1891–1900	1901–1910	1911–1920	1921–1930	1931–1940	1941–1950
All countries	3,687,564	8,795,386	5,735,811	4,107,209	528,431	1,035,039
Europe	3,555,352	8,056,040	4,321,887	2,463,194	347,566	621,147
Austria-Hungary	592,707	2,145,266	896,342	63,548	11,424	28,329
Austria	234,081	668,209	453,649	32,868	3,563	24,860
Hungary	181,288	808,511	442,693	30,680	7,861	3,469
Belgium	18,167	41,635	33,746	15,846	4,817	12,189
Czechoslovakia	—	—	3,426	102,194	14,393	8,347
Denmark	50,231	65,285	41,983	32,430	2,559	5,393
France	30,770	73,379	61,897	49,610	12,623	38,809
Germany	505,152	341,498	143,945	412,202	114,058	226,678
Greece	15,979	167,519	184,201	51,084	9,119	8,973
Ireland	388,416	339,065	146,181	211,234	10,973	19,789
Italy	651,893	2,045,877	1,109,524	455,315	68,028	57,661
Netherlands	26,758	48,262	43,718	26,948	7,150	14,860
Norway-Sweden	321,281	440,039	161,469	165,780	8,700	20,765
Norway	95,015	190,505	66,395	68,531	4,740	10,100
Sweden	226,266	249,534	95,074	97,249	3,960	10,665
Poland	96,720	—	4,813	227,734	17,026	7,571
Portugal	27,508	69,149	89,732	29,994	3,329	7,423
Rumania	12,750	53,008	13,311	67,646	3,871	1,076
Soviet Union	505,290	1,597,306	921,201	61,742	1,370	571
Spain	8,731	27,935	68,611	28,958	3,258	2,898

Region and Country of Last Residence	1891–1900	1901–1910	1911–1920	1921–1930	1931–1940	1941–1950
Switzerland	31,179	34,922	23,091	29,676	5,512	10,547
United Kingdom	271,538	525,950	341,408	339,570	31,572	139,306
Yugoslavia	—	—	1,888	49,064	5,835	1,576
Other Europe	282	39,945	31,400	42,619	11,949	8,486
Asia	74,862	323,543	247,236	112,059	16,595	37,028
China	14,799	20,605	21,278	29,907	4,928	16,709
Hong Kong	—	—	—	—	—	—
India	68	4,713	2,082	1,886	496	1,761
Iran	—	—	—	24112	195	1,380
Israel	—	—	—	—	—	476
Japan	25,942	129,797	83,837	33,462	1,948	1,555
Korea	—	—	—	—	—	107
Philippines	—	—	—	—	528	4,691
Turkey	30,425	157,369	134,066	33,824	1,065	798
Vietnam	—	—	—	—	—	—
Other Asia	3,628	11,059	5,973	12,739	7,435	9,551
America	38,972	361,888	1,143,671	1,516,716	160,037	354,804
Canada & Newfoundland	3,311	179,226	742,185	924,515	108,527	171,718
Mexico	971	49,642	219,004	459,287	22,319	60,589
Caribbean	33,066	107,548	123,424	74,899	15,502	49,725
Cuba	—	—	—	15,901	9,571	26,313
Dominican Republic	—	—	—	—	1,150	5,627
Haiti	—	—	—	—	191	911
Jamaica	—	—	—	—	—	—
Other Caribbean	33,066	107,548	123,424	58,998	4,590	16,874
Central America	549	8,192	17,159	15,769	5,861	21,665
El Salvador	—	—	—	—	673	5,132
Other Central America	549	8,192	17,159	15,769	5,188	16,533
South America	1,075	17,280	41,899	42,215	7,803	21,831
Argentina	—	—	—	—	1,349	3,338
Colombia	—	—	—	—	1,223	3,858
Ecuador	—	—	—	—	337	2,417
Other South America	1,075	17,280	41,899	42,215	4,894	12,218
Other America	—	—	—	31	25	29,276
Africa	350	7,368	8,443	6,286	1,750	7,367
Oceania	3,965	13,024	13,427	8,726	2,483	14,551
Not specified	14,063	33,523	1,147	228	—	142

APPENDIX
G

Chronology of Significant Events, 1890 to 1945

1890   Congress enacts the Sherman Antritrust Act

1890   Massacre at Wounded Knee occurs

1892   The People's Party (the Populists) is founded

1892   Ellis Island immigration depot opens

1894   The Pullman strike occurs

1895   Booker T. Washington delivers His "Atlanta Compromise" speech

1896   *Plessy* v. *Ferguson* is rendered

1898   The Spanish-American War is fought

1898   Hawaii is annexed

1899   War breaks out in the Philippines

1899   John Hay announces the Open Door policy

1900   Theodore Dreiser's *Sister Carrie* is published

1900   U.S. troops join an international expeditionary force to suppress the Boxer rebellion in China

1901   President McKinley is assassinated; Vice President Theodore Roosevelt assumes presidency

1902   The federal government sues the Northern Security Company for antitrust violations and wins

1902   The Platt Amendment is imposed on Cuba

1903   The Panamanian revolution begins, supported by the United States

1903   The first power-driven airplane flies at Kitty Hawk, North Carolina

1903   The first World Series takes place

1904   Construction of the Panama Canal begins

1904   Ida Tarbell publishes her exposé of Standard Oil

1904   The Roosevelt Corollary to the Monroe Doctrine is proclaimed

1905   The National Education Association is formed

1905   Theodore Roosevelt mediates the Russo-Japanese War

1906   U.S. troops intervene in Cuba

1906   Upton Sinclair's novel *The Jungle* is published

1907   William James publishes *Pragmatism*

1908   The U.S. "Great White Fleet" sails around the world

1908   Henry Ford manufactures the first Model T

1909   U.S. Marines are dispatched to Nicaragua

1910   The Mexican revolution begins

1910   The NAACP is founded

1911   Irving Berlin writes "Alexander's Ragtime Band"

1913   Henry Ford installs the first moving assembly line

1913   The Sixteenth Amendment establishes the income tax

1913   The Seventeenth Amendment provides for the direct election of senators

1914   U.S. troops intervene in Vera Cruz, Mexico

1914   World War I begins

1914   U.S. troops intervene in Haiti

1914   The Panama Canal is completed

1915   D. W. Griffith produces the first movie spectacular, *Birth of a Nation*

1915   HMS *Lusitania* is sunk by a German submarine

1916   Mexican general "Pancho Villa" invades the United States

1916   U.S. troops invade Mexico

1916   Margaret Sanger founds the New York Birth Control League

1917   The United States enters World War I

1917   Congress enacts a literacy test for new immigrants

1917   The Soviet revolution occurs

1918   World War I ends

1919   The Treaty of Versailles is signed

1919   The Eighteenth Amendment establishing prohibition is ratified

1920   Prohibition goes into effect

1920   The Nineteenth Amendment enfranchising women is ratified

1920   the U.S. Senate rejects the Treaty of Versailles

1920   The first commercial radio station, KDKA in Pittsburgh, begins broadcasting

1921   The first Miss America is crowned in Atlantic City, New Jersey

1921   Margaret Sanger founds American Birth Control League

1921   Washington Naval Conference takes place

1922   "The Wasteland" by T.S. Eliot is published

1922   *Babbitt* by Sinclair Lewis is published

1923   The Teapot Dome scandal occurs

1923   *Time* magazine is founded

1924   The National Origins Act is enacted

1924   George Gershwin composes "Rhapsody in Blue"

1924   The Dawes Plan is implemented

1925   *The Great Gatsby* by F. Scott Fitzgerald is published

1925   *The New Negro* by Alain Locke is published

1925   The Scopes Monkey Trial takes place in Dayton, Tennessee

1926   *The Sun Also Rises* by Ernest Hemingway is published

1926   Rudolph Valentino dies of ulcers

1927   The first Academy Awards are announced

1927   The first sound motion picture, *The Jazz Singer,* is released

1927   Charles Lindbergh flies solo across the Atlantic, from New York to Paris

1927   Babe Ruth hits 60 home runs

1927   Sacco and Vanzetti are executed

1928   The Kellogg-Briand Pact is negotiated

1928   Herbert Hoover is elected president

1929   Hoover proclaims the Good Neighbor policy

1929   The Great Stock Market Crash occurs

1930   The Hawley-Smoot Tariff is enacted

1931   The Great Depression begins

1931   President Hoover declares a moratorium on international debt payments

1931   Japan invades Manchuria

1932   Bonus Marchers descend on Washington, D.C.

1932   The Pecora Committee investigates Wall Street

1932   The Reconstruction Finance Corporation is established

1932   The Farmer's Holiday Association is formed

1932   Franklin Delano Roosevelt is elected president

1933   Guiseppe Zangara tries to assassinate President-elect Roosevelt

1933   Hundred Days legislation, the New Deal begins

1933   Black blizzards create the Dust Bowl in the Great Plains

1933   Cuba cancels the Platt Amendment

1933   Prohibition is repealed

1933	13 million are unemployed, about one-quarter of the work force
1934	The Securities and Exchange Commission is created
1934	The American Liberty League is formed
1934	The Indian Reorganization Act is enacted
1934	Nye Committee hearings begin
1934	Southern Tenant Farmer's Union is formed
1934	Hollywood implements the Motion Picture Production Code
1935	Hollywood produces the first color film
1935	The Supreme Court Nullifies the NRA
1935	The WPA is created
1935	Social Security is enacted
1935	The National Labor Relations Act is enacted
1935	Huey Long is assassinated
1935	The First Neutrality Act is enacted
1935	Italy attacks Ethiopia
1936	The Congress of Industrial Organizations is created
1936	UAW initiates the sit-down strike
1936	The Supreme Court nullifies the first AAA
1936	Germany reoccupies the Rhineland
1936	Jesse Owens wins four gold medals at the Olympic Games
1936	The Spanish Civil War begins
1936	Roosevelt is reelected
1937	SWOC organizes U.S. Steel workers
1937	The Memorial Day Massacre occurs in Chicago
1937	Roosevelt's efforts to "pack" the Supreme Court fail
1937	Joe Louis becomes heavyweight boxing champion
1937	Japan invades northern China; World War II in Asia begins
1937	Roosevelt delivers his "quarantine the aggressor" speech
1938	the Fair Labor Standards Act is enacted
1938	The New Deal ends
1938	The Munich Conference takes place
1939	Marian Anderson sings at Lincoln Memorial

1939	Germany occupies Czechoslovakia
1939	The Nazi-Soviet Pact is signed
1939	Germany invades Poland; World War II in Europe begins
1939	The New York World's Fair is held
1939	*Gone with the Wind* premieres in Atlanta
1940	The Fall of France occurs
1940	The Battle of Britain occurs
1941	Roosevelt and Churchill sign the Atlantic Charter
1941	Pearl Harbor is attacked; the United States enters World War II
1942	Japanese Americans are interned
1942	The Battle of the Coral Sea takes place
1942	The Battle of Midway takes place
1942	Allied troops invade North Africa
1942	The Manhattan District Project begins
1943	Soviets win the Battle of Stalingrad
1943	Roosevelt and Churchill announce unconditional surrender policy at Casablanca
1943	Allied forces invade Italy; Italy surrenders
1943	Race riot occurs in Detroit
1943	The Battle for Guadalcanal occurs
1943	The Big Three meet at Teheran
1944	D-Day: The Allies invade Normandy
1944	Paris is liberated
1944	The Battle of the Philippine Sea takes place
1944	The Battle of Leyte Gulf takes place
1944	The Battle of the Bulge takes place
1945	The Big Three meet at Yalta
1945	The Battle of Iwo Jima takes place
1945	Roosevelt dies; Harry S. Truman becomes president
1945	Adolph Hitler commits suicide
1945	Germany surrenders
1945	The Philippines are liberated
1945	The Battle of Okinawa takes place
1945	The Potsdam Conference is held
1945	Two Japanese cities are bombed with atomic weapons
1945	Japan surrenders; World War II ends

Photo and Map Credits

PHOTOS

CHAPTER 1   The Museum of Modern Art, 7; Library of Congress, 10; Library of Congress, 14; Hampton Institute, 19; Library of Congress, 21; Library of Congress, 34.

CHAPTER 2   Library of Congress, 44; Brown Brothers, 46; Library of Congress, 51; Library of Congress, 52; The Schlesinger Library, Radcliffe College, 55; National Archives, 61; Metropolitan Life Insurance Co., 63.

CHAPTER 3   Library of Congress, 73; National Archives, 78.

CHAPTER 4   Bettmann, 113; National Archives, 116; National Archives, 118.

CHAPTER 5   National Archives, 136; Michigan State Archives, 138; AP/Wide World Photos, 151.

CHAPTER 6   The Museum of Modern Art/ Film Stills Archive, 161; Library of Congress, 163; Library of Congress, 167; Bettmann, 173; New York Public Library, 176; National Archives, 178.

CHAPTER 7   James N. Rosenberg, "Painting of 1929 Crash." Philadelphia Museum of Art. Purchased: Lila Dowin Peck Fund, 185; Library of Congress, 192; Bettmann, 193; Library of Congress, 194; Public Domain, 195; National Archives, 201.

CHAPTER 8   FDR Library, 215; Bettmann, 217; FDR Library, 219; National Archives, 226; Library of Congress, 229; FDR Library, 239.

CHAPTER 9   James Van Derzee, 255; Library of Congress, 259; National Archives, 268.

CHAPTER 10   National Archives, 275.

CHAPTER 11   National Archives, 302; Bettmann, 312.

CHAPTER 12   National Archives, 317; National Archives, 321; U.S. Army Photograph, 326; National Archives, 327; U.S. Army Photograph, 330.

CHAPTER 13   FDR Library, 350; National Archives, 354; National Archives, 358; National Archives, 363.

CHAPTER 14   National Archives, 376; Joint Army Navy Task Force One Photo, 380.

MAPS

Maps on the following pages are from Winthrop D. Jordan and Leon F. Litwack, *The United States, 4th ed. (Brief Edition)*. Englewood Cliffs, NJ: Prentice Hall, 1994. Drafted by Alice Thiede: pp. 3, 16, 25, 56, 115, 128, 304, 322, and 340.

Maps on the following pages are from George Donelson Moss, *America in the Twentieth Century, 2nd. ed.* Englewood Cliffs, NJ: Prentice Hall, 1993: pp. 29, 31, 33, 43, 95, 101, 133, 144, 207, 221, 237, 287, and 292.

Maps on the following pages are from Irwin Unger, *These United States: The Questions of Our Past, 5th ed.* Englewood Cliffs, NJ: Prentice Hall, 1992: pp. 85 and 335.

Index